# ARIUS ON CARILLON AVENUE

# ARIUS *on* CARILLON AVENUE

More than a Memoir: A Trinitarian Saga

*Peter Carnley*

CASCADE *Books* · Eugene, Oregon

ARIUS ON CARILLON AVENUE
More than a Memoir: A Trinitarian Saga

Cascade Books
An Imprint of Wipf and Stock Publishers
199 W. 8th Ave., Suite 3
Eugene, OR 97401

www.wipfandstock.com

PAPERBACK ISBN: 978-1-6667-6518-2
HARDCOVER ISBN: 978-1-6667-6519-9
EBOOK ISBN: 978-1-6667-6520-5

## *Cataloguing-in-Publication data:*

Names: Carnley, Peter, author.

Title: Arius on Carillon Avenue : More than a Memoir: A Trinitarian Saga / Peter Carnley.

Description: Eugene, OR: Cascade Books, 2023 | Includes bibliographical references and index.

Identifiers: ISBN 978-1-6667-6518-2 (paperback) | ISBN 978-1-6667-6519-9 (hardcover) | ISBN 978-1-6667-6520-5 (ebook)

Subjects: LCSH: Jesus Christ—History of doctrines. | Trinity—History of doctrines. | Jesus Christ—Divinity—Biblical teaching.

Classification: BT109 .C30 2023 (print) | BT109 (ebook)

Cover design: A photograph of the pavement mosaic of Solomon's Knot from the ruins of the first-century synagogue at Ostia, the ancient Port of Rome. Jewish workmen were involved when the Emperor Claudius undertook a major reconstruction of the port facility. The ruin of the synagogue at Ostia is located on the ancient waterfront, at the edge of the city, just a little to the East of the Porta Marina through which Paul would have passed when he arrived in custody around the year 58. Although it is extremely likely, whether Paul actually visited the synagogue is one of the unanswered questions of history.

For the Bishops

of

the Anglican Church of Australia
who shoulder the onerous responsibility

of

maintaining the Church in truth.

# Table of Contents

# Preface

THE TRAUMATIC SPREAD OF the coronavirus in the first months of 2020 understandably precipitated a spate of dramatic governmental directives advising people around the world to "shelter in place," to avoid going out unless for some essential reason, and to self-isolate. The rudely intruded necessity of "social distancing" into our lives, sporadically punctuated as it was by enforced lockdowns, put a distinct damper on the possibility of visiting the homes of friends, let alone eating meals out at restaurants, or going to the cinema, or concerts, or even to church. As a consequence, many of us were confronted with the challenge of having to fill the new-found empty spaces and silence of our lives with some productive and worthwhile enterprise. I found myself thinking that the time of lockdown might be a good time to start writing a memoir.

With this purpose in mind, I began to flip through folders of bits and pieces that, over the years, had found their way into my filing cabinet—perhaps fortuitously in preparation for this eventual future project. In a file marked "Primatial Years"[1] I happened across a copy of an email that had been sent to me in 2005 by Tom Frame, whom I had personally appointed in my role as Primate of Australia to be the first full-time bishop to the Australian Defence Force. At the time of this email, Tom, an accomplished historian, was working on a contribution to a collection of essays in honor of Bruce Kaye, who had been general secretary of the General Synod of the Anglican Church of Australia, in which he focused on difficulties of theological debate within the Australian context.[2] He wanted to ask some questions about the circumstances surrounding a theological controversy concerning the orthodoxy or otherwise of some

1. I was Anglican Primate of Australia from 2000 to 2005.

2. Tom Frame published this as "Dynamics and Difficulties of Debate in Australian Anglicanism." This was followed by a book in which he expanded on this theme, *Anglicans in Australia.*

propositions made in 1999 by the Doctrine Commission of the Diocese of Sydney, and to which I had made passing critical reference in a book entitled *Reflections in Glass,* which had itself been published in the year before the email, 2004.

The Sydney Doctrine Commission's problematic proposals related to the Trinity. They had to do with what was alleged to be a "relational" or "functional" subordination of the Son to the Father in the internal or immanent life of the Trinity, which, because of the standing orthodox insistence on the uncompromised equality of the persons of the Trinity in nature, dignity, and status, naturally triggered a good deal of initial puzzlement and gentle questioning before blowing out in public controversy. This idiosyncratic Trinitarian proposition about the interpersonal subordination of the Son to the Father is to be found in a report entitled "The Doctrine of the Trinity and its bearing on the relationship of men and women," which had been presented to the Sydney Diocesan Synod in 1999. My passing comments on it, some five years later, were to be found in a chapter of *Reflections in Glass* entitled "Women in the Episcopate?"

However, the apparent theological mismatch between the Sydney notions of interpersonal subordination in the immanent life of the Trinity and the traditional and orthodox insistence on the equality of the Trinitarian identities had already been very forcefully signaled much earlier, most notably by the Melbourne evangelical theologian Kevin Giles. In a book entitled *The Trinity and Subordinationism,* which was published in 2002, Giles was not coy in suggesting that the Sydney Doctrine Commission's position was a form of the ancient heresy of Arianism.[3] He also addressed the question of the propriety of appealing to a problematic paradigm of interpersonal domination and submission within the eternal life of the Trinity to justify the male domination of men over women, both within families and in the ministry of leadership in the church.[4]

3. This was clearly perceived in Sydney. Robert Doyle, a senior lecturer at Moore Theological College, for example, noted that Giles said: "It is to be conceded . . . that none of these evangelicals is a true Arian. They all repeatedly insist that they believe in the full divinity of the Son and the Holy Spirit." While not seeing themselves as Arians it remains a question as to whether their position does not lead them in that very direction, and Doyle was himself well aware that Giles's criticisms amounted to the charge of Arianism: "Basically, although it is conceded that the targets of this book are not true Arians, . . . nevertheless, by the end of the book the clear implication is that we are heretics, and of the nastier Arian kind." Doyle, "Use and abuse," citing Giles, *Trinity and Subordinationism,* 81.

4. Women had been ordained as deacons in the Anglican Church of Australia, and the first women deacons were admitted to the priesthood in 1992. This development

Though this initial pairing of the topic of the Trinity with gender politics might at first sight appear to be somewhat unlikely, there is no doubt that debate about the place of women in the leadership structures of the church's ministry was actually the point of entry into a public discussion of Trinitarian principles. If the subject of the Trinity was dividing evangelical minds, it was therefore no abstract discussion of an abstruse theological point that might be deemed to be far removed from life; on the contrary, its relevance to one of the most contested moral and ecclesial questions facing the whole national Church at the time was fully appreciated. It was from the very start clear that the apparently highly speculative theological topic of interpersonal subordination in the immanent Trinity was believed to have a bearing on live issues of gender equality. For this reason alone, the wider community of committed Anglicans around Australia, not to mention members of the general public, naturally took interest in it. Perhaps many perceived it as something of a curiosity that the question of the admission of women to the episcopate could somehow be perceived to be connected with fourth-century speculation about the interrelations of persons in the eternal Trinity. Certainly, a controversy that had initially started between opposed evangelical minds within the Anglican Church of Australia concerning the orthodoxy or otherwise of some propositions about the internal relations of the persons of the Trinity soon began to secure some purchase across the entire national Church. In 2004 I found that I had myself been somewhat clumsily drawn into it.

⌇

The rediscovery of Frame's email in 2020, with its questions about this episode, immediately suggested a possible starting point for the writing of some memoirs. Even though one might usually be inclined to commence a personal memoir with an account of family origins and reminiscences of childhood, there was some point in starting with events of closer temporal proximity. Generally speaking, my privileged experiences as Primate of Australia between 2000 and 2005 were very positive, richly rewarding, and agreeably enjoyable; but even so, some of the inevitable negatives had been traumatic and stressful enough to continue to bulk

---

continues to be resisted within the Anglican Diocese of Sydney along with some other regional dioceses in Australia.

menacingly large and clear in memory. Given that it was not possible in the early days of the coronavirus lockdown to leave the house to go to a library or sift through boxes of archival material now located far from home in the Diocesan Archive, it seemed reasonable enough to start with what I actually remembered with some clarity, aided by what I still had already on hand in the drawers of my own filing cabinet.

At the same time this exercise in revisited memory provided an opportunity to try to unscramble some of the confusion and crossed wires of theological controversy, the verbal precipitate of a time when, as Tom Frame pointed out, people vehemently defended long-cherished set positions and confidently held views, and so tended to talk past each other and out the window. In Frame's estimation, people responded to the essays I had published in *Reflections in Glass* simply by withdrawing into their burrows. As a consequence, he judged the book to be a failure; he contended that the discussion went nowhere, basically because he believed that a commercially available publication was an inappropriate medium for what he imagined I had proposed as an agenda of theological topics for serious discussion across the national Church. A better strategy for fostering in-house theological discussion might have been to tug on somebody's sleeve and have a quiet word in a corner. Frame may well have underestimated the complexity of the issues at stake, which demanded more than a mere chat. This was particularly so given that, as Sydney folk defensively responded to Giles's criticisms, many of us from the start sensed a distinct reluctance on their part to engage in debate. A confident conviction of the unassailable rightness of the Sydney Doctrine Commission's position appeared to act as a disincentive to the serious examination of the issues, even if some others did happen to think them problematic. In any event, whether Frame's analysis and assessment of the futility of attempting theological discussion in a commercially available book is accurate or not is immaterial. The point is that many issues were not adequately resolved at the time of my retirement in 2005. This meant that misunderstandings and misrepresentations remained unaddressed. I myself was at one point charged with being more interested in intra-church politics than the pursuit of theological truth![5] However, now, in the time of COVID lockdown, there was an opportunity to revisit some of the puzzling and unresolved points of theological issue that were once sensed to be "not quite right" but that were never properly

5. Adam, "Honouring Jesus Christ," 11.

examined. Certainly, this could not be a purely historical exercise; there was an opportunity at least to try to unpick the tangle of unresolved issues that seemed, like Solomon's knot, to be impenetrable.

⌁

From my own point of view, the original failure to pursue the issues through to some kind of closure was in large part the inevitable result of the priorities of work at the time. Apart from the administration and pastoral care of the Church in a rapidly expanding city, there were pressing international and national issues to be tackled. Certainly, I was fully involved in the discussion of a wide-ranging set of public concerns. Ecumenical dialogue was high on my agenda: from 2004 I was the Anglican co-chair of ARCIC,[6] which was in the final stages of completing an agreed statement on Mary in the life and worship of the church. At the same time, the issue of how best to minister to homosexual people had necessarily to be addressed as a highly contentious but important issue, both nationally and internationally. Indeed the divisive questions of the blessing of gay relationships and the ordination of openly gay people was threatening to fracture the international life of the Anglican Communion. I found myself in the role of chair of the Archbishop of Canterbury's Panel of Reference, which was charged with meeting with dissident groups around the world, hearing their grievances, and then reporting on the issues that appeared to be most confronting and disturbing to them, and offering some tentative advice as to how the discussion might be advanced. All this, while at the same time maintaining the highest degree of communion.

Over this period, there were also hotly contested social issues within Australian society—the bioethics of stem cell research, in vitro fertilization and surrogacy, Aboriginal land rights and reconciliation, the dangers of global warming, and the nation's handling of refugees and asylum seekers. Inevitably, this meant that some of the troublesome technical theological issues internal to the life of the Church had to be left in the "too-hard" basket.

The advent of more tranquil years since retirement in 2005 and now, somewhat fortuitously, the enforced circumstance of not leaving home during COVID lockdown, meant that they could at last be scrutinized

6. The Anglican-Roman Catholic International Commission.

more carefully, and hopefully brought to more adequately considered judgment. Perhaps, in the cooler light of the passing of time it might even be possible to identify what originally had actually been at stake with a little more precision than could be achieved at the time; what the debate was really all about might at least be clarified so as to allow us all to move towards some sorely needed theological closure.

This book is thus more than a memoir of "what happened when." Rather than just a dig in intellectual archaeology, it touches down in past occurrences and experiences as the springboard for some continuing serious theological reflection and argument.

As I began to work on the question of exactly what was wrong with the projection of notions of interpersonal subordination into the understanding of the internal relations of the persons of the Trinity, and the question of the relevance or otherwise of this to the issue of the subordination of women in domestic arrangements and in the life of the church, I became increasingly aware that a third doctrinal strand was also begging to be acknowledged as also being relevant to the presenting theological discussion. This involved an issue that had actually surfaced right at the beginning of my time as Primate, indeed, even before this ministry was formally inaugurated, shortly after Easter in 2000. In fact, the indignant hostility triggered by so much as questioning the orthodoxy or otherwise of the Sydney Doctrine Commission's views of the Trinity in *Reflections in Glass* in 2004 had by and large been expressed by Sydney bishops at national bishops' meetings, usually at some remove from public gaze. This was a comparatively minor flurry compared with the tsunami of pullulating angst and foot-stamping that spilled from the life of the church into full public display early in 2000.

The unbecoming and very public skirmish at that time initially focused, not on the doctrine of the Trinity, but (more appropriately at Easter) on the meaning of the cross. I had been asked to write a reflection on the significance of Easter in a journal article for the Australian newsmagazine *The Bulletin,* which I was more than glad to do. As it transpired, its publication met with a wave of negative responses, mainly emanating from within the Anglican Diocese of Sydney, though certainly not confined to it. As I now peruse the huge volume of ensuing press comment, cartoons, and letters to the editor that appeared right across the country in national outlets of the Australian media, it is fairly obvious that those who found fault with what I had written were not only responding to language that was somehow strangely unfamiliar to them as a way of approaching the meaning of the cross of Christ, though that may have to some degree been the case. Rather, the chief complaint was that *The Bulletin* article did not canvass a specific theory of the atonement, which many (mostly Sydney folk) clearly thought to be mandatory in the proclamation of the Christian gospel.

This was the "penal substitution theory," which, briefly put, holds that God the Father intentionally sent the Son into the world to die upon the cross, so as to bear the punishment deserved by all humanity in the wake of the rebellious disobedience of Adam. According to this theological theory, by suffering the penalty of death instead of others, Christ satisfied the need of a righteous God not to turn a blind eye to human sin and evil, but to take it seriously and, in fact, to deal with it himself by exacting an appropriate punishment in order to satisfy the just requirements of the law. Already, in his thumbnail sketch of the doctrine we may detect hints of the operation of a presupposed interpersonal dynamic of command and willing obedience, expressive of a relation of domination and submission between the Father and the Son.

The alleged transaction between God the Father, who could not be thought to be indifferent to the just demands of the law, and his only begotten Son whom he sent into the world for the specific purpose of meeting its demands, thus expresses in time something of the eternal "functional" or "relational" subordination of the Son to the Father in the internal life of the Trinity. If the notion of a demanding Father exacting the penalty of death on his innocent Son for the crimes of others may seem morally gross, and indeed, patently unjust, something of its presenting offensiveness is mitigated by the fact that the Son is said willingly and thus voluntarily to accept his fate in docile obedience out of his great love for humanity. Indeed, given that the Son is divine, there is a sense in which God, rather than inflicting a required cruel punishment on a third party, takes the punishment for human sin and evil upon himself.

In this way, there is a sense in which the penal substitution theory of the atonement involves the acting out in history of the eternal subordination of the Son to the Father as this had been set forward by the Sydney Doctrine Commission in its Report of 1999. Obviously, this theory of the atonement positively requires the willing obedience of the eternally subordinate Son in order to neutralize the suggestion that the Father grossly imposes a penalty on the unsuspecting and entirely innocent and sinless Son in a way that *prima facie* appears morally reprehensible and, in fact, anything but just. However, for some committed self-consciously evangelical Christians this is the essence of the Christian good news, because Christ's willing payment of the penalty for the sin and evil of the world means that those who appropriate its benefits in trusting faith are saved from having to bear the same punishment themselves. It is understandable that to some minds this article of faith is of the very essence of the Christian gospel;[7] if it is assumed to be mandatory, then the total absence of reference to it in a journal article on the meaning of the cross in the Easter edition of *The Bulletin* in 2000 can more clearly be seen to be an impeachable offence.

⟜

This means that, from the point of view of the particular theological mindset in which "eternal functional subordination" is a foundational plank, we are invited to deal with a total package comprised of three distinct but interrelated strands:

1. The eternal "functional" or "relational" subordination of the Son to the Father in the internal or immanent life of the Trinity.

2. The use of this as a model or paradigm for understanding the alleged creational intention of God with respect to the interpersonal relations of husbands and wives in families, and to men and women generally, especially with respect to the "headship" of men over women in the leadership of the church.

3. The historical playing out of this same relationship of fatherly command and willing filial obedience, in the drama of redemption insofar as it is expressed in Christ's obedient offering of his life to

---

7. Thus, Wayne Grudem forthrightly declares: "in the atonement Christ actually bore the wrath of God against sin that we deserved. This is the heart of the gospel message, and the gospel message is the primary message of the entire Bible. To attack the idea of penal substitutionary atonement is to attack the central message of the Bible." Grudem, *Systematic Theology*, 1398. As recently as 2022 the Synod of the Christian Reformed Church in the United States, in affirming the centrality of this belief, actually "walked up to the edge of declaring the denial of penal substitutionary atonement as a heresy." See Libolt, "Synod Affirms Penal Substitutionary Atonement."

God the Father, even unto death on the cross, in payment of a justly required penalty for the sins of the world.

In this book I seek to examine the first of these three interrelated theological themes in the light of my own experience of encounter with fellow Anglicans for whom they are clearly of enormous importance. If the novel proposals of a complementarian understanding of intra-Trinitarian relations fails as a legitimate alternative to orthodox Trinitarian egalitarianism, then its capacity to render support for the proposition that women are subordinate to men in a relation of domination and submission simply dissipates. I leave it to others to pursue the implications of this for contemporary discussion of gender politics.

A companion volume, *The Subordinate Substitute*, will be devoted to an examination of the third theological issue—the outworking of belief in a complementarian doctrine of the Trinity in which the Son is said to be "eternally subordinate to the Father" for the theology of salvation. This second, forthcoming book will thus focus upon the "penal substitution theory" of the atonement and whether it can really be sustained in the light of orthodox Trinitarian theology.

My own view is that the theological propositions relating to the subordination of the Son to the Father, with which we have to do in this book, are seriously flawed, even to the point of attracting the critical judgment of being sub-Trinitarian and out of kilter with the doctrinal norms of historical Christian orthodoxy. Indeed, we have frankly and candidly to face the unavoidable possibility, upon which Kevin Giles has insisted with terrier-like tenacity for just on two decades, that we are grappling with a contemporary form of the ancient Christian heresy to which, for good or ill, the arch-heretic Arius originally gave his name in the first half of the fourth century.

⌒

For this reason, the working title for this book started out as *Arius in Australia*. Somehow the assonance attracted. However, I have come to see that this might mislead some into thinking that this is a problem that has the entire Anglican Church of Australia in its thrall. Though in terms of its geographical spread Trinitarian subordinatonism is an Australia-wide problem, given that people who think in this way are found dispersed around the country, in fact, this package of delinquent theological ideas is nevertheless confined to a clearly identified and well-defined strand of thought within the broad spectrum of Anglican inclusiveness. It is not difficult to pin it down. It is well-known that worshippers of the Anglican Diocese of Sydney stand for a remarkably conservative approach to the interpretation of Scripture, and a characteristic style in their articulation of the Christian gospel. It has to be acknowledged that this can be clearly and powerfully presented. Understandably, many refer to themselves self-consciously as "Sydney Anglicans" in the clear knowledge that not all other Anglicans are of the same mind.[8] Certainly, there is little doubt that within Australia the powerhouse for the generation of the distinctive theology in which the three interrelated strands of my present concern are found is Moore Theological College, which has been historically located on Carillon Avenue, now at its junction with King Street, Newtown in Sydney.

On the other hand, it is important to emphasize that the distinctive set of theological views with which I wish to engage is not confined to a single geographical location. It is certainly not confined to the city of Sydney, even if this is where it is most clearly defined and institutionalized. Even within the Anglican Diocese of Sydney there are certainly Anglican Christians who do not subscribe to these three doctrinal and moral propositions. I therefore hesitate to speak of them as the views of "Sydney Anglicans."

Admittedly, it is usual to identify this theological package by applying the label "evangelical." However, this is a descriptive word that even catholic-mined Christians may rightly want also to own. Furthermore, not all who would call themselves "evangelical Anglicans" would subscribe to the set of three theological propositions centered upon subordinationism or the complementarian doctrine of the Trinity with which I am here concerned. Kevin Giles is himself one of them. For this reason, we appear to be in need of an alternate identifying name to denote what is in fact a highly distinctive or even partisan expression of evangelicalism. Given that its most vocal champions have been centered in Moore

---

8. Tom Frame appears to imagine that I coined this epithet. That is not the case. Sydney Anglicans regularly speak of themselves in this way. See sydneyanglicans.net/about: "About our Diocese. Sydney Anglicans belong to a network of churches encompassing the Sydney Metropolitan, Blue Mountains, Southern Highlands, South Coast and Illawarra areas." Likewise, Michael Jensen has apparently happily published *Sydney Anglicanism*. See also Judd and Cable, *Sydney Anglicans*.

Theological College, "Carillon Avenue theology" suggests itself as an appropriate identifying label.

I am inclined therefore to use "Carillon Avenue" as a metaphor. It is employed as a code word for signaling a clearly defined strand of theological thinking that runs around various parts of Australia and that may even be found in other regions of the world as well. It may certainly be found in various parts of New South Wales outside of Sydney. "Carillon Avenue" in a sense also runs diagonally across the country from the Diocese of Tasmania, and—as though going underground—pops up again in the Diocese of North West Australia. Those traveling on "Carillon Avenue" may also be discerned in parish groups dispersed in identifiable pockets dotted around the country—a few may probably be identified in Queensland and at least a few also in Adelaide, and certainly many more in Melbourne. Indeed I know from my own direct personal experience that this explicit theological package may also be found, for example, in a number of Perth parishes.

One of the attractions of employing this "roadway" metaphor is that it signals that those whose thinking it denotes are on a journey. As in the case of the rest of us, the theological views of those on "Carillon Avenue" are always subject at least to the possibility of intellectual movement and development. After all, human intellectual life is dynamic and rarely static—we are as humans always capable of growing, changing our minds, and expanding our horizons. Indeed I think it may have been Somerset Maughan who once said that "only mediocre people are at their best all the time." It is always possible to glimpse some signposts that previously were inadvertently or perhaps deliberately overlooked, or perfunctorily considered and passed by, and so to change direction—and even to get off "Carillon Avenue" altogether.

Clearly, the changing of one's mindset at least from time to time, is not to be set aside as little more than a theoretical and merely remote possibility. Among Christians it is in fact judged to be eminently advisable to examine one's views as a matter of regular practice, so as to avoid falling unwittingly into a rut—and to note the Irish saying that "the only difference between a rut and the grave is its depth." In other words, this is an exercise that is often recommended for the ultimate good of one's soul.

As John Henry Newman once said: "To live is to change, and to be perfect is to have changed often."[9]

On the other hand, some might be inclined to argue that there is a sense in which the quest for theological truth, explicitly when it is focused on the nature of deity, is a futile exercise. Peter Adam, for example, in contending that the questioning of the views of others does nothing more than divide people, appeals to the ultimate mystery of God and then goes on to argue that if our God "is an unknown God, how is it possible to lay down the law about the internal relations of the Trinity?" "To be blunt," he says, "if God is a mystery, how can anyone be sure that Sydney is wrong?"[10] In other words, it is not really possible "to attack any particular view of the relationship of the Father and the Son." To do so is said to be divisive and can be nothing more than a purely political exercise: if ultimately it cannot hope to arrive at theological truth, it must therefore be politically motivated. Better to let sleeping dogs lie.[11]

In a similar vein, in the course of the debates of 2004 to 2005, the late David F. Wright expressed some impatience with a reliance on orthodox Trinitarianism to settle controversial issues when Scripture itself is either opaque or, alternatively, incapable of settling those issues on its own terms. He asks "whence derives the remarkable confidence with which so much resurgent Trinitarianism speaks about the inner life of the Godhead, on which Scripture scarcely provides fulsome instruction?"[12]

---

9. Newman, *Essay on the Development of Christian Doctrine*, sec. 2.

10. Adam, "Honouring Jesus Christ," 11.

11. This appears to be a recipe for an ultimate form of liberalism—just as in liberal democratic societies individuals are free to entertain their own religious and moral point of view so long as it does not impact negatively on the right of every other individual to entertain his or her point of view. If one view is as good as another, this means that liberal democratic societies survive on an awkward truce in which all individual points of view must be tolerated. Unfortunately, this means that the question of truth goes out the window. On the other hand, Adam's argument that theological truth regarding the internal life of the Trinity eludes us cuts both ways: If it is not possible for anyone ever to "be sure that Sydney is wrong," then Sydney itself cannot really be sure that it is right. Certainly, it cannot be sure enough of its appeal to an alleged interpersonal subordination within the internal life of the Trinity to justify relations of domination and submission within the home and the leadership structures of church and society. Clearly, the abandonment of the quest for theological truth is a high price to pay in favor of Adam's contention that the motivation for critiquing theological views proposed by others must be purely political.

12. Wright, "Dr. Carnley on T. C. Hammond and Arianism," 48.

Then, somewhat confusedly, he says that Scripture itself is to be preferred over "supra-scriptural theological constructs."

It is understandable that evangelical Christians are naturally inclined to place their confidence in Scripture, and so avoid the more constructive discipline of systematic theology in coming to terms conceptually with the mystery of God's internal Being. Alas, Scripture itself often has to be interpreted, and interpretations of the meaning of scriptural texts regularly differ. It has to be admitted that Scripture itself may not contain a ready-made answer to everything.

As though this is not difficulty enough, the transcendence of God entails the ultimate unknowability and incomprehensibility of God, and this reminds us that there are certainly limits to religious knowledge. The Infinite is by definition beyond any finite image that may be employed to construe and refer to God; the divine transcendence entails that all finite images of God are less than the Infinite reality to which they are intended to point. Among other things, this means we are obliged to speak of God in metaphors and analogies that in the final analysis are irreducible to a set of clear and distinct propositions.

Even so, given belief in the self-revelation of God, not least in Christ, which Peter Adam is at least willing to affirm, some images that may be formed of God, even though it is acknowledged that God is a surpassing mystery, may be judged to be more appropriately used than others. The images of God as King, Shepherd, and Father may quite certainly be preferred over the images of God as Tyrant, Ruthless Bully, and Gestapo Prison Guard. Indeed, what is deemed to be unhelpful and misleading and even condemned as a heresy that is best avoided altogether, is not measured against a pretended detailed knowledge of the inner life of God as God is in God's self; rather the church in her wisdom has authoritatively determined that some humanly formulated conceptions of God are to be positively judged to be beyond the boundaries of Christian orthodoxy, and hence to be consigned to oblivion. Given its fundamental convictions about how God is perceived to be, the doctrine of the Trinity certainly seeks to speak of the interpersonal mystery of the love of God in a way that positively excludes other possibilities that are thus judged to be erroneous. In other words, the doctrine of the Trinity does not purport to say everything that might be said about the being of God in a patently clear and distinct kind of way; but what it does say is in the first instance intended to exclude possibilities that are judged to be incompatible with orthodox Trinitarian belief. Thus we may readily acknowledge the mystery with which we have to do when we insist upon belief in the full and equal sharing by all three divine persons of the very same divine nature in one Unity of Being.[13] At the very least, however, this *prima facie* appears to exclude the possibility of thinking of the interpersonal relations of the Trinitarian identities in subordinationist or complementarian terms. This is positive gain.

Moreover the identity of the church entails that it must have boundaries of this kind. These are normally set by dogmatic definitions of the whole church, such as those enshrined in the Christian creeds. The doctrine of the Trinity is such a definition. Clearly, the quest for theological truth, and the church's struggle to discern what may be authoritatively defined and identified as an acceptable statement of belief by at least pointing towards truth, by contrast with what should as a consequence advisedly be avoided, is *par for the course* in the life of the church. Likewise, from time to time, we are obliged to judge whether a specific statement of doctrinal belief or moral stance is in fact incongruent with the historical tradition of Christian orthodoxy and not a legitimate development of it.

⟿

That said, a lively discussion of alternative approaches to a broad range of doctrinal matters seems almost inevitable in the church, given that a good deal of latitude may be allowed in relation to many such matters. This freedom is often achieved by distinguishing clearly between required articles of faith or dogmatic definitions and things that may be categorized as matters that are "indifferent." Moreover, generally speaking, in the contemporary world of religious liberty a strict intellectual conformity in matters of religious belief does not carry a very high premium. Once nonconformity was feared as a threat to social cohesion. It was even nervously and brutally put down as a token of treason. But in the modern world we are less challenged and threatened by alternative points of view than our forebears undoubtedly were. Today the welter of diverse religious opinion is not to be feared but to be understood. When we understand more, we naturally fear less.

13. As defined at the Council of Nicaea in 325 as the Son's being *"homoousios"* or "of the same substance" as the Father.

This means that even what has historically been labeled "heresy" is not today regarded as the fearsome enemy that it once was. In the fourth century, once Arius was deemed to be in error he was sent into exile. In the seventh century, Maximus the Confessor likewise went into exile, though not before having both hands cut off to prevent him from writing and his tongue cut out to prevent him from speaking (about Christ having two wills, one divine and one human). In the sixteenth century, Ursinus, whom we shall meet in chapter 2 of this book, was removed from his teaching post in the University of Heidelberg when it was determined to switch from Calvinism to Lutheranism. Indeed, there was a time in the sixteenth century when to deny the Trinity or to misconstrue it was punishable by death. In England at least eight anti-Trinitarian heretics were burned at the stake between 1548 and 1612.[14] John Milton, who almost certainly espoused a form of Arianism, escaped such a fate, perhaps by the skin of his teeth.[15]

Sadly, the history of the church is strewn with such horrors, but, mercifully, civil authorities do not enforce conformity of belief in the world of religious liberty of today, certainly not in the Christian West. Even so, it admittedly remains true that, when property is held in trust for the benefit of legally defined religious bodies it cannot be alienated. This entails that, when those who occupy church buildings cease to adhere to the ruling principles and fundamental declarations of a legally constituted religious body the right of continuing occupation of trust properties may occasionally become the subject of civil legal proceedings.[16] Sometimes this is unavoidable. Unfortunately some find them-

14. See Lieb, "Milton and 'Arianism,'" 197; Rumrich, *Milton Unbound*, 87; and Nuttall, *Alternative Trinity*, especially 136–42.

15. Milton's Arianism only became clearly apparent upon the publication of *Treatise on Christian Doctrine* by Charles R. Sumner in 1825, but Michael Bauman has shown that there was a chorus of voices complaining of heresy even in *Paradise Lost*. Charles Leslie already in the late seventeenth century provides a paradigm example of such complaint. See Bauman, *Milton's Arianism*, 279; Leslie, *History of Sin and Heresy*, 117–18.

16. As has been the case in the United States, where some parishes of the Episcopal Church have been obliged to surrender their former property, given their declared dissent from ruling decisions of the Church's General Convention—for example, in relation to the ordination of women, the blessing of same-sex unions, and the ordination of openly gay people. From 2004 when I was the chair of the Archbishop of Canterbury's Panel of Reference, which was tasked with responding to dissident parishes and dioceses that had appealed to him for help, I found myself regularly advising them not to announce that they were "no longer Episcopalians" for, given that the

selves in a kind of exile from the properties which they formerly had a right to occupy. However, generally speaking, while dissenting voices may sometimes have to surrender their legal right to occupy property, for most denominations of contemporary Christianity strict conformity of belief is no longer enforced by "thought police." Certainly, the threat of Arianism no longer haunts the modern mind in the way that nonconformity did in the sixteenth and seventeenth centuries.

Despite this obvious civilizing improvement in the modern world, interpersonal animosity towards those who disagree is not unknown in the theological debates of today. Sadly, it is all too easy to "shoot the messenger" in the mistaken belief that this is an acceptable substitute for robust debate based upon a carefully considered assessment of the relevant available evidence. We may well learn from history that vilification of the kind that Arius suffered, even if today it is by comparison of a very minor or humdrum kind, is inappropriate in intellectual debate amongst Christians. It is perhaps salutary also to remember that Maximus the Confessor, who for a time received the same treatment as Arius, was ultimately judged to be right and was thus vindicated. A little caution may be in order before engaging in a rush to be right.

That does not mean that the earnest and even passionate quest for truth is not important. It does mean that the candid assessment even of firmly held views is not to be mistaken for permission to engage in low grade *ad hominem* abuse.

⤳

Fortunately, despite occasional lapses, we are today more likely to be positively appreciative of the important role of earnest debate about the conflict of ideas; even views that in the long run turn out to be judged to be erroneous may ultimately have a positive role to play in the cut and thrust of debate and not least in the ultimate discernment of truth. We cannot fail to grasp a clearer definition of what *is* to be believed than by discerning what is certainly *not* to be believed.

In fact, if anything, even the arch-heretic Arius has to some extent been rehabilitated in recent times. Maurice Wiles in an article entitled

---

church property they occupied was held in trust for Episcopalians, this could have dire consequences in courts of law. Sadly, this turned out to be the case in more than a few instances.

"In Defence of Arius,"[17] pointed to Arius's sincerity and spirituality as a corrective to his usual vilification as a troublemaker and radical enemy of the church, even an antichrist. Subsequently in *Archetypal Heresy*, Wiles pointed out that the sense of Scripture "viewed as a whole" is not all that simple to determine[18] and that we should have some sympathy for those on both sides of the debate in the fourth century as they sought to answer questions for which the evidential material is a less than a clear resource.[19] In actual fact, Arius could legitimately point to some scriptural texts which, when read in a literal or plain sense, seemed clearly to confirm his convictions.[20] Even Newman, in his hostile portrayal of Arius, pointed out that it was the liturgical reality of the fact that Christ was worshipped as divine, rather than an appeal to a transparently clear scriptural warrant, that ultimately caused laypeople to stay away from services of worship led by Arianizing bishops, and that this played a key role in their ultimate marginalization.[21]

Rowan Williams makes an additional point that is even more pertinent for us to take note of today. Williams points out that the church's discernment of theological truth is an arduous process, involving a good deal of careful argument. Inevitably, despite misgivings about its futility of the kind expressed by Tom Frame and Peter Adam, it is a process that in fact positively requires the need for alternative and competing points of view to be entered into the arena of public debate, where they must be seriously analyzed and candidly assessed. Often the innovative and disturbing emergence of a challenging set of ideas provides the language that is then taken up and fashioned by opponents into an acceptable response. This as a consequence means that in the process of the discernment of

17. Published in 1962.

18. Wiles, *Archetypal History*, 171.

19. Wiles, *Archetypal History*, 185.

20. Not least Proverbs 8:22 ("The Lord created me as the first of his work") to which he gave some priority, so that texts relating to the Son's "being begotten," by the operation of some deft footwork, were accommodated to it. Likewise, Milton understood Christ to be the first of the things that God created (*De Doctrina Christiana*, I, vii, 303). Milton could cite 1 Corinthians 8:6 ("There is but one God, the Father") and Ephesians 4:6 ("One God and Father of all") to affirm that the Father alone is self-existent. See *De Doctrina Christiana*, I.v, 216 and 218.

21. Newman, *Arians of the Fourth Century*, 445. This was a key consideration in the formation of Newman's contribution to the role of the laity, and the importance of a doctrine of "reception" in the discernment of truth, which he originally began to signal in an appendix to *Arians of the Fourth Century*. In 1859 he developed these insights more fully in *On Consulting the Faithful in Matters of Doctrine*.

truth what is eventually authoritatively defined and dogmatically taught by the church actually relies upon the articulation of points of view that eventually get labeled as theologically unacceptable or even "heretical."

It is not a rare occurrence that sincerely held positions turn out to be polar opposites that in a strange way are mutually illuminating and defining. Thus, there is a sense in which Athanasius could not have articulated the position that ultimately triumphed at Nicaea in May of 325 and eventually at Constantinople in 381 had it not been for Arius's passionate and determined attempt to promote his alternative view of things. In a sense, truth is discerned only in relation to what is eventually regarded as error, and cannot really be clearly discerned without it. In fact, in theology, as a matter of course, we regularly follow the *apophatic* or "negative" way: it is easier to say what is *not* to be countenanced, and as something therefore to be carefully avoided, than to state clearly and distinctly what is positively the case. Such is the nature of the ultimate mystery of the Infinite with which we have to deal within limits imposed by the only available resource of a language designed for reference to finite things.

From this point of view those who have sought publicly to defend what I have called "Carillon Avenue theology" have done us all a service insofar as they have forced many of us to address a set of issues that otherwise would have remained ill-defined and only vaguely expressed, and to a great extent largely hidden from view in the shadows of obscurity. I have personally learned a great deal about the doctrine of the Trinity as a result of having to engage with and respond to the key proposals of "Carillon Avenue theology." My hope is that readers of this book may have a similar experience.

+Peter Carnley
Fremantle, WA, December 1, 2022.

# Acknowledgments

I WISH TO THANK all those near and dear to me, who have helped and supported me in the course of the writing of this book and also its companion volume, *The Subordinate Substitute*. First, I want to express my profound thanks to my wonderful wife, Ann. I have been known to say (with apologies to Bette Midler) that Ann is "the wind beneath my wings." This is certainly an apt metaphor specifically in relation to the description of her supportive encouragement in the course of this writing project over the last few years. I am enormously appreciative of her constant love and care. This is especially so, since I am fully aware of the fact that she has writing projects of her own that she is anxious to tackle, but too often these get pushed aside as she devotes her energies to me and to so many others, both family and friends, who depend upon her support.

My United States friends Beth and Mikael Salovaara challenged me over the dinner table to say in a few words what the main thrust of the argument of these books was, and why I thought it important to the future life of the Christian church to get them into publishable form. They then generously volunteered also to read the manuscripts with a critical eye. I am grateful for their continuing friendly interest. On the other side of the Atlantic, a number of long-suffering librarians, who were previously entirely unknown to me, have helpfully assisted me in accessing bibliographical information that is hidden away in the rare book rooms of various Cambridge colleges. I am particularly indebted to William Hale, Jane Sinnett-Smith, Helen Carron, Emily Dourish, Sophie Pittock, and Hellen Weller, whose patience and ingenuity has helped me to overcome the frustrations of the tyranny of distance. I must say that to have had firsthand experience of the cooperative working of the Theological Federation at Cambridge has been a delight; the detailed excellence of the cataloguing of the university library a dream.

Other long-standing friends have been closer at hand. In Perth, David Wood has generously given his time and energy to the reading of manuscripts for the purpose of identifying the inevitable typing errors or missed words, and to highlight sentences that have often been either too long or just too opaque! I am very grateful also to Bill Leadbetter, who has been meticulous in spotting problems in what I imagined was a more or less completed manuscript—such as a plethora of maverick punctuation marks, and particularly my overuse of commas and semicolons—as well as suggesting more felicitous ways of expressing things. Bill has been over generous with his time and I am enormously appreciative. Apart from practical help of this kind, I have also to acknowledge the experience of something in the writing process of a less tangible kind: given the logical knots and challenges of any deep dive into the doctrine of the Trinity and the constant call for stamina in the pursuit of theological truth, the supportive companionship and encouragement of like-minded friends is of more value than might be imagined.

Finally, it must be said that it has been a pleasure to deal with such a user-friendly and professional publishing enterprise as Cascade Books. The chief editor, K. C. Hanson, may be justly proud of his assistants, Matthew Wimer and George Callihan, whose friendly and superefficient handling of the initial administrative work in relation to this project, often with a promptness that is breathtaking, is much appreciated. I am also greatly indebted to Jorie Chapman on the administrative side of things, and to E. J. Davila especially for exercising patience in assembling material for the back cover when this turned out to be more of a challenge than was first anticipated, to Jesselyn Clapp for guiding this book through its format checking stage, and especially to Rodney Clapp for his expert editorial skills and painstaking attention to detail in the work of getting the manuscript into acceptable shape through the closing stages of the publishing process. Finally, I have to thank Heather Carraher who, as typesetter, has wrought the miracle of turning a welter of errors and changes into the smoother wine of the completed text. If it is true that it takes a whole village to educate a child, it is equally true to say that it takes a whole community of people, all "on the same page," with a wide-ranging set of skills, and all dedicated to excellence, to produce a book. I know full well that I am myself only one player in this exercise and am grateful to all those who have played a part in it.

+Peter Carnley
Fremantle, July 2023.

# Abbreviations

| | |
|---|---|
| ATF | Australian Theological Forum |
| CBMW | Council of Biblical Manhood and Womanhood |
| EFS | Eternal Functional Submissiveness |
| FOAG | Faith and Order Advisory Group of the Church of England |
| GAFCON | Global Anglican Futures Conference |
| *NPNF* | *Nicene and Post-Nicene Fathers* |
| *PG* | *Patrologia Graeca* |
| SBL | Society of Biblical Literature |
| SPCK | Society for the Propagation of Christian Knowledge |
| *WUNT* | *Wissenschaftliche Untersuchungen zum Neuen Testament* |

*Chapter 1*

# The "Evangelical War" on the Trinity

THE YEAR 2016 WITNESSED a quite extraordinary flurry of theological activity. The historical evidence relating to this episode may be found, not so much in a paper-trail of journal articles and other hard copy publications (though there have been some), as in an electronic trail of telltale blog posts and tweets, many of which, fortunately, are still available to be scrutinized.[1] These make for extraordinarily interesting reading.

The contributors to this electronic debate were Christians, overwhelmingly of evangelical persuasion, and for the most part located in the US. It is abundantly clear that this theological exchange was colored by a degree of angst and emotional heat, not to mention some quite vitriolic expressions of interpersonal hostility among those entertaining radically different opinions. Indeed, the obvious passion with which logically competing views were expressed is probably an indicator of the fact that the points of contention at that time actually touched an uncomfortably raw theological nerve of some kind. As we shall see, much more was at stake than a cool and purely rational theological discussion of alternative views.

A recent US commentator, Glenn Butner, has characterized the episode as "an evangelical war on the Trinity."[2] Dr. Kevin Giles, who kept a keen watch on these US developments from afar in Melbourne, eventually

---

1. These were triggered by Liam Goligher in "Is it Okay to Teach a Complementarianism Based on Eternal Subordination?," posted on June 3, 2016 by Aimee Byrd on *Housewife Theologian* at the blog *Mortification of Spin*, which may still be consulted electronically. Joshua R. Munroe posted an extensive bibliography of articles relating to the 2016 debate on March 7, 2018. This was compiled by John T. Jeffery and is available at http://www.booksataglance.com/blog/trinity-debate-bibliography-complete-list.

2. Butner, *Son Who Learned Obedience*, 1.

wrote up an account of the whole episode, also characterizing it as an "evangelical civil war."[3] As one who had already devoted a good deal of his time and energy to the discussion of almost identical issues in Australia for more than two decades, Giles came to the discussion well prepared.[4] Indeed, as we shall see, he has, almost single-handedly and with terrier-like determination, pursued the technical intricacies of the doctrine of the Trinity in Australia over that period of years so as to highlight the shortcomings of subordinationism.

⤸

The theological exchange of 2016 came to focus on the doctrine of the Trinity because of what has come to be codified as an "eternal functional submissiveness"(EFS)[5] that was alleged to characterize the relation of the Father and the Son in the internal (or immanent) life of the Godhead.[6] By contrast with the traditional view that the three persons of the Trinity operate *in tandem* in accordance with an absolutely undivided single will and purpose, the proponents of "eternal functional submissiveness" in effect (and perhaps unwittingly) appeared to postulate two eternal divine wills, one expressing the commanding purpose and intention of the Father, and the other, giving expression to the Son's submissive obedience to the Father's determinative will. Despite the obvious initial problem of suggesting an implicit tritheism just as soon as the persons of the Trinity appear to be assigned identifiably individual wills of their own, an unfortunate dynamic of domination and submission was also obviously introduced into the doctrine of the Trinity. Many found this troubling.

---

3. Giles, *Rise and Fall*.

4. See for example, Giles, *Trinity and Subordinationism; Jesus and the Father;* and "Trinity without Tiers."

5. A notion said to have been invented in 1977 by George Knight III in *New Testament Teaching on the Role Relationship of Men and Women.* Knight spoke of a "chain of subordination" between Father, Son, men, and women (33). In the face of Liam Goligher's incisive comments on his blog, Wayne Grudem and Bruce Ware were amongst the early defenders of "eternal functional submissiveness" in 2016; very quickly some fifty scholars and innumerable "men and women in the pew" became involved.

6. The internal or immanent life of the Trinity (as God is in God's self) is often contrasted with what is humanly known of the life of the Trinity through historical revelation in divine works of creation and redemption and sanctification, or in the "economy" or management of salvation, which is therefore spoken of as the "economic Trinity."

Even though the proponents of "eternal functional submissiveness" non-chalantly thought their position to be thoroughly biblical, their disturbed opponents were quickly gripped by the view (which they expressed with a degree of alarm) that this was regrettably a step on the way to the heresy of a kind of neo-Arianism.[7]

Given an implied fundamental inequality of status and authority in the resulting divine relationship between the divine persons, it seemed to entail the *un*equal subordination of the Son to the Father.[8] Indeed, instead of the *equality* of persons in the Trinity, the proponents of EFS openly and candidly insisted that the relationship of Father and Son could be said to express a kind of *complementarity*. Hence, when Kevin Giles came to write up the episode in 2017, he quite understandably published his account of it under the title of *The Rise and Fall of the Complementarian Doctrine of the Trinity*.

Alas, as it has turned out, talk of the "fall" of a subordinationist understanding of the interpersonal relations of the Trinity, may have been a little premature. For some of its leading proponents, have since mounted defiant attempts at self-defense. Chief amongst these is Wayne Grudem, who has championed Trinitarian subordinationism at least since the publication of his *Systematic Theology* in 1994. In a revised edition of this work in 2020, he has endeavored to answer his critics. Even if this appears to be a classic exercise of whistling in the dark, it amply demonstrates that belief in the "eternal functional subordination" of the Son to the Father in the immanent life of the Trinity has still to be laid to rest.[9] As we shall see, the same situation prevails also in Australia amongst Carillon Avenue theologians, many of whom remain implacably wedded to Trinitarian subordinationism and complementarianism.

---

7. Goligher's co-host of *Mortification of Spin*, Carl Trueman, spoke of "a likely staging post to Arianism" in a blog entitled "Fahrenheit 318" (http://www.alliancenet.org/mos/postcards-from-palookaville/fahrenheit-318#0). Kevin Giles has recently been candid in openly suggesting that Trinitarian complementarianism is a form of Arianism. See *Rise and Fall*, 6: "I and a very few other evangelical egalitarians argued against this teaching, claiming it was simply a reworded form of Arianism."

8. Apparently contrary to the Nicene doctrine of the *"homoousion"*—asserting the equality of substance without difference in essence or being of the Father and the Son (and the Spirit).

9. See a classic restatement of Trinitarian subordinationism in Grudem, *Systematic Theology*, 601–3. Originally published in 1994, this book boasts bestseller status, with over 750,000 copies having been sold. No one should underestimate the importance of Grudem's contribution to the promotion of Trinitarian subordinationism.

⤸

Clearly, in June 2016 this somewhat emotionally fraught electronic debate quickly came to focus on the orthodoxy or otherwise of the notion of the alleged "eternal functional submissiveness" of the Son to the Father, and specifically, whether this fell short of the church's authoritatively defined understanding of the internal life of the Trinity.

Notwithstanding that the internal or immanent life of the Trinity is, by definition, something that must ultimately be acknowledged to fall within the category of the incomprehensible "mysteries" of the life of God that are "known to no-one" (1 Cor 2:11), the church in its wisdom has dogmatically defined some preferred formulations of its understanding as, at the very least, a less misleading way in which the divine Trinitarian relations should be conceived and expressed than others. Traditionally, the essential equality of persons rather than a kind of hierarchy of persons of unequal status, authority, and dignity within the Godhead, has prevailed as the church's authoritatively defined, and thus orthodox, Trinitarian description. Insofar as Scripture allows finite human minds to conceive them and to speak about them, these teachings have historically come to be enshrined in the church's creeds and confessions of faith. Hence, the Athanasian Creed says: "In this Trinity none is before or after the other, none is greater or less than another . . . the three persons are coequal."

By contrast, in the fourth century, Arius was condemned as an entirely mistaken arch-heretic for what was understood to be his teaching of the subordination of the Son to the Father. Instead of being of "the same substance" (*homoousios*), the position that came to be attributed to Arius was that the two divine persons were at best "*homoiousios*"— of similar or like substance, rather than the very same substance. The *homoousion*[10] has been the authoritatively defined Christian orthodoxy since the Council of Nicaea in 325, though in modern translations the philosophical category of "substance"[11] has tended to be avoided in favor of speaking of the Son and the Father simply as "one in Being." Either way, it is clear that the unity of God is what is at stake when it is suggested that one of the persons of the Trinity is subordinate to the other, or of different "substance" from the other.

---

10. The accusative singular form of the term.
11. Deriving ultimately from Aristotle.

It has to be said, however, that those who postulated an eternal "functional" submissiveness of the Son to the Father imagined that this could be entertained without compromising the essential divine nature that was believed to be secured by affirming the *homoousion*. Somehow, an equality of divine "substance" or essence was thought to remain unsullied, even despite the candid promotion of "functional" inequalities implicit in a form of subordination that was understood in purely relational terms. In other words, it was believed that a defensible form of subordination could be held alongside of the affirmation of the essential equality of the Trinitarian identities.

Whether a purely *functional* or *relational* subordination could be maintained without affecting an understanding of the essential being (or ontology) of the Trinitarian identities, given that these identities are defined relationally, appears to be a problem. For the eternal Father has his specific identity as Father, and can only be understood as Father, in relation to the eternally begotten Son, and *vice versa*. Whether a relational or functional inequality could somehow be quarantined from leading to an inequality in terms of the being of the persons engaged in such an unequal relationship is the question.

It is understandable that talk of "*eternal* functional submissiveness," as distinct from what might appear to be some kind of occasional or passing subordination between persons of essentially equal status and dignity, was heard to contain an uncomfortable contemporary echo of fourth-century Arianism. Clearly what was heard by many was a candidly expressed challenge to the orthodoxy of the formulation of a quite central Christian belief. This was bound to trigger a good deal of emotional heat.

The electronic discussion of June 2016, however, was also colored by some additional complications of a less abstract and much more grounded kind. Talk of the *complementarity*, rather than the *equality*, of the relationship of the persons of the Trinity of Love, became a hotly debated and sensitive issue especially for those who wished to argue for the gender complementarity of husbands and wives in the contractual and covenantal relationship of marriage. In other words, the *prima facie* New Testament teaching that wives are to be submissive to their husbands (as for example, in Ephesians 5:22) and the institutionalization of this in a hierarchical social arrangement of domination and submission, could be said to find its justification as a human and temporal echo of the alleged eternal complementary functional relationship between the persons the Trinity. Even if, in the light of the gospel, the relationship between husbands and their wives could of course be said to be necessarily informed by love—at least among people "filled with the Spirit" (Eph 5:2,18)—an unequal-but-complementary model of relations between the persons of the Trinity appeared to sanction a fundamental principle of male "headship" that implicitly suggests a kind of gender superiority of men over women as their inferiors. Indeed, in 1 Corinthians 11:3, Paul is said to have explicitly made this very human-divine connection in a kind of chain of submissiveness when he declared: "But I would have you know, that the head of every man is Christ; and the head of the woman [is] the man; and the head of Christ [is] God."

Whether St. Paul, as a man of his time, might simply have reflected a Stoic norm for the good ordering of society, which he clearly saw as being transformed by the love of Christ, is a moot point. But insofar as Genesis speaks of a purposive divine activity in which humans are made, male and female, in God's "own image" (Gen 1:27) it is theoretically possible to argue that this kind of social ordering is somehow "creational." That is to say, it is divinely intended in accordance with God's creative purpose.[12] When it is noted that in one Genesis creation narrative God made Adam *first*, with Eve then being made as a helpmate out of Adam's rib, Scripture could be held to teach, not only the gender priority of males to females, but a kind of male superiority to females in hierarchical terms, with males being said to be somehow "over" females in terms of authority. This might then accommodate the power dynamic of a continuing relationship of domination and submission.[13] In other words, just as the Son is alleged to be set under the authority of the Father in the ordering of the Trinity, so in marriage women are set under the authority of men.

Those whose theological mentality was schooled in the eternal and unchanging *equality* of persons of the Trinity naturally found this a scary warrant for unacceptable alpha-male dominant behavior, and even a troubling step on the way to the social horror of domestic violence and abuse. One can understand that a seemingly innocuous and highly speculative articulation of belief concerning the internal life of the persons

12. Hence, this Genesis text is said to establish a fundamental principle about the divine intention with regard to a social ordering based upon gender difference. Whether a "creational" principle was also involved in God's first creating light, and only afterwards the sun, is a pertinent question.

13. A classic treatment of this will be found in Jewett, *Man as Male and Female*. Also see Grudem, *Systematic Theology*, chapter 22.

of the Trinity really did touch a raw nerve in the hotly disputed arena of contemporary gender politics.

A second raw theological nerve, especially in the world of evangelical Christianity, apparently had to do with the prevailing evangelical understanding of the basic thrust of the gospel message. Insofar as Christ is proclaimed as a "personal savior," he is often represented as one who submissively went to the cross on the world's behalf out of obedience to a God-given vocation received from the Father. In other words, God "so loved the world" that he gave his only Son, precisely in satisfaction for the world's many sins and shortcomings. It was the vocation of the Son obediently to carry through this God-given task, even unto death on the cross. This means that a specific understanding of the doctrine of the atonement is often accepted in evangelical circles as gospel truth, almost as though it is to be classified as a required dogma, even though as a matter of fact this, unlike the internal relations of the Trinity, has never been formally defined by the church. According to this characteristic evangelical doctrine, Christ pays the penalty as a kind of substitute for all sinful humans, who through their disobedience to God deserve to die, but who thus escape punishment, and find their salvation in Christ. His unwavering obedience to the will of the Father, insofar as the Father wills the redemption of humanity, is a fundamental given of much evangelical preaching of the gospel.

This characteristic evangelical understanding of atonement is of a forensic kind that relies upon the need for the justice of God to be satisfied by an appropriately perfect and once-for-all offering. This is often justified by employing an apparently literal reading of such apparently metaphorical biblical intimations of how the salvation of Christ was humanly felt, such as "being freed from bondage" by the "payment" of a "ransom" (Mark 10:45/Matt 20:28), or as the "satisfaction" for a debt, or the imposition of a penalty by God the Father to meet the demands of justice.

Thus, in this way of thinking, it is held that a kind of penalty has to be paid by humanity for Adam's disobedience. The Son pays this penalty as the Second Adam through his perfect obedience to the Father's will. The "penal substitution theory" of the atonement thus requires the Son to submit to what are alleged to be the perfectly just requirements of the Father.[14] Alternatively, drawing upon Old Testament notions of animal

14. For a transparently clear account of this evangelical doctrine of the atonement see Grudem, *Systematic Theology*, chapter 27. For example, he declares: "Christ's death

sacrifice, Christ's sacrificial death may be interpreted, following motifs of the Epistle to the Hebrews, as the once-and-for-all vicarious sacrifice for sin.

Even if the resulting conflation of biblical metaphorical imagery into a kind of systematized theory somewhat awkwardly suggests that God was somehow bound to act in accordance with provisions of justice that he himself had set up, this transactional account of the action of God in the economy of salvation then tends to get projected onto a heavenly screen in talk of the "eternal functional submissiveness" of the Son to the Father in the internal or immanent life of the Trinity. Thus, the submissive obedience of the Son to the Father is said to be no less appropriate on an eternal heavenly stage as it is when perceived in what are understood in faith to be divinely orchestrated historical events of this world in the economy of salvation.

In other words, though it might be thought that the scriptural language about the submissiveness of the Son to the will of the Father refers to the earthly, historical life of the humanly incarnate Jesus, this kind of language may be said to be of a piece with the kind of relationship of divine fatherly command, matched by perfect filial obedience, that complementarians argued obtains eternally within the internal (or immanent) life of God. Submissive obedience is thus not just something exhibited by the *human* Jesus and belonging to the "economy of salvation," but to the essential nature of the *being* of the divine persons. What is seen in the incarnate life of the historical Jesus, is simply the acting out in time of an eternal state of affairs as far as intra-Trinitarian relations are concerned. Christ is said to have "come down from heaven" in obedience to the Father's will in order to fulfill a requirement that was necessary for the salvation of the world, and this he obediently and steadfastly did right through his historical life even to his obedience-unto-death on the cross.

This fundamental doctrine of "substitutionary" atonement that is so characteristic of evangelical Christianity thus implicitly enshrines principles of divine command and filial obedience, fatherly domination, and the Son's dutiful submission to what is demanded of him. As a consequence the notion of "eternal functional submissiveness" could easily be

---

was 'penal' in that he bore a penalty when he died. His death was also a 'substitution' in that he was a substitute for us when he died. This has been the orthodox understanding of the atonement held by evangelical theologians, in contrast to other views that attempt to explain the atonement apart from the idea of the wrath of God or payment of the penalty for sin" (1395).

perceived to be intrinsic to a standard evangelical way of presenting the gospel of God's saving grace. A challenge to the orthodoxy of this notion of the eternal filial submissiveness of the Son to the Father's will, could therefore be perceived to cut to the quick as a threat to the very identity of much evangelical Christianity. It was almost bound to generate some emotional heat and not a little vitriol.

⮌

The Australian experience of a similarly emotionally charged discussion focused on essentially these same Trinitarian issues somewhat earlier, right at the very beginning of the twenty-first century. Unlike the "evangelical war" of 2016, this did not take the form of a debate amongst otherwise like-minded evangelical Christians belonging to various denominations, but was instead an in-house debate within the life of the Anglican Church of Australia.[15]

This involved a good deal of quite informal face-to-face passing comment, but sometimes discussion in scheduled meetings, whether called together explicitly for the purpose, or meetings of the national Church whose agenda became hijacked by the felt need to address this specific issue. This in-house discussion has left a modest paper trail of published material in journal articles and books, of which the sustained contributions of Kevin Giles, to which reference has already been made, are without doubt the most significant.

The Australian debate was initially triggered by a Report of the Doctrine Commission of the Anglican Diocese of Sydney, which was formally received, apparently without dissent, by its Diocesan Synod in 1999.[16] Very significantly, this was entitled "The Doctrine of the Trinity and its bearing on the relationship of men and women." As with the electronic debate of 2016 in North America, the discussion of the internal relations

15. Though initially the chief protagonists were well recognized evangelical Anglicans, such as Kevin Giles and Robert Doyle, others of us were inevitably drawn into the debate so that it soon began to gain purchase well beyond the ranks of those who thought of themselves as evangelicals.

16. This report may be accessed on the website of the Anglican Diocese of Sydney at Sydney Diocesan Services (SDS): https://www.sds.asn.au/reports-received-synod-1999, Reports to Synod, document 18. It is also published in a slightly different format in Giles, *Trinity and Subordinationism*, Appendix B. The reformatted report was arranged in numbered paragraphs, whereas the original version was divided into sections. Both methods of referencing will be sustained below.

of the persons of the Trinity touched down in earthy reality insofar as the heavenly model of divine interpersonal subordination was perceived to have an important bearing on the interpersonal relations of husbands and wives, and on the question of whether the admission of women to ministerial priesthood, not to mention leadership roles in the episcopate, was somehow contrary to the intended natural ordering of gender difference by God from the time of creation.

The report thus outlined an uncompromisingly complementarian approach to the understanding of male-female relationships by defending a parallel model understanding of the interpersonal relationships of the persons of the Trinity, in which the Son was explicitly said to be eternally submissive and, indeed, "subordinate" to the Father. The report specifically denied any suggestion that scriptural references to the submissiveness of the Son only applied to the historical life of the incarnate Jesus.[17] It was not just that the *human* Jesus was subject to the sovereign divine authority of God the Father in the course of his incarnate historical existence; rather, this kind of subordination was projected onto a heavenly screen from all eternity. The Second Person of the Trinity in his divine nature was declared to be eternally subordinate to the person of the Father.

I must confess that many of us were perplexed at the time by this apparent departure from the traditional orthodox understanding of the Trinity. Apart from openly espousing a form of subordinationism, the Sydney Doctrine Commission appeared to repudiate the notion of an indivisible single divine will, eternally shared without differentiation by all three persons of the Trinity, as well as the consequent inseparability of their operations in the economy of salvation. Hence many of us were immediately troubled by the implicit difficulty that this may have constituted a form of Arianism, though the primary focus at the time had more overtly to do with the vexed question of the admission of women to ministerial priesthood and the episcopate in the Church, and whether this fell under a kind of prohibition given the possibility that Scripture could be held to embody a principle of exclusive "male headship."

In 2002, however, Kevin Giles published his spirited critique of the fundamental complementarian case for the kind of hierarchical ordering within the life of the Trinity that *prima facie* seemed to be implicit in the thinking of the Sydney Doctrine Commission and, at the same time,

17. Report of the Sydney Doctrine Commission, 1999, sec. 4.2/para. 18.

questioned its use as a methodological principle for justifying both the submissiveness of wives to husbands, and the exclusion of women from ministerial priesthood and episcopal leadership in the life of the church. This was entitled *The Trinity and Subordinationism*.

In explicitly addressing the notion of the eternal subordination of the Son to the Father that had been argued by the Sydney Doctrine Report, Giles warned that this constituted a serious departure from the historical norms of Christian orthodoxy as these have been authoritatively defined in the creeds and confessions of faith. In doing so, he pulled no punches in declaring forthrightly that the position adopted by the Sydney Doctrine Commission report failed to represent "historic orthodoxy."[18] That is to say, by logical implication it could be classified as a Christian "heresy." Indeed, although Giles tended to distance this Christian deviant from the classical expression of Arianism by Arius himself in the fourth century, Giles's meaning was not lost on his readers. Robert Doyle, one of the original authors of the Sydney Report, in reviewing Giles's work lamented that "by the end of the book the clear implication is that we are heretics, and of the nastier Arian kind."[19] Without doubt, the hostile reaction that followed, and Giles's own self-defensive responses about the legitimacy of the concerns he had raised, certainly prepared him for a clear and spontaneous engagement with what transpired electronically especially amongst United States evangelical theologians in 2016.[20]

⤷

At the time of Giles's initial critique of the Sydney Doctrine Commission's report, I was Primate of Australia, having been elected on February 3, 2000. I well remember the intense reaction triggered by Giles's criticisms of the report amongst those in leadership positions in the Diocese of Sydney, including one notable occasion, which I think occurred during the luncheon recess at a national meeting of the Australian Church—possibly

18. Giles, *Trinity and Subordinationism*, 25.

19. Doyle, "Use and abuse."

20. See the review of Giles's book in the blog, "Trinity and Subordinationism," prepared by "Anglican Media Sydney staff," November 26, 2002, https://sydneyanglicans. net/search/6e175ead2a122a7713de46d45ed70042, and Doyle, "Are We Heretics?," *The Briefing*, 307, 11–19, and again under the title of "Use and abuse" on the Sydney Diocesan website; also Grudem, *Evangelical Feminism*, 426, and Ware, "Trinity and Subordinationism," 355. For an alternative, more positive review see Reid, "Trinity and Subordinationism."

a meeting in Sydney of the Standing Committee of the Church's General Synod. At this impromptu gathering Dr. Peter Jensen, who had originally been a member of the Sydney Doctrinal Commission and thus one of the 1999 report's joint authors, and who by this time had been elected and assumed office as Archbishop of Sydney, sought leave to read a paper in which he proceeded to discredit Giles's work. If anything, Jensen relied less on arguing matters of theological principle in relation to the doctrine of the Trinity, and instead preferred to focus on cataloguing the historical support of like-minded adherents of a form of subordinationism as a way of insisting on the legitimacy of marrying this with affirmations of orthodox belief in the equality of the Trinitarian identities. Beyond this, he tended to highlight the identification of errors in the technical apparatus of the footnoting in Giles's presentation, apparently in order to suggest that his case should not be taken too seriously. I recall wondering at the time if typographical errors and the occasional mistake in footnoting may have been more of an indication that Giles had done his work without the help of a research assistant than evidence of actual flaws in his Trinitarian argument.

Strangely, there was little, if any, serious engagement with substantive theological issues at that particular gathering. Instead, in the course of mounting a spirited defence of the commission's work, Dr. Jensen was content to insist that the idea of the submissiveness of the Son to the Father was in accordance with Scripture, and that, as it was often affirmed historically in theological writing, it therefore could not justifiably be condemned as a form of Christian heresy.

At this gathering interested parties were accordingly furnished with a photocopied compendium of twenty-five numbered excerpts from published works by a range of theological authorities. Apart from a couple from the writings of Kevin Giles expressing the contrary position, all of these excerpts were presented as evidence of the legitimacy of maintaining belief in the eternal subordination of the Son to the Father. This collection of documents did not, however, form the basis for entering into any explicit discussion of the actual issues involved. Rather, the motivation behind the production of this collection appears to have been simply to affirm that the subordination of the Son to the Father could be accepted almost as self-evident, by perusing the assembled documents and accepting them as authorities that supported belief in the continuing validity of the Sydney Doctrine Commission's arguments.[21]

If there was a shortfall in terms of the level of actual Trinitarian debate around this time, this was largely owing to the fact that the Sydney complementarians were already firmly convinced that they were defending a position that was taught in Scripture, even if others of us were prepared to countenance the possibility that Giles might be right in contending that historic Christian orthodoxy had actually been compromised by the Sydney Doctrine Commission. Insofar as talk of the "eternal functional submissiveness" of the Son sounded alarmingly like a new form of Arianism, the fundamental point that Giles had endeavored to make certainly seemed *prima facie* to warrant being taken seriously.

Though I had not actually had time to study Giles's 2002 book in any detail, nor even to examine the catalogue of theological authorities that had been assembled in Sydney in answer to him, in 2004 I ventured to comment on the Sydney Doctrine Report of 1999 in the context of a discussion of the role of women in Christian ministry, and specifically in the episcopate. This was little more than a passing reference in a chapter of *Reflections in Glass*, which was published in that year.[22] After noting the teaching, regularly assumed to have originated with Arius, that the Son is subordinate and thus inferior to the Father, I observed that insofar as the members of the Sydney Doctrine Commission held that the Son is "incapable of doing other than his Father's will" "from before creation" as something "imposed by the inner reality of personhood" they appeared to endorse a position remarkably reminiscent of these sub-Trinitarian views. Indeed I ventured to repeat what many others had been saying— that the Sydney Doctrine Commission Report "seem prepared openly to embrace this heretical position."[23]

As it turned out this passing expression of support, effectively for the position that had been forthrightly taken for some years in the

---

21. My copy of this compendium is bound together in a spiral folder, under a plastic cover. A yellow front page bears the identifying crest of the Diocese of Sydney. It was otherwise without a title. I shall return to the discussion of this collection of documents in chapter 4.

22. Women had been admitted to ministerial priesthood in Australia since 1992, though the Anglican Diocese of Sydney has steadfastly resisted moving in that direction. *Reflections in Glass* was reviewed by Robert Forsyth, "It's Negative Theology," *Market-Place*, April 8, 2004, and Robert Doyle, Review of "*Reflections in Glass*, Chapter 7."

23. Carnley, *Reflections in Glass*, 235.

pioneering work of Kevin Giles, turned out to trigger a spate of negative reactions. The Archbishop of Sydney, Dr. Peter Jensen took me aside from one national gathering to tell me that, "unlike many others," he was not at all pleased with *Reflections in Glass*, and registered his consternation that I might actually agree with Kevin Giles in thinking that Sydney Anglicans might be seriously in error. He was clearly disturbed that the theological orthodoxy of the Sydney Doctrine Commission Report was publicly being called into question. Given that he had been one of its joint authors, this was entirely understandable.

Some time later when I was asked by the Australian Bishop to the Forces, Tom Frame,[24] if I was surprised by Sydney's collective, and Peter Jensen's personal, hostile response to the contents of *Reflections in Glass*, my reply was, "Yes, I was surprised—given that others had written about the Sydney position, and the idea that the report was doctrinally faulty had been explored at length by Kevin Giles." Indeed, as the matter had been an item of public comment on and off for nearly five years, and, as my words in *Reflections in Glass* were really just a passing reference in a chapter that was essentially about the admission of women to the episcopate, I was surprised at the degree of negative reaction to it. I ventured the suggestion to Frame that perhaps the reason was that, while there was a tendency to write Kevin Giles off as quite simply mistaken, the fact that the Primate of Australia was now prepared to say something similar, even in a passing comment, was probably what was disturbing—i.e., it was *the Primate* who was expressing a doubt about Sydney orthodoxy!

It was only some time later that I discovered that the compendium of alleged theological authorities that had been assembled in support of Sydney subordinationism against Giles had actually included in its entirety a brief article that I myself had written on the significance of the doctrine of the Trinity for understanding the role of the bishop in the hierarchical ordering of the ministry of the church as "first amongst equals." In other words, unbeknown to me, I myself had two years prior to this conversation been corralled to the support of subordinationism! Clearly, the fact that I stated in *Reflections in Glass* that I was in effect inclined to agree with Giles's charge of Arianism probably came as something of an unwelcome surprise. Having been unwittingly press-ganged into the support of Sydney subordinationism it now appeared that this was not

24. In his email communication of July 4, 2005. Tom Frame subsequently published "Dynamics and Difficulties of Debate in Australian Anglicanism" in *Agendas for Australian Anglicanism* (see 94, 106, and 142–59), and *Anglicans in Australia*.

actually the case, and that, on the contrary, I had publicly declared a hand in support of Giles's critique of the very position I had previously been assumed to support.[25]

⟿

It fairly quickly became clear that the wider Anglican community was taking an increasing interest in what had been discussed. Inevitably, the question of the orthodoxy of Sydney complementarianism became much more wide-ranging than just a dispute among theologians and bishops in semi-private gatherings. What was being perceived as a serious theological debate was known to be simmering across the national Church. Unfortunately, the differences of opinion amongst bishops was leaked to the Sydney press, which ran an unsympathetic article in criticism of Sydney's alleged misogyny. This in turn triggered a spate of letters to the editor, and led bishop Robert Forsyth to produce a defensively negative review of *Reflections in Glass*. Although I was unaware of the specifics of any of this at the time, for I was on the other side of the country and certainly not in the habit of following the coverage of "Church news" in the Sydney press, I was certainly more generally aware that the issue of the problematic nature of the theology that had been expressed in the Sydney Doctrine Commission's Report of 1999 was now no longer just a passing item of discussion amongst the national House of Bishops.

In view of the public broadening of the debate, I came to the conclusion that people generally needed to be as well informed about what actually was at stake as possible. I well knew that in my own Diocese of Perth there were valued evangelical parishes, some with very lively and indeed large congregations, with theological sympathies fed by a historical connection with Moore College in Sydney. The last thing we needed was for them to fall, simply by default, into the possible Arianism of the "wise men from the East." Moreover, as we were all at the time grappling with the question of the role of women in ministry with which Trinitarian complementarianism had been so deliberately and clearly linked, there was a clear need in Perth to reach a common mind across differences of theological and missional emphases.

25. In a lecture in Dublin in June 2005, Dr. Jensen rehearsed this alleged implicit support of hierarchical ordering amongst the persons of the Trinity. He declared that I was "in print supporting a notion of monarchy in the Trinity with an application to church government by bishops." See Frame, "Dynamics and Difficulties," 157.

On the other hand, the fate of women in ministry across the whole Australian Church was at stake. It became clear enough, for example that, at least within the life of the national Church, people were, if not puzzled and perplexed, then fascinated, not only by the somewhat speculative debate about the immanent Trinity, but because they were well aware that this was impinging on the then hotly debated issue of whether Australian Anglicanism might embrace the practice of consecrating women as bishops. The relevance of the issue to the then hotly contested discussion of the admission of women to the episcopate meant that subordination-ism and complementarianism could not be quarantined as somewhat esoteric and speculative items of Trinitarian description, but had quickly become more general matters of public interest. It was no longer an op-tion to imagine that this could just be allowed to fade away into oblivion.

I was therefore faced with the question of whether I in fact had a responsibility to pursue the public discussion of the issues further, being well aware that it is the job of a Primate, indeed, as it is the task of all bishops in the exercise of their teaching office, to call maverick theologi-cal adventurers back to the fold. This is an explicit responsibility of the episcopal teaching office that flows from the solemn ordination promise to correct and exhort, and particularly to forewarn those at the precipice of error. The widespread conversation within the Anglican Church of Australia, and even beyond it, about an apparent tendency to Arianism, thus posed a particular challenge to those of us committed to the mainte-nance of the Church in all truth. I was therefore instinctively disinclined just to "blow an out-of-range dog whistle" that could not be heard by men and women in the pew and the general public. Clearly, it was important that the national Church should not just be allowed to drift into a kind of Arianism by default—and certainly "not on my watch" as Primate.

Moreover, any report of a Doctrine Commission is, after all, essen-tially a study document; its very purpose is to stimulate public discussion and debate. The work of any one Diocesan Commission is bound to be noted beyond the boundaries of the diocese that has produced it. Those responsible for the publication of such reports usually accept that they must anticipate the possibility, even the probability, that they will pro-voke robust critical comment. If rationally assessed, and discussed with a modicum of civilized good will, a nationwide consideration of the seri-ously held subordinationism and of the complementarian doctrine of the Trinity as it was set out in the Sydney Doctrine Commission Report of 1999 seemed to be a good thing.

I therefore facilitated the calling of a public colloquium in Melbourne with the aim of bringing interested Anglicans more generally up to speed in relation to the matters at issue. Melbourne seemed the obvious place, given that Kevin Giles was on hand to lay out his concerns in relation to the position espoused by the Sydney Doctrine Commission and to be given the opportunity to submit his critique to questioning. Given that there had been a tendency simply to dismiss him and his expressions of concern, it was important that he be heard and his arguments submitted to peer review. The hope was (although this may have been wishful thinking) that a full day of serious discussion based on some papers prepared by opposing theological minds might be able to make some headway towards identifying the real nub of the problems at issue, so as at least to help people move some way towards achieving a common mind. This colloquium was held at Trinity College in the University of Melbourne on August 20, 2004. About fifty people, including both clergy and laypeople, attended. From the outset, however, Dr. Peter Jensen signaled that he was not interested, and unfortunately there was no formal presence of the members of the Sydney Doctrine Commission who had authored the report. A pity.

‿

In introducing the topic at this meeting, I endeavored to broaden the discussion by deflecting attention away from a narrow focus on the Sydney Doctrine Commission Report itself that might inevitably be heard as accusatory and even suggestive of an inquisition, to a more general consideration of the broader theological and missiological commitments that seemed to me to underlie the conservative evangelical fascination with "subordinationism." For some time, I had entertained a sneaking suspicion that the seminal theology that had become domiciled at Moore College in Sydney could be sheeted back to its most influential principals—most notably Dr. Broughton Knox, who was principal from 1959 to 1985, and, in the generation before that, to archdeacon T. C. Hammond, who had come from Ireland to be the college principal in 1936.

Hammond, particularly, enjoyed a prestigious reputation as the theologian who had set the Diocese of Sydney on a very distinctive theological course, not least by producing a handbook of basic Christian doctrine, which he in fact prepared for publication during the course of the sea voyage to Sydney. This was published under the title of *In*

*Understanding Be Men*. It was destined to become a basic theological text, second only to Calvin's *Institutes of the Christian Religion* for years to come at Moore Theological College.

It is of enormous significance that in this theological primer Hammond forthrightly and unequivocally declared that there were three essential ingredients of the doctrine of the Trinity:

> In short, the full Christian doctrine demands all three of the following
>
> 1 The unity of the Godhead.
> 2 The full deity of the Son (who was "begotten") and of the Spirit (who "proceeds" from the Father and the Son).
> 3 The subordination of the Son and the Spirit to the Father.[26]

Interestingly, in the 1999 Report of the Sydney Doctrine Commission appeal is made explicitly to this passage in claiming the support of Hammond's authority to clinch the legitimacy of the idea of the Son's eternal subordination to the Father. In the first published editions of the report in the Diocesan Synod Minutes of 1999 this passage from *In Understanding Be Men* is quoted at the end of a paragraph which cites some cautious words of H. E. W. Turner: "There is an orthodox subordination in the sense that the Trinity must begin with the Father or lead up to the Father, but this is concerned with the order of thought and unity in derivation and does not affect the ontological status of the three persons."[27] There is no suggestion that Hammond's words are to be understood to constitute anything more than an endorsement of these words of Turner.

However, the report was apparently at some later stage reformatted, which resulted in Hammond's words being separated from this quote from Turner and assigned a separate numbered section in their own right. Thus, the version that is still available on the Sydney Diocesan Services website was obviously amended; the end of the preceding paragraph that originally quoted T. C. Hammond was subsequently made into a new separate paragraph (No. 15) exclusively in its own right, perhaps to highlight the perceived pivotal importance of the authority of T. C. Hammond in relation to the subordinationist thesis.[28]

---

26. Hammond, *In Understanding Be Men*, 56.

27. Turner is cited in Richardson, ed., *Dictionary of Christian Theology*, 329.

28. See the version published with permission as "Appendix B" in Giles, *Trinity and Subordinationism*, 138.

Understandably, the very same subordinationist quotation from Hammond is also included in the collection of theological authorities that were gathered in support of Sydney subordinationism and distributed in the wake of Archbishop Jensen's rejoinder to Kevin Giles's publication of *The Trinity and Subordinationism* in 2002. In this set of photocopied documents it appears as the final authority of twenty-five excerpts. In other words, the last word of the collection is assigned to Hammond so as roundly to conclude that an essential ingredient of the doctrine of the Trinity is "the eternal subordination of the Son and the Spirit to the Father."

Clearly, any attempt to probe the historical antecedents of the subordinationist position espoused by the Sydney Doctrine Commission necessarily has to begin with this statement of T. C. Hammond. As it happened, at a National Heads of Churches meeting in Canberra in 2004, I shared this suspicion about the seminal importance especially of the theology of T. C. Hammond for understanding Sydney subordinationism with my opposite number in the Uniting Church, the Reverend Professor James Haire. In the course of a casual conversation about the rumble that *Reflections in Glass* had triggered, I mentioned the reference in chapter 7 about the apparent willingness amongst Sydney folk to embrace a form of Arianism, and my inclination to think that this might well be sheeted back to the seminal influence of T. C. Hammond. Haire, who was himself an Irishman, immediately volunteered that T. C. Hammond was a typical "federal theologian," and (semi-jokingly) that there was a sense in which "all the Ulster federal theologians were Arian." Indeed, James Haire helpfully pointed me to Alan J. Torrance's book, *Persons in Communion: Trinitarian Description and Human Participation*, where I would find a useful discussion of federal theology.[29] As it happened, we were standing outside St. Mark's Library in Canberra at the time. At the opportunity of the next meeting break I took myself inside to consult Torrance's book. This was my introduction to federal theology, which in turn informed the paper that was read at the Melbourne Colloquium. In the following year, 2005, this was published under the title of "T. C. Hammond and the Theological Roots of Sydney Anglicanism" along with other papers of the Colloquium, in *St. Mark's Review*.

In a presentation in response to my attempt to place the issues that faced us in a historical context, Dr. Peter Adam, an evangelical theologian

---

29. Torrance, *Persons in Communion*. The relevant section on federal theology is found on pages 60–62. See also Weir, *Origins of the Federal Theology*.

and principal of Ridley Theological College in Melbourne, immediately expressed two major complaints about the holding of a colloquium at all. Even though he was nevertheless prepared to participate in it, he first charged that the colloquium was political and deliberately intended to divide people, and so "Christ was not being honoured."[30] Adam pointedly asked why it was that Archbishop Peter Jensen was not present—the suggestion apparently being that he had not been invited. Clearly, something of the angst that marked the electronic "evangelical war on the Trinity" of June 2016 in the United States was not absent from this Australian sneak preview of essentially the same debate in 2004. Indeed not a little *ad hominem* vitriol appeared to lurk just below the surface. I was fortunately able to point out that Dr. Jensen had been invited but had chosen not to attend, not being really interested in a colloquium on the Trinity. It was clear that he was not enthusiastic about engaging publicly with the theological issues that Giles had been pursuing.

Adam's second complaint related to what was represented as an "attack" on T. C. Hammond. When he published his account of the views that he had expressed at the Melbourne Colloquium in *St Mark's Review*, he declared that it was inappropriate to impugn the reputation of T. C. Hammond by suggesting that he might have been the root cause of the efflorescence of views of problematic orthodoxy. "I was particularly distressed," he said, "to discover that Archbishop Carnley chose this occasion to launch an attack on the late T. C. Hammond, a figure of virtually iconic significance in the Diocese of Sydney." It is gratifying that at least there is agreement about the fact that T. C. Hammond is much revered, almost to the point of being venerated as a kind of cult hero, amongst Sydney Anglicans. Whether this should justify a tendency to tiptoe around his published views as though they are somehow theologically untouchable, however, is surely problematic. This is particularly so in view of the very fact that Hammond appears to hold the key to understanding the origins of the contentious Sydney subordinationist position. Unfortunately, Adam made no attempt to respond to the actual theological points at issue or to challenge the ultimate role of federal theology in the formulation of Hammond's quite unequivocal articulation of what may be the initial and defining expression of the subordinationist thesis amongst Sydney Anglicans. This was simply bypassed.[31]

30. See Adam, "Honouring Jesus Christ," 11–18.

31. Likewise, a more recent commentary on the theology of T. C. Hammond baldly asserts, but without any discussion: "There was no hint of unorthodoxy with regard

In the wake of the Melbourne Colloquium, a number of published pieces in a follow-up number of *St Mark's Review* indicated that any interest in pursuing the Trinitarian issues was likewise eclipsed instead by a flurry of concern to close ranks behind T. C. Hammond and to defend the orthodoxy both of his subordinationist position and of those who have followed in his footsteps.

One writer who was summoned to the public defence of T. C. Hammond was David F. Wright, from New College in Edinburgh, who had revised and republished a new edition of *In Understanding Be Men* in 1968. Rather than address Hammond's actual theology of the Trinity, Wright declared that he had not noticed that any sign of Arianism that had crept into Hammond's theology. Despite Hammond's unequivocal espousal of belief in the subordination of the Son to the Father as one of the three essential things that are needed in Trinitarian theology, Wright was content simply to volunteer: "I am however puzzled that, after studying patristics as an undergraduate at Cambridge and a postgraduate at Oxford and teaching it for a few years in New College, University of Edinburgh, I should have failed in the later 1960s to discern Arianism lurking in *In Understanding Be Men*."[32] Even despite the clear declaration of Hammond's own words relating to the eternal subordination of the Son to the Father, Wright was prepared to declare that he had found no suggestion that the Son is somehow eternally submissive or subordinate to the Father in a way that would compromise the Nicene insistence on the equality of the divine persons. Indeed, he went so far as to say, "It is nothing short of outrageous to accuse T. C. Hammond of Arianism or Arianising tendencies. The accusation would not stand up in any kind of court of fair judgement. Whatever he had to say about the relations between the three persons cannot be read as cancelling out what he affirms, in line with the creeds of confessions, in the most unambiguous terms about the full co-equal divinity of the Son and the Spirit with the Father in the one Godhead."[33] Clearly, Wright was of the view that so

---

to the Trinity and the relation of the persons so mistakenly alleged by the Anglican Archbishop of Perth in 2005." McIntosh, *Anglican Evangelicalism in Sydney*, Kindle ed., loc. 7781.)

32. Wright, "Dr. Carnley on T C Hammond and Arianism," 46.

33. Wright, "Dr. Carnley on T C Hammond and Arianism," 47. Wright heavily relies upon the making of authoritative assertions of this kind. It nevertheless remains the case that there is still a question to be proved: whether what Hammond had to say in relation to the subordination of the Son and the Spirit to the Father "cancels out" or compromises what he had to say about their equality is precisely the question we

long as it was first affirmed that the Father and the Son were equal, it is possible also to affirm that the Son was subordinate to the Father. Exactly how the Son could be thought of as being both equal to the Father and at the same time subordinate to the Father without self-contradiction is the question at issue.

⁓

The hallowed authority of T. C. Hammond is, without doubt, of seminal importance in the historical development of the subordinationist theology of the Trinity in Sydney. The very fact that questioning the theological orthodoxy of this aspect of T. C. Hammond's theology clearly touched a raw nerve is a poignant indication that there is much more to this story than we have yet been able to unfold. In the next chapter we will further unpack the basic elements of federal theology, along with an account of its role in the thinking of T. C. Hammond as a key index for understanding what lies behind the infamous Report of the Sydney Doctrine Commission of 1999.

Meanwhile, it is sufficient to observe the unmistakable parallels between this conversation amongst Australian Anglicans through the first decade of the twenty-first century and the electronic debates of the "evangelical war on the Trinity" in the United States in the northern summer of 2016. It is noteworthy that in both cases this was initially a debate between evangelical Christians. Others of us were only gradually drawn into it. Apart from the obvious linkage that was made at the outset in both cases between a consideration of the internal relations of the persons of the Trinity and the gender politics involving the alleged subordination of wives to their husbands, and the implications of this, not only for a Christian understanding of the dynamics of family life, but in considering the possible role of women in the ministry of Christian leadership, the issue of the subordination of the Son to the Father also appears to be linked with some cherished evangelical sensibilities relating to the very understanding and presentation of the gospel of reconciliation. Clearly, something more appears to be involved than a dispassionate and purely speculative consideration of issues of Trinitarian description.

---

have to pursue. Furthermore, whether this amounts to a form of Arianism is yet an open question.

⌐⌐

Given the intensity of the continuing disturbance in Sydney, and even levels of resentment at the very suggestion that its Doctrine Commission might be in error, at Dr. Jensen's kind invitation I agreed to meet with members of the commission at Dr. Jensen's house, Bishopscourt, at Darling Point in Sydney on September 11, 2004, to try to communicate why it was that so many of us were now seriously concerned. Unfortunately, Robert Doyle, who had been one of the original authors of the report and who specialized in systematic theology at Moore Theological College, was unable to be present. Bishop John Harrower of Tasmania was, however, in attendance to represent the interest of the National Bishops' Conference in the discussion.

By this time the membership of the Sydney Doctrine Commission of some five years earlier had changed. Apart from Dr. Jensen himself and Dr. Robert Doyle, who was absent, the people with whom I met were members of a newly constituted commission, though, just as had been the case previously, it was composed of theologians drawn largely from Moore Theological College,[34] who were understandably committed to the loyal defense of the earlier commission's now much talked about report of 1999. Only one member of this new commission had been in attendance at the Melbourne Colloquium.[35]

This group of predominantly like-minded Carillon Avenue theologians heard me courteously, as they earnestly sought to defend the functional subordinationist position to which the clear majority of them were implacably wedded; indeed, it seemed that they found it very difficult even to think that the Sydney Doctrine Commission Report of 1999 was anything but orthodox because of their confident belief that its teaching was thoroughly in accordance with Scripture. In a sense, while they were convinced that they still conformed to the church's historic dogmatic tradition, this was for them of less significance than the authority of Scripture. On the other hand, it became fairly clear (admittedly, if only to me) that the members of this group as a whole tended to begin their thinking about the Trinity by starting first with the idea of divine substance (*ousia*) to secure a claim to orthodoxy by affirming the equal divinity and unity

34. The clergy training facility of the Diocese of Sydney.

35. The Revd. Dr. Ivan Head, warden of St Paul's College, within the University of Sydney. Although at the time "from Sydney" he was hardly "of Sydney," having come originally from the Diocese of Perth.

of the three Trinitarian identities (the *homousion*), and then, on the basis
of this commitment, they moved on to speak secondarily of the functional differentiation of three divine persons, whose essential divinity
had to their mind therefore already been established and affirmed. This
meant that it was possible for them to argue that the three persons shared
equally in the same divine substance (*ousia*), while their individual functional roles were held to be identifiably different and complementary. For
example, they reaffirmed section 4.1/paragraph 17 of the report where it
was stated that the persons of the Trinity were equal, even though it also
affirmed that subordination "belongs to the eternal relationship between
the persons of the Trinity, and not only the humanity of Jesus in the incarnation . . ." and that "This applies to the Spirit as well as the Son (Jn.
14/26)."[36]

When I tried to point out that, insofar as they spoke of the Son and
the Spirit as being subordinate to the Father, I thought they were thinking
of the three identities of the Trinity as three individuals rather than three
interrelated persons,[37] this clearly cut no ice; this suggestion was simply
greeted with blank looks. When I went on to characterize the relationality of persons within the Trinity as a "perichoretic mutuality of self-gift"
between equals, it was pointed out that this was not scriptural language,
whereas the idea of submissiveness (*hupotasso*) certainly was (at least
between husbands and wives). Unfortunately, they seemed to overlook
the fact that the term "*ousia*" upon which they so heavily relied was not
a biblical term either.

I also noted that, the methodology of beginning by according a
logical priority to the idea of substance (*ousia*) so as first to establish
the equal divinity of all three persons of the Trinity *before* moving on
to speak of their interpersonal relationality appeared to echo a basically
Augustinian approach to the Trinity, which perhaps represented a somewhat problematic drift away from the original Cappadocian insistence on
beginning with the person of the Father as the divine origin both of the
divinity of the only begotten Son, and of the Spirit who proceeds ineffably

36. Sec. 4.1/para.17.

37. The difference being that whereas an individual is conceived in separation from
others, a person is conceived in relation to others. Thus, it is intrinsic to being a person
to be able to address others and to anticipate a similar response from them. Persons
are persons by virtue of the fact that they are involved in interpersonal give and take.
This essential relationality was one of the great discoveries of the Cappadocian fathers
of the fourth century, and a huge step forward in the history of ideas.

from the Father.[38] In this way the Cappadocians were able to ground the shared divinity of all three persons in their mutual relationality so as to constitute the divine essence of their unified shared being or *ousia*. In other words, it was not possible to separate the shared divine being and nature from the relationality of persons. However, in noting an Augustinian rather than Cappadocian style of theologizing, I did not at the time drop to the fact that this probably holds the key to untangling the issue of the legitimacy or otherwise of the functional submissiveness of the Son to the Father with its implication of subordinationism. I shall return to this later in this book.

For the moment, it is important to note that this meeting was very much controlled, with those sitting around the table being invited to make a point or raise a question in turn, strictly at the invitation to speak of the Archbishop. It was hardly a free-flowing discussion, but rather a very well-modulated, though friendly and civilized, exchange of alternative and logically competing views.[39] Though the free airing of views alternative to those expressed in the Sydney Doctrine Commission's 1999 Report was not encouraged, at one point it was admitted by one of those present that the language of the report might have been a little misleading. Indeed, he confessed that he had himself tried to rewrite the report, though without much success. In response to this I attempted to suggest that some rewriting, perhaps with a view to preventing the kind of reading of the report that I and many others had found troubling, might be a very worthwhile enterprise. This seemed to have no appeal as a good idea to the chairman of the meeting, who remained very convinced that the report as it stood reflected the teaching of Scripture.

It is pertinent to note that, though I was not myself then aware of it at the time, a rejoinder to the chapter of *Reflections in Glass* to which exception had originally been taken had been published by Anglican Media Sydney the week before this meeting (on September 3, 2004). This had been written by Dr. Robert Doyle, who was unable to be present at the meeting. In this very critical, though somewhat journalistic piece, Doyle insisted on defending the notion of the "eternal functional

38. The fundamental point being made by H. E. W. Turner in the words already quoted.

39. Bishop Harrower later reported, in a letter to all bishops of the Anglican Church of Australia, dated September 17, 2004, that "The meeting was conducted in a spirit of politeness, graciousness, and with a high level of lively intellectual interaction and attentive listening. . . .The conversation was gracious and is ongoing."

submissiveness" of the Son, while at least acknowledging that an ontological or essential subordination of the Son to the Father "would be
Arianism." His conclusion that the Sydney Doctrine Report had successfully avoided this pitfall was based on the claim that the report only affirmed the functional and not an essential or ontological submissiveness
of the Son, and also that an alleged functional submissiveness was fully
in accord with a logically prior affirmation of the equal divinity of the
Son which was shared with the Father and the Holy Spirit (the *homoousion*). There is little doubt that members of the group of Carillon Avenue
theologians with whom I met on September 11 had been bolstered in
confidence and were thoroughly confirmed in their belief that the eternal
functional submissiveness of the Son to the Father was in accord not only
with Scripture but with Christian orthodoxy. They were clearly wedded
to the same position that I only later discovered had been articulated in
published form by Doyle the previous week; certainly, they appeared to
be firmly set in their thinking.

This is not to say that they were entirely and unanimously of one
mind, but the environment was hardly conducive to the expression of a
dissenting voice, other of course, than my own. At the end of the meeting
we simply parted amicably, agreeing to differ. Had I been aware of Dr.
Doyle's media posting of the previous week in which he had critically
reviewed *Reflections in Glass* I might have been able to understand where
these men were coming from and why it was that the subordinationist
thesis was so attractive to them. At the time I found myself thinking that
"you win some and you lose some" and that we just have to agree to differ.

Within a couple of the weeks following the meeting, Dr. John Wood-
house, the then chairman of the Sydney Doctrine Commission, wrote to
Dr. Jensen declaring that the commission was of the opinion that "no
substantial case had been made that the 1999 Report on the Doctrine of
the Trinity is in serious error."[40]

⤸

In March 2005, at a regularly scheduled National Bishops Conference
in Adelaide I came prepared to introduce the discussion of some altogether different topic, but at the very beginning of the meeting was pre-
vented from doing so at the urging of some of those present for whom

40. This letter, dated September 27, 2004, is quoted by Tom Frame, "Dynamics and
Difficulties," 155–56.

the spokesperson was Bishop Philip Huggins of Melbourne. Philip had previously served as one of my assistant bishops in Perth before returning to his home diocese of Melbourne. Tom Frame has reported that, on February 8, 2005, Dr. Jensen had written to Bishop Huggins (and to Bishop John Harrower, also of Melbourne) to ask them "to communicate the conclusions of the Sydney Doctrine Commission" in response to the criticisms of the 1999 Report that had been raised over the previous twelve months.[41] I was caught entirely off guard at that meeting as I had not come prepared to discuss my comment on the Sydney Doctrine Commission Report, and certainly did not produce "a paper on what (I) thought was 'wrong' with the Report," as Frame suggests.[42]

In any event, it became clear that more than just the communication of the commission's response to criticisms was on the agenda. As ever the peacemaker, Huggins proposed that we should first address the contentious issue specifically which *Reflections in Glass* had raised in relation to the views of the Sydney Doctrine Commission. Given that this had so traumatized the Sydney bishops, the contention was that it clearly called for some group work to restore the harmony of the national episcopal fellowship. It was immediately made clear that the Sydney bishops present were alarmed, if not indignant, at having their orthodoxy called into question by the suggestion that the Sydney Doctrinal Commission Report, which at least two of them had had a part in writing,[43] explicitly aligned them with a brand of Arianism. Although, as far as I was aware, this assembly of national bishops was not really prepared for a considered theological discussion of the interpersonal relations within the immanent life of the Trinity, it was clear that the issue had to be addressed head-on. The scheduled agenda of the meeting was thus effectively hijacked.

By this time, and providentially, I had at least revisited the Sydney Report a number of times to check what it had to say, and was able to outline its basic problem as I saw it: though the report started by affirming the belief that the three persons of the Trinity were equally divine in being, dignity, and status through sharing the same divine substance, insofar as it then went on to speak of the distinct identities of the Trinity

41. See Frame's account of this episode in "Dynamics and Difficulties," 156.

42. Frame, "Dynamics and Difficulties," 156.

43. Dr. Glenn Davies, who was then an assistant bishop in Sydney, and Dr. Peter Jensen himself. Assistant bishop Paul Barnett, who was the chair of this Doctrine Commission, retired in 2001, but assistant bishop Robert Forsyth may also have been present.

and the complementarian differentiation of their roles, these initial affirmations appeared to me to be seriously compromised.

In laying out the case for the eternal functional submissiveness of the Son to the Father, the report had relied heavily on an essay of Dr. Thomas R. Schreiner, who had argued that one can pursue a different function from another person and still be equal in essence and worth. Thus, "Women are equal to men in essence and in being; there is no ontological distinction, and yet they have a different function . . ."[44] The report itself took the principle that "in personal life equality and subordination can co-exist"[45] and applied it in doctrinal terms: the same may be said of the persons of the Trinity. This seemed to be the nub of the problem: for it was hard to see that an eternal differentiation of function did not inevitably (i.e., by a kind of logical necessity) lead to ontological implications in a way that in turn negated the proposition that the three persons shared equally in the same divine substance (*ousia*). In other words, the question is, can one person of the Trinity be equal with another and at the same time act (or function) unwaveringly in a way that speaks of an inequality in divine status and authority? By defining an identity by appealing to what he or she characteristically *does*, using functional language, we appear to be logically bound to draw some ontological implications.

How is it possible, for example, to describe a person who gardens very regularly, and as one who habitually functions *as* a gardener, but not go on to describe him or her as *being* a gardener? Or how is it possible to describe a person who has committed serial murders, but not go on to identify him or her as *being* a serial murderer? Likewise, how is it possible to say that the Son eternally functions as a subordinate of the Father without *being* a subordinate? Just as, by exercising a dominant will, the Father appears to *be* a dominant person, so the Son tends to become *a being who is* eternally submissive to the will of the Father. This quite unavoidably seems to imply the Father's *being* of different status and authority with respect to the Son. It is thus clearly dangerous to assert differences of function within the immanent life of the Trinity without this impinging negatively upon the nature of the very *being* of the three persons in their essential nature. This means that statements of function

44. Schreiner, "Head Coverings, Prophecies and the Trinity," 190–91. Schreiner's full text is: "One can possess a different function and still be equal in essence and worth. Women are equal to men in essence and in being; there is no ontological distinction, and yet they have a different function or role in church and home."

45. Sec. 5.2/para. 30.

cannot somehow be isolated by a kind of logical quarantine from their ontological entailments. Perhaps this is why traditional expositions of Trinitarian description insist upon the *undifferentiated functioning* of the three persons of the Trinity in the economy of salvation, in accordance with a single undivided divine will. The unity and simplicity of God demands this.

Furthermore, I was able to point out that the report *itself* could not avoid the ontological implications of its own functional language, insofar as it actually went well beyond talk of the *functional* submissiveness of the Son to the Father, to speak in fact of differences of an ontological kind—i.e., eternal differences not just of function but of essential being. The Sydney bishops very vocally protested that this was just not so. I held to the view that I was sure it was. "Show us!" they said.[46]

A copy of the Sydney Report, which had been published in the *Sydney Diocesan Yearbook* for 2000, was produced. Unfortunately, given that I had not come to the meeting prepared with exact paragraph references at my fingertips, in the heat of the moment I could not immediately point to the crucial sections of the report that I had in mind, even while holding fairly confidently to the view that I knew they were there somewhere in print for all to see. "Show us!" was the repeated reply. Fortunately, it was time for a morning recess, so we adjourned in some disarray for coffee. Clearly, we all needed a shot of caffeine by this time . . . and a little time to consult the text of the report.

When the meeting resumed, I was able to point out that the report actually says that the functional subordination of the Son as it had been expressed by Dr. Schreiner was only "true as far as it goes."[47] Thus "a second and more profound exposition of the doctrine of the Trinity in its biblical context" was said "to be required" in which "the equality and subordination which 'subordinationists' see in the Trinity *belongs to the very Persons themselves in their eternal nature . . .*" (my italics).[48] Thus, the submission of the Son to the will of the Father was explicitly said not to be only "voluntary, temporary and personal"; rather, it reflects "the essence of the eternal relationship between them."[49] Thus, the report

46. I clearly remember Bishop Glenn Davies being very vocal at this point.

47. Sec. 5.4/para. 32.

48. Sec.5.5/para.33,

49. Sec.4.9/para.25. See also sec. 4.2/para.18. Sec 4.5/para. 21 even goes so far as to say: "According to Scripture, the submission of Christ does not express a temporary and arbitrary arrangement, but the very nature of God in himself."

declares roundly that "The Son's obedience to the Father arises from the very nature of his being as Son."[50] In other words, it is asserted that there are "essential differences" in "the eternal nature" respectively of the Father and the Son. Clearly, this was being declared to be a matter of theological ontology and not just an incidental matter of occasional function.

In this way the logical move from a purely "functional" or "relational" subordination to an ontological subordination of the Son to the Father had been made.[51] After the identification of these disastrously incriminating passages, the meeting moved quietly on to the next item on the agenda, leaving the Sydney bishops studying the 1999 Report in puzzled, stonelike silence.

It was apparently difficult for them to appreciate the disastrous ontological consequences of the actual words of their Doctrine Commission's report, or even to believe that words that they had had a part in writing were actually embedded in the text. Undoubtedly, this was because they were so sure that the subordinationist position they were advocating was in accord with Scripture. They appeared to be oblivious to the fact that the report moved well beyond a merely functional subordination to argue explicitly for a kind of subordination of an ontological kind that was even said to be of the eternal essence of the relationship of the Father to the Son insofar as "submissiveness" arose from the very being of the Son as Son.

Before the close of this meeting of the National Bishops Conference it was agreed that all bishops would "walk" together in this continuing dialogue concerning the doctrine of the Trinity.

In June 2005 when, in a Dublin lecture on the life and significance of T. C. Hammond, Dr. Peter Jensen referred to the fact that I had raised the issue of T. C. Hammond's possible Arianism, he reported that "the Sydney Doctrine Commission gave careful consideration to these charges, and rejected them decisively." In a subsequent publication, Archbishop Jensen again defended the thinking of the original Sydney Doctrine Report, even to the point of claiming that the then current Sydney Doctrine Commission, "having heard Dr Carnley personally, having studied his writings and having given itself afresh to the consideration of the matter, remains entirely convinced that there is nothing Arian about the original

50. Sec. 4.2/para. 18.
51. See also secs. 4.1, 4.2, 4.5, 4.6, 5.4/paras. 17, 18, 21, 22, 32.

report." From this point of view the report explicitly repudiates Arianism and there is nothing in it which falls outside orthodox Trinitarianism.

⌇

Without doubt the solidification of this position was largely owing to the contribution of Robert Doyle, who is to be credited with the most sustained published theological discussion of the actual issues. His media posting of September 3, 2004 containing his defensive and critical review of *Reflections in Glass*, chapter 7,[52] had been very aggressively subtitled "Arianism of Straw Men and Fabrication." Doyle sincerely believed that the 1999 Sydney Doctrine Commission Report had made a careful distinction between essential subordination and a purely functional subordination in the relations between the three persons of the Trinity, and that it "clearly affirms that all three Persons are equal in substance or essence." This allowed him to declare that "There is no essential subordination," but only a functional subordination of the Son to the Father.

Indeed, in defending the accusation that I had fabricated an image of members of the Sydney Doctrine Commission as "men of straw," Doyle charged that in *Reflections in Glass*, chapter 7, I had not so much as noted the important distinction between functional and essential subordination; he boldly declared that my presentation of the Sydney Doctrine Commission's Report had said "not a word" about these distinctions in assessing "the acceptability of the report's position." "Carnley," he said, "is able to treat all the report's statements about functional subordination as if they are statements about the essence of God."

In addition, he (correctly) insisted that: "Carnley criticises 'Sydney' for reading back the functional subordination of the Son in the economy of salvation into the eternal or immanent life of the Trinity." In other words, the subordination of Jesus' earthly actions in response to the Father's will were equated with a subordination in the being of God as God is in all eternity. Thus, the charge was that the authors of the Sydney Doctrine Commission Report were (to use Doyle's own words) guilty of "pushing what is true of created time back into the timeless eternity of God." Somehow it seems that Doyle was oblivious of the fact that these very statements that he himself was quoting from *Reflections in Glass* demonstrated that a distinction between functional and essential

52. Posted by Anglican Media Sydney on the SDS (Sydney Diocesan Services) website.

submissiveness is made there after all. This is even though he had earlier charged that "not a word" was made of this important distinction.

Clearly, Doyle's assessment is somewhat confused, for my chief point in *Reflections in Glass* was that talk of the functional submissiveness of the Son is very difficult to isolate from logical entailments of an ontological kind, and that this kind of logical slide from functional to ontological statements may be observed already in the Sydney Doctrine Commission Report itself. He appeared unaware of what was actually said in the report at Section 4. 2/paragraph 18 about the Son being subordinate to the Father's will, and its contention that this arises out of the "very nature of his being." Though Doyle charged me with fabricating "straw men," this is something that is clearly demonstrable from statements of the Doctrine Commission Report itself. It was pointed out in *Reflections in Glass* that it appeared very difficult for the authors of the report both to speak of the obedient submissiveness of the historical Jesus in the economy of salvation, and also to resist the temptation to attribute the very same obedient submissiveness of his historical human life to his timeless pre-incarnate life in his eternal relation to the Father as the divine Second Person of the Trinity.[53]

By resorting to some unfortunately provocative and condemnatory language, Doyle thus resorted to the making of assertions that were by and large unsupported by evidence: for example, not only that I had constructed "men of straw," but that the charge of Arianism had been "manufactured" and "fabricated." This is even in the face of the report's own clear assertion that the obedient submissiveness of the Son arises out of "the very nature of his being as Son," which on Doyle's own admission amounts to a form of Arianism: "To assert that," he said, "would be Arianism and contrary to the teaching of Holy Scripture."

In any event, though *Reflections in Glass* had embodied little more than a passing remark on the apparent Arianism of the Sydney Doctrine Commission Report of 1999 in its chapter on the question of the admission of women to the episcopate, Doyle's published review had the effect of broadening the debate from a semi-private discussion between a few theologians and bishops and catapulted it into a more open arena. The ensuing notoriety ensured that sales of *Reflections in Glass* doubled initial

---

53. Thomas Schreiner openly pursues this methodology in "Head Coverings, Prophecies and the Trinity," when he says, "Whenever Scripture says that God sent the Son into the world (e.g., John 3:17), we see subordination in role: the Father commands and sends; the Son obeys and comes into the world to die for our sins" (192).

expectations; and I am gratified that regular "notifications" coming from my subscription to *academia.com* indicate that even today it is still being read and referred to in journal articles and doctoral research theses in places as diverse and as far away as Tasmania, Poland, and South Africa.

But this is not to say that the fundamental issue of Trinitarian relations has been adequately addressed. Whether it is theologically possible to affirm the *homoousion* and to remain true to orthodox Trinitarian belief in the essential equality of the three persons of the Trinity in being, status, and dignity, and at the same time to argue that the Son and the Spirit are functionally and relationally subordinate to the Father within an eternal interpersonal dynamic of domination and submission, fatherly command and filial obedience, without this leading to some kind of self-contradiction, remains unresolved and problematic.

~

Whether this involves a form of the ancient heresy of Arianism is still another matter. For, we have to note that some have become convinced of the theological pitfalls of "eternal functional subordination" but have resiled from categorizing it as a form of Arianism. Glenn Butner, for example, has exposed a problem concerning the introduction of talk of two wills under the cloak of the defence of complementarian subordinationism. The need of subordinationists to speak of the commanding will of the Father and the complementary submissive will of the Son, is judged by Butner to be a step on the way to a sub-Trinitarian tritheism, but he is reluctant to condemn it as a form of Arianism.[54]

Even so, by contrast with the unresolved nature of the Australian debate about the Trinity between 1999 and 2005, Kevin Giles has written the history of "the rise" of complementarian subordinationism within international evangelical circles and of its "fall" in the wake of the electronic debates of 2016.[55] His account is understandably colored by an unmistakable sense of vindication and even a well-deserved glow of triumph. After nearly two decades of having to endure hostile responses to his arguments in defence of Nicene orthodoxy, and often disparaging remarks from the pens of declared functional or relational subordinationists, we

---

54. Very notably Butner, *Son Who Learned Obedience*, 4. Butner's arguments will be examined in chapter 3 of this book.

55. Giles, *Rise and Fall*.

do not begrudge him the satisfaction of his sense of coming out on top of this debate.

Some former adherents of the complementarian subordinationist thesis have certainly declared their change of heart and mind on this issue;[56] others have apologized to Giles for "rough handling" of him in opposing his claim that complementarian teaching on the Trinity breaches Nicene orthodoxy.[57] Indeed, in celebrating the "fall" of complementarian subordinationism, he has signaled the "defeat" of two of his arch-opponents on the international field of battle.[58]

Alas, one of these, Wayne Grudem, has since published his revised *Systematic Theology* in which he certainly does not concede defeat. In fact, Grudem vigorously reargues the case for subordinationist complementarianism, even to the point of contending that it is possible to speak both of a single shared divine will of God (as required by the early defenders of Christian orthodoxy) and at the same time of a difference of willing between the persons of the Father and the Son. On the face of it, this sounds as though a case might even be made for holding monotheism and tritheism simultaneously! An initial reading of the relevant chapter of Grudem's revised *Systematic Theology*[59] also discloses some howlers that suggest Grudem is involved in a desperate clutching at straws. For example, Grudem even fails to distinguish the human willing obedience of the incarnate Jesus from an alleged "eternal functional submissiveness" within the internal life of the Trinity. "Surely,'" he says,

> there must be some kinds of distinction in the one will of God because there is a difference between the Father's willing to send and the Son's willing to be sent. There is a difference between the Father's willing to pour out divine wrath against sin and the Son's willing to bear that wrath for our sake. There is a difference

56. Giles mentions as a notable example Dr. Denny Burk, the president in the US of the Council of Biblical Manhood and Womanhood (CBMW) and declares that complementarian subordinationism "has been abandoned even by many of its once most ardent supporters and advocates." "The about-turn of Dr. Denny Burk, . . . a long-time dogmatic supporter of the eternal subordination of the Son and of the argument that women's subordination is grounded in the life of God, proves the point." Giles, *Rise and Fall*, 2.

57. Giles, *Rise and Fall*, 6.

58. Wayne Grudem, professor of theology and biblical studies at Phoenix Seminary, Phoenix, Arizona, and Bruce Ware, professor of systematic theology at Southern Baptist Theological Seminary, Louisville, Kentucky. Giles, *Rise and Fall*, 3.

59. Grudem, *Systematic Theology*, chapter 14.

between the Father's will to say "You are my beloved son; with you I am well pleased" (Mark 1:11) and the Son's will to receive such approval as the beloved Son. There is a difference between the Son bringing requests before the Father (Heb. 7:25) and the Father hearing those requests.[60]

But Grudem fails to demonstrate that these may be references to the willing obedience of the human Jesus in undertaking his vocational mission in the world, with little (if anything) to do with the eternal functional submissiveness of the Son to the Father in the internal life of the Trinity.

Furthermore, Grudem's own failure to observe the distinction between the willing of the human Jesus and the alleged eternally submissive willing of the Son in the internal life of the Trinity, is imported into his reading of the early church fathers. To take one example: though he admits the theological tradition amongst the fathers that affirms the unitary importance of the single undivided will of the Godhead, he insists that some of the fathers speak of the subordinate will of the Son in relation to the will of the Father, quoting as an example Hilary of Poitiers. Alas, here once again the question of the submissive human will of the incarnate Jesus to God the Father is not in dispute; it is the projection of this into the internal life of the Trinity that is at issue; and it is well known that Hilary did not so much as consider the question of whether the incarnational willing of the human Jesus might be more than incarnational and in fact eternal.[61] Although Grudem triumphantly points, by way of example, to the alleged support of Hilary of Poitiers, it is clear enough that when Hilary wrote *On the Trinity* he was concerned to affirm the full divinity of the Son by reference to the unitary nature of the works of the historical Jesus and the works of the Father: "That they are the same works proves his nature."[62] If anything this proves the Son's equal divine status with the Father, and the harmony of his human willing and action with that of the Father. It has nothing whatever to do with the alleged "eternal subordination of the Son to the Father."

---

60. Grudem, *Systematic Theology*, 616.

61. R. P. C. Hanson in *Christian Doctrine of God*, 478, notes that Hilary "insists that the Son's (incarnational) activity is the Father's, but he allows that the Son has an independent (human) will of his own, which he voluntarily aligns with the Father's will. He never raises the interesting question, whether this will of the Son is a human or divine will."

62. Hilary of Poitiers, *On the Trinity*, vii.18.

Grudem's desperate attempt to shore up the case for subordinationism in the wake of the electronic debates of 2016, even if unconvincing,
does at least demonstrate that some still remain to be convinced, even
despite Giles's talk of its "rise and fall." Certainly "defeat" has not been
universally conceded, and this is not least the case amongst Carillon Avenue theologians on Australian shores. Rather, defensiveness, colored by
a sense of mild resentment that their position has even been put under
scrutiny at all, has, by and large, continued to be the order of the day among
Australian subordinationists. We might be forgiven for suspecting that
many, particularly within Australia, who have been schooled in Carillon
Avenue theology, comfortably continue to be self-confident "functional
subordinationists" and remain entirely unconvinced that their commitment to and promotion of this position harbors any real problems at all.
Undoubtedly, there are still others who have simply moved on to engage
with new and more absorbing theological and moral preoccupations, and
so are content to allow the once highly contentious Trinitarian issues of
the first decades of the current century to gather dust. The pity is that, by
leaving the untidy threads of this unfinished debate to recede into dim
obscurity in a foggy harbor of unresolved theological questions, a latent
reliance on the doctrinal commitment to Trinitarian subordinationism is
allowed to continue to inform and support a parallel commitment to the
legitimacy of complementarian notions of domination and submission
between husbands and wives in families, and between men and women
in the ministerial and leadership structures of the church. And this is
not to mention the continuing assumption that a relation of fatherly
command and filial obedience may still legitimately be called upon as an
unchallenged principle of the divine life to support and warrant a penal
substitutionary theory of the atonement. All this remains identifiably
alive and well in many parts of Australia.

Furthermore, we still have some way to go in trying to understand
the logic of how so many became so convinced of the rightness of their
complementarian subordinationism as to give the impression that they
were barely touched by any felt need to reexamine it, let alone bother
seriously to engage with and respond to their critics. Kevin Giles ventures
to suggest that the root problem is a methodological appeal to scriptural
texts alone, detached from the interpretative directives of the dogmatic
traditions of Christian orthodoxy. According to Giles, their flawed methodology is encapsulated in the slogan, "All my theology comes directly

from Scripture."[63] While it may in part be the case that the confident belief that complementarian subordinationism is supported by a specific approach to the reading of Scripture, my own view is that a foundational commitment to the systematic theological package, to which I refer as Carillon Avenue theology, with historical roots in scholastic Calvinism, may also help us all understand the basic reluctance of complementarian subordinationists seriously to countenance that they may be wrong. We shall look more closely at this possibility in the next chapter of this book.

Since the electronic debate of 2016 enormous progress has been made. Kevin Giles is right to celebrate the fall of the complementarian subordinationist view of the Trinity. It no longer presides from the self-confident commanding position it once enjoyed in the theological agenda of international evangelicalism. Even so, the persistence of unresolved arguments and the consequent reluctance of many Australian Carillon Avenue theologians to loosen their grip on the package of complementarian and subordinationist systematics in which they have been well schooled, means that the question of the theological legitimacy of "eternal functional or relational subordination" within the immanent life of the Trinity has yet to be finally laid to rest. Clearly, we still have some way to go in the quest for theological truth.

63. Giles, *Rise and Fall*, 3–4. As an alternative to those who say "we have no creed but the Bible," Giles explains his own methodological commitment: "In reply, I outline a better methodology, one followed by the sixteenth-century Reformers and articulated in modern times by the best of confessional Reformed theologians. This gives primacy to Scripture yet acknowledges that working out what is foundational and central in the varied comments in Scripture, or what should be inferred from Scripture when it does not speak explicitly on an issue, is not self-evident. This methodology also listens carefully to the doctrinal tradition, authoritatively outlined in creeds and confessions. This informs theologians on what the church in the past has agreed is the teaching of Scripture. And this methodology gives place to reason enlightened by the Spirit in the 'doing' of theology." *Rise and Fall*, 4.

# Chapter 2

# T. C. Hammond and Federal Theology

I WENT TO LIVE in Sydney in 1956, towards the end of my first year after leaving school, in order to pursue the study of law while working in the Petty Sessions Branch of the New South Wales Department of Attorney General and of Justice. My first city job was at what was then known as the Central Court in Liverpool Street, which handled criminal matters, and this was followed by a variety of different legal experiences—in the recovery of debts at the Philip Street Small Debts Court, which was also located in the Sydney CBD; and a wide-ranging introduction to initial contact litigation and the administration of family law in suburban courts at Lidcombe, Campbelltown, and Kogarah as well as some brief country excursions to Leeton, Queanbeyan, and a more lengthy stay at Orange in the Central West of New South Wales.

During those years in Sydney I boarded at Concord West, where the local parish church was dedicated to the Holy Trinity. Although I showed up there occasionally for worship, I somehow sensed that it was not really my cup of tea. I had been brought up in the country town of Young in southwestern New South Wales, in the Diocese of Canberra-Goulburn, where I was confirmed in 1952, on the day before my fifteenth birthday. My confirmation occurred in the Anglican Church of my baptism, even though with my parents' consent, I had been taken by a friendly neighbor to her Methodist Sunday school during my primary school years.

The officiating bishop at my confirmation was the great Ernest Henry Burgmann, who had put a quite distinctive stamp on his diocese with his uncompromising zeal for social justice,[1] mixed with a progres-

1. During the Depression he actually led a march of protesting steelworkers,

sively minded and intellectually robust theology, which was fearless in its embrace of biblical criticism.[2] By contrast the biblical literalism and strangely narrow focus on individual salvation that I encountered at Holy Trinity, Concord West suffered in its appeal as somehow trite and, intellectually speaking, pathetically shallow. When, at a parish fundraising dinner I was invited to sign up to a stewardship pledge, I found myself obliged to decide where exactly I would most comfortably belong and best direct my (admittedly meager) contribution to the offertory plate.

A Petty Sessions colleague, Ian Pike, with whom I worked on the front counter at Central Court in Liverpool Street, and who eventually became the chief stipendiary magistrate for New South Wales, introduced me to the Young Anglican Fellowship, which met in the crypt of the central city Church of St. James on King Street in Sydney on Friday evenings. I soon took myself there on Sundays as well. An additional day of commuting into central Sydney from Concord West by electric train each week was not inhibiting, as I found that the preaching and liturgy, not to mention the interpersonal communion of its parish fellowship, had a life-giving and magnetic appeal.

At this time T. C. Hammond was still rector of another of Sydney's inner-city churches, St. Philip's, on York Street, located a little west of Circular Quay in the vicinity of the very early colonial settlement of The Rocks.[3] I did not ever worship there, but T. C. Hammond was well known by reputation as a somewhat hard-line conservative evangelical of decidedly Calvinist leanings. There is no doubting that he was a very skilled apologist for Reformed theology and, correspondingly, was an unmuzzled critic of the "errors" of the Church of Rome, having schooled himself in this trade in his earlier Dublin days. Under the umbrella of the Society for Irish Church Missions in Dublin, he appears to have been as concerned with the conversion of Roman Catholics to the "true faith" of his Reformed tradition as with the conversion of sinners to Christianity.[4]

---

demanding double the dole, down the streets of Newcastle.

2. Burgmann had the initial vision to establish a national theological library which he dedicated to St. Mark in Canberra. This dedication was not an accident, given that St. Mark's Day coincides with Anzac Day, which Burgmann believed should really be celebrated as Australia's national day.

3. Hammond's appointment as principal of Moore Theological College also included parish ministerial responsibilities as rector of St. Philip's, York Street.

4. Witness the polemical emphases of Hammond, *One Hundred Texts*, first published in 1939.

Indeed, it may not have occurred to him to draw this distinction. I therefore first came to know of him by reputation as a somewhat controversial figure with clearly defined quasi-sectarian religious convictions. Even during his time of living in Australia, he was known as a card-carrying Orangeman, who served as chaplain and finally, in the year prior to his death, as grand master of the Grand Orange Lodge of New South Wales.

〜

I quitted the ink and blotting paper of my originally envisaged legal career in 1960 in response to the insistent call to Holy Orders. At my bishop's direction, I enrolled at St John's College at Morpeth, which was located in the Diocese of Newcastle to Sydney's north, as a prospective ordinand for the Diocese of Bathurst.[5] My hero Burgmann had in fact been warden of St. John's prior to his election as a bishop. It was there that his distinctive package of social justice and progressive theology came together in what he referred to as "the Morpeth mind."

As providence would have it, in 1961 I was selected to go, along with a fellow ordinand, Harvey Dineen, who was an ordination candidate for the Diocese of Melbourne, on a student exchange from Morpeth to Moore Theological College in Sydney.[6] We were cordially received into a two-day taste of Sydney evangelicalism with the welcoming local cohort of Moore College students, who were clearly relying on Hammond's systematic presentation of basic Christian doctrine in *In Understanding Be Men* for the fundamental orientation of their thinking. If they held Calvin's *Institutes of the Christian Religion* in one hand, *In Understanding Be Men* was firmly gripped in the other.

Hammond had apparently written this "handbook of Christian doctrine" in 1935, and proofchecked it on board the ship during the long journey from Ireland to Australia to take up the appointment as principal of Moore College early in 1936. This book had clearly become a basic theological resource for Moore College students, and without doubt played an important role in securing Hammond's place as perhaps the single most significant theological influence in the formation of Sydney's distinctive style of doing theology. Between 1936 and 1976, *In*

5. I was working at the Court of Petty Sessions in Orange, in the Diocese of Bathurst, at the time.

6. In a reciprocal arrangement two Moore College students got a taste of "the Morpeth mind," as Burgmann used to refer to it, at the same time.

*Understanding Be Men* was reprinted no less than twenty-five times. Even so, I came away without a copy from the Moore College bookshop, and it was actually some years before I eventually mustered enough enthusiasm to purchase one, let alone sit down to read it. As it happened, on November 16 of that same year, 1961, T. C. Hammond died.

It was not until 2004 that I took my copy of this celebrated theological primer from the shelf,[7] and began to study it with care, prompted as I then had been by James Haire's tip to check out the Ulster roots of Hammond's distinctive brand of Calvinism. The hunch was that Anglican theology in the first decades of twentieth-century Ireland exhibited a family likeness to the doctrinal stance of pre-Barthian Ulster Presbyterianism, with a shared historical origin going back beyond that to the Scholastic Calvinism of federal theology, which, as I had come to learn,[8] entered Britain early in the seventeenth century and took on a definitive importance in the wake of the *Westminster Confession* of 1646. I thus read *In Understanding Be Men* with a keen eye for any clues as to the possible influence of federal theology and the Westminster tradition and was, naturally, particularly interested to discover whether Hammond's Trinitarian thinking, especially in relation to the alleged "eternal obedient submissiveness of the Son," might have had its origin as a remnant survival of this pre-Barthian form of Calvinistic scholasticism in the Church of Ireland.

Federal theology had its origin in the Palatinate in the mid-sixteenth century when Zacharias Ursinus,[9] who was professor of theology at Heidelberg University, and Caspar Olevianus, the preacher to the royal court, were commissioned by the pious Elector Frederick III to produce a manual of instruction for "guiding pastors and teachers" in the instruction of basic Christian doctrine, particularly to youth, so that the Reformed faith might be clearly understood and maintained. This was at a stage in Heidelberg's history when the city was in a Calvinist, rather than a Lutheran, phase.[10]

7. My edition is a printing of the version, edited and revised by David F. Wright, and published in London by Inter-Varsity Press, 1976.

8. In Torrance, *Persons in Communion*, 62.

9. Born July 18, 1534, died May 6, 1583. Ursinus was a friend of Melanchthon.

10. Heidelberg reverted to Lutheranism in 1576, at which time Ursinus moved to

Ursinus produced what became known as the *Heidelberg Catechism* although, in fact, there were actually two complementary documents that were probably written at around the same time.[11] The first, the *Major Catechism,* apparently dates from 1562, though it was not actually published until the year after Ursinus's death in 1584. Its delayed publication may possibly have been due to the fact that it was an unapologetically technical work originally intended only for students of theology in the University of Heidelberg, rather than for general congregational use.

The second work, the *Catechism of the Christian Religion,* was synodically endorsed and publicly released in 1563 with the intention that it would be systematically used for the Sunday afternoon instruction especially of young people, by outlining questions and answers for each of the fifty-two Lord's Days of the year. The Great Synod of Dort in 1618–19 declared that the Heidelberg Catechism was in all respects in harmony with the Word of God, and so adopted it as "a completely accurate compendium of orthodox Christian doctrine, adapted with singular wisdom not only to the level of tender youth, but also for the proper instruction of adults . . ."[12] The Synod issued directives for it to be used by parents in teaching their children, instructors in schools, and by pastors on each Lord's Day afternoon.

With the help of John Cocceius,[13] who is usually credited with systematizing the insights originally attributed to Ursinus by giving them their classical form in his *Summa doctrinae de foedere et testamento Dei* (1648), the *Heidelberg Catechism* became the most widely used and influential catechism of the Reformation period right across the Reformed churches of Europe.[14]

Neustadt as the former Calvinist faculty dispersed.

11. If David Weir is correct. See Weir, *Origins of the Federal Theology.*

12. See Sinnema, "Heidelberg Catechism at the Synod of Dort," 5.

13. A Dutch theologian born in Bremen (August 9, 1603–November 5, 1669).

14. The Heidelberg Catechism was translated into almost every European language. In The Netherlands, the Heidelberg Catechism was approved by the Synods of Wesel (1568), Emden (1571), Dort (1578), the Hague (1586), as well as the Great Synod of Dort (1618–19). This Great Synod, which was attended by a significant delegation from England, not only authorized and commended the Heidelberg Catechism but incorporated its characteristic teaching into its own canons.

～

Its life in England may be attributed to Ursinus's student at Heidelberg, Thomas Cartwright, and his assistant and disciple, Dudley Fenner, who in fact first coined the term *foedus operum,* or "covenant of works" in the course of unpacking the fundamental elements of federal theology in the context of the rise of English Puritanism.[15] This was said to be a prelapsarian covenant of a contractual kind that God, allegedly, made with Adam, but which Adam in rebellious disobedience violated, thus incurring the inevitable and justly deserved penalty of the kind that normally attaches to broken contractual arrangements. His was clearly no "small debt" to be settled in a Court of Petty Sessions, for the disastrous outcome of Adam's disobedience then flowed on to all humanity of every succeeding age, given that Adam was understood to be the representative "federal" or "contractual" head of the human race. Thus, Adam by his disobedience earned, not just for himself, but for all humanity after him, the supreme penalty of death. The apparently intractable problem that ensued for all humanity was only then remedied with the coming of Christ, who in submissive obedience to God the Father reversed Adam's disobedience, thereby faithfully enacting a "covenant of grace" by paying the penalty for Adam's fall, as the "federal head of the new humanity." As James B. Torrance puts it, "Adam as such is not a private individual but the federal head of the race. Thus when he disobeyed, he brought a curse not only upon himself, but on all for whom he contracted. However, God in his sovereign grace does not destroy the human race, but elects out of the mass of fallen mankind a number for himself and makes a covenant of grace for them in Christ."[16]

Even Christ himself as a human being was subject to the penalty of death as a consequence of the broken "covenant of works" entered

15. For the original use of the term *"foedus operum,"* see Fenner, *Sacra theologia, sive veritas quae est secundum pietatem,* 88. Fenner does not speak explicitly of the *foedus operum* as prelapsarian, but Genesis 2:17 is cited as a prooftext, so an event prior to the fall is implied. John Calvin writes of a probationary period for Adam and a promise of life for obedience, and the federal headship of Adam, but he does not write of "a covenant of works." It is not referred to as a covenant in the opening chapters of Genesis, but Fenner implies as much also by citing Genesis 2:17 as a prooftext, and it is referred to as a covenant in Hosea 6:7: "But like Adam, they transgressed the covenant; there, they dealt faithlessly with Me." See Letham, *Westminster Assembly,* 227–28, and *"Foedus Operum,"* 458n15.

16. Torrance, "Covenant or Contract?" This essay is also found as Appendix A in Tilling, *Beyond Old and New Perspectives on Paul.*

into by Adam. However, by fulfilling its conditions in his holy life and by undergoing its curse against all human beings for their involvement by contractual implication in the breach of its requirements, Christ satisfied God's justice and merited God's mercy. As the Scottish theologian and churchman Robert Rollock was to put it in 1597: "Christ himself as man was subject to the covenant of works and, by fulfilling its conditions in his holy life and by undergoing its curse against us for our breach of its stipulations, he satisfied God's justice and merited God's mercy for us."[17]

It is important to note that this notion of a prelapsarian contract, or as Ursinus spoke of it, "covenant of creation" between God and Adam, is explicitly found only in the theologically technical *Major Catechism* of 1562, rather than in the *Heidelberg Catechism* proper of 1563, though it was of course tacitly presupposed in this more popular companion document. However, once the *Major Catechism* itself actually became widely available in published form in 1584, and with the help of the codifying language of the *foedus operum* coined by Fenner in 1585, it quickly took off, and by 1590 the notion of the prelapsarian contract that was understood to have been disastrously broken by Adam became normative in the belief systems of Reformed Christianity across Europe. As Barth observes, "in the second half of the 17th century it was the ruling orthodoxy of the Reformed Church."[18]

With the publication of the treatise entitled the *Tractatus de vocatione efficaci* in 1597, Robert Rollock produced an impressively mature treatment of the relatively new notion of the *foedus operum*, the contract of works, which brought a crucial phase of development of this brand of covenant theology to a climax in Scotland.[19] From early in the seventeenth century federal theology had thus become domiciled both within English Puritanism and in Scottish Presbyterianism. From Scotland it quickly found a home also in neighboring Ulster.

⌐∽

The signature doctrine of the *Heidelberg Catechism* is today often identified, following David Weir's pioneering and magisterial work,[20] as the

17. Rollock, *Select Works*, 1.52–54.

18. Barth, *Church Dogmatics*, IV.1.55.

19. See Letham, "*Foedus Operum*," 457.

20. First in his PhD thesis of 1984, subsequently published as *Origins of the Federal Theology in 16th-Century Reformation Thought*, in 1990.

belief in this prelapsarian contractual covenant between God and Adam. According to this dogmatic schema, God made Adam the child of nature, who could discern the laws of nature by the light of reason. As a prerequisite for such a contractual covenant, the first human beings were understood to have been created by God capable of entering into such a covenant of a legal and natural kind. The *foedus operum* was therefore understood to have been revealed in legal and propositional terms and was understood to be naturally discerned using human reason. "God's justice required that, as a prerequisite for such a covenant, man be created pure and holy and be endowed with God's law in his heart."[21] This in turn called for a response of obedience, dare we say, "submissive obedience," the polar opposite of Adam's rebellious disobedience. Thus, the Westminster Confession of Faith of 1646 enshrined this basic covenantal article of faith in contractual terms: "The first covenant made with man was a covenant of works, wherein life was promised to Adam, and in him to his posterity, upon condition of perfect and personal obedience."[22] Prior to this Robert Rollock had produced his mature treatment of the then relatively new notion of the *foedus operum*. According to Rollock, "all the word of God appertains to some covenant; for God speaks nothing to man without the covenant."[23] This covenant of God consists of a promise, conditional upon a specified response on the part of humans.

Though David Weir has put the focus on this prelapsarian covenant with Adam as the identifying doctrine of federal theology, it is more specifically the contractual nature of this arrangement and the penalties incurred by the conditional nature of contracts generally, that is of real significance.

Some semantic confusion has in fact arisen because the Latin "*foedus*," which means "contract," is often also translated into English simply as "covenant." The *foedus operum* is therefore also known in English as the "*covenant* of works" made with Adam, which Adam foolishly fractured to his own disadvantage. However, given its contractual connotations of conditionality insofar as a penalty has to be paid for any "breach of contract," it is properly speaking contractual rather than covenantal.

Strictly speaking a covenant relationship, by contrast with a contract, is without legal penalties. In other words, it involves a promise that

21. Rollock, *Select Works*, 1. 34.

22. *Westminster Confession of Faith*, chapter VII.ii.

23. Rollock, *Select Works*, 1.33.

is entirely *unconditional*. In federal theology, however, on the basis of the alleged contractual arrangement that God was understood to have entered into with Adam, it took the form of a kind of social contract, similar to that found between a sovereign and his subjects, so that, only *if* Adam obeyed the laws of nature (which are the laws of God) and so fulfilled the conditions of the contract, would he gain eternal life. This element of conditionality gives federal theology its most characteristic identifying quality. Indeed, this constitutes the essential defining nature of the *foedus naturale,* the contract of nature, or contractual "covenant of creation" as Ursinus originally spoke of it. Subsequently Fenner was to define it as *"foedus operum,"* which came to be referred to in English as the so-called "covenant of works"[24] upon which all society under God was said to be based. Thus, even though the term "covenant" is used in English, it is assumed that it is conditional upon a specified response on the part of humanity, and is thus contractual, rather than strictly speaking "covenantal."

Despite the use of the term "covenant" this contractual style of thinking was thus what the *Westminster Confession* inherited from the federal theology of Ursinus. Inevitably, particularly given the defining expository work of Robert Rollock, it first became domiciled in Scottish Presbyterianism, and from Scotland infiltrated Reformed theological minds in Northern Ireland.

This means that, even though the Latin *"foedus"* may be translated into English promiscuously by either of the words "contract" or "covenant," it is therefore important to appreciate that if "covenant" is employed then it is not to be construed without contractual connotations of conditionality. Thus, sometimes when "covenant" is used in federal theology, as for example in the *Westminster Confession of Faith,* "contract" would be less confusing, and in fact preferable. Hence, in the *Westminster Confession,* which like the *Heidelberg Catechism* begins by first citing the problem bequeathed to humanity by Adam, it is explicitly stated that "life was promised to Adam, and in him to his posterity, *upon condition of perfect and personal obedience.*"[25] In order to preserve this aspect of it, I will tend to speak of it as a "contract" or "contractual covenant" rather than simply as a "covenant."

24. "So-called" because in federal theology covenantal arrangements are always contractual.

25. *Westminster Confession,* VII, 2. As prooftexts Genesis 2:17 and Galatians 3:10 are offered.

It is the conditional nature of the original contractual arrangement specified in the *foedus operum*, and not just the bare fact of an initial prelapsarian "covenant" that is thus of most significance here. Indeed, the logical priority of its conditional nature in turn colors the "covenant of grace" established by Christ. Another identifying characteristic of federal theology is therefore that even the "covenant of grace" that Christ initiated as the "federal head of the new humanity" also took on an aspect of conditionality: it could itself only be appropriated on condition of obedient faithfulness.

⸻

Unfortunately, a commitment to the operation of a principle of justice within the contractual arrangements of federal theology thus entailed that Reformed theology had begun to crystallize the notion of law as *prior to and determinative of grace.*[26] Indeed, one of the key identifying tokens of federal theology is that it began a trend in Reformed theology that characteristically conceived of God's grace in legal terms. In this way, federal theology has necessarily come to be characterized by an idiosyncratic understanding of grace conditioned by its framing in the context of the operations of justice and legal principle.

Because the covenant of God with Adam consists of a contractual promise, conditional upon a specified response on his part, but implicating all humans after him, it follows that the covenant of grace executed by Christ is also to be understood in legal and contractual terms. Theological sense is made of Christ's covenant of grace when it is seen as the fulfilling of the broken contractual arrangement God originally made with Adam; because the original arrangement was conditional upon Adam's obedient response it inevitably entails that the remedy must be conceived in terms that are equally legal once it is broken. In this way, just as soon as the covenant of works is broken, the fundamental legal principles that underpin it necessarily flow on into its remedy.

The contract said to have been made with Adam, which was conditional upon his obedience, is therefore crucially important in allocating an ultimate salvific value to Christ's total obedient submissiveness and faithfulness to his God-given vocation.

---

26. Letham, "*Foedus Operum*," 467.

The principles of justice upon which the *foedus operum* with Adam was based, even though being presupposed rather than explicitly stated in the *Heidelberg Catechism*, in this way then condition the understanding of the covenant of grace. Given that it is presupposed that a penalty had to be paid in order to remedy a broken contract as the natural requirement of justice, this means that the idea of grace is also necessarily conceived in a legalistic framework. The whole *schema* is thus conceived on the basis of principles of justice and the fulfillment of a legal requirement.

It is this twofold juxtaposition of the contractual "covenant of works" and the equally contractual "covenant of grace" and the issues of justice and legal principle that underpin the rationale of their interdependence that gives federal theology a very distinctive identity. This means that, though a prelapsarian contract is often cited as the idiosyncratic identifying doctrine of federal theology, it is important to emphasise that federal theology involves a more extensive set of interrelated and highly distinctive theological ideas. Even if the prelapsarian contract or *foedus operum* may not be explicitly referred to, it is, however, presupposed, by the articulation of a theology of grace that is logically dependent upon it, as indeed it was in the *Heidelberg Catechism* itself. Thus, this doctrinal *schema* came naturally to refer to Christ as "the federal head of the new humanity."

~

Apart from the element of conditionality that characterizes contractual arrangements, another quite crucial logically associated background notion is, therefore, that of God's justice. As with broken contracts generally, in the specific case of the violation of the initial contract God is said to have made with Adam, it is God's justice that is said to demand the requirement that a penalty must necessarily be paid. This understanding of things means that Adam's contractual transgressions cannot be left unpunished. That would signal that God did not respect the requirements of his own standards of justice. As with broken contracts generally, justice demands that a penalty must be paid as a matter of necessity. The penal substitution theory of the atonement finds its basic rationale precisely here.

It would, however, be *unjust* for God to punish a human being for the misdeeds of another. Thus, the Father is said in a sense to be obliged to take the burden upon himself, and therefore requires his own Son, born without sin, to pay the penalty incurred by Adam. In this case, there is a sense in which the violation of the initial contract God made with Adam has to be remedied by God's grace, not as a freely bestowed act of divine generosity, but in accordance with principles of justice.

The "covenant of grace" initiated by Christ is therefore represented as a work of perfect *obedience* that is necessarily only really understood in relation to the *disobedience* of Adam and the ensuing demands of justice in relation to this infringement of God's law.

Given that the operation of God's grace is therefore inevitably understood contextually in legal terms, it is not difficult to see that the "penal substitutionary theory" of the atonement could easily incubate and flourish in this intellectual matrix. In contrast to the entirely free gift of God's love, an understanding of grace informed by notions of justice and legal principle means that God's grace is understood to involve something that a righteous God is in a sense constrained wrathfully to enact in accordance with the demands of his own principles of justice. Furthermore, the saving role of Christ is not understood in terms of something done simply *on behalf* of humanity, but explicitly in *substitutionary* terms. The sinlessly innocent Christ pays a legally required penalty *instead* of other humans, who are the ones deserving of punishment precisely because of their rebellious sinfulness. T. C. Hammond is helpfully clear in his definition of the concept of a "substitute." It is simply "One who takes the place of another."[27] A direct line may therefore be drawn from the presupposed "covenant of works" to the theory of atonement expounded as the payment of a penalty in satisfaction of the demands of justice.

It likewise becomes second nature in federal theology to represent God not so much as a welcoming and forgiving God of generous and unconditional love, but more often as "a God of wrath" who is said to "hate sin" (even while loving sinners) and who thus unwaveringly requires the payment of a penalty, not only for the disobedience of Adam but for the sinful disobedience of all humanity after him. This justly deserved punishment that is said to have been required by God's justice is therefore in turn naturally linked with the notion of the "wrath of God." Hence

27. Hammond, *One Hundred Texts*, 534, Hammond gives three examples: (1) The ram for Isaac; (2) Jonah for the sailors; (3) Christ for sinners. But he then cites Isaiah 53, even though Isaiah's suffering servant as the man of sorrows who takes the infirmities of others upon himself may not necessarily do so as their substitute, but may simply do so vicariously *on their behalf.* Thus, Isaiah's words "By his stripes we are healed" are not necessarily substitutionary; the servant's suffering may simply be for the ultimate benefit of others.

the *Heidelberg Catechism* itself asks in Question 10: "Does God permit disobedience and rebellion to go unpunished?" Its forthright answer is: "Certainly not. God is terribly displeased with the sin we are born with as well as the sins we personally commit."

Unfortunately, if God must attend to the amendment of Adam's transgression in such a way that he must himself act in accordance with the dictates of justice, there is a sense in which God therefore does not act freely to bestow the gift of his grace. Instead of making a free and generous gift of grace, God is somehow constrained by principles of natural justice to orchestrate the payment of the penalty that justice itself is said to demand. In a sense God becomes captive to his own principles of justice. Many will find this uncomfortably anthropomorphic, modeled as it is on the workings of human legal systems. In any event, all this presupposes with the *foedus operum* the alleged prelapsarian covenant of a natural and legal kind, that is both contractual and conditional, that God is originally said to have made with Adam, as the "federal head of the human race."

ᔐ

By contrast, many Christians think of themselves less as the condemned children of Adam, and more often as the richly blessed "children of Abraham" who, because of the work of Christ, are inheritors of the promises made to Abraham.[28] The "covenant of grace" is understood already to have been promised in the *protevangelium* of Genesis, announced to Abraham, and fulfilled by faith in Christ amongst the inheritors of the promises made to Abraham. It is important to note that these promises are not conditional upon human conformity to a legal code of conduct. Indeed, the *unconditional* nature of God's covenant with Abraham is almost the polar opposite of the contractual, and thus conditional, nature of the contract said to have been made with Adam, which allegedly led to the imposition of the penalty of death as the necessary satisfaction for his breach of faith and broken promise. In other words, in a truly covenantal arrangement, as against a contractual one, the promise is entirely unconditional. Whereas a broken contract may incur a penalty that must be paid in order to win back the goodwill of one's contractual partner, a covenant is by contrast based upon a commitment of faithfulness to keep

28. Following Paul in Galatians 3:6–9.

one's promises "come what may." As in the covenant of marriage, it is "for better or for worse." Thus God faithfully promises to Abraham to be the God of Abraham and his descendants, the people of Israel, and assures them that they will be his people *despite their faithless shortcomings*. Even in the face of their all-too-apparent breaches of promise, God is always faithful to his covenantal promise, and steadfastly generous and changelessly unwavering in the almost wanton distribution of his love. This is entirely unconditional. It naturally evokes a thankful human response of faithfulness and love, but is not conditional upon it.

In this way, the free gift of grace is bestowed on the beloved in Christ even though the *covenant* made with him has nothing of the contractual conditions so characteristic of federal theology. Clearly, God's *covenant* with Abraham is, in this way, fundamentally different from the theological considerations that ensue from the idea of an alleged legal *contract* that is said to have been made by God with Adam.

⌒

Much contemporary evangelical Christianity, perhaps without knowing it, characteristically presents the gospel in such a way as to tick many of the boxes that were characteristic of federal theology. The heavy reliance on the legal requirement of a kind of retributive justice involving the necessity of the payment of a penalty for Adam's sinfully rebellious disobedience leads on, with a kind of logical necessity, to the development of a redemptive schema in which concepts of justice and legal principle bulk large, even to the point of developing an understanding of God's grace itself in terms of a just requirement—the just requirement of the payment of the penalty for human sin and evil. It is at this very point that, perhaps unwittingly, the contractualism of federal theology harbored a tendency to drift into a form of Arianism, for in accounting for the Son's obedience to the Father in fulfillment of the legal penalty for Adam's fault it was effectively obliged to embrace the notion of "eternal functional submissiveness" with the exercise effectively of two divine wills, the Father's commanding will and the obedient response of the Son to the Father, all in the interests of fulfilling the requirements of justice, for an obediently subordinate Son is required to satisfy the just demands of the Father. The fundamental redemptive purpose of the Father's sending of the Son into the world, and the Son's obedient compliance in carrying out that purpose even unto death on the cross, which is understood in the context of the juxtaposition of Adam's disobedience and Christ' perfect obedience, presupposes a relation of interpersonal domination and submission. This is expressive of the subordination of one to the other in the form of the Father's command and the Son's filial obedience in response. In all this the juxtaposition of what became widely known as the "covenant of works" and the "covenant of grace" becomes quite necessary if the entire schema is to hang logically together with any rational conviction.

On the other hand, the germ of the sub-Trinitarian idea of two divine though complementary wills (one the commanding will of the Father and the other, the compliant will of his submissively obedient Son) may already be discerned in this widely accepted understanding of the divine remedy for Adam's violation of what Dudley Fenner originally defined in England in 1585 as the *foedus operum* or "covenant of works."[29]

∽

The pressing question before us now becomes whether this theological tradition of federal theology offers any help in understanding the thought of T. C. Hammond, particularly with regard to his conviction that the theology of the Trinity requires belief in "the subordination of the Son and the Spirit to the Father"? Given that Hammond's actual words expressing this unequivocal theological conviction are much quoted, and indeed appear to be quite pivotal, both to the argument of the Sydney Doctrine Commission Report of 1999 and to the published Sydney responses to the charge of its apparent Arianism since this possibility was first mooted in the wake of Kevin Giles's critique from 2002 onwards, this becomes a crucial question. Was Hammond the conduit from "Ulster federal theology" to the tendency to the kind of neo-Arian subordinationism that lurks behind and finds expression in contemporary Carillon Avenue theology?

It is already abundantly clear that the very suggestion that T. C. Hammond's distinctive theology is even to be understood as a derivative of "Ulster federal theology" has been met with vigorous pushback. The

29. In North America this "covenant theology," with a distinctive contractual and conditional coloring, was articulated by the highly influential Princeton theologians Charles Hodge, who taught theology at Princeton for fifty years, and his son A. A. Hodge. For a nineteenth-century exposition of "federal theology" and a clear if somewhat fanciful account of the original "Covenant of Works" that God is said to have made with Adam, see A. A. Hodge, *Outlines of Theology*, chapter xvii, "The Covenant of Works"; also, 362–66, 482–86.

spirited defense of Hammond by Peter Adam in response to the paper I delivered at the Melbourne Consultation on the Trinity of late 2004, followed by both Peter Jensen and David F. Wright in their published responses to the same paper in 2005, provide unmistakably clear examples of this.[30]

Alas, apart from an *ad hominem* tendency to "shoot the messenger," the rush to come to the defense of T. C. Hammond has not been productive of a great deal by way of advancing the discussion of the salient theological points that bear upon the issue at hand. These responses have instead involved a good deal of hand-wringing about the alleged impropriety of even daring to engage in a public questioning of such a hallowed figure as Hammond, let alone the questioning of the orthodoxy of the theology inherited from him more generally. Unfortunately, this has led Hammond's defenders to rely on a catalogue of unsubstantiated assertions and denials instead of rising to the challenge of serious theological argument. This has certainly communicated the nervous impression that if Hammond were to be classified as a federal theologian, this would be a bad and unwelcome thing; but we are not sure exactly why. A chorus of assurances of the orthodoxy of Hammond's position actually leaves the question unresolved. Sometimes the attempt to mount some kind of argument even exhibits the appearance of a desperate clutching at straws.

For example, Peter Jensen, Crawford Gribben, and Tom Frame were all quick to urge that Hammond cannot be classified as an "Ulster federal theologian" because he was in fact not from Ulster, but from Southern Ireland, and, indeed, from Dublin itself.[31] This is a remarkably unconvincing argument, if argument it is intended to be. When we speak of "Ulster federal theology" we are not thinking in terms of a geographical qualification for membership of a local gentleman's club in Northern Ireland, but of a fashion of Reformed theological thinking that, though characteristically found in Ulster, was hardly locally quarantined there by some kind of geographical constraint. To suggest that T. C. Hammond cannot have been a federal theologian because he did not actually reside in Ulster is akin to saying that somebody cannot have been an exponent

---

30. Jensen, "T. C. Hammond No Arian," and Wright, "Dr. Carnley on T. C. Hammond and Arianism."

31. Jensen, "T. C. Hammond No Arian," 44; Jensen quotes a letter from Dr. Crawford Gribben of Manchester as saying "he was a southerner through and through." Frame, "Dynamics and Difficulties," 147: "Hammond was actually born in Cork and ministered in Ireland's south and not Ulster."

of the Westminster theological tradition because he or she did not reside in the vicinity of Westminster Abbey.

On the other hand, when the late David F. Wright reminded us of his own impressive academic credentials in the study of patristics as a Cambridge undergraduate and a post-graduate at Oxford, and as teacher of patristics for a few years at New College, Edinburgh, this was to preface the declaration that it is puzzling, given this academic background, that he did not pick up any hints of any Arianizing tendency "lurking in *In Understanding Be Men*" in the course of editing his revised edition of the work in the late 1960s.[32] We are apparently meant to conclude from his qualifications and firsthand work of editing Hammond's writing that no Arianizing tendency was therefore there to be detected.

In June 2005 Dr. Peter Jensen pursued a similar style of argument in a lecture, which he delivered in Dublin, on the life and significance of Hammond. While Jensen correctly acknowledged something of the undoubted breadth and enduring importance of Hammond's influence over a couple of generations, he argued that "to Arianise Hammond is to say that the Intervarsity movement, the Diocese of Sydney, and Evangelicals everywhere, have been instructed in doctrine by an Arian theologian for seventy years."[33] This is repeated in "T. C. Hammond No Arian": "His alleged Arianism has passed without controversy for seventy years." It is as though for this reason Hammond's unquestioned orthodoxy should instead be self-evident to everyone.[34] However, it happily remains the case that error does not miraculously become truth simply because it is either overlooked, or widely embraced, or because its embrace is sustained over a long period of time. Certainly, longevity of error does not make for theological truth.[35] After all, there was a time in the first decades of the fourth century when a very significant portion of the church "woke up to find itself Arian." This deviation from Christian orthodoxy could only be corrected by intentional discussion of the relevant evidence in seriously

32. Wright, "Dr. Carnley on T. C. Hammond and Arianism," 46.

33. This is reported by Tom Frame, "Dynamics and Difficulties," 157.

34. Jensen, "T. C. Hammond No Arian," 46. "His alleged Arianism has passed without controversy for seventy years."

35. I am reminded of Cyprian's reply to Pope Stephen's famous mid-third-century assertion about the importance of tradition. Stephen said: "Nihil innovetur nisi quod traditum est" ("Let nothing be introduced that has not already been handed down"), to which Cyprian replied: "Consuetudo sine veritate, vetustas erroris est" ("Custom without truth is but the longevity of error")!

intensive debate, eventually at the General Council at Nicaea between May and August of 325. Clearly, the certainty of assent to theological truth is ultimately only confidently achieved as the product of the apprehension of the logical necessity of the specific conclusions of a cogent argument. Perhaps we find ourselves facing a similar challenge today.

On the other hand, though James Haire was of the view that "Ulster federal theologians" tended typically, though perhaps unwittingly, to lean towards a kind of Arianism,[36] this obviously does not mean that every Ulster theologian, whether actually resident in Ulster or otherwise, is definitely to be corralled and labeled "Arian." This is the kind of judgment that can only be made by looking closely at what specific individuals have actually said. This means that the question of T. C. Hammond's orthodoxy in particular, as James Haire himself is reported to have observed under the close questioning of Tom Frame, "can be established only by referring to Hammond's books and lectures."[37]

Even this is not to say, of course, that, when Hammond's actual writing is examined, we can immediately expect an outcome of settled unanimity. Peter Jensen has firmly expressed the view that "the attempt to link Hammond to 'Ulster federal theology' is doomed to failure because there is no evidence that he belonged to such a school of thought."[38] Almost as if joining in a kind of defensive duet, David F. Wright likewise echoed the same categorical refrain: "there is no trace in *In Understanding Be Men* of what Dr Carnley identifies as one of the basic elements of federal theology."[39]

Clearly, we must necessarily attend to the consideration of this alleged evidential deficit with candor, and with a good deal of care.

⌒

When we go to Hammond's actual writings, not least *In Understanding Be Men*, we find that the story is somewhat different from the chorus of denial that his defenders urge us to hear and accept. Any dispassionate

36. Tom Frame reports that Haire expressed the view that "Hammond, like many Anglicans at the time, was influenced by what was known as 'federal Calvinism' and that many 'federal Calvinists' were accused of Arianism at different times." "Dynamics and Difficulties," 147.

37. Frame, "Dynamics and Difficulties," 147.

38. Jensen, "T. C. Hammond No Arian," 45.

39. Wright, "Dr. Carnley on T. C. Hammond and Arianism," 46.

and attentive reading will uncover ample evidence of his federalist sympathies.

From the start, Hammond's acquaintance with Protestant Christianity was colored by the uncompromising commitment to the identifying characteristics of federal theology that were enshrined in *The Westminster Confession of Faith*. This was already domiciled in the Ireland of his youth. Apart from his inclination to supplement his reliance on the Anglican *Thirty-Nine Articles of Religion* with *The Westminster Confession of Faith,* and to regard these two documents almost as a composite product of "British Isles" theology,[40] Hammond generally presents the Westminster tradition in a favorable light. Indeed, he had some early sympathies with Presbyterianism. Shortly after his conversion, when he already seemed inclined to study for Christian ministry, "there is even a hint that he felt attracted to the Presbyterian ministry,"[41] and in his early days as an itinerant preacher he certainly had direct contact with communities of Presbyterian worshippers. Cookstown in County Tyrone in Northern Ireland, which Hammond described as "a strong presbyterian village," is obviously one of them. Although he came to embrace Anglicanism and its episcopal ordering with enthusiasm, his declared militant "Protestantism" meant that he naturally found theological allies amongst Irish Presbyterians.

Hammond's conversion occurred during his time at the YMCA in Cork, while he was a member of a group led by John McNay, a son of pious Scottish Presbyterian parents.[42] In later life in Australia Hammond contributed regularly to *Evangelical Action*[43] which was edited by W. R. McEwen, a good friend and fellow exile, and a Reformed Presbyterian minister.[44]

We also have to remember that in political terms there was an independent Ireland separate from Ulster only from 1922 onwards. Hammond knew it only over the last fourteen of the years that he lived in

---

40. Hammond, *In Understanding Be Men*, 21: "[T]he British Isles produced the Thirty-Nine Articles and the Westminster Confession." Much later, in *New Creation* (1953) it is significant that, in commending the federal theology of Hodge (*Outlines of Theology*, 362, 357), approving mention is made specifically of "the Synod of Dort and the Westminster Assembly." *New Creation*, 89.

41. Nelson, *T. C. Hammond*, 43.

42. Nelson, *T. C. Hammond*, 36.

43. Earlier *Good Tidings*.

44. Nelson, *T. C. Hammond*, 119.

Ireland. During the earlier years of his life Ireland was unitary. Furthermore, the Church of Ireland to which Hammond belonged covered the whole of Ireland as a single unit, as it does to this day. Though he saw himself as a man of Cork, he quite naturally belonged also to the Ulster Protestant Association.[45]

The Ireland of the second half of the nineteenth century was one in which Protestantism increasingly became self-consciously aware of its distinct differences with Roman Catholicism. As heir to a "Second Reformation," this Protestantism was marked by evangelical revivals, such as a notable 1859 revival that "brought great blessings to Northern Ireland, some of which overflowed southward into Protestant churches" and gave birth to the YMCA of which Hammond was an active member in Cork from 1890, and the Irish Church Missions that Hammond was to be intimately associated with in Dublin from 1895. Clearly, the unbecoming denial involved in suggesting that Hammond was "a southerner through and through" and somehow closeted in Cork in a way that quarantined him in his formative years from the contagion of the federalist influence of *The Westminster Confession* hardly assists the cause of truth.

$$\backsim$$

When we begin to look for the origins of Hammond's own Calvinist theology, and how it was that he came to embrace the contractual coloring put on it by the federal theology that he appears so comfortably to have shared with *The Westminster Confession* of his Ulster Presbyterian friends, we need look no further than to the primary influence of James Ussher.[46] In an article on "Post-Reformation Theology in Ireland" that he contributed in 1932 to the 1,500th anniversary celebrations of the arrival of St. Patrick in Ireland, Hammond referred to Ussher as the "greatest of the sons" of the Church of Ireland,[47] who had in turn "modelled his outlook upon the great questions on the Reformed interpretation of the sage of Hippo."[48] In Hammond's view it was only right that as a theologian "the

45. Nelson, *T. C. Hammond*, 23.

46. James Ussher (1581–1656), Archbishop of Armagh (1625), described in the *Oxford Dictionary of the Christian Church* as a Calvinist theologian and a historian "of vast learning."

47. Hammond, "Post-Reformation Theology," 105.

48. Hammond, "Post Reformation Theology," 98. The reference is to St. Augustine of Hippo.

incomparable Ussher"[49] was able to "command the respect of all time."[50] From him the church had learned that "the Scriptures of God" were "the proper object of faith," and that justifying faith was fixed "solely on Jesus Christ and him crucified."[51]

Significantly, already in a booklet entitled *Authority in Religion* (1916), Hammond capped off a discussion of the authority of Scripture by quoting *The Westminster Confession of Faith* on the internal testimony of the Holy Spirit.[52] He explicitly declared his appreciation of the *Confession*, which he proudly noted was chiefly the work of Church of England clergy, very importantly aided by the work of the Irish Archbishop James Ussher, who had been appointed to the Westminster Assembly as the member for Oxford. Though Ussher as a Royalist refused to attend the assembly that began to meet on July 1, 1643, many of its divines admired him and drew upon his theological support.[53] Amongst his closest contacts amongst members of the assembly was his colleague Joshua Hoyle, the assembly member for Cumberland from 1643–49 and the unofficial representative of Trinity College, Dublin. Very importantly, Hoyle was a key member of the assembly committee charged with the drafting of the *Confession of Faith*. On the other hand, Ussher was actually quoted by Thomas Goodwin, who went down in history as the third most vocal of all assembly members,[54] and with Hoyle was also an active member of the committee for the *Confession of Faith*. Another member of this committee, Jeremiah Whitaker, a staunch Presbyterian, is known to have quoted views of Ursinus relating to the sacraments.[55]

49. Hammond, "Post-Reformation Theology," 98.

50. Hammond, "Post-Reformation Theology," 98.

51. Hammond, "Post-Reformation Theology," 98, citing James Ussher, *Answer to a Jesuit*, 448.

52. Hammond, *Authority in Religion*, 298–99, quoting the *Westminster Confession*, Chapter 1, "Of the Holy Scripture," 5.

53. See *Minutes and Papers of the Westminster Assembly*, I.141: Ussher was "widely respected by assembly members and parliamentarians in spite of his episcopal and royalist convictions." In 1648 the House of Lords considered inviting him to the assembly for a second time. For Hammond's comment on Ussher's contribution to the Westminster Assembly, see "Post-Reformation Theology," 98, quoting Ussher, "Answer to a Jesuit," 702, 721.

54. Notching up some four hundred addresses to the assembly. He referred to Ussher in positive terms at Session 102.

55. At Session 566 of the assembly on January 5, 1645.

It is not by accident that Ussher was an enthusiastic exponent of the characteristic federal doctrine of an alleged "covenant of nature" or "covenant of works" as the relevant clause enshrined it in *The Westminster Confession*.[56] A recent commentator on Ussher has noted that the "covenant of works" was "integrated . . . throughout his theological system,"[57] further observing that this doctrine "taught that God made a covenant with Adam, the first person, and in this covenant offered him eternal blessings *if he rendered perfect obedience* during a period of probation."[58] As such the "covenant of works" is said to have become the "linchpin of his theological system."[59] The contractual and conditional nature of this "covenant of works" should not evade our attention.

A clear indication of the fact that by the time of the Westminster Assembly Ussher had long since embraced the key federal tenets of scholastic Calvinism may be found in Sermon V of his "Eighteen Sermons Preached in Oxford" in 1640. While demonstrating that Ussher did not draw his federal theology from the deliberations of the Westminster Assembly but was already well versed in it, this sermon at the same time indicates that Ussher did not draw these beliefs out of Scripture either, but injected them into his reading of the texts! Sermon V was based on Galatians 3:22: "But the Scripture hath concluded all under sin, that the promise by faith of Jesus Christ might be given to them that believe." Surprisingly, Ussher found "in this excellent portion of Scripture" a hidden reference to "the two covenants of Almighty God: to wit the covenant of nature, and the covenant of grace." He went on to expound the "covenant of nature" that God was alleged to have made with Adam, which was said to have been "written by God in man's heart." This is said to be "the holy law of God, by virtue whereof a man was to continue in that integrity, holiness and uprightness, in which God had first created him, and to serve God according to that strength he first enabled him with, that so he might live thereby."[60] Then "when man had broken this covenant, and entered into a state of rebellion against God, he is shut up in misery, but not in misery for ever"[61]—for God is said to make a way for escape

---

56. Clause 7.ii

57. Perkins, *Catholicity and the Covenant of Works*, 1.

58. Perkins, *Catholicity and the Covenant of Works*, 1. My italics.

59. Perkins, *Catholicity and the Covenant of Works*, 4.

60. Ussher, *Whole Works*, 60.

61. Ussher, *Whole Works*, 60.

and deliverance and for "entrance into the second covenant of grace." Somehow, Ussher imagined that he found all this in Galatians 3:22!

The 1640 Oxford sermon published immediately prior to this, Sermon IV, also shows that Ussher was already working with a clear reliance on the signature beliefs of federal theology: the characteristic notions of the alleged prelapsarian covenant between God and Adam, the "covenant of nature or works" that Adam, as the federal head of natural humanity was said to have breached, resulting in the imposition of the penalty of death on all humanity after him. Thus, Ussher says, "So in Adam, he being the head of the covenant of nature or works, that is, the law, if he had stood, none of us had fallen; if he fall, none of us all can stand." In this sermon Ussher goes on to explain how it was that Adam's contractual obligations flow on to all subsequent humanity: "He is the peg, on which all the keys hang: if that stand, they hang fast; but if that fall, they fall with it. As we see in matter of bondage; if the father forfeit his liberty, and become a bondman, all his children are bondmen to a hundred generations, here is our case. We were all once free, but our father (Adam) hath forfeited his liberty; and if he become a slave, he cannot beget a freeman."[62] Clearly, the theory is that, as the offspring of slaves are automatically also slaves, so all of sinfully disobedient humanity is said also to bear the penalty of death imposed on Adam for his disobedience.

There is thus a clear historical link between the federal theology of T. C. Hammond's hero, Archbishop Ussher of Armagh, and the notoriously federalist *Westminster Confession,* not least the idea of a prelapsarian contractual "covenant of works" with Adam as this is set out in Article 7(ii), as fundamental to the theological posture of the militant Protestantism that Hammond shared as a matter of course with his Irish Presbyterian friends.

---

62. Ussher, "Eighteen Sermons Preached at Oxford," 53. Ussher speaks of Adam and Christ as "two head-men, two fathers of all other men. There were but two, by whom all must stand or fall, but two such men. By the fall of the first man we all fell; and if we rise not by the second man, we are yet in our sins. If he rise not, we cannot be risen. We must rise or fall by him. He is the mediator of the second covenant. If he rise and we are in him, we shall rise with him; but if not, we are dead still. So it is in the first Adam, we all depend on him, he is the root of all mankind." Clearly the "second covenant" to which Ussher refers presupposes the "covenant of works" with Adam after the manner of Ursinus's schema in *The Heidelberg Catechism.*

⌐⌐

Understandably, in *In Understanding Be Men,* Hammond declared that he was naturally prepared to hold up the tradition of the Reformation and English Puritanism, along with "nations such as Scotland and Holland," as exemplars of the moral power of Calvinism.[63] As it happens, historically these were three of the world's most important hubs of "federal Calvinism." Even if Hammond did not reside permanently in England, Scotland, or Holland, we should not be surprised to find indications of federalism in Hammond's own professed Calvinist theology. His own direct familiarity with Ursinus's classic expression of scholastic Calvinism is evidenced by the fact that he not only quoted, with approval, directly from the *The Heidelberg Catechism* of 1563 in a section on "Puritans and Sacraments" in his last book, *The New Creation,*[64] but in that his discussion of baptism also went on explicitly to declare that he believed that the "federal view" was "the best way of combining the scriptural evidence in a coherent whole."[65] In relation to this, Hammond quoted A. A. Hodge's commendation of federal theology's understanding of Adam as "the federal head and representative of his race" and the parallel understanding of our union with Christ. Hodge believed that this was accepted as the general consensus amongst all brands of Christians.[66]

Very significantly, Hammond also cited both Calvin and Ussher as exponents of the "federal theory" whereby "the arranging party" of a covenant or mutual compact enters into an arrangement on behalf of others: "When there can be no direct contact someone must be found who will undertake the negotiations, fulfil the necessary conditions, for a satisfactory arrangement. In such circumstances the arranging party is a mediator."[67] Hence the authority of Adam to enter upon the "covenant of works" as the federal head of natural humanity, and of Christ, the mediator of the "covenant of grace," as the federal head of the new humanity. We should not be surprised to find that the key elements of Ursinus's

63. Hammond, *In Understanding Be Men,* 93.

64. Hammond, *New Creation,* 161: "The sacraments are holy visible signs and seals ordained by God . . . that He may more fully declare and seal . . . the promise of His gospel unto us . . ." See "Heidelberg Catechism," Question 66. John McIntosh speaks of this as Hammond reaching "into his treasure-store from the Reformation." *Anglican Evangelicalism in Sydney 1897 to 1953,* Kindle ed., loc. 8299.

65. Hammond, *New Creation,* 47.

66. Hodge, *Outlines of Theology,* 362, 357.

67. Hammond, *New Creation,* 39.

brand of scholastic Calvinism in fact inform Hammond's systematic theology specifically with respect to redemption and grace understood through the lens of justice and legal principle.[68]

Even so, David F. Wright throws down the gauntlet at this point: "I defy anyone to read *In Understanding Be Men*, and derive from it a concept of grace . . . worked out in terms of the logically prior category of law."[69] Alas, the indications are that the actual evidence may well demonstrate that it would be obtuse, if not impossible, to avoid such a reading. We must therefore turn to Hammond's own declared position in relation to the importance of matters of justice and legal principle in coming to an understanding of the operation of God's grace.

It is initially significant that, in *In Understanding Be Men*, Hammond's theological priorities explicitly focus on the theme of God's justice, which is elevated to a level of importance with divine love and forgiveness. Thus, speaking of the attributes of God, he roundly declares that the remission of sins "is as much derived from His *justice* as His love."[70] Indeed, in terms of the logic of his argument, love and forgiveness tend to assume a kind of subsidiarity to justice by being accommodated to it. So, under the heading of "The Justice of Retribution" Hammond declares that "Punishment is an inevitable sequel to sin" that may be understood on analogy with "a form of judicial dealing" such as the "punishment prescribed by a human magistrate."[71] This punishment is understood to achieve the "vindication of God as the Lawgiver."[72]

This somewhat unusual preferential characterization of God as "Lawgiver" in *In Understanding Be Men* is in turn not in the context of a discussion of the importance of the Torah or Mosaic law, but in the

68. Citing Jude v. 6 as a support to Galatians 3:22, Ussher assures his hearers that this is "no new doctrine devised by us, but it is the course and method of the Scripture: for it begins in this great work with imprisoning and shutting up. The law is as a justice of peace, by his mittimus (warrant of arrest) commands us to prison. It is a sergeant that arrests a man, and carries him to the gaol." Sermon V, *Whole Works*, 60–61.

69. Wright, "Dr. Carnley on T. C. Hammond and Arianism," 47.

70. Hammond, *In Understanding Be Men*, 119. Hammond's italics.

71. Hammond, *In Understanding Be Men*, 85.

72. Hammond, *In Understanding Be Men*, 85. This statement about Christ's punishment being the vindication of God as Lawgiver is repeated on pages 119 and 126 where it is notable that God is characterized primarily as a Lawgiver (125–26).

context of a discussion of "the law of contract" and the contractual implications of the disobedience of Adam and of all humanity after him. It
is within this specific context that Hammond speaks of "infringed legal
liabilities"[73] and of the work of Christ that "made propitiation and discharged all our legal liabilities."[74] His theology of atonement consequently
emphasizes that it was "Our Lord's perfect obedience" that extended "to
voluntary submission to death" and "vindicated the Lawgiver." By assuming "our legal liability" Christ "gave full satisfaction to the Upholder of
the moral laws of the universe."[75]

In all this Hammond shows himself to be the devoted pupil of his
hero James Ussher, whose Calvinism is not without the fundamental reliance on themes of justice and legal principle that he shared with the
Westminster tradition of his time and that was ultimately inherited from
Heidelberg. Thus, Ussher characterized Christ's priestly office chiefly in
terms of his self-offering "for the satisfaction of God's justice."[76] Indeed,
an echo of the presupposed broken contractual arrangement with Adam
of federal theology may be heard in his understanding of the redemptive
work of Christ: "Christ therefore, because Adam did not fulfil the law, he
undertook to fulfil the same to relieve us, and that God's justice should
not be in vain." Accordingly, Christ pays "the penalty due to the breach
of the law."[77] The Godhead and the manhood are said to have performed
this work "in full obedience unto God's justice."[78] In a sermon preached
on Ephesians 4:13, Ussher encapsulated this juridical understanding of
Christ's atoning work: ". . . the satisfaction which our High-Priest was
able to make unto his Father's justice, as well by his passive as by his
active obedience . . . behoveth him also to fulfil the law and all righteousness, that so he be the end of the law for righteousness to everyone that
believeth."[79]

73. Hammond, *In Understanding Be Men*, 124.

74. Hammond, *In Understanding Be Men*, 126.

75. Hammond, *In Understanding Be Men,* 119–20. Once again, "our Lord's death
offered to God the full satisfaction of obedience to the divine law . . . Hence the emphasis came to be placed on man's debt to the Lawgiver, and the guilt of sin came to be
measured by the dignity of the Lawgiver."

76. Ussher, Sermon IX, *Whole Works*, 128.

77. Ussher, Sermon IX, *Whole Works*, 512.

78. Ussher, Sermon IX, *Whole Works*, 516.

79. Ussher, Sermon on Ephesians 4:13, published in *Answer to a Jesuit*, 692.

Without doubt the formative influence of James Ussher is of enormous importance in understanding Hammond's determination to work out a theology of redemptive grace in which issues of justice and legal principle are fundamental. This makes a feature of the self-conscious determination not to place love above law, and still less to allow a treatment of God's love to dispense with law.

⤸

Whereas Hammond regarded the tendency to elevate God's love above the importance of law as the fatal error of liberalism and modernism, for Ussher it was the perceived growth of antinomianism in his time that was judged to be the chief theological foe in relation to this. The Westminster Assembly had been convened in 1643 to advise the Long Parliament on religious issues, with an agenda including such practical matters as the perceived moral failure amongst members of the clergy, and the Church's ineptitude in relation to the examination of candidates for ordination, as well as ecclesiological issues of a structural kind, along with the theological need to revise the *Thirty Nine Articles of Religion* and produce new catechetical materials and a new definitive statement of faith. At the very beginning of the assembly, apart from the nervous need to address "overexposure to papists,"[80] the threat of a perceived growth in antinomianism and the fear of social disorder that it might harbor bulked large as a prevailing concern on all sides. Briefly put, at that time, the view that the new covenant of grace had eliminated the effect of the law was based on the antinomian view that "if Christ have fulfilled the law," then humanity was "not bound to fulfil the law."[81]

A petition was presented to the House of Commons on August 10, 1643 against antinomian teachers out of the fear that they might "cast off the whole moral law of God"[82] and a summary of antinomian errors followed on September 23, 1643. A measure of the seriousness with which the threat of antinomianism was viewed is indicated by the fact that in the following year, on August 23, 1644, the assembly established a committee for suppressing the antinomians. As Robert Letham has observed, this was particularly urgent, because antinomianism "was the real perceived

---

80. Van Dixhoorn, ed., *Minutes and Papers of the Westminster Assembly*, I, 2 (Document 42).

81. Van Dixhoorn, ed., *Minutes and Papers of the Westminster Assembly*, II, 95.

82. Van Dixhoorn, ed., *Minutes and Papers of the Westminster Assembly*, V, 2.

threat, not only to the church but to civil society."[83] And while members of the assembly were united in their opposition to the merits of good works given the perceived importance of justification by faith alone, they were concerned not to give any encouragement to the antinomians. Hence, this was a relevant consideration in the doctrinal approach of the assembly's discussions of covenant, law, and liberty that led to the carefully worded texts of the Confession of Faith and the Catechisms.[84]

This same struggle to suppress antinomian views reinforced the theological approach of the scholastic Calvinism with the characteristic twist of the "federal theory," which both Ussher and his admirers amongst the Westminster divines self-consciously embraced in their presentation of the essence of the gospel of God's grace. An understanding of human redemption based upon the foundation of God's justice, and the need for a penalty to be paid for human disobedience following the fracture of the "covenant of works" by Adam, then invited the response of faithful believers to appropriate the benefits of forgiveness and grace followed by the living of regenerate lives in accordance with the moral law. Similarly, Ussher was very adamant that only the regenerate could please God.

The reliance on a legal framework, starting with the "covenant of works" that God was imagined to have made with Adam, and ending with Christ's payment of satisfaction for the breaking of this contract, understood in terms of the alleged divinely imposed punishment of the penal substitutionary theory of atonement, was thus no purely incidental or inadvertent development, but the product of an agenda that was entirely deliberate, and, originally, self-consciously pursued in answer to antinomianism. The determination to fight against the dual threat of popery on one hand and antinomianism on the other was what set Ussher on common ground with the predominantly Presbyterian sympathies of the divines of the Westminster Assembly. Indeed, Ussher had already made no bones about where he stood on this issue: "Know . . . that law is the highway to the Gospel, the path that leads to it, that way which must be trodden in: we are still out of our way, till we have begun our walks in this path: and if thou art not terrified by the law, and the sight of thy sins, been at thy wits end, as it were, weary of thy condition and bondage, thou art not in the way yet."[85]

83. Letham, *Westminster Assembly*, 119.

84. See Letham's sensitive discussion of the theology of the Assembly in *Westminster Assembly*, chapter 6.

85. Ussher, Sermon V, *Whole Works*, 65.

Given the high regard that T. C. Hammond had for Ussher, it is entirely understandable that he shared his views. We hear something more than a distant historical echo of all this in his Calvinist views and in the Carillon Avenue theology generally, which began to flourish under his watch at Moore Theological College and thereafter became domiciled there. Indeed, to this day for many these themes constitute the "pulsating heart" of their presentation of the gospel.[86]

◦

Unsurprisingly, when Hammond attempts a definition of the law, he does not speak of the role of law in securing a basic standard of behavior necessary for society to hold together with a degree of security and peace, so as then to go on to speak of the call of religion to live by grace in accordance with a standard over and above what the law requires.[87] Rather, he conceives of law in interpersonal and subordinationist terms that are logically congruent with his preferential characterization of God as "the Lawgiver." Accordingly, the law is defined as "Something laid down by a superior for the guidance of an inferior."[88] Already we perceive in the background here the motif of a relationship of domination and submission that informs Hammond's understanding of the relation of God to humanity, as well as the relationship of fatherly command and filial obedience in his understanding of the dynamics of the divine life of God itself and in the outworking of the economy of salvation. His understanding of the law and of justice already bulks large in his thinking as the controlling motif of his theology of human redemption.

Understandably, in expounding the need for the incarnation, Hammond therefore argues that almost every New Testament reference to incarnation suggests that "redemption is its purpose": "In order to become 'the Last Adam', the covenant Head of a new race of redeemed men, our Lord must needs take a body similar to ours, and as Man offer the fullest

---

86. See for example Michael Bird's *Evangelical Theology*, 677–83, for a discussion of Adam in which he argues that all humanity is condemned because of Adam's sins. He says he takes the view of the place of Adam outlined by H. Blocher in *Original Sin*, 77, where Blocher says "in Adam all are placed in a 'covenant of creation' and so are culpable."

87. As in the thinking of Lord Patrick Devlin in *Enforcement of Morals*.

88. Hammond, *One Hundred Texts*, 531.

obedience to the divine claims."[89] In the ensuing redemptive schema, God's love is then shown primarily and definitively in the giving of his own Son to bear the required punishment for human sin, thus paying the penalty that justice requires in order to neutralize the disobedience of Adam. The sacrificial overtones usually associated with the notion of propitiation (e.g. as found in Romans 3:25), even sometimes in relation to the cooling of an alleged divine anger, are replaced by a more juridical understanding of propitiation, that Hammond apparently found more congenial: by bearing the justly deserved punishment instead of a sinner, the death of Christ "entirely removes his legal liability."[90] The propitiating mystery of the Savior's death, understood in this juridical way, is said to be "the crowning wonder of the grace of God, the most superb gesture of the Godhead to men, and the very heart of Christianity."[91] This "crowning wonder of grace" as the propitiating fulfillment of a legal requirement is in turn cited as a condition of the possibility of salvation, for the receiving of divine forgiveness is based upon it and cannot proceed without it: there can be no reconciliation with God prior to the atonement for sin and evil understood in this specific way.

It is entirely congruent with this emphasis on understanding the atonement in terms of the fulfillment of legal principle that Hammond interprets the key words "propitiation," "offering," and "sin-bearing" and the phrases "the Just for the unjust" and "the obedience of One" as all having "a very definite content." Through the lens of his theological federalism "propitiation" compels us to picture "outraged Justice and the great need of securing mercy."[92]

In fact, Hammond's fundamental appeal to the requirements of justice and legal principle in a way that renders his understanding of the gift of God's love and forgiveness as being dependent upon it, and thus in logical terms subservient to it, means that his understanding of God's redemptive grace is misunderstood without it. Hence, Hammond notes

89. Hammond, *In Understanding Be Men*, 97. His reference to "covenant Head" here is of course not insignificant.

90. Hammond, *In Understanding Be Men*, 120. The "infringed legal liabilities" (124) have to be dealt with by God, the doctrine of justification by faith being understood by the Reformers by putting an emphasis largely of forensic aspects found in the Epistle to the Romans. Hence, Romans 3:25 is interpreted with a legal coloring: "Christ has made propitiation *and discharged all our legal liabilities.*"

91. Hammond, *In Understanding Be Men*, 117.

92. Hammond, "Significance of the Death of Christ," 49.

that the Reformers were chiefly concerned with the legal aspects of the atonement and its relation to their central teaching of justification by faith. In order to interpret the death of Christ the first Christians are said to have unlocked "the very treasures of Greek thought and of Roman jurisprudence . . . to unfold for us something of the glory and the majesty of this sacrifice of the Eternal Son for the sons of men."[93] This is why "the Reformers put an emphasis largely on forensic aspects as given in the Epistle to the Romans—viz., since Christ has made propitiation *and discharged all our legal liabilities*"[94] (my italics).

As has already been noted, in *The New Creation*, which Hammond published in 1953, he put his federalist sympathies on the table by declaring that he thought that the "federal theory," which he attributed to Calvin and Ussher, was "the best way of combining the scriptural evidence in a coherent whole."[95] In coming to this conviction the influence of the publications of Charles and his son A. A. Hodge is also important, not least A. A. Hodge's *Outlines of Theology* (1860) where the fundamental themes of federal theology are clearly expounded in some detail along with its history. Hammond himself acknowledges his sympathies with Hodge's federalism in *The New Creation*, on page 89.

In this work he explicitly emphasized the importance of elevating law over love, lamenting the "very bad" moral effect of the "vials of wrath poured on 'legalistic ideas'" by liberal Christians, who claimed to transcend law by "the higher principle of love."[96] This to Hammond's mind was the great mistake of theological liberalism. It was his firmly held conviction that the view of liberals and modernists achieves nothing positive but only "transforms Christ into an ideal Example."[97] In other words, an ideal example of love accomplishes nothing in terms of the actual

93. Hammond, "Significance of the Death of Christ," 47.

94. Hammond, *In Understanding Be Men*, 126.

95. Hammond, *New Creation*, 39–47. See also, John A. McIntosh's discussion of *New Creation* in *Anglican Evangelicalism in Sydney, 1897 to 1953*, chapter 12. It is not insignificant that Ussher was, if not a participant in the Westminster Assembly of 1643–49, a kindred theological spirit, or that Hammond enthusiastically celebrated Ussher's contribution to Irish theology. Among other things this was because Ussher himself held that "the regenerate person only is 'alive unto God'; the unregenerate person being unable to please God" (Ussher, *Answer to a Jesuit, Works*, 448). See Hammond, "Post-Reformation Theology," 98.

96. Hammond, *New Creation*, 68.

97. Hammond, *New Creation*, 72.

payment of the penalty that the law demands as a contractual obligation, given the disobedience of Adam.

⤸

Furthermore, in unpacking the outworking of the justice of God in God's dealing with sin and evil, and in lockstep with the classical expressions of federal theology, Hammond makes no distinction between the meaning of "covenant" and of "contract" but moves somewhat promiscuously between the two.[98] Indeed, he lumps together the "covenants" with Adam, Noah, and Abraham[99] in a way that assumes that all were qualitatively monochrome and, indeed, "contractual." This means that the notion of the *protevangelium*, and the unconditional nature of the covenant between God and Abraham, is entirely missing from Hammond's theology.

Instead, in the manner of federal theology as it developed in the wake of the seminal work of Ursinus, Hammond concentrates on Adam, whom he is inclined to view as a historical figure, apparently the first human being to emerge from whatever may have gone before in the evolutionary process,[100] and who is understood to have implicated all humanity after him in his disobedience. As in Ursinus's *Heidelberg Catechism* of 1563, though there is no explicit mention of a *prelapsarian* covenant in *In Understanding Be Men*, it is nevertheless clearly presupposed that Adam had entered into a covenant[101] that can only be prelapsarian, and that this is understood in contractual terms, the fulfillment of God's promise of love and life being originally conditional upon Adam's obedience.[102] In *In Understanding Be Men* Hammond in this way works out his

98. This may be observed, for example, in the central paragraph on page 84. This is entirely parallel to A. A. Hodge's treatment of covenants. See especially chapter xvii on "The Covenant of Works" in his *Outlines of Theology*.

99. Hammond, *In Understanding Be Men*, 87.

100. Hammond, *In Understanding Be Men*, 68: "Adam was as much an historical person as our Lord Himself . . . By no process of literary interpretation can . . . references to Adam be made to mean other than that he was considered as much a person as the patriarchs."

101. Hammond, *In Understanding Be Men*, 87.

102. Hammond, *One Hundred Texts*, 2. Text 20–21: "With what sad fact does St. Paul connect this truth of universal sin? With the fact that Adam broke God's law. What does the connection with Adam's sin teach us? That all who are born of Adam are sharers in his sin." Compare *The Westminster Confession of Faith*, 7:ii: "The first covenant made with man was a covenant of works, wherein life was promised to

doctrine of redemption along the lines of the penal substitution theory of the atonement, in which the operation of grace is necessarily construed in legal terms, the need for Christ's death being explained on the basis of the legal requirements of God's justice relating to broken covenants understood specifically as broken *contractual* arrangements. Thus the "supreme covenant" is said to have been made between the Father and the Son, and "made 'on our behalf' who were incapable of keeping any *contract* between God and man"[103] (my italics).

Very importantly, as in federal theology, Adam acts in the role of a representative head, thus implicating all whom he represented in his failure to fulfill his contractual obligations. This means that Hammond explicitly defines the notion of the covenant that was entered into by Adam on behalf of all humanity in contractual terms involving the fulfilling of conditions. In Hammond's *One Hundred Texts* a "Covenant" is said to be "an agreement between two persons. That arrangement between God and man by which God engages to give *on certain conditions* certain blessings to man" (my italics).[104] Furthermore, Hammond imports this notion of contractual headship into the internal dynamics of the divine life by telling us that God the Father made a contract with the Son, by virtue of which the Son becomes the "Covenant Head" of the human race, capable of acting representatively, precisely to restore the human race, the position of "Covenant Head" being explicitly defined as "that position which Christ holds as Representative of His People in virtue of a covenant between the Father and the Son."[105]

Because Adam is said to have been contractually required to be obedient or else undergo death, death is understood to be the deserved punishment, not only for his rebellious disobedience, but a punishment suffered by all sinfully rebellious humanity after him. In other words, given that he was disobedient and thus fell from grace, it was precisely because of his position as the representative or federal head of the human race that all humanity therefore fell with him. Once again, as in Ursinus's *Heidelberg Catechism*, this is clearly presupposed also by Hammond insofar as his account of Christ's "covenant of redemption" does not hesitate

Adam, and in him to his posterity, *upon condition* of perfect and personal obedience." (My italics.)

103. Hammond, *In Understanding Be Men*, 87 (my italics).

104. In support of this Hammond cites Hebrews 8:7, 9, and 10. See Hammond, *One Hundred Texts*, 529.

105. Hammond, *One Hundred Texts*, No. 16, 529.

to speak of Christ, not just as the "Covenant Head" of the redeemed human race (where covenant is understood in contractual terms), but quite explicitly as the *"federal* head of the new humanity."[106]

Accordingly, it is as a contractual or federal head that Hammond understands Paul's participatory language of being "in Christ." The concept of being "in Christ" means being "in union with Him as our head, united as a branch to a vine."[107] The reliance on this particular understanding of the "headship" of Christ is of enormous importance to Hammond's theology of salvation because it explains how "the obedience of the new Head of the race is able to benefit those who receive him as their Head." This is in turn because it is by virtue of the new contractual covenant entered into by Christ with the Father that "the penitent sinner who acknowledges him as his Head is assured of all that Adam and the race could ever have attained had original righteousness not been lost."[108]

It is understandable that the notion of Christ as "the federal head of the new humanity" appears in *In Understanding Be Men*, not just once but twice,[109] in addition to such semantic equivalents as "the new Head of the race"[110] and "the Covenant head of a new race of men."[111] Surely all this is quite unmistakable evidence of the residual influence of federal theology in T. C. Hammond's thinking. So much for the contention that there is "no evidence" to support the view that he belonged to such a school of thought!

⌒

In his insistent desire to distance Hammond from federal theology the important distinction between "contracts" and "covenants" is also lost on David F. Wright. Wright, indeed, categorically insists that "covenant" is

106. Hammond, *In Understanding Be Men*, 84: "As from Adam men derive sin and guilt, so from Christ the new *federal* Head of the race, we derive forgiveness and righteousness" (my italics).

107. Hammond, *One Hundred Texts*, 531. In support of this Hammond cites John 15:4, 5; 1 Cor 15:18, 19; and 2 Cor 10:17.

108. Hammond, *In Understanding Be Men*, 79.

109. Hammond, *In Understanding Be Men*, 84: Christ is spoken of as "the new federal Head of the race"; on 116: Christ's death is spoken of as *exemplary* and also *representative*, "that is, as being that of the federal Head of the new race of men."

110. Hammond, *In Understanding Be Men*, 79.

111. Hammond, *In Understanding Be Men*, 97: "In order to become 'the last Adam', the covenant Head of a new race of redeemed men . . ."

"scarcely a prominent theme in the book and undoubtedly not an organiz-ing motif" of *In Understanding Be Men*.[112] In advancing this contention Wright is in one sense correct. The unconditional nature essential to a covenant, particularly in the paradigm of God's covenant with Abraham, is very effectively passed over by Hammond. Strictly speaking the motif of a genuine "covenant" as an unconditional agreement therefore certain-ly does not appear in *In Understanding Be Men*. But this is not because the word "covenant" is rarely used as of no importance;[113] rather it is because covenants generally are treated by Hammond not as essentially uncon-ditional promises but precisely as legal contractual arrangements that impose conditions on their fulfillment. Though Dudley Fenner's explicit phrase "*foedus operum*" or "covenant of works" is not used, Hammond does speak explicitly of a creational covenant with Adam. And, even though this "covenant with Adam" is indiscriminately bundled together with the covenants with "Noah and Abraham," which are all in turn said to be "illuminative of and lead[ing] up to" the "supreme covenant" of Christ, all the while an assumed contractual and legal coloring is presup-posed in covenantal arrangements. All these "covenants" are assumed to be "contractual" in nature.[114] No attempt is made to distinguish the kind of contractual covenant that is conditional on obedience, and which brings with it the imposition of a penalty should it be broken, as in the case of the alleged prelapsarian contractual covenant with Adam, from the wholly unconditional "promise without penalty" of the thus radi-cally different quality proper to covenants, such as that God made with Abraham in which God is always and unalterably faithful to his promise, regardless of the shortcomings and failures of the human parties to the covenant. Indeed when Hammond defines the concept of a covenant in *One Hundred Texts*, he explicitly refers to its contractual and conditional nature: a covenant is said to be not just "an agreement between two per-sons" but that arrangement between God and man by which God engages to give certain blessings to man "*on certain conditions*."[115] This definition almost certainly contains an echo of *The Westminster Confession of Faith*

112. Wright, "Dr. Carnley on T. C. Hammond," 46.

113. David Wright ("Dr. Carnley on T. C. Hammond," 46) notes that the word "covenant" "appears in a title only for one sub-subsection (on 86–88), where the real subject is election rather than covenant."

114. Hammond, *In Understanding Be Men*, 87.

115. Hammond, *One Hundred Texts*, 529 (my italics). He cites Hebrews 8:2; 9:10; and chapter 10.

7.ii: "The first covenant made with man was a covenant of works, wherein life was promised to Adam, and in him to his posterity, *upon condition of perfect and personal obedience*" (my italics).

As with federal theology generally, the important issue of whether God's covenants are conditional or unconditional is not explicitly discussed either by Hammond, or by Wright in his defense of Hammond. Instead, all "covenants" appear quite simply to be assumed to be conditional and contractual, even including the covenant of Christ, which, though it is "for all men," is said to be conditionally operative only when appropriated by those humans who align their lives in faith with Christ as the new head of their race and opt to live in obedience to him. Thus, "the obedience of the new Head of the human race is only able to benefit those who receive him as their Head." As Hammond expounds this, it is by virtue of the new covenant that the penitent sinner who acknowledges Christ as his head is assured of all that Adam and the race could ever have attained had original righteousness not been lost. Thus, though the work of Christ "was equal to the needs of the whole world, he had definitely in view only those who would believe and receive him."[116]

The fundamental importance of the presupposed idea of a contractual covenant with Adam as the representative federal or covenant/contractual head of the human race can thus be very easily demonstrated here. As T. C. Hammond might himself have put it, despite the protestations of David Wright, the broken contract resulting from Adam's disobedience is quite fundamental to the theological quest to make more intelligible "the unifying purpose that governs the whole" of his approach to Christian doctrine.[117]

This means that in *In Understanding Be Men* clear appeals are made to covenant theology at significant "moments" in Hammond's discussion, such as in this section explicitly on "The Father's Electing Grace and Covenant,"[118] as well as (in the manner of *The Heidelberg Catechism* itself) its methodological presupposition, throughout the whole work where the disastrous disobedience of Adam's contractual violation of God's law is matched by the obedience of Christ as "the new federal Head of the race." Hammond, thus, explicitly declares his hand: "As from Adam men derive sin and guilt, so from Christ, the new federal Head of the race we derive

116. Hammond, *In Understand Be Men*, 125.

117. Hammond, *In Understanding Be Men*, 13.

118. Hammond, *In Understanding Be Men*, 86–88.

forgiveness and righteousness."[119] Clearly, Wright's categorical denial of there being any trace of federal theology in Hammond's writing appears to be whistling in the dark. The same may be said of Peter Jensen's contention that "the attempt to link Hammond to 'Ulster federal theology' is doomed to failure because there is no evidence that he belonged to such a school of thought."[120]

༄

Alas, though David Wright in his defense of T. C. Hammond, provocatively defied anyone to read *In Understanding Be Men* and derive from it a "concept of grace . . . worked out in terms of the logically prior category of law,"[121] the clear evidence of Hammond's own words constrains us to conclude exactly what Wright apparently judges to be impossible. In fact, if anything, such a reading of *In Understanding Be Men* is surely impossible to avoid. Clearly, the utterly free gift of divine love and generosity tends rather to be replaced by the required payment legally demanded by a righteous God's justice. It is only in a very qualified sense as a somewhat equivocal "manner of speaking" that it may be spoken of as "freely given" for it is systematically presented as a requirement of justice. Unfortunately, although Wright insisted that "a grotesque caricature of a doctrine of grace . . . worked out on the basis of a logically pre-existing understanding of a contractual or legal obligation" is something which has to be imported into the reading of Hammond, and "which is simply not there," Hammond's own federalist words about the priority of law to love in the operation of grace in his understanding of the *ordo salutis* are in fact transparently clear.

Indeed T. C. Hammond even moves the characteristic motifs of federal theology on to a new idiosyncratic level of his own. Insofar as Hammond distinguishes the roles of the Father and the Son, he exhibits the usual characteristic implication of speaking of two separate personal operations within the Trinity that are matched by two separate and

119. Hammond, *In Understanding Be Men*, 84. In *One Hundred Texts* Hammond thus speaks of the meaning of being in Christ in terms of Christ as contractual head. His explanation of the meaning of "in Christ" reads: "In union with Him as our head, united as a branch to a vine. *John* xv. 4, 5; *I Cor.* xv. 18, 19; *2 Cor.* x. 17." (*One Hundred Texts*, 531.

120. Jensen, "T. C. Hammond No Arian," 45.

121. Wright, "Dr. Carnley on T. C. Hammond," 47.

complementary wills. In sending his own Son to execute his will, the Father is even said to initiate his redemptive plan with the Son, whose willing response of obedience is necessary to achieve the Father's redemptive purpose. Thus, in the interests of achieving the redemption of fallen humanity, the Father is said to have chosen "the atoning sacrifice of Calvary as its necessary means." Hammond then goes so far as to say that "the Father is the Author of the plan; the Son . . . performs the redemptive will of the Father."[122] Clearly, we cannot fail to detect here the seeds of a division of what the Sydney Doctrine Commission Report came to speak of as two "complementary" wills within what in orthodox theology is spoken of as the entirely undivided life of the Trinity in the unity of a single will and purpose. We will return to the discussion of the serious implications of attributing two wills to the Godhead in the next chapter.

‹⌐

If anything, in Hammond's case the dangerous logical possibility of implying two divine wills, the commanding will of the Father and the complementary and submissively obedient will of the Son, is pushed beyond the need to deal with the self-assertive rebellious disobedience of Adam by its juxtaposition with the perfection of Christ's submissive obedience. Astonishingly, Hammond is even prepared to draw on the motif of "contractual covenants" to declare, not only that God made a covenant with redeemed humanity *through* the work of Christ, but that God the Father made a covenant *with* Christ the Son in order to carry through the work of redemption! This is Hammond's take on the *pactum salutis* of the Reformers with the distinctive coloring of his own federal theology, given that the covenant between Father and Son is conceived in contractual terms, by virtue of which the Son must obey the Father in order to pay the penalty for the breaking of the contract of works by disobedience of Adam.[123] Unlike the shared agreement of all three Trinitarian identities

122. Hammond, *In Understanding Be Men*, 87

123. Already in the seventeenth century the Oxford Nonconformist theologian John Owen highlighted the problem that the covenant of redemption could not be "properly federal" because a contractual covenant requires the willing consent of at least two parties, while God's acts are acts of a single and undivided will. See "Federal Transactions between the Father and the Son" (1668), 77. Owen went to considerable lengths to expound an understanding of the *pactum salutis* in terms that avoided the Son's subordination to the Father understood as a personal property of the Son, and instead insisted on the free redemptive act of the undivided divine nature.

to pursue the redemption of humanity of the Reformed tradition of the *pactum*, an appeal is made to the concept of an alleged heavenly contract between the Father and the Son.

When the inevitable question is raised concerning the biblical basis of this somewhat speculative theory of the Father's making a contractual covenant with the Son in heaven and keeping it in store until the fullness of time,[124] we may find ourselves somewhat perplexed. There is an all too apparent want of clear biblical evidence for this alleged heavenly contract between the Father and the Son based upon the obedience of the Son as a personal property of the Son in response to the commanding authority of the Father as a property that is personal to the Father, just as there is also a lack of biblical evidence for the contractual covenant that God is said to have made with Adam at creation.

Historically, in relation to Adam, federal theologians made a good deal of Genesis 2:17, which was interpreted to be much more than a warning of the dire ultimate consequences of death "on the day of eating of the tree of the knowledge of good and evil." Death, for example, could not be understood as a natural consequence of self-confident and self-assertive determination to "go it alone" in the world without the tutelage of God,[125] but was assumed to carry a hidden burden pertaining to its legal implications and the inevitable punishment that would result from an alleged broken contract. On the other hand, in relation to Christ, the Father's "sending of the Son" into the world, in John 3:16, was simply assumed to lend itself to the importation of speculative contractual implications for the good purpose of achieving the human redemption of all that Adam lost. However, it is hard to find concrete indicators to confirm this explicitly legal interpretation in the biblical textual tradition. Indeed, as we shall see in the next chapter, the interpretation of John 3:16 from Augustine onwards has had to examine what the "sending" of the Son might mean in Trinitarian terms, especially given that the Son, as "the Word through whom all things were made," was in the world already before being "sent." To imagine that a baggage of contractual implications might somehow be implicit in this "sending" goes well beyond the meaning that the actual text is capable of delivering.

124. Hammond, *In Understanding Be Men*, 87.

125. As, for example, in the theodicy of the great Archbishop William King of Dublin, *De Origine Mali* in 1702, translated into English with extensive notes by Edmund Law in 1731 as *An Essay on the Origin of Evil*.

⟜

In view of the lack of a clear and uncontested biblical textual tradition, Robert Letham has sought to account for the emergence of federal theology in the mid-sixteenth century by appeal to other conditioning factors.[126] Letham suggests that the missing piece of the jigsaw is the philosophy and methodology of Peter Ramus (1515–1572), who drew on a principle of "dichotomous subdivision" to map the entire field of knowledge, theology included. What was at first a pedagogical principle, designed to organize material to make it manageable and comprehensible, unwittingly soon began to generate assumptions and expectations relating to the *content* of what was to be learned.

While Ramist pedagogical theory was at first taken up principally in Germany,[127] it quickly became all-pervasive across Europe, gaining a firm foothold in Oxford, and especially in Cambridge where it increasingly became identified with Puritanism. Under the reforming zeal of Andrew Melville, educational reforms on Ramist lines were introduced in Scotland at the University of Glasgow (1570), Kings College, Aberdeen (1575), and the University of St Andrews (1578). Indeed, Letham notes that it was only two years after the reordering of the curriculum according to Ramist principles at St Andrews that Robert Rollock became director of the arts faculty there (1580). It is therefore not an accident that an unmistakable Ramist scheme is followed through the course of Rollock's summary of theology in his influential *Tractatus de vocatione efficaci*. Rollock, for example, summarizes the content of theology on the basis of a series of dichotomies: theology consists of two heads, God and the works of God. Under the first head are two sub-divisions: the nature of God and the Trinity. Under the second head are two sets of subjects: the work of God from eternity and the work of God in time.

Letham points out that the all-pervading popularity of the Ramist pedagogical principle of drawing dichotomies and antitheses coincided precisely with the emergence of federal theology, which amply demonstrates the same propensity. For example, the understanding of Christ as the new Adam on the basis of the biblical appeal to the Adam motif, by drawing a dichotomous antithesis between Adam and Christ, disobedience and obedience, the covenant of works and the covenant of grace, both in historical time, and then in the immanent life of the Trinity, even

126. See, Letham, "*Foedus Operum.*"

127. Where Ramus had made a triumphant tour in 1568–1570.

by speaking of the will of the Father and the will of the Son explicitly in terms of the antithetical distinction between the Father's command and the Son's dutifully obedient response. It is not difficult to discern the origin of Trinitarian subordinationism precisely here.

Letham's thesis is therefore that in the absence of clear biblical warrants for the dichotomous exposition of the "covenant of works" and the "covenant of grace," the educational schema based on Ramist principles takes over by default and helps to generate a theology in terms that are neatly antithetical. The result was that, under the pressure of the popularity of the Ramist organizational principle, the idea of the covenant of God naturally fell into two dichotomous parts. Given this methodological principle of the organization of material, it is understandable that a procedure of drawing antitheses and dichotomies led federal theology quite naturally to contrast the covenant of works and the covenant of grace. Thus, the federalism of Rollock: "The covenant of God generally is a promise under some one certain condition. And it is twofold: the first is the covenant of works; the second is the covenant of grace."[128]

Certainly, instead of speaking of a "covenant of grace," T. C. Hammond speaks more characteristically of a "covenant of redemption."[129] This is said to be "the one supreme covenant" which is described by Hammond as having been kept secret until "the time had fully come" when Christ was "revealed to be its Mediator and Surety."[130] It is in this context that this alleged covenant is described as being "between the Father and the Son, that is to say 'made on our behalf' who were incapable of keeping our side of any *contract* between God and man."[131] This is said to elevate humans to "a position far higher than Adam had attained when he fell." It is in this context that the Son's death is said to be properly regarded "as *exemplary*, that is, as the supreme example of obedience to the will of God, and *representative*, that is, as being that of the federal Head of the new race of men who, realizing their failure under the old covenant, find life and power in the new covenant given in His blood."[132]

---

128. Rollock, *Select Works*, 1.34. Letham points out that already in 1585 Dudley Fenner had said not only *"Foedus operum est, in quo Deus promittit vitam aeternum homini . . ."* but also that *"Foedus duplex est: Operum foedus/Grauitae promissionis foedus."* Letham, "*Foedus Operum*," 458 and 467.

129. Hammond, *In Understanding Be Men*, 88, 125.

130. Hammond, *In Understanding Be Men*, 87.

131. Hammond, *In Understanding Be Men*, 87 (my italics).

132. Hammond, *In Understanding Be Men*, 119.

Alas, without clear biblical warrant, we have to contend with the possibility that such talk of the Father entering into such a contractual covenant with the Son in heaven is entirely fanciful; indeed, as has already been noted, even the seventeenth-century Puritan, John Owen, a thoroughgoing federal theologian, observed that talk of a heavenly contractual arrangement between the Father and the Son "per modum foederis" is problematic. He observed that a contract involves two parties but because heavenly acts "are single acts of the same understanding and will, they cannot properly be federal."[133]

Today some would say that such talk of a contract between the Father and the Son is "mythological." Unfortunately this naturally invites a question as to whether talk of the Father making a heavenly contractual covenant with the Son may be pure mythology, reminiscent of Zeus entering to a contract of marriage with his first wife the Oceanid Metis.

 

Certainly, given unmistakably clear indications from Hammond's own pen, it would be obtuse for us to accept the claim that T. C. Hammond's theology was entirely untainted by the legal principles and contractual requirements so characteristic of federal theology. Insofar as his soteriological conclusions about propitiating justice as the fundamental basis of the need of the Son to be obediently submissive and thus subordinate to the will of the Father, we are obliged to acknowledge that Hammond's theology may rightly be understood as a remnant survival of the federal theology of scholastic Calvinism with roots going back to Ursinus and *The Heidelberg Catechism* of 1562/3.

So much for the assertion that "the attempt to link Hammond to 'Ulster federal theology' is doomed to failure because there is no evidence that he belonged to such a school of thought."[134] Clearly, the fond assertion of Hammond's defenders that, "there is no trace in *In Understanding Be Men* . . . of the basic elements of federal theology" is entirely without warrant. On the contrary, the evidence unavoidably suggests that a "close

133. Owen, "Federal Transactions between the Father and the Son", 77. Owen is careful to expound the covenant between the divine Father and the historical human Jesus in terms of a mutual agreement or compact entered into voluntarily by both parties, while resisting the temptation to project a federal transaction into the immanent life of the Trinity.

134. Jensen, "T. C. Hammond No Arian", 45.

encounter" with "Ulster federal theology" played a significant role in leading Hammond into the infamous assertion that the Christian doctrine of the Trinity demands the "subordination of the Son and the Spirit to the Father."[135] Whether this amounts to a form of Arianism we have yet to determine. But first we must address the question of what exactly it is that is wrong, both with Hammond's talk of "the subordination of the Son and the Spirit to the Father" and more generally with belief in the "eternal functional submissiveness" of the Son to the Father that has become so securely domiciled in Australian Carillon Avenue theology, and that also featured so centrally in the electronic debates of "the evangelical war on the Trinity" principally in North America in 2016.

135. Hammond, *In Understanding Be Men*, 56.

# Chapter 3

# What Exactly Is Wrong with the Eternal Subordination of the Son to the Father?

It was a fundamental premise of T. C. Hammond's theology of the Trinity, as he presents it in *In Understanding Be Men*, that the affirmation of belief in interpersonal subordination within the immanent life of the Trinity is perfectly acceptable provided one first affirms the equality of the three divine persons.[1] Furthermore, this is a widely held view, at least among some evangelical Christians. This coupling of the otherwise logically competing notions of interpersonal equality and interpersonal subordination is said to be made possible by drawing a clear distinction between "being" or "essential nature" on one hand, and "function" or "role" on the other. In this way, it is said that equality of "being" or "essential nature" does not conflict with belief in subordination in terms of "function" or "role."

It is imagined that it is in accord with orthodox Christian belief that both propositions may be held together as simultaneous truths. Wayne Grudem has even insisted that "the idea of eternal equality in being but subordination in role" has been essential to the Church's doctrine of the Trinity "since it was first affirmed in the Nicene Creed."[2] Alas, this purported historical pedigree may turn out to be the product of a bit of wishful thinking, but we may certainly accept the proposition that this particular belief nevertheless occupies a place of prominence in the canon of evangelical doctrine, where its assumed orthodoxy has remained unquestioned for a very long time.

1. Hammond, *In Understanding Be Men*, 56.
2. Grudem, *Systematic Theology*, 251.

David F. Wright, for example, indicated that he clearly believed that, in some circumstances it is possible to hold *both* to the affirmation of the equality of the Trinitarian identities *and* the affirmation of the subordination of the Son to the Father, as though no real difficulty arises by way of logical tension between the two. Thus, in defending the alleged orthodoxy of T. C. Hammond, Wright declared that there is no way in which Hammond affirmed the Son's subordination to the Father "in a way that compromises his equality with the Father." While Wright implicitly acknowledged that there is a noxious form of subordinationist belief that is unacceptable (as for example, historically, in the traditional understanding of Arianism), he believed even so that there is a legitimate way of affirming belief in the subordination of the Son to the Father that does not impact negatively on the equality of the essential nature of their persons. He is therefore able to say that "Hammond's careful use of 'subordination' nowhere threatens his patient and ubiquitous Nicaeno-Constantinopolitan Trinitarianism . . ."[3] Then, rehearsing the customary subordinationist distinction between "being/nature" and "function/role," he adds: "Hammond is right to insist that there is a subordination in order of relation, but not in nature."[4] At this point Hammond's actual words on page 54 of *In Understanding Be Men* are being quoted, where it is said that there is a "subordination (in order of relation, but not in nature . . .)."

Clearly, the kind of subordination of the Son to the Father that is alleged to be perfectly acceptable and in no way threatening to the affirmation of belief in the equality of the Son and the Father (and the Spirit) is a subordination that is said to pertain to their "relational order," and not to the being or essential divine nature in a way that might damage the fundamental equality of the persons of the Father, the Son, and the Spirit. All three divine persons remain One in Being, or "of the same substance" as first dogmatically defined at Nicaea in the *homoousion*.

⌒

This theological insistence on the possibility of holding "equality" and "subordination" together by appeal to the distinction between "being or nature" and "function or role" has enjoyed a long history of acceptance within Australian evangelicalism, most notably on Carillon Avenue since, at least, 1936 through the seminal influence of T. C. Hammond.

3. Wright, "Dr. Carnley on T. C. Hammond and Arianism," 48.
4. Wright, "Dr. Carnley on T. C. Hammond and Arianism," 48.

Understandably, the authors of the Sydney Doctrine Commission Report of 1999 calculate that Arius's problem was simply that he "overestimated" the element of subordination in the New Testament presentation of the life and work of Jesus.[5] The implication of this statement is that it is possible to avoid the subordinationist pitfall of Arianism so as to be able to continue to entertain subordinationist notions in relation to the persons of the Trinity, provided that such notions are not "overemphasized" to the point where their essential unity and equality is compromised by making the Son appear less than fully divine. Rather, the implication seems to be that the essential equality of the divinity of the Son (and the Spirit) and the Father is maintained if the element of subordination is only affirmed in some kind of "lite" or doctrinally inoffensive way. This delicate maneuver is accomplished methodologically by first affirming the equality of the persons of the Trinity in terms of their essential nature (the *homoousion*), *before* then proceeding to talk of a degree of subordination. The hope is that, so long as it is insisted that the specific kind of subordination that is envisaged is a purely functional or relational subordination, the charge of Arianism may be held at bay.

The basic distinction between subordination "in order of relation" and the equality of the "being" or "essential nature" of the Trinitarian identities that is now domiciled in Carillon Avenue theology and found in many parts of the Anglican Church of Australia, also featured prominently in the thinking of those who promoted "eternal functional submissiveness" in the lead-up to the electronic debates in North America in mid-2016. Apart from Wayne Grudem's insistence on "the idea of eternal equality in being but subordination in role,"[6] Thomas Schreiner already sought, as early as 2006, to justify this version of Trinitarian belief by appealing to an anthropological analogy, even despite any qualms that might arise from the practice of fashioning God in a human image: just as human persons can be said to be equal in terms of their shared human nature while there are nevertheless occasions when one human is obliged to be submissive (or subordinate) to another, so it is within the life of the Trinity.[7] Clearly, it has for a long time been believed that the

5. "The Arians over-emphasised the subordinationist elements of the NT presentation." (Sydney Doctrine Commission Report, 1999, sec. 4.6/para. 22).

6. In Grudem, *Systematic Theology*, 251.

7. Schreiner, "Head Coverings, Prophecies and the Trinity," 128: "One can possess a different function and still be equal in essence or worth. Women are equal to men in essence and in being; there is no ontological distinction, and yet they have a different

essential equality of the persons of the Trinity through being "of the same substance," and as a consequence their sharing of the same divine nature, was something that could happily be affirmed in accordance with historic Christian orthodoxy, while at the same time affirming a purely functional or relational submissiveness of the Son to the Father that was said to pertain to the personal interactions within the divine life, no less than in the social interactions of humans.

꒦

Whether it is possible first to salute the *homoousion* by affirming the equal divinity of the three Trinitarian identities in terms of their essential being, and thus the equal and unchallenged status and dignity of their shared divine nature, and then proceed to talk of the "eternal functional submissiveness" or "relational subordination" of the Son to the Father, is the burning question. When it is said that the Son's submissive obedience to the Father must be an unwavering and perfect obedience of an eternal rather than a purely occasional kind so as to warrant talk not just of "eternal functional submissiveness" but, as in the case of T. C. Hammond and the Sydney Doctrine Commission, of the eternal "subordination" of the Son to the Father, as something that arises out of "the very being of the Son," then alarm bells begin to sound.

The first difficulty with this "*both* equality *and* subordination" proposition appears to arise from the methodology of working from an anthropomorphic analogy. For example, when Thomas Schreiner says that human persons may be equal in terms of their shared human nature, and thus be of equal status and dignity as a result, even though in functional terms one may be submissively obedient to the other, we may well ask whether this very human analogy will really hold in relation to the understanding of the Being of God. We obviously know from the concrete experience of the life of human beings that, in the hierarchical ordering, let us say, of commercial enterprises, there are bosses and those who are subordinate to them, while they all equally maintain their shared genetic inheritance and equal rights as members of the human race. But the difficulty of drawing this analogy with the divine life of the Trinity is that equality understood in terms of membership of the human species, and the consequent sharing of the same human nature by all individual

---

function or role in church and home. Such differences do not logically imply inequality or inferiority, just as Christ's subjection to the Father does not imply His inferiority."

members of the species, does not happily carry over into the divine life, precisely because the persons of the Trinity are not individual representatives of a species. In other words, the three persons of the Trinity do not share membership of the species that can somehow be labeled "divine" in the same way that human individuals belong to the species that is labeled "human." It is not that the three persons of the Trinity may be understood as three individual representatives or instances of the same nature, because they all belong to the same divine race or species. There are not three Gods, or three divine individuals sharing a common membership of a divine species, so that each may be said to be an instance of the same nature pertaining to that species or race. Rather the three *hypostases* of the Trinity share one single and undivided nature, for God is One, not three instances of "divinity" as three equally divine individuals nor, in other words, three Gods. It cannot therefore be said that the divine nature is something shared by three individual members of the same divine species who function together in a way that permits the subordination of one to the other, without unwittingly entering into some kind of tritheism.

As a consequence, orthodox Trinitarianism has insisted that the three *hypostases* or *personae* (as they were referred to by Tertullian, and hence in both the East and the West from the fourth century onwards), in the unity of One God share a single divine nature and operate according to a single power to achieve things, a single divine will. Even an alleged "functional" or "relational" subordination of one person to another therefore introduces division into the divine life, for, as three different instances of that divine nature they would possess three different, if complementary, wills. As Glenn Butner has succinctly summarized this issue: "Language of the Father demanding and the Son obeying divides and separates a divine operation into two operations. Submission itself seems to require . . . not just a distinction in mode of willing, but a distinction of wills."[8] In this case, a quite disastrous fracture is introduced into the understanding of the Godhead that very seriously compromises the divine unity of Being. It is pertinent to note that even Robert Letham, who was originally an enthusiastic supporter of "eternal functional submission," frankly acknowledged this problem: "To speak of three wills," he said, "is heterodox, implying tritheism."[9] While correctly affirming the orthodox Christian commitment to belief in a single and undivided will within the divine nature, Letham then had to face the challenge of trying

8. Butner, *Son Who Learned Obedience*, 53.
9. Letham, "Reply to Kevin Giles," 340.

to maintain his original commitment to subordinationism. Eventually he seemed to move significantly away from it.[10]

Basil of Caesarea, in his treatise *On the Holy Spirit* (374) suggests that it is not that the Father and the Son possess separate and identifiably different wills, even if they are of a harmonious and complementary kind. Rather, for Basil the Father finds his own will reflected back to himself by the Son "like the refection of an object in a mirror."[11] There is thus in the Trinity not a complementarity of willing, but a coincidence of willing. The Father and the Son and the Spirit being "of one substance" and sharing the very same undivided nature, are of one heart and mind, and exercise one will with a single power to accomplish things, by virtue of which they all act together simultaneously and in perfect harmony. If the Father wills the redemption of humanity, the Son wills the redemption of humanity, and so does the Spirit. There are not three complementary wills, but one will, exercised by all three *hypostases* together in perfect unity.

In the eighth century this orthodox position was restated with uncompromising clarity by John of Damascus:

> For there the community and unity are observed in reality, through the coeternity of the Hypostases, and through their having the same essence and energy and will and concord of mind, and then being identical in authority and power and goodness—I do not say similar but identical (ταυτότητα)—and then movement by one impulse. For there is one essence, one goodness, one power, one will, one energy, one authority, one and the same, I repeat, not three resembling each other. But the three Hypostases have one and the same movement. For each one of them is related as closely to the other as to Himself: that is

10. As reported by Kevin Giles, *Rise and Fall*, 58. Robert Letham, in *Holy Trinity* "accepts that the hierarchical ordering of the divine persons is heresy"—at least if it involves notions of rank: "The idea of rank is certainly heresy, . . ." (475). However, this is not entirely accurate. It is not rank or even hierarchy as such that is the problem (e.g. as in references relating to Trinitarian order as "the first, second, third Person of the Trinity"). Rather, it is the subordination of Christ's nature to that of the Father that is heresy.

11. Basil of Caesarea, *On the Holy Spirit*, 20. John Owen perceived this very clearly in the seventeenth century: "The *will* is a natural property, and therefore in the divine essence it is but one. The Father, Son, and Spirit have not distinct wills. They are one God, and God's will is one, as being an essential property of his nature; and therefore are there two wills in the one person of Christ, whereas there is but one will in the three persons of the Trinity." ("Federal Transactions", 87).

to say that the Father, the Son, and the Holy Spirit are one in all respects (κατὰ πάντα ἕν), except those of not being begotten, of birth and of procession. But it is by thought that the difference is perceived (ἐπινοίᾳ τὸ διῃρημένον).[12]

It is therefore not possible to affirm the *homoousion*, thereby securing the equality of the divine persons, and then introduce even a tiny hint of functional subordination into their respective willing, as they relate and function together, for to speak as though they exercised different if complementary individual wills necessarily falls into a kind of tritheism. By contrast orthodox Trinitarianism insists upon adherence to belief in One God, with three *hypostases*, not understood in the manner of three individual members of a race, each of whom is an instance of the same nature, but three *hypostases* who in the mystery of the One God, share a single and undivided divine nature as persons in the unity of one interpersonal communion.

⤙

It may well be asked why it is that those who assent to the notion of the subordination of the Son to the Father in the internal life of the Trinity tend to be so firmly wedded to it and so apparently confident in this belief? Apart from the persuasive authority of inherited evangelical teaching, especially that of such a revered and influential teacher such as T. C. Hammond undoubtedly was in the Australian context, it is important to take note of the congruence of this idiosyncratic Trinitarian belief with notions of the alleged moral propriety of forms of subordination in the interpersonal relationships of husbands and wives, and in the ministerial structures of the church.[13] This is not to mention the importance of the notion of the obedient submission of the Son to the Father in the penal substitutionary version of the theology of the atonement that is so central to the presentation of the gospel particularly among Carillon

12. John of Damascus, *Orthodox Faith*, 8.

13. Kevin Giles has noted this problem in the thinking of Robert Letham. "What we learn from Dr. Letham is that the minute the doctrine of the Trinity and the relationship of the sexes get mixed up, good theology goes out the door" (Giles, *Rise and Fall*, 23). Though Letham is now inclined to reject Trinitarian subordination, Giles notes, "For him, the traditional ordering of the sexes remains of huge importance and he is still drawing this into his work on the Trinity in 2015. See his chapter in *One God in Three Persons*, 124–25. So far he has not been able to separate these two matters." Giles, *Rise and Fall*, 66.

Avenue Christians. Somehow assent to belief in the "eternal submissive-ness" of the Son to the Father or the "eternal subordination" of the Son to the Father, and those characteristic evangelical postures relating to the dynamics of family life and the ministry of the church, as well as to a distinctively evangelical approach to an understanding of the economy of salvation, go hand in hand as a total package. It is understandably dif-ficult to surrender one without casting a problematic shadow over the validity of the others.

Over and above this difficulty, which is basically a matter of theo-logical logistics, it has been my experience that the fundamental and un-wavering commitment to the notion of the subordination of the Son to the Father is firmly grounded in the belief that this is the clear teaching of Scripture. Robert Doyle, for example, in responding to Kevin Giles's *The Trinity and Subordinationism,* not only accuses Giles of misrepresenting the historical tradition, but spends a good deal of time on the herme-neutical question of how the Scripture works in relation to the doctrine of the Trinity, insisting on the principle of *sola scriptura* to ground the belief that apart from the cultural conditioning of scriptural interpreta-tion "texts have their own objectivity."[14] Doyle believes that the textual evidence clearly supports belief in the eternal subordination of the Son to the Father.

Unfortunately, when the actual scriptural texts that are said to sup-port belief in the eternal subordination of the Son to the Father are closely examined, the outcome is far from encouraging. As we shall see, what Doyle thinks is the objective meaning of the New Testament texts that are deemed to be relevant to belief in "eternal functional subordination" ap-pears in fact to be subjectively grounded in a problematic interpretation from the idiosyncratic perspective of Carillon Avenue.

᠆

We are hugely indebted to D. Glenn Butner for a very thorough analy-sis of the relevant scriptural material. This is found in the context of a carefully argued case against the proposition that Scripture actually does teach the "eternal functional submissiveness" of the Son (and we may add by logical extension, the eternal relational subordination of the Son). In *The Son Who Learned Obedience,* which was published in 2018, a chapter subtitled "The Missing Scriptural Case for Eternal Submission" sets out

14. Doyle, "Use and abuse," Methodological and theological errors 1.

the results of his examination of the suite of biblical texts that are regularly interpreted as lending support to the "submissiveness" of the Son to the Father. While acknowledging that some scriptural texts are capable of being construed as being compatible with eternal submission, Butner painstakingly demonstrates that *none of these passages indisputably teach this doctrine.*[15] He concludes, rather, that the weight of the biblical evidence that has been summoned to the support of this comparatively recently minted item "is insufficient to justify overthrowing centuries of theological tradition."

Butner demonstrates that the great majority of texts that are said to be relevant to "eternal submissiveness" actually pertain, not to the internal or immanent life of God, but to the subordination and obedience of the human Jesus in the course of his earthly life even unto death on the cross. These allegedly key texts are therefore to be understood in the context of the economy of salvation to which they properly belong. Butner points out that they appear to have nothing to do with the question of the "eternal functional submissiveness" or "subordination" of the divine Son to the Father in the internal or immanent life of the Trinity.

Generally speaking, proponents of the "eternal submissiveness of the Son" come to grief because of the problematic methodology of assuming that scriptural statements that appear to refer to the incarnate Son, and the perfectly acceptable obedience with which, as a truly human subject he responded to the God whom he addressed as "Father," must also refer to his pre-incarnate life as the Eternal Word, the Second Person of the Trinity. In other words, biblical illustrations of his human obedience, appropriate to his human nature, and intentionally motivated by the exercise of his human will, are assumed to be legitimately projected back beyond time into his divine nature and the exercise of his divine will in the context of the eternal relations of the immanent Trinity.

It is possible to discern something of the reasoning behind this methodological commitment. Given that the *hypostatic* identity of the Eternal Son remained the same when he took on human flesh and became incarnate, this is that same divine Word "who was with God and who was God" before all worlds, and "through whom all things were made" (John 1:1). Somehow the humanly willing response of obedience of the incarnate Son is detached from his human nature and associated with the *hypostasis* of the Son, which does not change either side of the

15. Butner, *Son Who Learned Obedience*, 162 (his italics).

incarnation. This naturally invites a reading of the scriptural texts concerning the human obedience of the incarnate Jesus in historical time
that allows the application of the same obedience to the Second Person
of the Trinity through all eternity. Just as the historical Jesus obeyed the
Father's will and remained steadfastly true to his earthly mission to the
end, "even unto death on the cross," so the Eternal Word of God is said to
have eternally obeyed the will of his Father who "sent him into the world"
for this very purpose. Robert Doyle explicitly spells this methodology
out for us: "the incarnate Son says that he delights to do the Father's will
(John 4.34). If so under the conditions of incarnation, how much more so
in the immanent Trinity?"[16]

Proponents whether of "eternal submissiveness" or "eternal subordination" in this way tend to conflate statements relating to the obedience
of the human Jesus, the Word incarnate, and statements relating to the
alleged divine obedience of the Eternal Word in the immanent life of the
Trinity. As we shall see, this appears to have to do with the association
of the Son's willing obedience with the notion of his *hypostasis* rather
than with the notion of his two natures; indeed, there may even be an
assumption of a single divine/human nature in Christ and thus of a single
will of steadfast obedient submissiveness in all this.[17] Unfortunately, this
falls foul both of the Chalcedonian definition of two natures of Christ,
divine and human, and its insistence that these natures should not be
"confused."[18] Consequently, it is also out of step with the determinations

16. Doyle, "Use and abuse," Methodological and theological errors 2: Doyle roundly asserts, "Because . . . texts speak of the God incarnate, then even if they are strongly
economic, they must also with contextual propriety be allowed to say something of
the immanent Trinity."

17. A version of *monothelitism*.

18. The Council of Chalcedon in 451 declared: "We, then, following the holy Fathers, all with one consent, teach people to confess one and the same Son, our Lord
Jesus Christ, the same perfect in Godhead and also perfect in manhood; truly God
and truly man, of a reasonable [rational] soul and body; consubstantial [co-essential]
with the Father according to the Godhead, and consubstantial with us according to
the Manhood; in all things like unto us, without sin; begotten before all ages of the
Father according to the Godhead, and in these latter days, for us and for our salvation,
born of the Virgin Mary, the Mother of God, according to the Manhood; one and the
same Christ, Son, Lord, only begotten, to be acknowledged in two natures, incon-
fusedly, unchangeably, indivisibly, inseparably (ἐν δύο φύσεσιν ἀσυγχύτως, ἀτρέπτως,
ἀδιαιρέτως, ἀχωρίστως—*induabus naturis inconfuse, immutabiliter, indivise, insepa-
rabiliter*); the distinction of natures being by no means taken away by the union, but
rather the property of each nature being preserved, and concurring in one Person
(*prosopon*) and one Subsistence (*hypostasis*) . . ."

of the Third Council of Constantinople that condemned *monothelitism* in 681.[19]

⌐

Before we can come to judgment on these apparent methodological assumptions against the historical canons of Christian orthodoxy, it is important to examine some of the scriptural texts that are regularly held to teach the "eternal submissiveness" or the "eternal subordination" of the Son to the Father. One of the regularly cited texts for this view is 1 Corinthians 11:3.[20] This is Paul's articulation of a kind of chain of authoritative command, in which a principle of "headship" is expressed in a set of interpersonal relations of domination and submission, that are said to trickle down from God to Christ, from Christ to every man (humankind?), and from husbands to wives. This is a classic text for those who seek to demonstrate the validity of the so-called "headship" argument in which an interpersonal dynamic of command and docile obedience is relied upon to establish the unwavering gender subordination of women to men by grounding this in an appeal to an analogous "headship" of the Father in relation to the Son.

The interpretation of this text is fiercely contested. Glenn Butner argues very persuasively that when Paul said that God was the "head" of Christ, and Christ was the "head" of humanity, and that man is the "head" of the woman, he may well have meant the word "head" to have been understood simply to mean "source" without necessarily thinking in terms of power structures involving the exercise of authority and submissive obedience. Butner further suggests that, when Paul referred to man as the "source" of woman he may also have had in mind Christ as the Second Adam, precisely as the source of redeemed humanity just as the first Adam donated his rib as the source of Eve.[21]

Given, however, the patriarchal social arrangements of the ancient world, not least as they are found in Stoic household codes governing the behavior of younger men with respect to older men, slaves with respect to their masters, and wives to their husbands, it may be difficult to disengage the very similar household codes of the New Testament

19. Thus vindicating Maximus the Confessor, who steadfastly confessed the *dyothelite* belief in Christ's two wills.

20. See, for example, Fee, *First Epistle to the Corinthians.*

21. Butner, *Son Who Learned Obedience*, 186.

from the coloring of overtones of the power dynamics of domination and submission.[22] In this case the interesting theological question has to do with whether the conditioning impact of the values of the gospel had a transformative impact on the Stoic ethical codes of the prevailing culture of first-century Middle Platonism. We note, particularly, for example, that other less cryptic, more expansive household codes are found in the New Testament, especially in the later deutero-Pauline stratum of the material, and most notably in the Pastoral Epistles.[23] A classic example that appears in the Epistle to the Ephesians, and seems to be repeated in a closely parallel text in the Epistle to the Colossians, which even if Pauline authorship is disputed, is at least in the Pauline tradition. These codes also say that a husband is head of his wife, and that wives are to obey their husbands, but in addition insist that husbands are to love their wives (Eph 5:25, Col 3:19).[24]

Here at least the revelation of the unconditional love of God in Christ tempers the statements of male domination of the Stoic household codes.[25] In this case, Butner's attempt to disconnect Paul's references to "headship," particularly in the key verse 1 Corinthians 11:3, from the thought that it may be expressive of a principle of domination and submission by arguing that it may simply mean "source" and thus be entirely free of overtones of the exercise of authority in a divinely intended creational relation of "domination and submission," may be difficult to prove.

In any event, however, though Butner is inclined to favor the interpretation of "head" as "source," this is in a sense incidental to the main

22. The classic paradigm is Aristotle, *Politics*, Book I, XII–XIII.

23. This may reflect an increasing concern with ethical behavior in *this world* as the hope of the eminent eschatological return of Christ began to diminish in intensity.

24. Ephesians 5:21–24: "Be subject to one another out of reverence for Christ. Wives, be subject to your husbands, as to the Lord. For the husband is the head of the wife as Christ is the head of the church, his body, and is himself its Savior. As the church is subject to Christ, so let wives also be subject in everything to their husbands." The parallel in Colossians 3:18–4:1 reads: "Wives, submit yourselves to your husbands, as is fitting in the Lord. Husbands, love your wives and do not be harsh with them. Children, obey your parents in everything, for this pleases the Lord. Fathers, do not embitter your children, or they will become discouraged."

25. According to Robert Doyle this is a point apparently brought home to Moore College students by Broughton Knox. Doyle, "Use and abuse," sec. on Broughton Knox: "Broughton Knox, likewise conceptualized the asymmetricality of the man/woman relationship as the male having *the primary responsibility in serving the woman*." See Knox, *Selected Works* 1, 153–70 and *Selected Works* 2, 201–3.

thrust of his argument, in which he concludes that it is hard not to acknowledge that 1 Corinthians 11:3 is a text that has to do with creation and the economy of salvation, and that it has nothing explicit to say about the internal relations of the eternal Trinity. Whatever the interpretative impact of the meaning of head/source may be here, Paul's statement is in any case about the relationship of God to Christ (i.e., meaning the Messiah, or else being the proper name of the incarnate Jesus), rather than to the Eternal Word. After all, the text actually says that "God is the head of Christ" not "the Father is head of the Son, the Eternal Word." Clearly, however the meaning of the notion of "head" is construed, it is a bridge too far simply to assume that its meaning can simply be taken out of the context of its use in the economy of salvation where the reference appears to be to Christ as head or source of (redeemed) humanity, and then projected into the life of the immanent Trinity as a reference to the eternal Word.

A reading associated with the context of the economy of salvation certainly seems possible when 1 Corinthians 11:3 is compared with references to Christ's headship in Ephesians 5:23–24:

> Wives, submit to your husbands as to the Lord. For the husband is the head of the wife as Christ is the head of the church, his body, of which he is the Saviour. Now as the church submits to Christ, so also wives should submit to their husbands in everything.

Here it is made transparently clear that references to Christ as head of the church have to do with the economy of salvation. It is clearly a mistake to assume that when the author of Ephesians referred to Christ in these verses, he had in mind the Second Person of the immanent Trinity as one who was himself eternally obediently submissive to the Father. Rather, it is the humanly incarnate Christ, who in his human nature gave himself up for the church in obedience unto death, and who is the model for the ideal relationship of husbands and wives.

If Christ is explicitly "head of the church" here,[26] then it is not unthinkable that when Paul said that "Christ as the head of man" in 1 Corinthians 11:3 he did indeed have in mind the new humanity of which Christ was head as Second Adam. In this case we have to acknowledge the determinative historical context of the economy of salvation, rather than

---

26. Christ as "head of the church" is repeated in Ephesians 1:22, 5:23, and also in Colossians 1:18, 2:10.

the internal relations of the immanent Trinity.[27] Though the authoritarian model of Stoic household codes may certainly remain in the background here, the values of the gospel, and especially the transformative love of God, prevail. Thus Ephesians 5:25 goes on to declare: "Husbands, love your wives, just as Christ loved the church and gave himself up for her."[28]

The same may be said of 1 Corinthians 15:28. This text is perhaps the strongest candidate that has been brought to the support of "eternal functional submissiveness," given its explicit use of the verb *hypotasso*, (I submit) in relation to the eschatological destiny of the raised Christ. This particular text is therefore enormously important. It is understandable that Butner's extended treatment devotes some ten pages to the discussion of it. He points out that, in 1 Corinthians 15, Paul's understanding of the raised Christ's redemptive role as the Last Adam is a fundamental theme. By contrast with Romans 5, where Paul also treats the theme of Adamic Christology, Paul turns to the eschatological fulfilment of Christ's reign as God's vicegerent: the raised Christ, who as "second Adam has become a life-giving Spirit" (1 Cor 15:45) "must reign until he has put all his enemies under his feet" (1 Cor 15:25, echoing Ps 110:1). Then an echo also of Psalm 8:6 appears in 1 Corinthians 15:27, where Paul says again that "God has put all things in subjection under his feet." It is then that Paul says, significantly, in 1 Corinthians 15:28 that "When all things are subjected to him, then the Son himself will also be subjected to him who put all things in subjection under him, that God may be all in all." Paul is talking about the fulfillment of the role of the raised Christ: when his triumphant reign has put all in subjection under him, his reign as God's vicegerent will cease and "God will be all in all."

Clearly, this passage has nothing to do with the internal relations of the persons of the immanent Trinity, and everything to do with the final consummation of the work of the raised Christ, the Second Adam, when, having put all his enemies under his feet, all creation will then be subject to God with no longer any need of an Adamic mediator. The reference is

27. Paul C. Maxwell notes this same conclusion, along with the concurrence also even of professed complementarians such as Schreiner and Claunch: "First Corinthians 11:3 provides evidence for an economic authority relationship between the Father and Son (as Schreiner and Claunch admit), and the extrapolation of that authority relationship back into the immanent Trinity is merely speculative (a methodological assumption that does not receive satisfactory interrogation)." "Is There an Authority Analogy between the Trinity and Marriage?," 559. See Schreiner, "Head Coverings, Prophecies and the Trinity," 128–29; and Claunch, "God is the Head of Christ," 88–91.

28. A little earlier he had said: "He who loves his wife loves himself" (Eph 5:24).

to Christ in his raised and triumphant humanity and his completed role as God's vicegerent on earth.

Thus, Butner concludes, "It is certainly not the case that 1 Corinthians 15 demands acceptance of the idea of eternal submission."[29] On the contrary, "Simply put, the strongest potential candidate for direct scriptural endorsement of EFS fails to prove the eternal obedience of the Son."[30] We are therefore able to say that Paul's conviction was that, having completed this work as the vicegerent of God, the Son (and the Holy Spirit) will reign eternally with the Father, in an indivisibly shared divine eschatological act, for God will be all in all.

⤶

Those with whom Butner engaged in the wake of the debates of 2016 were not, alas, idiosyncratically innovative or isolated and alone in uncritically applying texts drawn from the context of the economy of salvation to the eternal context of the internal life of the immanent Trinity. The assumption that the *human* relationship of the historical Jesus to God could simply be read into the *divine* relationship of the eternal Word to the Father also appears to have already informed the methodology of the authors of the Sydney Doctrine Commission Report of 1999. When the actual use of Scripture in the report is carefully examined, indicators of the same fundamental mistake very quickly appear. Under the heading of "The Meaning of 'Subordination' in Orthodox Teaching," the report sets out the alleged "biblical roots" of this notion (sec. 4.1/para. 17). First, dutiful obeisance is paid to "the full humanity of the Son (1 Tim. 2.5) and his deity (John 1.1)." We are assured that "Jesus claimed unity and equality with God (John 10.30–33)." Then, as the initial step in seeking to ground belief in the eternal subordination of the Son to the Father, it is argued that such a relational dynamic is implicit in the fact that the Father sent the Son into the world (John 3:16–17). As we shall see, this statement may be about the appearance or manifestation of the historical Jesus in the world and hardly provides sufficient convincing grounds for believing that a relational subordinationism may therefore simply be imported to the internal life of the immanent Trinity. Certainly, the Father's sending of the Son into the world is insufficient grounds for a belief that

29. Butner, *Son Who Learned Obedience*, 172.
30. Butner, *Son Who Learned Obedience*, 172.

a subordinationist spin must necessarily be applied to the understanding of the relation of God the Father with the eternal Word who "in the beginning" was with God. In other words, a subordinationist reading of John 1:1 is hardly warranted by the problematic subordinationist reading of John 3:16–17.

As it happens, a subordinationist reading of John 3:16–17 was very effectively demolished by Augustine many centuries ago,[31] though the authors of the Sydney Report appear to have overlooked this in their enthusiasm to hurry on to clinch their argument by noting that Jesus "also said 'the Father is greater than I' (John 14.28)." Unfortunately, however, no consideration is given to the possibility that this text is also an utterance of the human Jesus in the context of the economy of salvation. Speaking from the point of view of his humanity, it is obvious that Jesus rightly acknowledged his inferior status in the face of the divine authority of the Almighty Father who is greater than himself. There is no warrant whatever for assuming that this text necessarily refers to the eternal subordination of the Eternal Word to the Father in the life of the immanent Trinity. Accordingly, John Owen rightly observed that the ancients expound John 14.28 unanimously to apply to Christ's "human nature only, to obviate the Arians, who ascribe unto him a divine nature, but made, and absolutely in itself inferior to the nature of God. But the inferiority of the human nature unto God or the Father is a thing so unquestionable as needed no declaration or solemn attestation . . . ."[32]

Even so, at this point the Sydney Doctrine Commission Report is prepared to sum up its view of the scriptural evidence: "The Scriptures thus themselves bear witness to a subordination which belongs to the *eternal* relationship between the persons of the Trinity, and not only to the humanity of Jesus in the incarnation, or even in the broader work of redemption. This applies to the Spirit as well as the Son (Jn 14.26)."[33] Alas, these Scriptures bear witness to no such thing.

This remarkably confident claim is based upon what must be acknowledged to be a less than thorough treatment of the biblical evidence that is deemed to be relevant for grounding belief in the eternal subordination of the Son to the Father. Nevertheless, it is apparently regarded as sufficient for the report to conclude:

31. Augustine, *On the Trinity*, iv.30.
32. Owen, "Federal Transactions," 84.
33. My italics.

> As far as revelation permits us to see in any temporal direction—from before creation (Eph. 1.4), to creation (1 Cor. 8.6) and to redemption (Jn 3.16–17; 12.49, 50), to the gift of the Spirit (Gal. 4.6), and forward to consummation (Jn 5.25–26) and beyond (1 Cor. 15.28)—unity, equality and subordination characterise the life of the Trinity.

Ironically, these words make it clear that texts that might be said to refer to the eternal subordination of the Son to the Father, as the divine Word, from all eternity and prior to creation, along with texts referring to the role of the historical Jesus Christ in the economy of salvation, are treated as a composite and sequential unity. This includes those texts referring to "redemption" and "the gift of the Spirit" along with texts that look forward to consummation of the good purposes of God "and beyond" in the eschaton. This is done without any consideration being given to the fact that the incarnational subordination of the *human* Jesus to God the Father, and the eternal functional subordination said to apply to the internal relations of persons of the Trinity, are two entirely different matters. In one case a perfectly acceptable obedience points to the subordination of humanity to divinity, whereas in the second an alleged subordination is said to be found in the eternal relationship of the divine persons themselves.

⌒

In expounding the orthodox view of the Trinity, Kevin Giles correctly observed, "Historic orthodoxy accepts the temporal subordination of the Son in the incarnation for us and our salvation; it rejects the eternal subordination of the Son and subsequently interprets Scripture with this in mind."[34] The Sydney Doctrine Commission Report, alas, fails from the beginning to observe this basic distinction in its treatment of the scriptural evidence, and as a consequence, the report must struggle to be taken seriously as a competent piece of theological argument.

Curiously, given that the report purports to set out the "biblical roots" of Trinitarian subordinationism, it is somewhat strange that this key paragraph of the report (sec 4.1/para. 17) does not make a great deal of the two texts that are regularly said to provide most help to the argument in favor of "eternal functional submissiveness/subordination": 1

---

34. Giles, *Trinity and Subordinationism*, 124.

Corinthians 15:28 and 1 Corinthians 11:3. In fact, there is no mention of 1 Corinthians 11:3 in the discussion of the scriptural basis for subordinationism in section 4.1/paragraph 17, though it is mentioned in section 4.4/paragraph 20 in an uncritical acceptance of the subordinationist views of Gordon Fee in his commentary on 1 Corinthians.[35]

Sadly, the contention that the weight of Scripture supports both the notion of the equality of the three persons of the Trinity *and* the notion of "eternal functional subordination" of the Son and the Spirit to the Father, appears to be very problematic indeed.

⤸

Even so, there are some additional arguments that have to be addressed. Proponents of eternal functional subordination regularly contend that even if notions of interpersonal subordination are not overtly expressed in specific scriptural texts, it is a doctrine that is implicit in some of the key affirmations of the Bible as a whole. One conditioning factor, for example, that seems to influence Carillon Avenue theologians in their confidently held belief that the Bible teaches the "eternal subordination of the Son to the Father" hinges on the very terms "Father" and "Son" when used throughout Scripture, and therefore with reference to the persons of the Trinity. For example, having dealt, apparently to its own satisfaction, with the biblical evidence which is thought to ground eternal subordination of the Son to the Father, the 1999 Sydney Doctrine Commission Report moves on to suggest that a dynamic of domination and submission may somehow be read from the Bible's use of the terms "Father" and "Son," as though "fatherly command" and "filial compliance" is natural (and perhaps even essential) to the interpersonal dynamic of fathers and sons generally. This means that just to use the terms "father" and "son" conjures up notions of commanding authority and filial obedience almost as a matter of logical necessity. More recently, Bruce Ware articulated this same kind of proposition when he insisted that "without question, a central part of the notion of 'father' is that of fatherly authority" and that this grounds the belief that "an inherent and eternal authority and submission structure exists" within the Godhead.[36]

---

35. Fee, *First Epistle to the Corinthians.*
36. Ware, "Equal in Essence, Distinct in Roles," 17.

Likewise, Robert Doyle, perhaps the most eminent systematic theologian amongst the authors of the Sydney Doctrine Commission Report, ventures to justify this relational dynamic of fatherly demand coupled with a corresponding response of filial obedience, by arguing that it is not only based on logical grounds implicit in the very titles of "Father" and "Son" but also that this may actually be demonstrated by appeal to the usage of these terms by Athanasius in the fourth century.

Once again, there is a hint of the noxious taint of anthropomorphism in his declaration that the Father is "the Lord eternally, ruling his creation, wielding 'universal providence', and therefore: eternally Father because 'providing/providence/rule' is what fathers do."[37] Whatever Doyle may mean by this, he fortunately does not actually go so far as to claim that the titles "Father" and "Son" are used literally of God, even though he does insist that God is a "real Father" and a "true Father," and that these terms are not being used in a merely figurative or metaphorical sense. Hence he says: "In this way the triune Father is a real father and the triune Son is a real son. Neither names are metaphorical."[38]

Many will find Doyle's language of a "real" and "true" Father and a "real" and "true" Son somewhat equivocal. Given that in this evangelical tradition the Bible is often said to be understood "literally," even though it is sometimes said "but not in a 'literalistic' way,"[39] there is a question about how exactly these terms are to be read. Thus, in his critical response to Kevin Giles's *The Trinity and Subordinationism,* Doyle argued that the early church fathers' response to the Arian heresy "was not only about the Son's nature and relation to the Father, but was set against the need to affirm and safeguard that the Father is really Father in himself; they contended that 'Father' as applied to God is not a merely figurative expression but names who he actually is eternally: the eternal Begetter of the Son, the eternal Source or Origin of divinity, the eternal Monarch."[40] Likewise, in his review of *Reflections in Glass,* he argued that, in responding to the views of Arius, Athanasius insisted that it was in order to safeguard the belief that "the Father is really Father in himself, that 'Father' as applied to God is not a merely figurative expression but

---

37. Doyle, "Use and abuse," section on Athanasius, 4.

38. Doyle, "Use and abuse," section on Athanasius, 4.

39. Whatever this qualification may amount to.

40. Doyle, "Use and abuse."

names who he actually is eternally."[41] Doyle then exchanges the reference
to a "real Father" for a "true Father": "by showing the Son is truly God,
Athanasius is also defending the eternal fatherhood of the first member
of the Trinity, for a father cannot be a true father eternally unless he has a
son eternally."[42] Doyle then repeated the same assertion originally made
in his response to Giles's *The Trinity and Subordinationism*: "The triune
Father is a real father and the triune Son is a real son. Neither names are
metaphorical."[43]

If the terms "Father" and "Son" when applied to the respective trinitarian identities are not to be read metaphorically as figures of speech,
then it might be thought that they must be taken literally. But this obviously cannot be the case. We cannot be talking about a physical or genetic relationship. Unfortunately, Doyle does not broach the possibility
that the terms "father" and "son," when used theologically, are neither
used literally nor metaphorically, but analogically. But perhaps he means
they are used "more or less" literally, or perhaps, even "more" rather than
"less" literally. In this case a question arises as to what specific qualities
of human fathers are "really" and "truly" in mind when God is called
"Father" and the Son is called "Son." Some analogical comparisons are
entirely inappropriate. Earthly fathers always precede their sons in a temporal sense; but obviously this is something that cannot apply to God, the
timelessly Eternal Father whose Son must also likewise be the timelessly
Eternal Son. Nor does God bring home a pay packet or pay taxes in the
way those who are referred to literally by the term "father" in this world
tend to do. Some aspects of fatherly behavior cannot apply to God, even
if God is said to be "really" and "truly" a father. But what more precisely
is being said when the analogy of fatherhood *is* applied to God? More
importantly, can it be claimed that authoritative command and obedient
submission is somehow essential to all father/son relations as though this
were a matter of logical necessity?

Traditionally, orthodox Christian theology has been cautious in trying to unpack the Father/Son analogy by affirming only what Scripture
will warrant: that the Father is identified as the one who "begets" the Son,
not in time, but eternally, and the Son is identified as "eternally begotten" of the Father. Even here the chief purpose was originally intended

---

41. Doyle, Review of "*Reflections in Glass*, Chapter 7," section on Athanasius, i.

42. Doyle, Review of "*Reflections in Glass*, Chapter 7," section on Athanasius, i.

43. Doyle, Review of "*Reflections in Glass*, Chapter 7," section on Athanasius, iii.

to exclude Arius's assimilation of the incarnation to the exercise in time of the creative will of the Father. Hence, the Creed of Nicaea affirms that Christ was "begotten *not made*"—but just what is involved in being "eternally begotten" lies hidden in the unknowable mystery of God. Notwithstanding this norm of traditional orthodoxy, Robert Doyle insists on projecting anthropomorphic notions of fatherly command and filial obedience as a form of interpersonal domination and submission into the meaning of these terms! The question that must therefore be faced is that, given the traditional theological practice of limiting the Father/Son analogy to the notion of begetting/being begotten, how can the importation of notions of domination and submission, with the logically consequent implication that two different and complementary wills are involved, be justified? Obviously without rational theological justification it is not possible to avoid the charge that talk of "eternal relational subordination" may be entirely arbitrary and, indeed, fanciful.

⌒

The basis of Doyle's logical move from the literal use of the terms "father" and "son," to the importation of a relation of domination and submission into the eternal relationship of God the Father and God the Son, seems to depend on the assertion that the Father is a "real Father" or a "true Father." It is as though the projection of notions of "subordination" into the relationship with the Son who is no less than a "real Son" and a "true Son" is warranted simply by the drawing of the analogy with human sons of this world. In other words, domination and submission is assumed to be something essential to the analogical use of these terms, given that it is based upon the general contention that it is essential to relations of fathers and sons. As Doyle says, this is "what fathers do."[44]

It is hard to avoid the suspicion that some kind of gratuitous selectivity is operating here. Doyle and others who draw on the analogy of humanly submissive and obedient sons in relation to the ruling or commanding will of a human father as something essential to this same kind of relationship also within the life of the Trinity, tend in practice to equate sonship with childhood, where "childhood" is understood, not as a permanent quality of the relation of parents and their children of whatever age, but as a defined period of life between infancy and adulthood, when

44. Doyle, "Use and abuse," section on Athanasius, 4.

children are naturally dependent and are expected to be obedient to their parents' direction. However, as Shakespeare astutely observed,[45] this kind of dependency does not necessarily carry over to the relationship of sons to their fathers once sons reach adulthood. Rather, the expectation of obedience diminishes as a child becomes an adult, and then actually disappears when later in life the roles tend to get reversed and fathers become dependent upon their sons (and daughters) in old age. This alerts us to the fact that what is said to be "natural" or "essential" to the relationship of fathers and sons is actually contingent rather than necessary, being selectively drawn essentially from the relations of parents to their children aged from about five to eighteen years of age. But why should an aspect of this particular segment of a child's life automatically carry into the life of the Trinity? Clearly, we cannot project notions of domination and submission drawn from a particular segment of human life that is characteristic of a particular temporally defined stage of growth and social behavior, and project that into the life of the Trinity as though this is a logical necessity. It is understandable that this logical move is made in the desperate quest to define an understanding of the eternal relationality of the three persons in terms of the dynamic of domination and submission, but we need to be clear that it does not follow with logical necessity from a consideration of the terms "father" and "son" when used literally in this world. This is purely arbitrary. Certainly, a subordinationist conclusion cannot be drawn simply because of the biblical use of the language of "Father" and "Son."

I am gratified to see that Glenn Butner has noted the analogical nature of the Father/Son relationship, but points out that submissiveness is not necessarily a defining or essential part of it. Butner begs to differ from a contention of Wayne Grudem[46] that, unless there are scriptural grounds for excluding some aspects of the human father/son relationship from applying also to the relationship of God the Father and God the Son, then all aspects of the relationship may simply be imported. In other words, Grudem's principle seems to be that there are good reasons for excluding

<hr/>

45. As famously described in the character Jaques's soliloquy in *As You Like It*. Here the lives of men and women in the world are compared to actors playing roles on a stage in the theater and in which the changes that take place over the course of a man's life are examined. Jaques divides the life of a man into seven stages: baby or infant, schoolboy or child, lover, soldier, justice or judge, old man, senile old person, again like a child.

46. Grudem, "Biblical Evidence," 231–32.

"genetic identity" from the divine Father/Son relationship, for God has "no body, parts, or passions." But unless there are explicit reasons such as this, then everything else that pertains to human fathers and sons may be said of the divine Father and Son. By contrast with Grudem's principle, Butner works from a minimalist point of view, by suggesting that only a restricted range of aspects of the father/son analogy may carry into our understanding of the immanent life of the Trinity, to the exclusion of other thinkable possibilities.[47] But that raises a question as to exactly what aspects of the human father/son relation are to be projected into the Godhead? And is the operation of a dynamic of domination and submission one of them?

In the tradition of Christian orthodoxy the answer to this question is decidedly "No!" Rather, the identity of the Father in relation to the Son, and hence the appropriateness of the use of the term "Father" referringly and denotatively, is defined by virtue of the fact that the Father eternally "begets" the Son. The Son is identified as the Son because he is "eternally begotten." There is clear scriptural warrant for this. Nothing additional needs to be said.

Unfortunately, this discussion between Grudem and Butner tends to forget that all aspects of the analogies and metaphors we apply to God, when we strive to express our understanding of the divine, are actually beyond our ken. In a sense they are all irreducible and cannot be unpacked and expressed in any clear and distinct, prosaic, or literal specification. The tradition of classical theism is cautiously *apophatic* at this point. The surpassing ultimate unknowability and incomprehensibility of a God, who is, by definition, infinite, means that we are obliged to bow before the mystery of God who transcends the limits of our necessarily finite understanding. This is why when we assent to the church's definition of the Son as "only begotten of the Father" we have to confess that we really have no notion of what being "eternally begotten" by the Father might be understood to mean in clear and distinct or literal terms, even though it is useful in excluding the Arian notion that the Son is part of the created order. Its dogmatic value is that it excludes Arius's contention

47. Butner, *Son Who Learned Obedience*, 190. Butner says "I must note that his [Grudem's] particularly maximalist account of the analogy between earthly sons and the divine Son may be flawed. Perhaps the biblical analogy is not intended to apply to all aspects of human sonship to the Father unless explicitly prohibited. Perhaps a minimalist account is superior, such that only a single attribute is in mind." His conclusion is that "there is not the scriptural warrant Grudem imagines for projecting submission into the Godhead."

that the Word was created by God at a specific point of time by a decision of the divine will. Hence, the orthodox Christian adherence to the creedal affirmation "begotten not made." This means that the Father/Son analogy is irreducible to precise, literal, and prosaic specification. What is more precisely involved in the Father's begetting of the Son is in a sense, something "other than" and beyond the limits of human understanding, for this is something known only to God.

The abiding importance and value of the affirmation of the eternal generation of the Son as the "only begotten of the Father" is not the exact precision of what it means to communicate, so much as what it intends to exclude. The creedal affirmation that the Son is "begotten *not made*" is intended to deny what Arius sought to affirm when he held that the Word came into being in time in relation to the created order, and in association with the materiality of creation as the Word "through whom all things were made." This allowed Arius to say that the Word was not eternal, and because of its intimate relation to the materiality of the created order, that the Word could not be consubstantial with the Father. This is primarily what is denied by the creedal affirmation of the *eternal* generation of the "only begotten Son" by the Father. Rather than the creation in time as a product of the creative will of God the Father, the eternal Word is "begotten from all eternity," not made in time at a point in a sequence. In this way the creedal formula inhibits the assimilation of the eternal Son to this created order and thus denies that he is less than equally consubstantial with the eternal God. It has nothing whatever to say about an alleged eternal functional subordination of one person of the Trinity to another. It is a mistake to assume, simply because of the identifying use of the terms "Father" and "Son" in relation to the divine persons, that an analogy may be drawn with an arbitrarily chosen aspect of the literal use of these words when they are used to refer to the fathers and sons of this finite world.

☞

Robert Doyle, as a professional theologian, is not unaware of the need to back up his argument by appeal to theological precedent. In his extended review of Kevin Giles's *The Trinity and Subordinationism*,[48] Doyle helpfully pointed to the Athanasian insistence on the fact that the Father is

---

48. Initially posted on *The Briefing* website on September 3, 2004.

Father from all eternity only because the Son is begotten from all eternity: "the Father in his Person is not just the unique King and Source of divinity in the economy of salvation, but, as Athanasius is at pains to point out, is so eternally, in the relations of the immanent Trinity." Thus, Doyle rightly points out that for Athanasius the eternal nature of the relationship is justified by saying that the eternal Father cannot be the Father without the Son; therefore the Son must be the Son eternally, and vice versa, the Son cannot be Son without the Father.

Apart from the strong biblical tradition of the use of Father/Son language to make this point, this allows Doyle to call upon Athanasius to support his own contention that there is an asymmetry in the relation of God the Father and God the Son that inheres in their respective identities as "Father" and "Son" from all eternity. To use Doyle's own words, this means "there is a profound and non-negotiable asymmetricality and hierarchy in the relations in the Trinity." Insofar as one cannot assume the identifying role of the other, for one is the eternal begetter and the other the begotten, this is correct. But Doyle insists that more than this is involved in Athanasius's use of these titles.

Although Athanasius did not necessarily mean to suggest the notion of obedient submission of the Son to the Father from all eternity, Doyle urges us to believe this is implicit in what Athanasius has to say. In addition to his affirmation of the need to understand the Father as a "real Father" or a "true Father" and the Son likewise as a "real" and "true" Son, Doyle seeks further to justify talk of the subordination of the Son to the Father by appeal to the notion of the "monarchy" of the Father as part of Athanasius's understanding of things. This is crucial to Doyle's case because, apart from the Father's begetting of the Son, and the Son's being begotten, the Father's "monarchy" is understood in terms of a relation of domination and submission "in which the Son as eternal Son shares by way of defining himself in subordination to that monarchy."[49]

In other words, Doyle argues that when Athanasius spoke of the "monarchy" of the Father it was not just for the purpose of insisting that the Father is to be understood as the eternal *origin* and *cause* of the Son and the Spirit, but that it also incorporates overtones of "rule" and therefore implies that the Father is the Lord and Master of the Son and the Spirit.[50] The necessary implication of the Father's "monarchy" is

49. Doyle, "Use and abuse."

50. Doyle: "This priority of the Father, which John's gospel and Paul's writings attest to, includes the Father's rule, his monarchy." "Use and abuse," section on Athanasius, 3.

therefore that both of the other two Trinitarian identities are "ruled" as subordinates of the Father. The biblical tradition of the Father's sending of the Son and the Spirit, and of the Son's "being sent" and the Spirit's being given as a gift, is an example of a "ruling" function within the exercise of the Father's will.

Doyle then pulls the rug from under his own argument by acknowledging that references to the "monarchy" of the Father in Athanasius only appear when Athanasius is quoting other authors, and are not integral to Athanasius's own regular vocabulary. Nevertheless, we are assured that even though "it may be true that Athanasius does not use the term 'monarchy' himself, except when quoting others . . . neither does he attack the term, but, on the contrary, seems to endorse the notion it contains."[51] Astonishingly, Doyle then goes on to say that "even without the term 'monarchy,' the concept of the single rule of the Father is not uncommon, especially when Athanasius is combating polytheism."

When we go to the text of Athanasius,[52] it is perfectly clear that Athanasius's appeal to the single rule of one God is to explain the harmony and order of the universe, as against the chaos which he believed would result from a multiplicity of competing gods. It has nothing to do with the relations between the Farther, Son, and Spirit, in the unity of the immanent life of the Trinity. If anything a divine rule of the universe in the sense that Athanasius felt important in order to exclude the possibility of the chaos of polytheism, is something equally shared by all three persons of the Trinity in the unity of Being of one God in dealing with the created order.

Nevertheless, Doyle would have his readers believe that he is justified in concluding, "The clear implication of this in Athanasius is that in the relations between the triune members, he is no 'egalitarian.'"[53] I have a sneaking suspicion that Athanasius would have read these words with some surprise, if not a good deal of consternation and alarm. Furthermore, on these grounds Doyle appears to believe that, given that Athanasius "does not attack the term 'monarchy'" Doyle is himself therefore free from attack in relation to his own proclivity for reading some kind of subordination or rule into the term "father," and then projecting this into the internal life of the immanent Trinity.

51. Doyle, "Use and abuse," section on Athanasius, 3.
52. Athanasius, *Against the Heathen*, 39–40; also 6–7.
53. Doyle, "Use and abuse," section on Athanasius, 4.

⌣

Furthermore, it has to be said that in orthodox Trinitarian theology the Son does not "define himself" as Doyle suggests, by being obediently submissive to the Father's commanding will. The Son is not defined, let alone does he define himself in behavioral terms by a decision of will. Rather, in orthodox Trinitarian theology the Son is defined as Son ontologically by virtue of the fact that he is "eternally begotten," and the Father is defined as the one by whom the Son is begotten, just as the Spirit is defined as the one who "proceeds" from the Father; and the Father is defined as the source *(arche)* or origin of both Son and Spirit. The dynamics of the interpersonal relationships of fathers and sons in this world, at some arbitrarily selected stage of life, have nothing to do with this.

We do well to remember that Athanasius's chief theological purpose in affirming that the Father is eternally the Father and the Son eternally the Son is precisely to insist on the *timelessly eternal* generation and hence the essential divinity of the Son, over against Arius's contention that the Word incarnate is to be associated with the created order, as the Word "through whom all things were made." Arius, in making this point was particularly impressed by the declaration of Proverbs 8:22: "He created me at the beginning of his work." It is therefore the eternal generation of the Son by the Father that is uppermost in Athanasius's mind, in order to secure the exclusion of linear time from the immanent life of the Trinity. Once again his purpose is to exclude the possibility of assimilating the Son to the created order as the product of the exercise of the Father's creative will. Doyle does not go so far as to say that the Son is the product of the exercise of the creative will of God the Father, and thus avoids this classic (mistaken) view of Arius in this respect, but he does import the noxious notion of the active exercise of the Father's commanding and ruling *will* with respect to the passive obedience of his Son's willing. Insofar as this is essential to his understanding of the defining quality of their eternal Father/Son relation, it also appears to introduce time into the immanent life of the Trinity, given that the exercise of a commanding will and then the obedient response to it, apparently at a point in a sequence, takes time. In this way talk of the Father's ruling command and the Son's response to it introduces time into the divine life, just as Arius introduced time into the divine life when he said that the Word came to be through involvement in creation. Orthodox Christian belief excludes talk of the exercise of identifiably separate wills of Father and

Son in some kind of temporal sequence. As Rowan Williams puts it in summing up Athanasius's chief purpose: "The Athanasian picture . . . absolutely rules out a 'history' in God; there are no transactions in eternity, and the Father and Son do not relate as active and passive principles."[54] A commanding will and a responsively obedient will is anathema, as is the notion of the eternal exercise of authoritarian rule on the part of the Father with respect to the submissively obedient Son.

We have to conclude that, if Athanasius accepted the use of the term "monarchy" by others it grounded the Cappadocian Fathers' belief in the Father as the *eternal origin* of the Son and the Spirit, but otherwise was used to insist on the unity of the creational activity of one God in three persons in their joint and undivided rule of the universe as against polytheism. Robert Doyle's attempt to import the notion of "rule" into an understanding of the monarchy of the Father for the purpose of justifying a relation of interpersonal domination and submission within the immanent life of the Trinity entirely fails.

⤙

Even so, Doyle has yet another argument to bring to his quest to bolster the contention that the Father's "monarchy" or "rule" involves more than the affirmation of the Father's identity as the one who eternally begets the Son, and therefore as the "origin" of the Son's divinity. A further excess of meaning, which is said to attach to the "ruling" power of the Father, is drawn from the biblical tradition that the Son is "*sent* into the world *by* the Father." This too is said to be asymmetrical: obviously, the Son does not send the Father.

Doyle's argument is that the language of "sending" and "being sent" may be taken to suggest the Father's directive or commanding will, and the corresponding obediently submissive will of the Son: "It is proper to the eternal personhood of the Son that he is sent, and likewise to the eternal personhood of the Father that he is the sender" and that this "sender/ sent" language supports the contention that the biblical tradition teaches subordinationism. Clearly, this is an important contention in Doyle's attempt to secure the eternal subordination of the Son to the Father.

54. Williams, *Arius*, 241. Williams notes that the notions of father and son is used by Aristotle in *Metaphysics* 5, 15 to illustrate the relation of agent to patient as it arises in consequence of a temporal event such as begetting.

This proposition is, however, not new. In the literature relating to the subordination of the Son to the Father, the sender/sent language, especially of the Gospel of John, has been widely assumed to carry persuasive weight over a considerable period of time. As early as 1990 Robert Letham argued for the asymmetrical nature of the interpersonal relationships within the Trinity: "the Father sends the Son and not vice versa . . . . The Son obeys the Father, the Father does not enter into a situation where obedience is owed to the Son."[55] In a similar way, Wayne Grudem, as perhaps the leading exponent of "eternal functional submissiveness" over a sustained period, was in the theological vanguard in confidently pointing to the importance of the Father's commanding role in the incarnation in his *Systematic Theology* first published in 1994.[56] In 2012 he was explicit in highlighting the significance of the Father's "sending" of the Son: "if one sends and the other is sent, then one commands and the other obeys."[57]

In the more recent second edition of his *Systematic Theology* he persists not only in maintaining a subordinationist position in the face of the sustained criticisms of Matthew Emerson and Luke Stamps[58] as well as Glenn Butner, but is even prepared to try to justify belief in a division of willing within the Trinity: "Surely there must be some kinds of distinction in the one will of God because there is a difference between the Father's willing to send and the Son's willing to be sent. There is a difference between the Father's willing to pour out divine wrath against sin and the Son's willing to bear that wrath for our sake."[59]

While there is no acknowledgment of dependence on Grudem's *Systematic Theology* in the 1999 Report of the Sydney Doctrine Commission, its thinking exhibits an unmistakable family likeness. When the report comes to cite the biblical evidence for belief in the eternal subordination of the Son to the Father, for example, it is quick to focus on the same sender/sent trope as it is expressed in the Gospel of John:

> In speaking of his relation with the Father, the Gospel of John
> refers to the way in which the world was made through him

55. Letham, "Man-Woman Debate," 68.

56. See his *Systematic Theology*, 600–606. See also the section on subordinationism in Grudem, *Evangelical Feminism and Biblical Truth*, 415–22.

57. Grudem, "Biblical Evidence," 245.

58. See Emerson and Stamps, "On Trinitarian Theological Method," 95–128 and 157–73.

59. Grudem, *Systematic Theology*, 616.

(1:3), and also the way in which he had been "sent" into the world for its salvation (e.g., 3:16–17). The Scriptures thus themselves bear witness to a subordination which belongs to the eternal relationship between the persons of the Trinity, and not only to the humanity of Jesus in the incarnation, or even in the broader work of redemption.[60]

It is important to note that, while John 3:16–17 is obviously regarded as a key text for this sender/sent argument, this kind of language is not confined only to one or two verses of John's Gospel. Bruce Ware has pointed out that the fact that Jesus was "sent" by the Father to accomplish his mission is mentioned some thirty times and that "his very coming to earth was itself in obedience to the Father."[61] In relation to this Ware cited Leon Morris, who also linked the obedient submissiveness of the Son to his God-given mission: "the very concept of mission, of being 'sent' contains within it the thought of doing what the Sender wills."[62]

The discussion of this biblical language of sender/being sent has tended to put considerable weight on the meaning of the verb *"apostello"* (I send) as this is found across a range of New Testament texts.[63] Bruce Ware, for example, argues that this term suggests that "the Father wills to send" and "the Son submits and comes."[64] Likewise, Grudem echoes this sentiment: "He was first 'sent' as Son, and then he obeyed and humbled himself and came."[65] Sometimes it is even argued that *apostello*, as used both in the Septuagint and the New Testament, had become a technical term with an implicit reference to the religious experience of being sent with a specific task by God. This, however, is disputed.[66] For one thing, the word is often used of the sending of inanimate things without overtones of a posture of human submissiveness—wheat, wood, barley, oil, wine,

---

60. Sydney Doctrine Commission Report 1999, sec.4.1/para 17.

61. Ware, *Father, Son, and Holy Spirit*, 77.

62. Morris, *New Testament Theology*, 251.

63. Matt 15:24; Luke 4:43, 9:48, and John 6:29, 3:17. Sometimes the alternative verb *pempo* is used, though with less of a sense of submission on the part of the one being sent than *apostello*. See Mercer, "*Apostellein* and *Pempein* in John."

64. Ware, "Equal in Essence," 17.

65. Grudem, "Biblical Evidence," 244.

66. In an entry under "Apostle" in *New International Dictionary of New Testament Theology*, D. Müller argues that "NT scholarship has not sufficiently considered the meaning of the vb. *apostello* . . . as a technical term denoting divine authorization" (134).

food, the ark of the covenant, and letters are all "sent."[67] It has to be said, however, that a context in which human willing is operative may import its own nuance of meaning in which the submissiveness on the part of one will to another *could* be an element in a way that does not apply to the sending of an inanimate object. On the other hand, even K. H. Rengstorf, who argued that *apostello* functions as a technical religious term at least when it is used in contexts that are religiously conditioned, qualifies this claim when it comes to John's Gospel, where submissiveness is said to be "excluded by the fact that between Jesus and the 'Father' is a unity in will and action (*John* 10.30; 14.9) which leaves no room for 'responsibility.'"[68] Furthermore, Rengstorf goes on to say that in John's Gospel when the incarnate Christ speaks of the Father as "the one who sends me," an effort is being made to highlight the unity of action between the Father and the Son, and that the word *apostello* is actually used by Jesus to justify his works by grounding them in the authority of the Father. In other words, the emphasis is on divine authority and commissioning, not on subordination.[69] In any event, while this has to do with the divine authority of the human works of the incarnate Word, it does not directly bear on the internal relations of the immanent Trinity. Butner is of the view that the New Testament "Sending language simply does not require acceptance of EFS."[70]

It also seems clear enough that Rengstorf's treatment of the biblical evidence was undertaken from the perspective of the essential unity of the Trinity and the need to adhere to the traditionally orthodox belief in the undivided single divine will and action to the exclusion of talk of a division of willing represented by the commanding will of the Father in "sending" the Son and the compliantly submissive will of the Son who is said dutifully to obey.

Curiously, Robert Doyle, though a systematic theologian, exhibits no sense of any need to conform to this norm of the theological tradition of Christian orthodoxy. On the contrary, he clearly believes that, over and above his subordinationist reading of the biblical evidence, in highlighting the asymmetric division of roles between the Father and the Son he is himself picking up "the later language of Augustine." Certainly,

---

67. 2 Chr 2:8; 2:15; Joel 2:19; Neh 8:10; 1 Sam 6:3; 2 Kgs 5:5.

68. Rengstorf, "*apostello (pempo)*," 405.

69. Rengstorf, "*apostello (pempo)*," 404–5.

70. Butner, *Son Who Learned Obedience*, 183.

St. Augustine had already responded to this very "sender/sent" biblical tradition at some length in *On the Trinity*, especially in Book II. Doyle is therefore right in pointing to the seminal Augustinian discussion of this sender/being sent language. It is important to note, however, that at the very beginning of *On the Trinity*, Augustine declared that his chief purpose in undertaking the project at all was to tackle the troublesome issues raised by biblical texts *that seemed to stand in opposition to traditional orthodox Trinitarianism*! In actual fact, in that work he argued very vigorously *against* the subordination of the Son to the Father that was apparently being said, even in his own day, to be signaled by the New Testament's "sender/sent" language.

⮜

The alleged problem posed by the biblical tradition of the "sending of the Son by the Father" therefore naturally bulks large in Augustine's exposition of John 3:16–17. Augustine's point is that, in the context of a more expansive appreciation of the total biblical revelation, this "sending/being sent" language cannot simply be taken at face value, still less can notions of domination and submission be imported into it. It is clear at the outset that Augustine was troubled by the fact that the send/being sent language tended to import an apparent division of willing between the Father and the Son. That the incarnation cannot involve a straightforward "sending and being sent" was clear to Augustine, since the sending of the Word incarnate into the world has to be held together with the belief that the Word was in the world already: "the Word was in the world, and the world was made by Him, and the world knew Him not" (John 1:10–11). Thus, Augustine pertinently observed that "He was sent therefore thither, where He already was" (see Wisdom 8:1). This seemed to him to mean that the said "sending" of the Son into the world, was more in the nature of the "making manifest" of the already present Word in a unique way in the person of the incarnate Jesus Christ. Clearly, in this case notions of fatherly command and filial obedience, which would also suggest the operation of two identifiably distinct wills, may not be part of the meaning of the Father's sending of the Son at all.

Augustine further declared that to have a right understanding of the incarnation and nativity of the Virgin, "wherein the Son is understood as sent," it is necessary to understand this "to have been wrought by one and the same operation of the Father and of the Son indivisibly; the Holy

Spirit certainly not being thence excluded, of whom it is expressly said, 'She was found with child by the Holy Ghost.'" Augustine goes on:

> [P]erhaps our meaning will be more plainly unfolded, if we ask in what manner God sent His Son. He commanded that He should come, and He, complying with the commandment, came. Did He then request, or did He only suggest? But which-ever of these it was, certainly it was done by a word, and the Word of God is the Son of God Himself. Wherefore, since the Father sent Him by a word, His being sent was the work of both the Father and His Word; therefore the same Son was sent by the Father and the Son, because the Son Himself is the Word of the Father.[71]

Clearly, far from using the language of "sender/sent" to try to justify some kind of division of wills, involving the complementarian operation of the commanding will of the Father and the obediently responsive will of the Son, Augustine in effect argued strenuously against subordina-tionism precisely because he perceived the theological importance of maintaining belief in the unity of a single divine will, shared by all three identities of the Trinity, and their resulting indivisible, single divine ac-tion in the world.[72] Thus, "to have a right sense of these things" from an Augustinian point of view, it cannot simply be said that the incarnation was the subordinationist outcome of the commanding will of the Father and the obedient response of the Son, because "the will of the Father and the Son is one, and their working indivisible."

Likewise, Augustine noted that "His Spirit, too, is everywhere, yet when the invisible Spirit was said to appear in visible tokens of the form of a dove, and cloven tongues of fire and a sudden rushing wind at Pen-tecost, He was understood also to be sent and given as a gift: Therefore, the Holy Spirit, too, was sent thither, where He already was" (Ps 139:1, 8).[73] "The Holy Spirit, then, is also said to be sent, on account of these corporeal forms which came into existence in time, in order to signify and manifest him, as he must needs be manifested, to human senses; yet he is not said to be less than the Father."[74] Thus, a "making manifest" of the Spirit does not carry any overtones of the subordinationism that might be read into the kind of sending involving the Father's command

71. Augustine, *On the Trinity*, II.5.7 (68).

72. Augustine, *On the Trinity*, II.5.9.

73. Augustine, *On the Trinity*, II.5.7.

74. Augustine, *On the Trinity*, II.7.12.

and the Spirit's obedient response. Augustine therefore insisted, "It is, then, for this reason nowhere written, that the Father is greater than the Holy Spirit, or that the Holy Spirit is less than God the Father."[75] The same holds of the relation of the Father and the Son.

The equal involvement of all three persons together in the incarnation is also seen in the work of redemption, for, as Augustine pertinently observed, Paul speaks of this as having been accomplished by *both* Father and Son, also acting together. Thus, Augustine noted that Paul says, that God "spared not His own Son, but *delivered Him* up for us all" (Rom 8:32) while elsewhere he speaks of the Savior himself, "who loved me, and *delivered himself* for me" (Gal 2:20). Clearly, the whole tenor of Augustine's discussion has to do with the defense of the unity of God and the indivisibility of the divine action, implemented not by different if complementary wills, but by the joint exercise of the single divine will that is equally shared by Father, Son, and Spirit as three identifiable *hypostases* in One Unity of Being.

Given that, generally speaking, evangelical expositions of the Trinity tend to follow the Augustinian pattern of starting with the unity of one God, using the idea of divine substance as the unifying ground of divinity, rather than the Cappadocian preference for starting with the person of the Father as the eternal origin of the divinity of the Son who is "begotten of the Father" and the Spirit who "proceeds from the Father," the omission from this evangelical discussion of a more careful consideration of Augustine's treatment of the biblical evidence is puzzling. Indeed, given that the biblical tradition of "God's sending of his Son, and of the Son's being sent" is so often cited as a key proof of the "eternal submission/subordination of the Son to the Father" this is very damaging to the subordinationists' cause.

⏑

How is it, then, that this Augustinian precedent is apparently overlooked by Robert Doyle specifically, and by Australian Carillon Avenue theologians and evangelical Christians generally, in their publicly espoused preference for subordinationism? And how are we to explain the modern popularity of subordinationism and the confident vehemence with which it is defended and promulgated? Furthermore, is it possible with a little

---

75. Augustine, *On the Trinity*, II.6.11.

more clarity to put a finger on what exactly it is that is wrong with the "eternal submissiveness and/or subordination of the Son to the Father"?

Kevin Giles suspects that we may reasonably assume that the popularity both of "eternal functional submissiveness" and "eternal relational subordination" must surely lie in a fundamental adherence to the supreme authority of Scripture, possibly also coupled with the belief that "the Bible interprets itself." His suggestion is that belief in *sola Scriptura* and the "perspicuity" of Scripture seems to entail that there is a diminished sense of need to attend to the cultural conditioning of texts, and the voice of alternative authorities, in favor of a reliance on "scripture alone." In this case, from the perspective of the subordinationist mentality the early fathers, and even the dogmatic definitions of the first four ecumenical councils of the church, while usually being formally accorded a certain authoritative status and deference, in actual practice assume a place of secondary importance to Scripture itself as its own self-sufficient interpreter.[76] Even though the irony here is that the authoritative determinations of ancient church councils were designed to define the most acceptable of disputed readings of Scripture and to anathematize alternative maverick readings as simply mistaken and unacceptable, a contemporary reading of Scripture alone in practice tends to prevail. As a consequence, for example, the theological implications of an initial affirmation of the Nicene *homoousion* tend to be neutralized in the enthusiasm to expound the alleged importance of "eternal subordination" in the life of the immanent Trinity on the basis of what is taken to be the clear teaching of Scripture.

If this assumption about the overriding methodological role of "Scripture alone" is correct, then this may explain the tendency that has been clearly demonstrated in practice among those who were committed, both to the promotion of "eternal functional submissiveness" in the debates of 2016 and to the "eternal relational subordination" of the Son to the Father as this has been espoused in Anglican Carillon Avenue theology through the last seventy years. This is the methodological practice, that we have already noted, of bundling together scriptural texts that

76. See for example, Giles, *Rise and Fall*, 75, where he says: "Before leaving this discussion on the contribution of Scripture in the theological enterprise I need to say that for the Reformers the Latin catch cry sola scriptura, by Scripture alone, did not mean, solo scriptura. It meant rather that Scripture alone is divine revelation and as such is uniquely authoritative in matters of faith and practice. The claim by modern evangelicals that it meant for them solo scriptura, 'Scripture only,' is simply mistaken."

are deemed to be supportive to the subordinationist cause, without first pausing to determine whether they might have to do with the incarnate Son's *human* response of obedience to God, and therefore without so much as raising a question as whether they have anything at all to do with the inner life of the immanent Trinity. On the contrary, it tends to be assumed that it is perfectly in order simply to begin with scriptural traditions relating to the obedience of the incarnate Jesus and then to import a corresponding obedience into the willing of the eternal Second Person of the Trinity.

By way of a concrete example: David F. Wright, in attempting to defend the subordinationism of T. C. Hammond, confesses: "It seems to me inescapable in the light of Scripture to talk in some terms of the Son being subject to the Father, at least in the context of the scheme of redemption. One would have to marginalize a good deal of the New Testament to reject all such language."[77] Wright does not seem to be aware of the fact that the issue relates explicitly to the eternal subordination of the Son to the Father within the immanent life of the Trinity. There is no rejection of New Testament texts "in the context of the scheme of redemption" that speak of the subordination of the human Jesus to God the Father in the course of his earthly life and ministry. This is not what is being called into question. But Wright appears to think that the submissiveness of the human willing of the incarnate Jesus may simply be projected back into the internal relations of the divine life of the Trinity. Hence, after signaling some perfunctory misgivings about whether the term "subordination" is the best word to spell out what is involved, a form of submissiveness or a kind of subordination is nevertheless said to be implicit in "the divine Word's being the Son of the Father, eternally being begotten from the Father, sent by the Father etc." He admits that "this issue is not so easy to settle . . . But it has to be settled by Scripture."[78] On the basis of the contention that a good deal of New Testament language suggests that the (human) Son is subject to the Father, Wright then declares that "Hammond is right to insist that there is a subordination 'in order of relation, but not in nature' . . . in the internal life of the Trinity."[79] Unfortunately, Wright does not address the question of the propriety of projecting texts that speak of the submissive human will of the incarnate Jesus into the

---

77. Wright, "Dr. Carnley on T. C. Hammond and Arianism," 48.

78. Wright, "Dr. Carnley on T. C. Hammond and Arianism," 48.

79. Wright, "Dr. Carnley on T. C. Hammond and Arianism," 48.

eternal relations of the immanent Trinity; rather, New Testament references to "the divine Word's being the Son of the Father, and eternally begotten of the Father, and sent by the Father, etc." are lumped together to indicate the legitimacy of the subordinationist case, as though this is somehow self-evident while admittedly at the same time being "not so easy to settle"!

On the other hand, though for the most part, those who have sought to defend "eternal functional subordination" appear to be oblivious to these unaddressed questions, Robert Doyle has actually even attempted to justify the validity of this methodology:

> Because these texts speak of the *God incarnate*, then even if they are strongly economic, they must also with contextual propriety be allowed to say something of the immanent Trinity. Why? Because . . . it is *God* who speaks, *God* who causes Holy Scripture to be written for our edification, *God* who takes on human nature and lives under our human conditions, and it is thus *God* who saves. So even the really hard economic text needs to also be read immanently, . . . they need to be allowed to speak of the relations between the Persons, because God's essence of substance is triune.[80]

This seems to hint at the possibility that it is the sharing of the same divine substance by the *hypostatic* identities of the Trinity that entails that what may be said of God incarnate may automatically be said to carry into the immanent life of the Trinity. It is thereby suggested that at the incarnation the divine *hypostasis* of the Son, who "takes on human nature and lives under our human conditions," assumes humanity, almost as though putting on a restrictively heavy overcoat, while his inner thought and power of decision-making, and his obedient submission to the will of the Father, remains that of his divine *hypostasis*.[81] This gives permission for the thought that the subordination of the incarnate Son to the Father may be conceived as a kind of continuation in history of a preexisting, eternal divine willing, or, as Doyle himself says, an eternally self-defining

---

80. Doyle, "Use and abuse," section on "How the Bible Functions in Trinitarian Theology."

81. Some traditional kenotic Christologies have appealed to the "putting on of humanity" to explain how it was that the divine powers of the Second Person of the Trinity were obscured or not brought into play in the course of the human Jesus' incarnate life. See a discussion of the inadequacies of this kind of Christology in Carnley, *Reconstruction of Resurrection Belief*, 293–96.

determination to be submissively subordinate to the Father. Conversely, this also appears to allow for the accounts of the dutiful subordination of the human Jesus Christ to his heavenly Father in the economy of salvation, of which we read in the historical record of scriptural texts, to be quite easily projected into the immanent life of the Trinity so as to ground belief in the eternal subordination of the Son to the Father.[82]

The same dynamic appears to be expressed when Doyle says that "the incarnate Son says that he delights to do the Father's will (John 4:34). If so under the conditions of incarnation, how much more so in the immanent Trinity?" Doyle seems here to be employing the "way of eminence" to take language applicable in a human context into a divine context. This theological strategy may also be seen in the observable readiness, both of Doyle himself and of the 1999 Sydney Doctrine Commission's Report, to import human characteristics of the relationship of fathers and sons generally into the eternal life of the Trinity.

There is even a suggestion that the Second Person of the Trinity, as God incarnate, may be understood to exercise the same divine will both in time, in the course of the historical life of Jesus Christ, and eternally, insofar as he is allegedly obediently submissive to God the Father, either side of his incarnation as it were. In other words, the willing obedience in the performance of his saving role in the economy of salvation is assumed to be essentially of a piece with the same willing commitment of obedient submissiveness to the Father prior to his incarnation, indeed from all eternity. Hence, Doyle is able to say that texts that "speak of God Incarnate . . . must be allowed to say something of the immanent Trinity."

The 1999 Sydney Doctrine Commission, of which Doyle was, of course, a member, argued in this way when in its now infamous report it said that "The Son's obedience to the Father arises from the very nature of his being as Son. His freedom consists in doing what is natural to him, which is to submit to his Father. He is incapable of doing other than his Father's will."[83] Even though the report started out by making a clear distinction between "being" or "essential nature" and a purely "functional" or "relational" subordination, the incarnate Son's willing obedience to the Father is now being said to be not so much a matter purely of function,

---

82. Doyle has undoubtedly been led into this methodological commitment because of his reading of "Rahner's Rule." A full discussion of this may be found in the companion volume to this book, Carnley, *Subordinate Substitute*, chapter 1.

83. Sydney Doctrine Commission Report 1999, sec. 4.2/para. 18.

but something that arises out of the "very nature of his being." Clearly, at the very least there is some confusion here.

This kind of thinking has two disastrous implications. First, insofar as Doyle says it is *God* who "takes on human nature and lives under human conditions" and "it is *God* who saves," the willing of the historical Jesus in the economy of salvation tends to be associated with the concept of his divine *hypostasis*, rather than with his human *nature*. Indeed, the exercise of the submissive will of the Son in response to God the Father's command prompts the suggestion that the incarnate divine *hypostasis* was exercising a composite divine/human will of filial subordination during his historical life, that seems to be at the expense of the exercise of an authentically human will as a property of an authentically human nature. In other words, in this case, there is a question as to whether the historical Jesus was an authentic human being, just like the rest of us, or whether he only *appeared* to be human for, deep down, as it were, he is understood to be a divine Person or *hypostasis*. Clearly, the danger of Docetism looms as a threatening problem here.[84]

Furthermore, the offering of perfect obedience to the Father, if it is a product of the willing of the Second Person of the Trinity, with his willing being associated with his divine *hypostasis*, seems to entail that the exercise of an authentically *human* wiling is missing from the incarnate life of Jesus. In this case the exercise of will in being perfectly obedient to the Father is no longer a *human* offering of perfect obedience, as a representative offering to God the Father on behalf of other humans, but an offering of the divine Second Person of the Trinity, or really the continuation in time of the alleged eternal subordination of the Son to the Father. Alas, if it is not an authentic *human* offering, it does not make good the imperfect offerings of the rest of humanity, and therefore does not fulfill the fundamental premise of Anselm's reasoning relating to "why God became man."[85] Indeed, there is a sense in which, as an offering of one divine *hypostasis* to another, the incarnation is rendered unnecessary and the atonement as the reconciliation of humanity with God becomes impossible. This is a congenital theological danger when behind-the-scenes transactions are said to take place at the expense of the significance of "front-of-house" historical events.

---

84. Docetism: the belief that Jesus only *appeared* to be human.
85. The thesis of Anselm in *Cur Deus Homo*.

The chief mistake here seems to be a methodological one. There appears to be a systematic tendency to attach the notion of "willing" to the divine person or *hypostasis* of the Son, both in his pre-incarnate life and in the incarnate life of the historical Jesus Christ, rather than to associate the notions of human and divine willing respectively with his divine and human natures. For this very reason, in orthodox Christology "willing" has historically not been understood as a property that is to be associated with the divine *hypostasis* of Jesus Christ as God incarnate, but rather with his two natures.

The first steps in this direction were taken by the assembled bishops or their representatives at the Council of Chalcedon in 451, which defined the christological dogma of two distinct natures in Christ. In the words of the Chalcedonian Definition, Christ was declared to be

> *homoousios* with the Father in godhead, and the same *homoousios* with us in manhood . . . acknowledged in two natures without confusion, without change, without division, without separation.

While the incarnate Jesus is to be thought of as a single *hypostasis*, Chalcedon insisted on the integrity of his two natures, one divine and one human, thereby charting the course of the ensuing reflection of the early fathers and the development of the tradition of Christian orthodoxy. Augustine, for example, perceived the importance of this distinction between the two natures very clearly. He was profoundly conscious of the fact that in his human nature, and exercising a human will, Christ related to the Father as "his God." Thus, he said, "Christ was born of a woman not as he is, the blessed God over all, but in that feeble [nature] which he took from us. . . . As man born of Mary, God was his God. As God the Word, eternally born, [his] relationship was to a Father."[86]

It would clearly be a mistake so to emphasize the divine action and will of the divinely and eternally submissive Son even in human form, and living "under human conditions," if this were to compromise the authentic human nature of the incarnate Son, including the authenticity of his human willing. In relation to the christological problem posed by the threat of a latent Docetism in emphasizing Christ's divine nature at the expense of his human nature, Joanne McWilliam has even observed that Augustine might have found the conversations between those of opposed views and even the eventual decisions of the Council of Ephesus

86. Augustine, *Contra Faustum* 3.6; *Enarratio in ps.21*, 10–11.

about Mary as *theotokos* (God-bearer) somewhat problematic: for Augustine it would have been "difficult, if not impossible, to join either side wholeheartedly."[87]

In any event, the gradual reception and processing of the Definition of Chalcedon, and the drawing out of the logical implications of its understanding of the two natures of Christ—"without confusion, without change, without division, without separation"—came to a climactic resolution at the Third Council of Constantinople in the year 681 with the authoritative definition of the two wills in Christ, a divine will and a human will, each associated respectively with his two natures (*dyothelitism*). In its uncompromising exoneration of Maximus the Confessor, the heroic proponent of Christ's two wills as against those who had argued for a single will in Christ (*monothelitism*), the Third Council of Constantinople insisted on the maintenance of the integrity of the Chalcedonian definition of Christ's two natures, with each will being understood as being a property of its respective nature, rather than a property of the divine *hypostasis* of the incarnate Christ.

The fundamental flaw of the *monothelite* position was that it rendered an understanding of Christ "incarnate in the flesh" but without an authentically human will. His free decision to remain faithful to his divinely appointed mission "even unto death," so important to the doctrine of atonement as the freely gifted perfect *human* offering of love and obedience as a representative of all humanity and on behalf of all humanity, is disastrously compromised.

Maximus had thus made explicit what was already implicit in the Chalcedonian Definition by upholding the doctrine of Christ's two wills, a divine will and a human will, each attaching respectively to his two natures. Maximus suffered terribly for his insistence, paying the price of standing resolutely for truth by having both his hands cut off so that he could no longer write, and his tongue cut out so that he could no longer talk, and exclusion from the community by being exiled. His posthumous vindication at the Third Council of Constantinople, and subsequent elevation to sainthood as Maximus *the Confessor*, secured the *dyothelite* doctrine of two wills in Christ in the orthodox understanding of the incarnation.

There is, unfortunately, a tendency in much Anglican and Reformed, and especially self-consciously evangelical, Christianity, to overlook the

87. McWilliam, "Augustine at Ephesus?," 56.

decisions of the Third Council of Constantinople by emphasizing only the decisions of the first four ecumenical councils—Nicaea, Constantinople I, Ephesus, and Chalcedon. The result is that this aspect of the historical consensus is overlooked and talk of the obedient will of the Son tends to be attributed not to the human willing of Jesus but simply to the *hypostatic* willing of the Second Person of the Trinity on either side of the incarnation—hence the "eternal functional subordination" of the Son to the Father within the immanent life of the Trinity.

As a general rule the churches of the Anglican Communion accept the authority of the first four general councils, while not necessarily claiming infallibility for their determinations. Indeed, Article 21 of the Anglican *Thirty-Nine Articles of Religion* declares that general councils "may err, and sometimes have erred." Nevertheless, provided conciliar determinations can be demonstrated to be in accordance with Scripture they are usually accepted without controversy.[88] A recent example of this has come from the Global Anglican Futures Conference (GAFCON) in a confessional statement formulated in Jerusalem in June 2008. This makes it clear that "The Bible is to be translated, read, preached, taught and obeyed in its plain and canonical sense," and then adds the important rider that this must be "respectful of the church's historic and consensual reading."[89] However, the landmarks of the church's "historic and consensual reading" then tend to be limited to what is found in upholding "the four Ecumenical Councils and the three historic creeds."[90]

The first four councils, which are usually accepted as authoritative, are not, however, exclusive; successive authoritative theological determinations of orthodox Christianity are not to be passed over, any more than the rich theological insights of the Reformers. Even in the sixteenth century Richard Field was hardly a lone voice in accepting the first six councils.[91] Moreover, there is a sense in which the *dyothelite* decisions of the Third Council of Constantinople are simply the logical extension of

88. The first four General Councils of the church were: the Council of Nicaea, the First Council of Constantinople, the Council of Ephesus, and the Council of Chalcedon.

89. See the Jerusalem Declaration of GAFCON, Article 3.

90. Also the Jerusalem Declaration, Article 3.

91. Richard Field (1561–1616). See *Of the Church*, in which he contended that Reformed Anglican piety and polity continued the pre-Tridentine Catholic conciliar tradition. He argued that all the essential doctrinal points of orthodox Christianity that had been agreed by conciliar authority had been sustained and defended constantly throughout the preceding centuries.

the determination of the Council of Chalcedon in 451, to which evangelical Christianity *is* at least formally committed, even if this may not always be strictly adhered to in practice.

Certainly, the doctrine of the two natures, given the logical implications as spelled out by Maximus in terms of two wills in Christ, picks up the Chalcedon teaching that they are not to be "confused" or, in other words, melded into a composite divine/human nature and will, which would be neither entirely and clearly divine nor entirely and clearly human. The implications of the incarnation of Christ are not to be understood in terms of a kind of single hybrid divine/human willing as a property of Christ's divine/human nature, but in terms of two identifiably different wills, a divine and a human, for, as Chalcedon concluded, Christ is *homoousios* with the Father and *homoousios* with humanity. The two natures are undivided and not separate, but neither are they changed or confused.

Even despite Chalcedon's definition of the two natures of Christ, and the drawing out of the implications of this at the Third Council of Constantinople (with the help of the teaching of Maximus) so as to arrive at the *dyothelite* definition of the two distinct wills of Christ, one divine and one human, some contemporary theologians persist in pursuing what appears to be a latent *monothelite* Christology. This is revealed in a tendency to talk of the *hypostatic* will with the resultant docetic implication that the element of human willing is minimized or even entirely eliminated from the picture.

We should not be surprised, for example, to find echoes of the operation of a tacit and latent *monothelitism* in the thinking of contemporary Carillon Avenue theology insofar as the biblical evidence that is cited in support of the "eternal relational subordination" of the Son to the Father tends to overlook the important consideration of whether specific passages refer to the historical incarnate Son and the exercise of his human will, or to the Eternal Son's exercise of his divine will whether in the economy of salvation or in his pre-incarnate life. There is, instead, a real danger in a tendency to conflate the divine and human willing of the Son, on the apparent assumption that the Son's willing is to be associated with the *hypostasis* of the Son. The problem is that the melding into a single will associated with the *hypostasis* of the Son effectively fails in practice to heed the Chalcedonian injunction to uphold the "two natures [of Christ] without confusion, without change, without division, without separation."

Likewise, Wayne Grudem says he supports belief in a single divine will of God, but nevertheless defends a kind of differentiated divine willing insofar as the "eternal functional subordination" of the Son to the Father involves making a distinction between the will of the Father and the subordinate will of the Son.

> Surely there must be some kinds of distinction in the one will of God because there is a difference between the Father's willing to send and the Son's willing to be sent. There is a difference between the Father's willing to pour out divine wrath against sin and the Son's willing to bear that wrath for our sake. There is a difference between the Father's will to say "You are my beloved son; with you I am well pleased" (Mark 1:11) and the Son's will to receive such approval as the beloved Son. There is a difference between the Son bringing requests before the Father (Heb. 7:25) and the Father hearing those requests.[92]

Once again, it appears to be assumed here that the Son's willing is associated with his *hypostatic* identity, for the doctrine of the two wills of Christ is apparently overlooked in these references that span the immanent life of the Trinity and the economy of salvation. Then, in the hope of avoiding the denial that there is one divine will, Grudem proffers the view that there can be "different expressions" of the one divine will in order to accommodate the distinction he wants to make. In other words, he says that the affirmation of one will in God does not mean that "there cannot be different expressions of that one will among the different persons in the Trinity."[93]

Grudem appears to mean that the one divine will just happens to be expressed differently by the Father in commanding and the Son in being submissively obedient to the Father's command. Thus, the commanding will of the Father and the obediently compliant will of the Son, are not to be understood as polar opposites, or different wills, but simply as "different expressions" of the one divine will! This means that the Father's commanding and the Son's dutiful compliance with commands are really just "different expressions," one active and the other passive, of the one divine will! This sounds remarkably like saying that the colors of green and red might appear to be different, and in fact opposite one another

---

92. Grudem, *Systematic Theology*, 616.
93. Grudem, *Systematic Theology*, 615.

on a color wheel, but are really not different colors but merely "different expressions" of something they have in common—that they are colors!

In the course of this the Son's divine willing, whether understood as eternal in the immanent life of the Trinity or expressed in the life of the incarnate Jesus in the economy of salvation, is handled as a single continuum of willing associated with the *hypostasis* of the Son; in this way the *dyothelite* doctrine of Christ's two wills is rendered unnecessary. Rather than a humanly submissive will and a divine will in all respects the same as the Father's will, we end with two "different expressions" of the divine will—the commanding will of the Father and the eternally submissive will of the Son. And furthermore, the eternally submissive will of the Son is exhibited both eternally within the immanent life of the Trinity and during the course of the incarnation in the economy of salvation.

This means that Grudem is necessarily obliged to stand loose to the *dyothelite* determination of the Third Council of Constantinople, and the teaching of Maximus the Confessor. It is clear that Grudem seeks to deflect the challenge to engage the conciliar determination in relation to Christ's two wills, by complaining that the council had nothing to say about his own suggestion of "different expressions" of the one divine will, as though this might have been considered as a viable option to *dyothelitism*.[94] Then, in responding to Butner's championing of *dyothelite* orthodoxy, Grudem says, "It is significant that Butner at this point appeals not to the official declarations of the Sixth Ecumenical Council"[95] but to the teaching of Maximus. Even though it is actually incorrect, for Butner does cite the determinations of the council,[96] this effectively allows Grudem to move quickly on from the determinations of the council. In any event, Grudem then damns Maximus with faint praise. First, he couples Maximus with Pope Agatho, who promoted what were essentially Maximus's views from the perspective of the West in the generation after

94. "The council declared nothing about how many different expressions of one will there could be with three persons, nor did they deny that the divine nature could have three distinctive expressions of the one will, all working in unity." Grudem, *Systematic Theology*, 618.

95. Grudem, *Systematic Theology*, 618. Also, 616: "I would say that, even if we affirm the existence of one divine will, that does not rule out the idea that each person in the Trinity can have different actualizations or different expressions of that will." Grudem then directs his readers to a previous section of his book on the unified will of God (*Systematic Theology*, 307–8).

96. Butner, *Son Who Learned Obedience*, 89.

Maximus's death.[97] Agatho then actually sent a delegation to the Third
Council of Constantinople to communicate the decision of a synod of
125 bishops in support of the definition of two wills in Christ. By way of
minimizing the importance of this whole episode in the history of orthodox christological reflection, Grudem speaks dismissively of Maximus
and Agatho as "two rather obscure figures from church history"[98] and
then roundly declares, "Their speculations regarding the doctrine of the
Trinity may be interesting, but to look to them as infallible authorities on
the Trinity is a procedure that is far removed from the direct authority of
the teachings of Scripture."[99] Once again, Grudem is confident about his
reading of what he takes to be the relevant scriptural texts relating to the
"eternal submissiveness" of the Son, and argues that "Butner's objection
that many passages that speak of the Son's obedience can be explained
with reference to his human nature only is not persuasive . . ."[100] He then
cites a number of verses. "For example," he says,

> God did not create the world "through" the human nature of
> the Son but through his divine nature (Heb. 1.2). The Father
> "chose us" in the Son "before the foundation of the world" (Eph.
> 1.4), which must refer to the divine Son (for the human nature
> did not exist at that time). When God "so loved the world that
> he gave his only Son" (John 3.16), it was not the human nature
> but the divine person of the Son whom the Father gave for
> our salvation. When God "did not spare his own Son but gave
> him up for us all" (Rom. 8.32), it was the divine Son, not just
> Christ's human nature, whom God did not spare. When Christ
> in heaven "is interceding for us" before the Father (Rom. 8.34;
> cf. Heb. 7.25), he is praying for the specific situations of millions
> of people around the world at the same time, something that
> only an infinite, divine person could do.[101]

Grudem seems to be jousting here with a man of straw. For whoever
imagined that the human nature and will of the incarnate Son was brought
into play in the creation of the world? On the other hand, when "God
gave his only Son" for the salvation of the world, how is this "giving" to be
judged to be eternal and not in history in the economy of salvation? And
it is the raised Jesus Christ who, as a result of his resurrection (which *does*

97. Maximus the Confessor died in 662; Pope Agatho was pope from 678–81.

98. Grudem, *Systematic Theology*, 618.

99. Grudem, *Systematic Theology*, 618–19.

100. Grudem, *Systematic Theology*, 619.

101. Grudem, *Systematic Theology*, 619–20.

surely involve the transformation and glorification of his human nature), now "ever lives to intercede for us." Butner's point is that these biblical references refer to Jesus the Son in his human nature and in the economy of salvation, and not necessarily to the pre-incarnate Word of God in the immanent life of the Trinity. Grudem hardly mounts a convincing response to Butner's contention that there are no uncontested biblical texts that refer to the immanent life of the Trinity rather than to the incarnate human Jesus in the economy of salvation.

⁓

Just as problematic as Grudem's entirely unconvincing appeal to these scriptural texts are the troubling dogmatic implications of Grudem's support for associating the Son's "different expression" of the one divine will with the *hypostasis* of the Son as his alternative to the orthodox tradition of two wills, one divine and one human, associated with the two natures of Christ. It is important to note a significant difference between the understanding of the concept of "wills" when associated on one hand with the two natures and when associated with the *hypostasis* of the Son simply as a "different (subordinate) expression" of the eternal divine will. When the exercise of will is associated with the *hypostasis* of the Son there is a certain indeterminate freedom of decision-making. In the case of the exercise of will associated respectively with the divine and human natures of Christ, there is an element of determinism insofar as the respective natures of Christ, whether human or divine, determine the properties appropriate to the willing respectively associated with each. The exercise of the human will of Christ, for example, is exhibited in such things as the historical Jesus' will to eat food in satisfaction of his hunger, or the will to activate his body parts (i.e., his legs) to walk from Galilee to Jerusalem. Such decisions of will are appropriate to his human nature. But they are not likewise appropriate to the divine nature that he shares with the Father. This is for the obvious reason that God has "no body, parts or passions" and his willing must take a form appropriate to his divine nature. Similarly, the miraculous exercise of the divine will, for example, to turn water into wine, is necessarily associated with Christ's divine nature.

When associated with the *hypostasis* of the Son, and dissociated from his two natures, there are no natural restraints, such as would require the willing to conform to one or the other of Christ's two natures.

Rather, the association of willing with the *hypostasis* of the Son allows for a kind of freedom in decision-making, such that "different expressions" of the one divine will become possible, whether in the internal life of the Trinity or expressed in the economy of salvation. There is a sense, then, in which nature is to necessity as *hypostasis* is to freedom. Grudem is certainly anxious to stress the free and voluntary nature of the Son's eternally obedient response to the Father.[102]

Now Grudem naturally emphasizes the element of freedom in willing decision-making associated with both the "different expressions" of will respectively of the subordinate Son and the Father.[103] However, Grudem himself had already introduced the concept of an ontological ordering of Father and the Son, which is expressed in these very terms. Unfortunately, the "subordination" or "submissiveness" of the Son is in accordance with his filial nature; it is not just randomly and freely chosen as an "expression" of the divine will by the Son. The Son is in a sense by nature programmed to be submissive. In other words, it comes naturally to the Son to be obedient, for it arises from his filial nature. In this sense, the Son's submissiveness is determined by his nature. This means that the divine nature of the Son is somehow different from the divine nature of the Father. But, if so, what has happened to the *homoousion*? Clearly, Grudem's defence of eternal functional submissiveness in response to Butner's critique leaves a great deal to be desired.

❧

Neither an eternal divine will clothed with human flesh, and a resultant human nature minus the element of human willing, nor a kind of hybrid single will of composite divine/human nature (which Chalcedon would have condemned as "confused") will ultimately be found to be christologically satisfactory. Neither of these options may be substituted for the orthodox view of the two natures and their corresponding respective properties of the two wills of Christ, a divine and a human, exercised in communion with one another, so that they are not divided or separated, but neither are they changed (by impacting negatively on one another) nor confused.

102. Grudem, *Systematic Theology*, 1327, 2792, 2794.

103. Grudem, *Systematic Theology*, 611, 616: "I would say that, even if we affirm the existence of one divine will, that does not rule out the idea that each person in the Trinity can have different actualizations or different expressions of that will."

We may, therefore, conclude that orthodox Christianity has correctly embraced the belief that the Incarnate *human* Jesus is subordinate to God, his heavenly Father. But we must be clear that this is a function of his human nature, which determines the exercise of a human willing obedience, even unto death on the cross. The divine Second Person of the Trinity, however, is not eternally subordinate to the Father, but fully equal with the Father, sharing the same undivided will with the Father, as the initiating power to accomplishing things in the world by acting indivisibly with the Father and the Holy Spirit. *Together* they may be said to will the redemption of humanity; but it is the vocation of the incarnate Christ by the determination of his human will to set his face towards Jerusalem as the one who "having loved his own, loved them unto the end," even unto death on the cross.

⌒

Those who wish to promote the notion of the eternal subordination of the Son to the Father, and who unavoidably introduce talk, whether of two different divine but complementary wills or "two different expressions" of the one divine will into the unity of the divine life, by talking of the commanding will of the Father and the submissively obedient will of the Son, stand responsible for promoting belief in a division of willing that is unfortunately vicious with respect to the unity of the divine life. In orthodox Christian belief, by contrast, there is but one divine will exercised in unity of action by all three Trinitarian identities as One God. This ensures that Christianity is essentially monotheistic. Talk of multiple wills within the internal life of the Trinity, or even multiple "different expressions" of the divine will, inevitably leads in logical terms to a kind of tritheism. This, at least in the first instance, is what is seriously wrong with belief in the "eternal subordination of the Son to the Father."

It is in the life of the incarnate Christ that it is properly said that there are two wills, a divine and a human, each belonging respectively to a divine and human nature, each with its own integrity. In his human nature the incarnate Christ is submissively obedient to the God whom he addressed as Father. Thus, the Second Person of the Trinity does not suffer in his divine nature any more than the Father suffers; it is the human Jesus in his human nature who suffers upon the cross. First Peter 4:1 makes this very clear when it is said that the Son suffers "in the flesh."

On the other hand, in his divine nature he remained unchanged as he ever was, equal with the Father. As the divine eternal Word he is not eternally submissive or subordinate to the Father, but equal (the *homoousion*). The interplay and communion of two wills in the life of the incarnate Christ are not to be projected into the interpersonal life of the immanent Trinity, so as to raise the unresolvable problem posed by trying to hold the logically competing notions of equality and submissiveness together in a (very confused) understanding of the immanent life of the Trinity.

It is simply not possible to argue that equality in terms of "being" or "essential nature" and the obvious inequality of interpersonal subordination in terms of eternal "function" or "relation" may be distinguished and held together at the same time. A major confusion is involved in holding that the willing involved in "willing obedience" that is said to be an eternal property essential to the divine nature, as something that "arises out of the very nature of his being" as Son or as something "essential to the definition of himself as Son," and at the same time to say that subordination does not belong to the being or essential nature of the Son, but is only functional. All this ultra-imaginative speculation is without biblical warrant. It is simply the result of a kind of faux theology from which we may be well advised to keep our distance.

The question that we must now face is whether adherence to this idiosyncratic belief on Carillon Avenue is rightly understood as a kind of Arianism, and as such something that should not therefore be countenanced but studiously and steadfastly avoided altogether. But first it is important to examine some additional important proposals, especially of Australian Carillon Avenue theology, in relation to the attempted justification of belief in the "eternal functional subordination" of the Son to the Father.

# Chapter 4

# "In Praise of Hierarchy"?

GIVEN THE WANT OF an uncontested biblical tradition relating to belief in the alleged "eternal subordination of the Son to the Father" in the immanent life of the Trinity, it is something of a puzzle to explain why the adherents of this problematic doctrine are so committed to it. One explanation obviously has to do with an apparent sense of historical loyalty to a theological tradition ultimately received from a hallowed teacher, which, at least in the case of Carillon Avenue theology in Australia, may be sheeted back to the federal theology of T. C. Hammond. But surely there must be some other agenda that makes the notion of "eternal relational subordination" so attractive and compelling as to lead its adherents to the mistaken conviction that the New Testament scriptural tradition actually supports it.

In the second half of the year 2002 through 2003 something of the theological reasoning behind the confident subordinationist commitments, specifically of Carillon Avenue theologians, began to surface in the life of the Anglican Church of Australia, insofar as there were indications that suggested that this novel Trinitarian teaching was logically related to an understanding of the "monarchy" of the Father. This, in turn, was linked to an expression of belief in a kind of hierarchy within the relational ordering of the Godhead. In other words, even though there may not have been many, if any, who were consciously aware of this at the time, in retrospect it can be appreciated that the Son's subordination to the Father was being conceived almost as a necessary logical outcome of the monarchical "rule" of the Father in what was in effect understood to be a hierarchy of Trinitarian persons. This was in turn thought to conform to historical Christian orthodoxy.

It was at this time that the collection of twenty-five photocopied excerpts from a variety of theological sources[1] was pulled together and distributed from the Diocese of Sydney. This document was produced in the context of mounting an immediate defensive response to the publication of Kevin Giles's *The Trinity and Subordinationism*, with its uncompromising and confronting charge of the implicit Arianism of the Sydney Doctrine Commission's Report of 1999. As has already been noted, this spiral-bound collection of excerpts was reproduced in photocopied form without a title, under a clear plastic cover over a yellow sheet that simply carried the coat of arms of the Diocese of Sydney. In this way, this document self-identified as a file of supportive material relating to the response of the Diocese of Sydney to Giles's accusations.

The collection was freely distributed to interested parties by Archbishop Peter Jensen himself, following his reading of a paper to a group of listeners who happened to be in Sydney from around Australia for a regular national meeting of Anglican Church administrative leaders.[2] Though I, for one, had not at that stage actually read Giles's book, and in this I suspect I was not alone, some twenty or so of us were happy enough to accept Peter Jensen's invitation to gather voluntarily to hear what he wanted to communicate. It was clear enough that Giles's charges were generating not a little angst within the diocese; this was obviously an important enough issue for Archbishop Jensen to want to take the opportunity of a break in the proceedings of this representative gathering of the national Church to mount an attempt to set the record straight in response to Giles's book. Needless to say, Jensen's paper was very defensive of the Sydney Doctrine Commission's Report of 1999.

Although the collection of brief excerpts was intended to support the thinking of the Sydney Doctrine Commission, it was not itself supported by a commentary of any kind; however, markings penciled in margins against selected passages, and occasional inked-in annotations, indicate that the collection was intended to garner support specifically for the legitimacy of Trinitarian subordinationism. More specifically, this document shows itself to have been designed to support belief in the

1. As mentioned in chapter 1, on p. 12 above. The excerpts are numbered 1 to 24, with one of these having two quotations—(a) and (b).

2. Possibly in 2003. It has already been signaled that this is likely to have been a meeting of the Standing Committee of the General Synod of the Anglican Church of Australia. One such meeting was held from November 8 to 10, 2003. The actual date, however, is not material.

equal divinity of all three persons of the Trinity even while maintaining, at the same time, belief in the "eternal relational subordination" of the Son and the Spirit to the Father in a set of relationships of a complementarian kind.

Having heard Jensen's paper in response to Giles, I accepted this handout and took it home to Perth where it was dutifully put away in a filing cabinet for future reference under the label of "Sydney Anglicans." There it has remained undisturbed for nearly twenty years. Upon examining it only very recently, I was frankly astonished to discover that a brief article that I had myself published prior to its production, in July of 2002, was actually included as one of the twenty-five numbered excerpts![3] Had I been aware of this at that time I would probably have taken a much more keen interest in Giles's contentions about Sydney Arianism, but at the actual time this appeared to be little more than an in-house spat amongst Australian evangelical Christians. There was not a great incentive for others of us to get immediately involved, and I had plenty of other pressing issues to claim my attention.

My own brief article was reproduced in the Sydney collection with the title "In Praise of Hierarchy"—the title under which it had originally appeared in the first edition of *Common Theology*, a journal sponsored at the time by some enterprising Australian women, and edited by Maggie Helass.[4]

I do not recall that permission was sought to reproduce it; indeed, its recent discovery in the Sydney collection of excerpts came as a complete surprise. Even so, the collection nonchalantly reproduced the entire article, apparently with no qualms about possible copyright infringement. This is not to suggest that I have any particular personal objection to its reproduction, for this was obviously without malice and was intended to serve the positive purpose of making the article easily accessible to anybody interested in the Sydney response to Giles's charges. That said, I have had quietly to bite my bottom lip, for whether what I had written in "In Praise of Hierarchy" in July of 2002 actually supports the complementarian propositions of the Sydney approach to the subordination of the Son to the Father in the immanent life of the Trinity is, at least to my own mind, entirely problematic.

3. Excerpt 21.

4. Although this journal is no longer being published, its archive of articles is still available online. See *Common Theology*, ed., Maggie Helass, 1/1, July 2002, at commontheology.com, Archive of vols. 1–3.

↜

This collection of theological excerpts has not been of great public consequence, given that it was privately circulated, initially to the small group
of people who heard Archbishop Jensen's response to Kevin Giles's critique, and otherwise possibly to an unknown number of people within
the Diocese of Sydney. It is of some interest today, however, as an index to
the thinking behind the obviously sincerely held commitment of Carillon Avenue theologians to complementarian subordinationism. This is
because an obvious common theme of the reproduced excerpts has to
do with the logical connection that was being forged at the time between
the "eternal functional subordination of the Son to the Father" and the
historical theological tradition of the "monarchy of the Father" as the
basis of a belief in the validity of a conception of the internal ordering of
the Trinity as a kind of "hierarchy."

Before we turn to examine the theological method and the argument
that I myself followed in "In Praise of Hierarchy," with a view to judging
whether it might legitimately be brought to the support of "eternal functional subordinationism" (which I very much doubt), it may be useful to
examine some of the other excerpts that were collected and republished
under the identifying crest of the Diocese of Sydney in 2002/3. In doing
so, we need to ask whether these collected excerpts in fact support belief
in the "eternal functional subordination of the Son to the Father."

It is, at the outset, worth noting that, while the authors of many
of these excerpts are certainly prepared to speak of the priority of the
Father as the "origin" and "cause" of the divine being of the Son and the
Spirit, and to accept this as the exercise of a kind of "monarchy" on the
part of the Father, these authors tend (at least in the quoted passages) to
steer well clear of explicit talk of any kind of "hierarchy" in the internal
life of the Trinity. Moreover, the capacity of these excepts to demonstrate
the validity of "eternal functional subordinationism" is certainly not immediately self-evident.

Admittedly, in appealing to the notion of the "monarchy" of the
Father in relation to the Son, many of the quoted authorities do seem
prepared openly to admit that this implies some kind of "subordination"
of the Son to the Father.[5] In doing so, however, they are careful to make

---

5. That *some kind* of subordination is involved is not contentious. John Ziziouslas,
for example, is prepared to say: "In making the Father the 'ground' of God's being—or
the ultimate reason for existence—theology accepted a kind of subordination of the

it perfectly clear that they are referring to a highly specific and nuanced kind of "subordinationism," rather than simply to subordinationism of an undifferentiated or generic kind that might then be said specifically to support the "eternal functional subordination" of the Son to the Father, particularly insofar as this involves the involvement of two wills, the commanding will of the Father and the obediently submissive will of the Son.

One of the quoted authors, Geoffrey Wainwright,[6] cautiously speaks, for example, of what he terms a *"measure of subordinationism,"* which, he says, "has its place in orthodox trinitarian doctrine, where the Father remains 'the fount of deity' in relation to the other two Persons." Similarly G. W. Bromiley[7] speaks of the same Trinitarian reality in terms of "a superiority and *subordination of order."* Clearly, a very specific kind of subordination is in mind.

Another of the authors, H. E. W. Turner, in an entry for "Subordinationism" that originally appeared in Alan Richardson's *Dictionary of Christian Theology,*[8] is similarly specific when he declares that there is an orthodox subordinationism "in the sense that the Trinity must begin with the Father or lead up to the Father." But he explains this as a kind of subordinationism only insofar as this is concerned with *"order of thought and unity in derivation* and does not affect the ontological status of the three Persons." Indeed, he might well have affirmed that the uncompromised sharing of the Father's divine nature with the Son and the Spirit by virtue of *its original derivation from the Father,* actually secures the ontological status and *equality* of the three persons!

In the same vein, Emil Brunner[9] affirms the traditional view that "God *gives* to the Son deity from all eternity." He then hastens to add: "This 'Subordinationism' does not eliminate the 'ομοουσιος.'" Indeed, far from not eliminating the Nicene definition of the *homoousion,* the Father's role as "origin" and "source" of the deity of the Son and the Spirit may be said to be precisely what secures the *homoousion.* In other words, the divine persons of the Trinity are one in Being (or of the same substance), not in spite of being three, but by virtue of being indivisibly

Son to the Father without being obliged to downgrade the *Logos* into something created." *Being as Communion,* 89.

6. Excerpt 10 in the collection.

7. Excerpt 7.

8. Excerpt 6.

9. Excerpt 2.

three, with all three Trinitarian identities sharing a common life and the very same divine nature because of their original derivation from a single source—hence the monarchy of the Father.

Likewise, some historical quotations reproduced from the seventeenth-century Anglican Bishop George Bull, in his *Defensio Fidei Nicaenae*,[10] affirm that "the divine nature and perfections belonged to the Father and the Son, not collaterally or co-ordinately, but subordinately . . . the Father is the fountain, origin and principle of the divinity which is in the Son." In addition, Bull says, "When the Son is said to be the next and second after the Father, the subordination of the Persons is expressed, so far forth as one has His origin from the Other." And it is important to note that Bull goes on to say that this is positively not to suggest "any inequality of nature in the Divine Persons." Rather, it is simply that "God the Father . . . is the fountain and origin, as of the Essence, so also of the Divine operations."

Without having to compile an exhaustive catalogue of similar references, it is already clear that the theological sources collected and republished under the identifying logo of the Diocese of Sydney regularly mention a specific *kind* of "subordinationism" in a highly cautious and circumscribed way. The authors quoted do not explicitly support the "eternal subordination of the Son to the Father" as something involving the exercise of two wills, the commanding will of the Father and the obediently compliant will of the Son, and there is no suggestion of an eternal relationship of domination and submission. Rather, the kind of subordination that these authors have in mind relates to the monarchy of the Father in the highly specific sense that the Father is the "origin" and "cause" of the Son and the Spirit, and thus the source of the *equally shared divine nature* of the Son and the Spirit. This is an unmistakable restatement of a basic point insisted upon by the Cappadocian fathers in the fourth century, and a reaffirmation of the importance of the Nicene *homoousion*. There is no joy here for those anxious to garner support for belief in the "eternal functional subordination" of the Son to the Father that grounds the contention that the Father commands and the Son dutifully obeys in an eternal relationship of domination and submission.

Even despite the obvious caution of most of the references in the Sydney collection, however, it seemed to be assumed that the use of the related terms "monarchy" and "subordination" in the specific context

10. Excerpt 14.

of the understanding of the relation of the Son as "begotten of the Father" and of the Spirit as "proceeding from the Father," were sufficient to warrant belief in a type of hierarchy of persons bound together in a set of functional relationships of a complementary kind. Furthermore, it seemed to be assumed that this involved the subordination of the Son and Spirit in their alleged eternal obedient response to the commanding authority of the Father. This is proposed even in the face of the fact that this is actually inimical to the orthodox insistence on the ontological equality of all three persons of the Trinity as this has been defined from Nicaea onwards at least. One of the excerpts actually spells this out: The reproduced entry under "subordination" in *Hastings Dictionary of Religion and Ethics*[11] quotes the doctrinal explanation of Nicene definition by R. L. Ottley, who noted that

> The Father (ὁ θεός, αὐτόθεος) is the fountainhead or root of Deity. . . . The Son and the Spirit, though co-equal and co-eternal, are subordinate in rank, because the divine essence in them is derived from the Father. So in the language of the Nicene theologians, the Father alone is ἀγέννητος, the Son is γέννητος: the Father αἴτιος, the Son αἰτιατός. . . . the Son is of divine essence (θεός). . . . As the original source of the Son's Deity, the Father may be termed "greater" than the Son. . . . The subordination is a τάξις not of time, but involved in the relationship of cause and effect. Such subordination is entirely compatible with equality of essence and majesty.

⸃

The one clear exception to the caution exhibited by most authors whose work is represented in these theological excerpts collected together by the Diocese of Sydney is that of T. C. Hammond, whose unqualified declaration of the subordination of the Son is included as the final excerpt in the collection.[12] He is, indeed, given the last word: the concluding excerpt of the collection, which was taken from Hammond's *In Understanding Be Men*, is his forthright assertion in clear and categorical terms, which is quoted as the last resounding flourish to the collection. In Hammond's words, the "full Christian doctrine" (of the Trinity) "demands all three of the following":

11. Excerpt 5.
12. Excerpt 24.

(a) The Unity of the Godhead.

(b) The full Deity of the Son (who was "begotten") and of the Spirit (who "proceeds" from the Father and the Son).

(c) The subordination of the Son and the Spirit to the Father.[13]

These words of T. C. Hammond were also quoted with approval by the authors of the 1999 Sydney Doctrine Commission Report, who clearly believed that they could hold all three propositions together in such a way as to affirm "eternal functional subordination" without compromising the equality of all three Trinitarian identities in being and nature, and hence in authority, status, and dignity. The absence of any explanatory commentary, however, means that just how propositions (b) and (c) above may be held together along with proposition (a) remains undefined.

At the outset, the 1999 Report of the Sydney Doctrine Commission asserted that the danger of heresy at this point is met by its prior insistence that the Son and the Spirit are "of one being" with the Father (the *homoousion*), and that there is therefore no "*essential* subordination" within the immanent Trinity but only a *functional* subordination. Curiously, insofar as the excerpts in this collection speak of a kind of subordination that inheres in the fact that the Father is the origin and cause of the Son and the Spirit and so ensures their equally shared divine nature, they are speaking ontologically but not functionally. Matters of ontological origin and subsequent relationality and functionality are obviously two different things. But in the thinking of Carillon Avenue theologians generally, including those who authored the Sydney Doctrine Commission Report, this is inverted. The Trinitarian identities are said *not* to be ontologically subordinate (even on the basis of the Father being the "origin" and "cause" of the Son and the Spirit?) but they are said to be functionally and relationally subordinate. Then, however, the report actually contradicts itself when it goes on to declare, "The Son's obedience to the Father arises from the very nature of his being as Son." In other words, it is natural to him "to submit to his Father" for what is natural is necessary to his identity. Indeed, the Son appears somehow to be ontologically programmed to function in a particular way in his inner being: "He is incapable of doing other than the Father's will." Clearly, these are

13. Hammond, *In Understanding Be Men*, 67 (56 of the edition quoted elsewhere in this book).

ontological assertions about the essential "nature" of the eternal being of the Son. The report is no longer speaking of obedient subordinate behavior in simply functional terms that are incidental to or independent of the "essential being" of the Son. But this is a kind of subordination that goes well beyond the fact that the Father is the "origin" and "cause" of the other two identities, thus ensuring their equal nature and authority. Indeed, by introducing functional or relational considerations involving domination and submission into the understanding of the divine life, inevitably presupposing two wills (the commanding will of the Father and the obediently subordinate will of the Son and the Spirit), interpersonal equality gives way to complementarianism.

We can, however, be very clear that none of this is actually supported by the theological authorities represented in the collected excerpts which were published under the badge of the Diocese of Sydney in 2002/3. Although this collection was made apparently with a view to defending the Sydney Doctrine Commission in the face of Kevin Giles's trenchant criticisms of its 1999 report in *The Trinity and Subordinationism*, the excerpts (like Giles!) are clear in their affirmation of belief in Trinitarian equality. To try to bring them to the support of complementarianism is highly problematic.

⌇

What then is to be made of the inclusion of my own brief article entitled "In Praise of Hierarchy" in this same photocopied set of excerpts from the writing of authors allegedly supportive of "eternal functional subordination"?

Given that this privately published collection of sources was without a supportive commentary, we have been obliged to infer that it was hoped that the accumulated thrust of these collected excerpts would build support for belief in the functional subordination of the Son to the Father. By putting two and two together, we can justifiably conclude that it was also assumed that "In Praise of Hierarchy" could likewise be brought to the support of complementarian subordinationism. In other words, the inclusion of this article in the Sydney collection does not appear to have been motivated by the need to provide some kind of balance, or alternative voice to sources thought to be supportive of subordinationism. It seems, rather, that it was apparently assumed to be self-evident that the bare mention of a kind of "hierarchy" was sufficient warrant for believing that it automatically also supported belief in the Son's eternal relation of obedient subordination to the Father, and furthermore, that this may be conceived in functional terms that are said somehow to be entirely independent of the ontological equality of the three divine persons. Alas, if this was so, it was an entirely mistaken assumption.

In actuality, "In Praise of Hierarchy" went to great lengths to make the point that references to *a specific kind of hierarchy*, one that is logically implicit in ontological talk of the monarchy of the Father as the "origin" or "cause" of the divine being of the other two persons, is designed in orthodox Trinitarian theology precisely to safeguard the essential ontological equality of the Son and the Spirit with the Father. It has nothing to do with the complementarian view of "eternal subordination of the Son to the Father" that is expressed in the Son's alleged willing compliance with the commanding will of the Father as his superior in a functional relation of domination and submission. This means that, in fact, "In Praise of Hierarchy"'is really of no positive use whatever as a support for the spurious thesis of complementarian subordinationism.

To the contrary, on any fair-minded reading of this brief *Common Theology* article it will be acknowledged that its purpose was entirely different. I had specifically taken issue with some ecclesiological proposals of Jürgen Moltmann, who had argued in his important book *The Trinity and the Kingdom* that hierarchically organized churches, with bishops and primates (not to mention the papal sovereignty of the modern Vatican State), had quite unjustifiably developed highly questionable models of Christian ministry on the basis of an insufficiently Trinitarian understanding of the nature of God. In other words, the hierarchically organized ministries of some churches were said by Moltmann to arise from a fundamental, but, in his view, mistaken, commitment to a "Christian monotheism" that was alleged to concentrate attention on the unity of the one God as the almighty ruler of all—whom Moltmann tended to conceive as a kind of autocrat.

Monarchical bishops were, evidently, thought by Moltmann to rule over their flocks in an analogous autocratic way. In place of the threefold episcopally led and hierarchically ordered ministry of bishops, priests, and deacons, he therefore proposed a more egalitarian model of Christian ministry, along with more democratically organized synodical methods of decision-making in the church.

To Moltmann's mind, it is the absolute monarchy of monotheism that "provides the justification for earthly domination—religious, moral, patriarchal or political domination—and makes it a hierarchy, a 'holy rule.'" "As long as the unity of the triune God is understood monadically," he says, ". . . a religious legitimation of political sovereignty continues to exist. It is only when the doctrine of the Trinity vanquishes the mono-theistic notion of the great universal monarch in heaven . . . that earthly rulers cease to find any justifying religious archetypes any more."[14] Molt-mann thus speaks of monotheistic Monarchianism as "an uncommonly seductive religious-political ideology" that the early church was only able to overcome through the doctrine of the equality of persons in the Trinity.[15]

In response to these provocative Moltmannian proposals, I had cited facets of the doctrine of the Trinity, over and above the fundamen-tal equality of persons within the Godhead, as indicators of an alterna-tive way of looking at things. In particular, I pointed to the importance of the traditional belief in the monarchy of the Father in relation to the other two persons, for it has been long held that the Father is the source of the divinity of the Son, who, as Scripture has it, "is the only begot-ten *of the Father*," and also the source of the equal divinity of the Spirit who "proceeds ineffably *from the Father*." This aspect of Trinitarian de-scription was cited in a quest to defend the legitimate place of bishops as "fathers-in-God" in the leadership of the church, as against a kind of an exclusively monochrome egalitarianism in ministry. The contention was that, even in churches with a long-established tradition of synodical decision-making, such as the national and regional churches of my own Anglican tradition, there is a place for the specific ministry of leadership of the bishop; such churches are "*synodically governed*, but *episcopally led*." This is the specific and highly nuanced kind of "hierarchy" to which appeal was made in the article bearing the title of "In Praise of Hierarchy."

〜

Kevin Giles, who in the course of his vigorous critique of Trinitarian subordinationism became an arch-critic of all forms of hierarchy, was

14. Moltmann, *Trinity and the Kingdom*, 197.

15. Moltmann, *Trinity and the Kingdom*, 131. As it transpires Moltmann appears to have acquired these views from Erik Peterson, *Der Monotheismus als politisches Problem* (1935). In 1971 Moltmann described Peterson's thesis as "magnificent" ("Po-litical Theology," 11). See Randall Otto's resounding critique in "Moltmann and the Anti-Monotheist Movement," 294 and 306–7.

invited to respond to "In Praise of Hierarchy" in the *Forum* section of
the Advent edition of *Common Theology* in the same year. He did so with
a piece entitled "In Praise of Egalitarianism," which in broad terms was
supportive of Moltmann's condemnation of any hierarchical ordering of
ecclesial ministry. This brief article was also reproduced in the Sydney
compendium as a concession to even-handedness, even if its conclusions
may not have been positively endorsed.[16]

In one way Giles's position is predictable, for in his sustained critique
of the alleged Arianism of the Sydney Doctrine Commission, he has been
consistently uncompromising in pointing to the equal status and authority of the persons of the Trinity as a token of Christian orthodoxy. In his
critique of subordinationist teaching he has, as a consequence, strenuously shunned all forms of hierarchical arrangement within the Trinity.
In relation to the egalitarianism of the ordering of ecclesial ministry,
although he himself ministers under the authority of a diocesan bishop
in Melbourne, he therefore assumed a position that was sympathetic to
Moltmann's proposals, and for basically the same Trinitarian-based reasons. On this occasion he was even prepared to declare that "Athanasius,
Augustine, Aquinas, Calvin, Barth, Rahner, and all the modern day expositions of the Trinity seem to be of one mind in rejecting hierarchical
ordering in the Trinity." Only what he spoke of as the "personal identity"
of the Son as given by the Father could be tolerated, for to be called "Son"
one must have a father—and vice versa, to be called "Father" one must
have a son (or daughter). The Father thus gives the Son a distinctive filial
identity, but, said Giles, the "divine being of the Son is derived from none.
He is God in his own right from all eternity."

Whether the early church fathers would have been prepared to accept the proposition that "the divine being" of the Son was not received
along with his filial identity as a consequence of the Father's begetting of
his "only begotten Son" from all eternity is a moot point. An immediate
problem may be detected here insofar as what appears to be the suggestion of a kind of Father-Son relatedness that is *incidental* to the Son's self-
generated "divine being." This could be taken to mean that the unity of
the three persons may be in danger of being compromised. If the *essential*
divine being of the Son, and of the Spirit, is not acknowledged to have
been received from the Father, with the simultaneous effect of sharing in
the very same essential nature by all Trinitarian identities, how are we to

16. Excerpt 22.

secure the essential unity of the Trinity? Furthermore, Giles's talk of the Son as one whose "divine being" is said to derive from no one may be troublesome insofar as it seems to suggest that the Son is somehow independently self-existent, which is in logical tension with his *origin* as the only begotten Son of the Father, and this inevitably leads to suggestions of a kind of tritheism. We shall need to return to this.

⤸

Meanwhile, it is understandable that Sydney theologians had apparently sought to corral my argument about a kind of hierarchy within the Trinity so as to use it as a weapon against Giles's egalitarianism, and hence as a support for their adamant refutation of his charge of Arianism. As a consequence, there was an understandable logic behind the reproduction of both these *Common Theology* articles, side by side in the Diocese of Sydney's collection of photocopied references. It certainly appears to have been assumed that *any* defense of a kind of hierarchy within the Trinity could legitimately be pressed into service as a support for the subordinationism of the original Sydney Doctrine Commission's Report of 1999, thus to assist the cause of helping the report to wriggle free from the charge of Arianism that Giles had raised against it.

Not long after, an Anglican Media Sydney posting of November 26, 2002 explicitly said as much. The following paragraph is notable:

> Archbishop Peter Carnley unwittingly in a recent paper rather provocatively entitled "In Praise of Hierarchy," argues that it is "an essential element within orthodox Trinitarianism" that there is a kind of monarchy within the Trinity, "the monarchy of the Father with respect to the other two persons within the Divine Unity." He has in mind the teaching that the Father "enjoys a certain priority as the 'origin' or 'sole cause' of the other two Persons," the very point made by the Doctrine Commission.'

This summing up of the basic contentions of "In Praise of Hierarchy" is fair and reasonable. Whether this was in fact "the very point" made by the Sydney Doctrine Commission is a moot point, particularly given the commission's determination to go beyond the biblical tradition of the Father as the one who "begets the Son" and the Son as his "only begotten" by adding the defining property of the power of command in the case of the Father and "obedient submissiveness to the Father" as the defining property in the case of the Son. Even so, while acknowledging that "Peter Carnley wants to draw implications for the leadership of bishops," the posting went on to say that the theological method of "In Praise of Hierarchy" "is not dissimilar" to that pursued by the Sydney Doctrine Commission!

Like it or not, I had been press-ganged into the support of a position with regard to which I actually entertain very serious reservations. The specifics of the appropriation of "In Praise of Hierarchy" in Sydney therefore obviously need to be carefully scrutinized. For whether it is in fact the case that the contention that the Father enjoys a certain logical priority with respect to the Son and the Spirit, as the *"origin"* or *"cause"* of their divine being, is really capable of justifying the kind of eternal *subordination* of the Son and the Spirit to the Father, in a moral and functional relationship of domination and submission, continues to be a matter of contention. And this is not to mention the attempt of the report of the Sydney Doctrine Commission, and of Carillon Avenue theology generally, to utilize this questionable Trinitarian teaching in order to justify a complementarian understanding of the interpersonal relationships of men and women.

᠊᠊ᡐ

Three years later (in 2005) there was a further twist in this minor episode, when Dr. Peter Adam published remarks sympathetic to complementarianism that he had originally made at the Melbourne Colloquium on the Trinity in September 2004.[17] He publicly announced that he had been told that I had since "retracted" the idea of a hierarchy within the Trinity—to assert the authority of bishops within the church.

While I do not consider this to be deliberately mischievous generation of misinformation, it was nevertheless a piece of "fake news." Unfortunately this is a measure of the fact that a regrettable carelessness characterized the handling of truth in theological conversation at the time. This is exemplified also in an account of this same episode by Michael Jensen in his book *Sydney Anglicanism: An Apology* (2012). In this book he goes beyond the rumor reported by Peter Adam, by imagining that an alleged "change of mind" on my part was actually triggered by Kevin Giles's forthright critique of the Sydney Doctrine Commission

17. To which reference has already been made in chapter 1, pages 19–20 above.

Report.[18] Obviously, without troubling to check the factuality of what he was reporting, Jensen said: "Australian Anglican Primate Archbishop Peter Carnley, who had originally outlined a hierarchical trinitarianism in support of a hierarchy of ministries, saw in Giles's accusation an opportunity too good to miss and so changed his mind, accusing Sydney of Arianism in his 2004 book *Reflections in Glass*."[19]

It needs to be said that this is entirely fanciful. If the truth be known, I had not actually had time to study Giles's book in any detail in 2004 when *Reflections in Glass* was written, let alone use it as "an opportunity too good to miss" to join Giles in a chorus of accusation directed at Sydney's alleged Arianism. There is only one passing reference to Giles in the relevant chapter of *Reflections in Glass*,[20] and no references to Giles's spat with the Sydney Doctrine Commission.

More importantly, I have never retracted the ecclesiological thesis of "In Praise of Hierarchy" and remain prepared to defend it as a legitimate alternative to Moltmann's use of a Trinitarian analogy to argue for a wholly egalitarian and democratic ordering of Christian ministry and ecclesial decision-making. My actual contention was, and still is, that the ordering of the Trinitarian identities may legitimately be drawn upon by analogy to argue for an episcopal ordering of ministry in the church. Insofar as the Father is the monarch, the eternal source of the divine Son (who is begotten of the Father), and the source also of the Holy Spirit (who proceeds ineffably from the Father), the Father has a logical priority as the *origin* and *cause* of the divinity of the other two trinitarian identities. There *is* a kind of hierarchy here: it is for this reason we thus speak of the Father as the First Person, the Son as the Second Person, and the Holy Spirit as the Third Person of the Trinity.

By analogy, this grounds the vision of an interpersonal ordering of ecclesial ministry in which the leadership of the bishop is exercised as the "first amongst equals." This is particularly the case when he or she acts as the minister of order and, in a certain sense, as the "origin" and

18. In Giles, *Trinity and Subordinationism*.

19. Jensen, *Sydney Anglicanism*, 134.

20. In chapter 7, on page 136, where the reference actually signals disagreement with Giles's contention that "the scriptural revelation can be trusted to 'accurately reveal the full truth about the triune God.'" Obviously even when revealed God is disclosed as a mystery that is beyond the limits of finite minds. Even the finite words of Scripture are incapable of revealing the "full truth" of the infinite mystery of the Triune God.

"cause" of the surrogate ministries of priests and deacons who, indeed, receive their holy orders by being ordained by him or her. A diocesan bishop is "the ordinary"—the source of order in this sense. This ministry is also exercised when he or she presides at worship and other church gatherings, and not least when he or she exercises a presidential role in community decision-making at a diocesan synod. This ministry of leadership is not exercised autocratically, however, but precisely as a service to the community.

In other words, contrary to Moltmann, the orthodox doctrine of the Trinity may actually provide us with the model of a legitimate *kind* of hierarchy within the life of the Christian community. However, whether this is the kind of moral hierarchy that is expressive of a relation of domination and submission, characterized by the power of command before which others must click their heels and make an obediently submissive response, is another matter.

This means, as we saw in the preceding chapter of this book, the kind of hierarchy that implies the interpersonal subordination of one person as the inferior of a superior in a relation of domination and submission, may rightly be resisted as inappropriate both in our perception of the divine life and by analogy in the ecclesial life of the interpersonal communion of the baptized.

We may well heed Moltmann's point, that a defective view of God should not be used to justify the imperfect and flawed interpersonal relationships of domination and submission in this world, wherever they may be found. But that does not mean that the church does not need leaders who are committed to a ministry of service for the good ordering and harmony of the life of the worshipping community. Likewise, the secular organizations of the world regularly need leaders in order to achieve their corporately shared goals. At the very least, we need to be careful not to import the fractured and imperfect interpersonal dysfunction within the human relationships of this world into the inner life of God.

⤿

From this perspective we may now say a little more by way of detailed amplification in response to the contentions of Moltmann about the ecclesial implications of the doctrine of the Trinity. The first thing to be said is that all the while Moltmann works with a very negative and highly stereotypical view of the single ruler, who is characterized, whether in church or state, chiefly in terms of the category of "domination." This is said to be projected into the Godhead. Indeed "the idea of the almighty ruler of the universe everywhere requires abject servitude," he says, "because it points to complete dependency in all spheres of life."[21] The monarchical episcopate, and its extension in the idea of primacy within a college of bishops, thus also tends to be associated with "political dictatorship" and "the terror of naked force" that keep people in abject and groveling servitude and dependency.

Moltmann's conviction was that this entirely unwelcome "political and clerical monotheism" in state and church respectively, which is rooted in what he regards as an entirely mistaken theology of the "universal monarchy of one God," could, however, be overcome by appealing to the doctrine of the Trinity. It is just not possible, Moltmann says, "to form the figure of the omnipotent, universal monarch, who is reflected in earthly rulers out of the unity of the Father, the Son and the Holy Spirit."[22] Rather, in the sphere of the state, the unity of the equal persons of the Trinity will be reflected in a spontaneously harmonious social consensus (one may be forgiven for suspecting Moltmann has the liberal democratic republicanism of the modern Western world in mind). Likewise, if the church is to be "a community free of dominion" it must be "without supremacy and without subjection."[23] It follows that "the presbyteral and synodal church order and the leadership based on brotherly advice are the forms of organisation that best correspond to the doctrine of the social Trinity."[24] The monarchical episcopate in a local church or diocese, and worse, the primacy of one senior bishop amongst diocesan bishops in a national or regional church, not to mention the universalist claims to immediate jurisdiction of an absolutist papacy, all fail to reflect the essential reciprocity of distinct persons of equal status and divinity in the unity of the Trinity.

╭╮

In terms of theological method, Moltmann acknowledges that it is difficult to track the exact nature of the interdependent relationship between

---

21. Moltmann, *Trinity and the Kingdom*, 192.
22. Moltmann, *Trinity and the Kingdom*, 197.
23. Moltmann, *Trinity and the Kingdom*, 192.
24. Moltmann, *Trinity and the Kingdom*, 202.

religious and political ideas. Whether economic and political realities of earth reflect and reproduce the superstructure of religion, or whether a projected religious and metaphysical reality is constructed on analogy with the economic and political world, is not easy to determine. Almost certainly, a reciprocal influence and conditioning is more likely, he says, in which affinities, correspondences, and interdependencies emerge.[25] That said, in the course of his argument it becomes obvious that Moltmann's *Tendenz* is to emphasize the conditioning of the political and earthly by fundamental religious and heavenly ideas and doctrines rather than *vice versa*. In other words, he begins with the Christian understanding of the nature of God, and then, secondarily, moves to speak derivatively of the nature of the church; indeed, for him ecclesiology is a subcategory of Trinitarian theology.[26]

This quasi-platonic approach to an understanding of the church, that emerges derivatively and not just analogically, from the doctrine of God, is said to be grounded in Scripture and the patristic tradition. It is not just the product of a modern gratuitously free-flowering of the analogical imagination. Thus, for example, in John 17 Christ prays that his disciples may all be one, "as I and the Father are one" and that they may be in the Father and the Son as "you, Father, are in me and I in you." This suggests that the newly created human communion in Christ is to be understood as being grounded in the communion of God. As 1 John puts it: our *koinonia* is not just with one another; "our *koinonia* is with the Father and his Son Jesus Christ" (1 John 1:3, 6–7). Cyprian could say, as a consequence, that "the Church is the people that draws its unity from the unity of the Father, the Son and the Holy Spirit." It is not just that the church "reflects" something of the divine in its own structures, for it is much more a matter of participation through baptism in an interpersonal relatedness that flows from the divine, the church being a creation of divine grace. The gospel is an invitation to have to do with God in trusting faith, and baptism into Christ is the means of incorporation into the divine life. As 2 Peter 1:4 puts it, in the church "we are partakers of the divine nature."

---

25. Moltmann, *Trinity and the Kingdom*, 193.

26. See for example, Moltmann, *Triunity and the Kingdom*, 191–92: "The notion of a divine monarchy in heaven and on earth, for its part, generally provides the justification for earthly domination—religious, moral, patriarchal or political domination—and makes it a hierarchy, a 'holy rule.'"

For Moltmann, this means that the doctrine of the Trinitarian nature of God should remind us that in God there is neither hierarchy nor inequality, neither division nor competition, but only unity in love amongst a diversity of distinguishable persons of equal status, and that the church should express the same reality in its life. On the basis of this kind of ecclesiological thrust Moltmann then goes on to argue that the unity of Being amongst the diverse persons of the Trinity is a quite different kind of unity from the absolute monarchy of the one God of "monarchical monotheism," and, very importantly, that it leads to a set of quite different ecclesiological and political implications from those that flow from a rigidly unitarian monotheism. Indeed, the "monarchical monotheism" to which Moltmann takes exception is said to be one of the ancient heresies that constitute "permanent dangers to Christian theology," for it leads right into what amounts to a form of political and ecclesial totalitarianism.

⮑

It is important to pause at this point to note, however, that, for Moltmann's conclusions to be sustained his argument involves a specific *kind* of Monarchianism. It is more precisely the kind of Monarchianism in the ancient church that sought to uphold the single and unitary nature of God by denying distinctions within the inner life of God. Such Monarchianism was a feature of theology, for example, in the third century at the height of the popularity of modalistic theories of the kind promoted by Sabellius, who reduced the distinctions between Father, Son, and Spirit to different and successive operations of the one God.

The same initial commitment to the absolute divine sovereignty of one God without any internal differentiation of persons was also understood to be a feature of the subordinationism attributed to Arius early in the next century. Insofar as Arius contended that the Word that was active in creation and incarnate in Christ was not "eternally begotten" but "made" by the exercise of the creative will of Father, and so found it impossible to classify the Word as being of the very same substance as the Father, he was in effect defending the ineffable and sovereign transcendence of the one God.

The kind of Monarchianism that Moltmann has in mind thus involves the heresy of, in one way or another, denying Trinitarian belief as in these classical ancient deviations from Christian orthodoxy. While we may accept this point, it is of some concern that at Moltmann's hands Ignatius of Antioch also tends to get tarred with the same brush! Indeed, Ignatius is explicitly identified as one who worked with the kind of defective Christian monotheism that Moltmann particularly has in his sights.[27] Ignatius is also said to provide a clear illustration of the ensuing ecclesiological error that Moltmann wishes to condemn, for at a number of points Ignatius draws an overt analogy between belief in the sovereignty of the one God and the monarchy of the bishop "presiding in the place of God," as the one in the local church or diocese "who rules over all." Whatever we may think concerning this assessment of Ignatius, it is clear that a Monarchianism, understood in the sense of the autocratic rule of a single person in the ancient church that accentuated belief in God as an absolute monad without distinctions within the unity, is the specific kind of monarchical belief that Moltmann contends gets reflected in dictatorial and domineering political leadership in the state, and in the similar tendency to the autocratic and authoritarian episcopal hierarchy of bishops in the church.

It is very important to observe, however, another kind of Monarchianism, which is entirely free of the taint of ancient heresy and which, indeed, is not only compatible with Trinitarian belief but, in fact, an essential element within orthodox Trinitarianism. This is precisely the more characteristically Cappadocian idea of the monarchy, not of one God with respect to the created order, but the mon-archy or "rule" of the Father precisely as the "origin" and "cause" of the other two persons within the Divine Unity. This is the kind of mon-archianism that, as we have seen, is tolerated and even spoken of as grounding a kind of circumscribed and qualified "subordinationism" with respect to the Son by the authors whose work was chosen for inclusion in the collection of references for the Diocese of Sydney, even if it was mistakenly assumed to be supportive explicitly of "eternal functional subordination." It is also analogous to the *kind* of Monarchianism within a hierarchically ordered episcopal ministry that was defended in "In Praise of Hierarchy."

Interestingly enough, exception is not actually taken to this kind of Monarchianism, even by Jürgen Moltmann himself. Thus, in his criticism

---

27. Moltmann, *Trinity and the Kingdom*, 200.

of the Western innovation of the double procession of the Holy Spirit from both the Father and the Son (or *Filioque*), Moltmann somewhat surprisingly, but unequivocally, affirms the sovereignty of the Father: "The uniqueness of the procession of the Spirit from the Father (and therefore the 'sole causality' of the Father in respect of the Spirit)," he says, "has in fact never been disputed by theologians of the Western Church."[28] Despite the Western *filioque* "there are not two sources of the Godhead." "It has never been denied in the West that the Son (John 16:27) and the Holy Spirit (John 15:26) proceed from the Father, each in his own way; and that therefore the Father is—in different ways—the 'origin' of them both."[29] This means that the eternal priority, or the "divine causality" of the Father with respect to both the Son and the Spirit is rightly maintained, and Moltmann therefore concludes that the "Filioque was never directed against the 'monarchy' of the Father."[30] Clearly, despite Moltmann's uncompromising critique of "monotheistic Monarchianism," there is in the doctrine of the Trinity itself an alternative expression of monarchy which even he judges to be acceptable.

It follows that, despite Moltmann's abhorrence of notions of "hierarchy," he does nevertheless admit that this *kind* of hierarchy is admissible within Trinitarian description: the Father enjoys a certain priority as the "origin" or "sole cause" of the other two persons. This means that "The Father, being himself without origin, was always the *first* Person in the Trinity"[31] (my italics). He is *autotheos*.[32] In other words, the *aseity* of God, the absolute uniqueness of his "being from himself" initially flows from the idea of the self-existing divine causality of the Father. It is of huge importance, however, to note that this species of divine causation and monarchy does *not* mean to suggest the kind of subordination of the Son to the Father, which expresses a moral relationship on the spectrum of domination and submission, command and obedience, that implies the complementarity of two divine wills. Rather, an essential divine nature is *equally* shared by the Father and the other two persons in such a way that both the Son and the Holy Spirit are "of the same substance" with the Father, and therefore of equal status and dignity; they are of one heart

28. Moltmann, *Trinity and the Kingdom*, 182.

29. Moltmann, *Trinity and the Kingdom*, 182.

30. Moltmann, *Trinity and the Kingdom*, 182.

31. Moltmann, *Trinity and the Kingdom*, 182.

32. Moltmann, *Trinity and the Kingdom*, 182.

and one mind, and function together in accordance with a single and undivided will.

It is important to say that there is a sense in which the Father does not somehow "possess" a divine nature that he then shares with the other two divine persons; rather, the timelessly eternal begetting of the Son and the eternal procession of the Spirit from the Father means that as divine persons together they "simultaneously" possess the same divine nature. Far from providing justifying grounds for the legitimacy of belief in the subordination of the Son and the Spirit to the Father, the kind of hierarchy that speaks of the Father as the "origin" and "cause" of the divine being of the Son and the Spirit thus secures their equality with him as sharers of one and the same divine nature (the *homoousion*). If the Father is spoken of as the *First* Person of the Trinity, he is the first among *equals*.

⌒

Now it is important to note that this notion of an admitted and legitimate monarchy of the Father within orthodox belief in a Trinity of distinguishable but equally divine persons leads to significantly different ecclesiological conclusions from those arrived at by Moltmann on the basis of his critique of what he calls "monotheistic Monarchianism." Indeed the priority of the Father as the eternal "source" and "origin" of the other two persons of equal dignity and status, finds its closest ecclesiological analogy in the episcopal principle of *primus inter pares*, or "first amongst equals." This principle in turn allows us to articulate an understanding of the role of the bishop in the church, and of a primate amongst other bishops, that is free of the falsely negative stereotyping engaged in by Moltmann.

The bishop is "first amongst equals" in the church in the sense that he or she is not separate from the church, for the bishop is shepherd and overseer *of* the church and minister of order *in* the church, but on the basis of a fundamental status equal to others as one of the baptized people of God. He or she is not necessarily present in the church in some authoritarian and offensively domineering way, as in Moltmann's stereotyping, but in a way that respects the equal dignity of every other baptized member and that serves the peace, well-being, and personal integrity of all, while facilitating the ministry of all. This particular ministry of service of the bishop as a baptized member of the church, rather than as a domineering and dictatorial ruler who is somehow outside of it and over it, can be appropriately described as a ministry of order; he or she is the "Ordinary" with the responsibility of safeguarding good order. As St. Paul says: "All things are to be done decently and in order" (τάξις).[33]

It is, indeed, not only that the bishop ordains and authorizes others for ministry, and who is thus the "origin" and "cause" of ordered ministry, or the one from whom, it might well be said, ministry in a sense "proceeds." As the "origin" and "cause" of the authorized and ordered ministry of others, the bishop in the church is thus the human source and sign of the unity of the church. Those baptized either by a bishop or by presbyters or deacons in ministry authorized *by* a bishop, become members of a eucharistic community that is in turn presided over *by* the bishop; all are in communion with one another by virtue of their shared communion *with* the bishop.[34] It is precisely in this way that the ministry of a bishop is to perform a specific and essential function of leadership and pastoral care in the life of the church as "first among equals." As the order for the consecration of a bishop appended to the Anglican *Book of Common Prayer* of 1662 has it, the bishop is exhorted to be "a shepherd and not a wolf."

Moreover, the principle of episcopal ministry as "first among equals" further informs the exercise of authority within the church. For example, in the Anglican way of doing things with which I am acquainted, in the process of decision-making at its synods, which was developed in the colonial Churches of the Anglican Communion from the time of the first Lambeth Conference of 1868 onwards (led by the insistent foresight of the great Bishop George Selwyn of New Zealand), this informing principle may be seen at work in the procedure of "voting by houses." This mechanism allows members of the synod to call for a vote on significant issues by separate "houses"—the three "houses" being constituted respectively by the diocesan bishop, the clergy, and the laity. A measure must win the support of all three houses voting separately in order to be passed. This procedure means that the bishop has a right of veto in relation to decisions affecting the life and worship of the church, but equally the "house of clergy" and the "house of laity" likewise have a similar power of veto. In this way, an arrangement of power sharing is securely grounded upon a principle of equality.

33. 1 Cor 14:40.

34. This is a central feature enshrined in the early second-century *Letters of Ignatius of Antioch*, in such maxims, for example, as "Where the bishop is, there is the Church." See *Ignatius to the Magnesians 2*, 6:1; 8:1, 9:1–2; *Ignatius to the Smyrnaeans, 8.*

While this kind of procedure may not prevail in all episcopally orga-nized churches, and while it cannot be denied that Moltmann's character-ization of the exercise of autocratic power may unfortunately sometimes be found, this nevertheless remains a contingent matter. It is not neces-sarily the case that it is a defect in all episcopally ordered ecclesial bodies.

The exercise of episcopal authority in decision-making and the re-sponsibility to act as "first among equals" is, once again, a concrete expres-sion of the bishop's monarchy, hence in some social/political contexts it is normal to speak of the "monarchical episcopate." The concept of "mon-archy" is sometimes also appropriately applied to the unique ministry of the bishop, because as teacher, the bishop is the one who must on occa-sion *rule* with respect to what is right and what is wrong in matters both of belief and Christian praxis. The accustomed function of the Ordinary with respect to the regulation of liturgy and worship, and the ordering of belief for the purpose of the maintenance of the church in truth both fall within his or her particular responsibility. As "spokesperson" for the church, moreover, the bishop does not act alone but performs as ministry of service in and for the church. It is ideally exercised in humility, with due regard to the equal dignity and human rights of all of the church's members, and with an appreciation of the need to consult, listen, and take advice, rather than operate in the utterly authoritarian and dictato-rial manner that Moltmann rightly finds so objectionable.

Hence the ecclesiological importance of the Trinitarian paradigm of the "first among equals" as the ground of the church's ministry of leader-ship is surely an alternative to what Moltmann mistakenly believes neces-sarily flows from "monotheistic Monarchianism." An authoritarianism informed by domination and submission does not flow without qualifica-tion into churches with episcopally ordered ministry.

It is this fundamental interpersonal insight, first articulated by the Cappadocian fathers of the fourth century in their determination to up-hold belief in the monarchy of the Father explicitly as the eternal "origin" and "cause" of the Son and the Spirit, that ensures the equal sharing of the very same divine nature, status, and dignity, that by analogy suggests that the bishop in the church should not act as an autocrat, but instead should exercise a ministry of service in which, indeed, "the first is last and the last first"[35] and "none is before, or after another; none is greater, or less than another."[36]

〜

The crucial question that must now be pursued a little further is whether this discussion with Jürgen Moltmann about the ecclesial implications that might be drawn by analogy from the doctrine of the Trinity, as this was originally set forward in "In Praise of Hierarchy," can rightly be turned to the support of the subordinationist and complementarian contentions of the Doctrine Commission of the Diocese of Sydney. Is the theological method pursued in "In Praise of Hierarchy" essentially the same as that pursued by the commission? And does it make "the very same point" as the commission itself in its report of 1999, as was declared to be the case in a posting of Anglican Media Sydney on its website on November 26, 2002? This means that a basic question has to be asked as to whether the acknowledged priority of the Father as the "origin" and "cause" of the deity of both Son and Spirit in orthodox Trinitarian description, as the basis for talking of the monarchy of the Father and the qualified kind of "subordination" of the Son that this might be said to imply, is in fact "the very same point" made by the Sydney Doctrine Commission. In other words, did "In Praise of Hierarchy" hold any joy for those committed to the complementarian understanding of an alleged eternal relation of subordination between persons of the Trinity and, in particular, did it provide the kind of support that might have justified its inclusion in the collection of theological references that were reproduced under the identifying crest of the Diocese of Sydney in 2002/3? Could the specific notion of Trinitarian hierarchy expressed in the maxim "first among equals" that was brought to ecclesiological use in "In Praise of Hierarchy" be of any legitimate assistance to the Sydney Doctrine Commission's attempt to ward off the charge of Arianism that was publicly being made against it at the time?

35. Mark 10:31, Matt 19:30, and Luke 13:30.
36. A clause of the Athanasian Creed.

⌇

It has to be admitted that, in the discussion with Moltmann, there appears to be a general theological agreement that at least "a *kind* of hierarchy" is implicit within an understanding of the immanent Trinity, but only insofar as the Father is accorded a specific kind of priority over the other two persons as the "origin" and "cause" of their divine being. At least, in this specific sense, when the Sydney Doctrine Commission Report acknowledges that "the position of the Father ensures a hierarchical mode of conceiving God," this is true enough. There is absolutely no dispute in relation to this. Robert Doyle, in defending the report, also speaks of this traditional theological theme. The logical priority of the Father has been normative in Trinitarian description at least since the time of the Cappadocians of the fourth century.

Just as importantly, however, the terms "monarchy" and "hierarchy" cannot be assumed to function always in a single and univocal sense. In different contexts they may well attract different nuances of meaning. In other words, "monarchy" is a term that is capable of taking on a specific nuance of meaning in accordance with the different semantic contexts of its use; the same may be said of the associated term "hierarchy" and also of the term "subordination" if it is used in reference to the Son. Certainly, in the particular context of Trinitarian description from the Cappadocian fathers onwards, these terms, if they are to be used at all, regularly bear a highly specific and circumscribed freight of meaning: *all have to do with and are restricted to* an authoritative and orthodox understanding of the ontological implications of the biblical teaching that the Son is "eternally begotten *of the Father*" and the Spirit "eternally proceeds *from the Father*." It is unwise to venture far from these biblical warrants. It is for this reason that it has to be appreciated that these concepts are not used in a generic sense, but in a highly nuanced and specific sense in relation to the Father's role as "origin" and "cause" of the other two Trinitarian identities.

The Father's "mon-archy," and the kind of "hierarchy" that is congruent with it, applies specifically and in a way that is appropriate to the exclusion of other possibilities in the Trinitarian description of the immanent Trinity. This means that it cannot be assumed that every possible entailment that might be imagined to flow from hierarchical language more generally will necessarily be valid. It certainly cannot be assumed that such language supports the particular proposals of the proponents of the "eternal functional subordination" of the Son to the Father; it certainly does not warrant the conclusion that two wills operate within the life of the Trinity, the commanding will of the Father and the obediently submissive will of the Son, in a relation of domination and submission. This goes well beyond anything remotely envisaged by the Cappadocian fathers in the articulation of the mon-archy of the Father as "origin" and "cause" of the shared divine life.

If the mon-archy or priority of the Father with respect to the Son and the Spirit is spoken of as a kind of ontological *order* that is appropriate to the being of the Divine, as distinct from a disorganized an-archy, and if this ordering is spoken of as a "kind of hierarchy" in the inner being of God, then it is not to be assumed that this language functions as though it has a single, univocal meaning so as then to warrant its use as evidence for the legitimacy of conceiving what would in fact be an essentially different kind of hierarchy—a hierarchy with morally offensive implications on the spectrum of relations of domination and submission, which is characterized by notions of the eternal willing submissiveness of the Son and Spirit in obedience to the commanding will of the Father.

It is necessary, therefore, to exercise a little caution before assuming that references to a "kind of hierarchy" in the immanent life of God, and the notion of a specific kind of "monarchy" that signals the logical priority of the Father with respect to the Son and the Spirit, may also then warrant a complementarian understanding of the Son's "eternal subordination to the Father," whether logical, ontological, or even in some ongoing functional and relational sense.

It needs to be noted, moreover, that in the specific context of unpacking what is meant when it is asserted that the Son is "eternally begotten" of the Father, as distinct from being the product of the creative will of the Father (which appears to have been one of Arius's fundamental mistakes), what is intended in orthodox Trinitarian description is the very opposite of any kind of subordination involving a diminishment of authority, status, and dignity amongst the three divine persons. For, in acknowledging that the Father is the "origin" and "cause" of the *hypostatic* identity, both of his only begotten Son, and of the Spirit which proceeds ineffably from him, the original intention amongst the Cappadocian fathers was to secure an ontological understanding of the sharing of the *very same* essential nature by all three together in one unity of being. Far from underpinning a complementarian and subordinationist understanding of things, the mon-archy of the Father ensures the essential *equality* of the Son and the Spirit with the Father. As a consequence of receiving their divine being from him all three together fully and equally share the properties of the very same divine nature, status, and dignity, undivided and undiminished. The mon-archy of the Father as the "origin" and "cause" of the equal divinity of the Son and Spirit in this way rules out of court any suggestion of interpersonal difference, whether in terms of nature, status, or dignity, let alone diminishment, whether "ontological" or merely "functional" of the kind promoted by the Sydney Doctrine Commission's notion of Trinitarian complementarianism as distinct from egalitarianism.

Likewise, appeal to a kind of hierarchy in the inner being of God is not to be thought to justify a hierarchy of nature based upon the fathers and sons of this world, in which one is conceived as always exercising a determining will with which the other must comply. By analogy this would suggest that God the Father is eternally the superior of God the Son and God the Spirit.

By contrast with these possible contentions, we have to conclude that, in orthodox reflection on the relations of the Father, Son, and Spirit, references to the "mon-archy" of the Father are designed simply to signal the ontological priority of the Father as "origin" and "cause" of the other two persons. This biblically based insight serves the important purpose of securing the ontological unity and equality of the shared deity of all three Trinitarian identities. We are therefore obliged to conclude that, in this context, the notion of "hierarchy," when used as a semantic entailment of "monarchy," is not to be assumed to signal anything that would compromise the equality and unity of the eternal divine being of all three divine persons. They are to be understood as equals, even if the Father is understood to be the "first among equals." But as soon as these same words are used in the context of affirming a relationship not of equality, but actually of a kind of inequality by *conceiving* a set of intra-Trinitarian relations on the spectrum of domination and submission, even if this is said not to be ontological but only an alleged moral and functional subordination of one to the other, then they take on an additional and entirely different freight of meaning.

↩

If Jürgen Moltmann was at least prepared to accept the logical priority of the Father as the "origin" or "cause" of the other two Trinitarian identities, and to speak of this as a *kind* of "monarchy" (even if he was reluctant to speak of this as a "hierarchy"), and if Kevin Giles more categorically resisted the use of the term "hierarchy" in any sense at all, then the opposite logical move may be discerned at various points in the defense of a subordinationism of a specifically complementary kind in the Sydney Doctrine Commission Report of 1999. The same may be said of published responses of the Diocese of Sydney to Giles's charge of the report's implicit Arianism.[37] Indeed, here the mere mention of the terms "hierarchy" and "monarchy" tends to be seized upon, almost as though they are self-evident indicators of the validity of complementarian and subordinationist points of view.

Just to light upon the use of the word "hierarchy" as it appears in the title phrase of the article "In Praise of Hierarchy" and then to assume that what it is intended to signal is a form of intra-Trinitarian relationships of a complementary kind between essentially different identities, expressing functionally different wills, is clearly a huge mistake. In speaking of it as a "kind of hierarchy" it has to be understood that it is *not* a hierarchy of individuals, *nor* a hierarchy of wills. Any talk of a hierarchical arrangement within the Trinity that flows from the notion of the "monarchy of the Father" has nothing whatever to do with "eternal functional submissiveness" or the "eternal relational subordination" of the Son to the Father.

Already it can be appreciated that the appeal to the specific form of the Father's monarchy as the "first among equals" in the Trinitarian description of God for the purpose of developing an ecclesiological analogy in relation to the ministry of bishops in "In Praise of Hierarchy" is of no relevance to the thesis of an alleged complementarianism in the immanent life of the Trinity.

⟳

When we go to the 1999 Report of the Sydney Doctrine Commission itself in search of an answer to the question of whether it makes "the very same point," and pursues a method "not dissimilar" to that which I myself pursued in "In Praise of Hierarchy," it soon becomes clear that neither of these claims can be substantiated. Indeed, in arguing for the "functional subordination of the Son to the Father" and in favor of the complementary nature of the relationship between them, and in appealing to the monarchy of the Father and therefore to a "kind of hierarchy"

37. Such as the Sydney Diocesan website posting of November 26, 2002.

amongst the Trinitarian identities to support these contentions, the Sydney Doctrine Commission actually deviates significantly from traditional orthodox Trinitarian theology. This outcome results from making some highly questionable assumptions in the mistaken quest to reach its own idiosyncratic outcomes.

First, in terms of method, in seeking to defend the notion of the "eternal functional subordination of the Son to the Father," it is assumed by the authors of the 1999 Sydney Doctrine Commission Report that any possible negative or logically toxic impact that the assertion of an alleged diversity of complementary functions might have on belief in the divine equality of status and dignity of the persons of the Trinity, could be satisfactorily dealt with simply by *first* making a logically prior verbal affirmation of the essential equal divinity of the persons.

In section 4.7/paragraph 23 of the report a passing acknowledgement is made of the Cappadocian insistence on the importance of the logical priority of the Father as "the source of the deity enjoyed by Son and Spirit." It is even acknowledged that the exercise of the monarchy of the Father in this way ensures the equal divinity and status of the other two identities. Thus the report says: "The danger of heresy is met by the insistence that the Son and Spirit are of one being with the Father." This seems to imply the admission that the subordination of the Son to the Father *would* be in danger of falling into heresy, but for the Cappadocian teaching of the sharing of the same substance in one unity of being. Even so, we are assured that "the position of the Father ensures a hierarchical mode of conceiving God."[38]

Then in section 4.8/paragraph 24, by contrast with this Cappadocian emphasis on the originating role of the Father, "the Western tradition, exemplified in Augustine," is said to have "as its starting point the Triune life itself in its oneness. The emphasis falls from the beginning on the single essence and hence the unity and equality of the Persons" rather than on the originating role of the Father.[39] The logically prior assertion

38. Report of the Sydney Doctrine Commission 1999, sec. 4.7/para. 23. Although the ordering implied by the Father's being the "origin" and "cause" of the Son and the Spirit may be spoken of "*a* hierarchical mode" of conceiving God, whether the same sense of the term is sustained when the subordination of the Son to the Father is spoken of as a "hierarchy" of personal properties, and the exercise of their corresponding functions by different wills, is another matter.

39. This is true of characteristically Western approaches to the doctrine of the Trinity. However, in fairness to Augustine, who is credited with being the author of this tradition, in starting with the unity of the Trinity and by emphasizing the sharing

of the equally shared divine substance (the *homoousion*) in accordance with this Western tradition is then thought to permit the next entirely innovative step that the authors of the report apparently imagine to be quite benign: a *functionally* different set of roles is brought into play, with the Father, Son, and Spirit then being spoken of as distinct hypostatic identities with different relational functions. It is as though the prior affirmation of the deity of all three persons will act as a kind of theological insurance to hold off the possibility of heresy. Furthermore, these "different functions" are said to be implicit in the concept of monarchy with respect to the Father, and subordination with respect to the Son. Thus, in methodological terms, an appeal is made *first* to the category of the shared substance to secure the unity and equality of the divine persons (the *homoousion*), and only then is a purely relational and allegedly functional understanding of intra-Trinitarian relations pursued, based upon an appeal to the unique properties of the distinct *hypostatic* identities. These are the different functions respectively of the Father's power of command and the Son's docile obedience, which are said to flow as implications from the concept of the Father's monarchy.

As it happens, but quite understandably, the report follows the methodological lead of T. C. Hammond at this point.[40] The deity of the three divine persons is first positively affirmed by declaring a belief in their sharing of the same divine substance, thus underlining the unity and equality of all three divine persons in "one unity of being." Only then is the subordination of the Son and the Spirit to the Father asserted. In methodological terms, however, when the unity and equality of the three persons is *first* said to be based on their sharing of the same substance as that which makes them "one in Being," and *then* the idea of the monarchy of the Father is used to secure his specific identity and to warrant the

---

of the same substance, Augustine was not actually in the same position as the Cappadocians. He was not systematically working up a doctrine of the Trinity from this starting point, as they were by starting with the monarchy of the Father. Rather, his concerns were apologetic. He began with his belief in the Trinity and its unity, and sought to defend this particularly in the face of some biblical texts that suggested the differences and distinctions between the hypostatic identities. The apparent division of willing in John's declaration that the Son was "sent into the world" by the Father, was one such example. Again, in *De Trinitate* Augustine was not so much developing a systematic theology of the Trinity as engaging in its apologetic defense.

40. The Trinitarian theology of T. C. Hammond is found in Part Two of *In Understanding Be Men* and summed up by him in a much quoted schematic outline on page 56.

notion of the Son's subordination to the Father, an illicit logical move has been made. Instead of the Father's monarchy being associated with the role of the Father as the ontological "origin" and "cause" of the *equal divinity* of the other two Trinitarian identities, this privilege is somehow shifted to an a-personal divine substance as the ground of the shared divinity of each of the three persons. Then the monarchy of the Father is called upon not to establish their equal divinity (for this has already been affirmed) but to establish their alleged essential *hypostatic* differences—the "subordination" of the Son and the Spirit that is said to correspond to, or to be complementary to, the Father's monarchy.

In other words, in this case, the notion of the *homoousion* actually takes the place of the monarchical role of the Father in first securing the equal divinity of the Son and the Spirit. Then, whereas in the orthodox discussion of the mon-archy of the Father in the theological thinking of the Cappadocian fathers the appeal is made precisely to the mon-archy of the Father as the "origin" and "cause" of the equal deity of the other two persons, by contrast in the thinking of subordinationist complementarians the acknowledged equal divinity of all three Trinitarian identities is first sheeted back to the *homoousion* (as distinct from the mon-archy of the Father). But then the Father's monarchical authority is appealed to, not to establish the equal divinity of the three persons (for this has already been stated), but to introduce and warrant the novel belief in the alleged willing subordination of the Son and the Spirit to the Father. In other words, the Father's monarchy is put to an altogether different purpose from its use in the theology of the Cappadocians. The resulting kind of hierarchy is not simply one that establishes the logical priority of the Father as "origin" and "cause," but harbors the introduction of the functional and relational differentiation of willing between the persons of the Trinity! This is probably one of the root problems of Carillon Avenue theology, and indeed, of complementarian subordinationism generally.

Furthermore, in methodological terms, when appeal is first to the notion of a shared divine substance to ground the unity of being of the Trinitarian identities, it is as though this may be thought of in a way that is logically independent of the hypostatic identities of Father, Son, and Spirit themselves. It is as though their divinity ensues from some kind of impersonal divine substance. In fact, however, in orthodox Trinitarian theology *what ensures the equality* of the *hypostatic* identities in terms of their divine being, nature, authority, status, and dignity is the mon-archy of the Father as the "origin" and "cause" of the divinity of the other two persons or hypostatic identities. The Son is equal to the Father *because* he is "*begotten* not made"; the Spirit is divine *by virtue of* an ineffable procession from the Father. Thus, the *homoousion* is the outcome, not the cause of the equally shared divinity of all three Trinitarian identities. When the Father is said to have a kind of priority as the source of the divinity of the other two persons (and when this is spoken of as a mon-archy, implying a *kind* of hierarchy) the definition of the *homoousion* is, logically speaking, the *outcome* not the *cause* of this divine state of ontological affairs.

This means that, in orthodox Trinitarian theology, the logical hierarchy between Trinitarian identities resulting from the monarchy of the Father is the kind of hierarchy to which appeal is made in order to explain and secure the ontological outcome of their essential divine equality. It is *because* the Father is the "origin" and "cause" of the Son and the Spirit that they are "one in Being" with the Father, and thus share a divine authority, status, and dignity equal to that of the Father. This is why orthodox Trinitarian theology is so insistent on affirming the monarchy of the Father as the "origin" and "cause" of the other two divine persons: the source of their very being is from a person rather than from an impersonal substance.

This is, however, far from signaling the *functional* subordination of the Son to the Father and a consequent *complementary relation between them,* that is imagined to be logically independent of the ontological equality of the three persons, so that this equality may be given a logical priority and asserted first as an insurance against heresy and then said to be sustained unsullied and undiminished. This means that the specific Cappadocian understanding of the notion of the monarchy of the Father is not a permission-giving ticket to entertain the notion of the functional inequality and subordination of the Son and Spirit to the Father. In fact, the very opposite is the case: the mon-archy of the Father is the key to securing the divine ontology of the Being of God involving the essential unity and equality implicit in the sharing of the very same nature, status, and dignity by all three persons in one unity of being.

Insofar as the methodology of "In Praise of Hierarchy" involved the drawing of an ecclesiological analogy based upon this fundamental principle of orthodox Trinitarian theology established by the Cappadocian Fathers relating to the mon-archy of the Father as "origin" and "cause" of the Son and the Spirit, thus establishing the fundamental principle of the "first among equals," this is illegitimately used to support conclusions that are arrived at in a way that is methodologically quite different. The

Report of the Sydney Doctrine Commission first affirms the equal divinity of all three Trinitarian identities (the *homoousion*) and then appeals to the monarchy of the Father for an entirely different purpose—to ground a functional or relational difference from the alleged subordination of the Son that this notion of the Father's monarchy is imagined to imply.

∾

We must conclude that the Cappadocian method of argument that begins with the notion of the mon-archy of the Father as the "origin" and "cause" of the Son and the Spirit, securing the equality of the three persons of the Trinity, and so grounding the principle of the "first among equals," has little in common with the Carillon Avenue quest to establish the eternal functional difference between the Father and the Son. In a sense, one methodology ends at the point where the other begins: whereas the Cappadocians appealed to the notion of the mon-archy of the Father in the interests of securing the unity and equal divinity of the other two Trinitarian identities, the Sydney Doctrine Commission, by presupposing the unity of being of the three divine persons based on their sharing of the same substance (the *homoousion*), then goes on to appeal to the monarchy of the Father as a unique quality of the Father's personal identity in contrast with the Son's alleged equally unique subordinate identity, so as then to warrant talk of an alleged complementary "eternal subordination of the Son to the Father." Indeed the Son's subordination is said to be logically entailed by the idea of the Father's monarchy.

It should therefore not surprise us to find that, far from making the same point as the Cappadocian fathers in their treatment of the monarchy of the Father, the actual point that was fiercely defended by the Cappadocians and the complementarian conclusions of the Sydney Doctrine Commission are light years apart, if not diametrically opposed. Clearly, the basic point being made by reference to the mon-archy of the Father as "origin" and "cause" in the orthodox Trinitarian description of the Cappadocians, is improperly used to warrant the talk of a specific kind of monarchy signaling an alleged *functional difference* of the kind proposed by complementarian subordinationism.

Likewise, the theological method employed in "In Praise of Hierarchy" that drew upon this specific aspect of Cappadocian trinitarian description to secure the notion of "the first among equals" as a basic principle for structuring ecclesial ministry, is illegitimately used to warrant the novel conclusions conjured up by the Sydney Doctrine Commission in its defense of complementary subordinationism. The article does not rely upon a methodology similar to that employed by the Sydney Doctrine Commission, nor does it make "the very same point" about the alleged Trinitarian hierarchy implicit in the commission's promotion of "complementary subordinationism."

~⌣~

Finally, it has to be acknowledged that the motivating intention behind the production of the collection of excerpts under the identifying crest of the Diocese of Sydney in 2002/3 has to be inferred from some annotations and markings in the margins of the reproduced texts, which draw attention to the concepts of the Father's monarchy and to a kind of hierarchy in the immanent Trinity. Apart from this, something of the thought processes about an alleged interpersonal Trinitarian hierarchy that was thought to justify belief in the "eternal functional subordination" of the Son to the Father is revealed in brief and somewhat cryptic comments of Sydney Diocesan media releases around the same time. However, a set of inferences that points to a reliance on a somewhat generic view of the Father's monarchy, and on the notion of an intra-Trinitarian hierarchy of persons of a specific kind that might support belief in "eternal functional subordination," does not amount to a cogent argument. For a more sustained argument in favor of the subordinationist case, and particularly for the reasoning that seeks to base the justification for it quite explicitly upon the notion of the monarchy of the Father, we must turn to the published work of Robert Doyle, who as senior lecturer in theology at Moore Theological College at the time, and one of the original authors of the 1999 Report of the Sydney Doctrine Commission, had by 2004 assumed the role of the report's chief public defender.

# Chapter 5

# Monarchy, Authority, and Rule

IN THE LAST CHAPTER it was observed that the quest to come to some understanding of the thought processes that appear to have led Carillon Avenue theologians to their confidently held belief in the "eternal relational subordination" of the Son to the Father is to some extent met by placing it in the context of a more general belief in a specific form of "hierarchy" amongst the persons of the Trinity. Indeed there is a sense in which the "eternal subordination of the Son to the Father" is simply one way of giving concrete expression to this alleged interpersonal Trinitarian hierarchy. Similarly, from the point of view of the Father, the obverse or complementary belief, also expressive of the same kind of interpersonal hierarchy, has to do with a specific understanding of the "monarchy" of the Father in relation to the Son and the Spirit.

The thinking behind the commitment of Carillon Avenue theologians explicitly to the alleged legitimacy of this form of belief in the monarchy of the Father is, fortunately, rather more transparent than was found to be the case with regard to their appeal to the alleged "hierarchy" of persons of the Trinity. Even though the collection of photocopied excerpts from the writings of theological authors that was produced in the Diocese of Sydney around 2002/3 was fairly obviously intended to support the 1999 Report of the Sydney Doctrine Commission, it has to be acknowledged that, in the absence of a supportive commentary, a little guesswork is necessary. In order to reach an estimate of the intended theological purpose of the collection of sources as a whole, we have been obliged to draw inferences, particularly from cryptic annotations against what were apparently thought to be significant comments and paragraphs of the reproduced texts.

This deficit of actual theological argument has been quite intention-ally addressed in the work of Robert Doyle, who brought his expertise in systematic and historical theology to the defense of the Sydney Doctrine Commission on various occasions through the first years of this century. In fact, given that Doyle at the time seemed to have assumed the mantle of the chief public defender of the commission's 1999 report, he is to be credited with the articulation of the most sustained and coherent de-fense of the subordinationist case. We are, as a consequence, very largely indebted to him for an understanding of the more detailed theological consideration of the Father's monarchy in Carillon Avenue theology.

⇜

In his long and disparaging review of Kevin Giles's *The Trinity and Sub-ordinationism*, which Doyle published in *The Briefing* on the website of Matthiasmedia[1] on April 1, 2004, he took the opportunity to rebut Giles's inferred charge of the report's Arianism by developing an argu-ment that is clearly informed by his understanding both of Scripture and the early fathers.[2] A second version of essentially the same argument was reproduced by Doyle in his equally hostile review of chapter 7 of my own *Reflections in Glass*.[3] In both cases Doyle spent a good deal of time endeavoring to defend the Sydney Doctrine Commission Report's complementarian understanding of the Son's subordination to the Father by following basically the same method of argument as the report itself, and once again following the methodological lead of T. C. Hammond in *In Understanding Be Men*. For example, in solidarity with other authors of the report, Doyle is initially careful formally to affirm his belief in the *essential* equality of all three persons of the Trinity. They are unequivo-cally said to be "of one being" in ontological terms, for they all share the same divine substance. Dutiful assent is thus registered with regard to the Nicene definition of the *homoousion*. This means that T. C. Hammond's requirement that the Christian doctrine of the Trinity initially demands assent to "the full Deity" of the Son and the Spirit is thus explicitly ac-knowledged. Only after this has been clearly affirmed does Doyle then turn to expound the alleged eternal *functional* or, as he preferentially

1. Matthiasmedia.com.au.
2. Doyle, "Use and abuse," April 1, 2004.
3. Doyle, Review of "*Reflections in Glass*, Chapter 7."

terms it, *"relational"* subordination of the Son to the Father, and to argue that these two beliefs may be simultaneously affirmed without logical competition.

Doyle also declares that any suggestion of an essential or ontological subordination of the Son to the Father is to be avoided for, as we have already noted, he rightly concedes that this *would* be to fall into the error of Arianism: "With the Creeds, the report clearly affirms that all three Persons are equal in substance or essence. There is no Essential subordination. To assert that would be Arianism and contrary to the teaching of Holy Scripture."[4] In this way, Doyle initially emphasizes what he sees as an important distinction between belief in the essential or ontological equality of the three divine persons, and at the same time what he believes to be an alleged legitimate, but purely relational or functional subordination, of the Son and Spirit to the Father.

In seeking to demonstrate that it is perfectly justifiable to entertain this belief in a subordinationist understanding of intra-Trinitarian *relations*, while hopefully avoiding any noxious implications that might subvert the ontological or essential equality of the shared divine nature of the Trinitarian identities, appeal is then made to the concept of the "monarchy" of the Father.

This is not, however, for the purpose of rehearsing the characteristically Cappadocian point that the notion of monarchy conveys an ontological truth about the identity of the Father as the "origin" and "cause" of the equally divine being of the Son and the Spirit. On the contrary, Doyle chastises Kevin Giles at this point for restricting his understanding of the Father's monarchy to this (historically) Cappadocian point of view. "Unfortunately," he says, "Giles seriously clouds the issue by interpreting the 'monarchy of the Father' *only* as the Father being the sole Origin or Source of Divinity"[5] (my italics).

For Doyle the "monarchy" of the Father clearly involves more than the ontological affirmation that the Father is the "origin" and "cause" of the other two divine persons. He is concerned to point out that this same concept of "monarchy" also means that the Father "rules" with authority in a functional sense. His role within the internal or immanent life of the Trinity is to order or command, and this in turn entails that the

4. Doyle, Review of *"Reflections in Glass,* Chapter 7."

5. The use of "source" here rather than "cause" need not detain us, even though it is unfortunate. The Father's monarchy is the freely exercised and intentionally *caused* work of a person, not something "sourced" as from an impersonal substance.

other two divine persons must dutifully obey. We may note that this is understood fundamentally as a relation of domination and submission. The monarchy of the Father, understood in this specific sense, therefore demonstrates the relational or functional subordination of both Son and Spirit to the Father. Thus, he declares that "the denial that authority and rule is included in the monarchy of the Father, and not just origin, has very serious implications for Giles's doctrine of God."[6]

Doyle contends, furthermore, that the Father does not hold his sovereign authority and power to himself, but shares this aspect of his monarchy with the Son and the Spirit, for the Father "*gives*" something of his "authority and rule" to them. At this point the theological waters begin to become decidedly muddied. For talk of the Father's sharing of properties of "authority and rule" that up to this point have been called upon to illustrate the essential character of the Father, apparently as incommunicable properties that are unique to his personal identity, are now being said to be "shared" and "given" to the Son and the Spirit. This would normally suggest that "authority and rule" as *shared* properties should not be thought of as incommunicable properties unique to the identity of the Father, but as communicable properties of the divine nature, that thus conform to the requirements of the Nicene definition of the *homoousion*. In other words, normally the divine "authority and rule" appropriate to the divine nature are equally shared as communicable properties belonging to all three Trinitarian identities from all eternity as a consequence of the begetting of the Son by the Father and the procession of the Spirit from the Father. No additional "giving" of something of the Father's authority and rule is necessary, or, indeed, even thinkable.

Doyle seems to be intent, however, upon reserving the properties of "authority and rule" as personal identifying properties of the Father, which though normally understood to be incommunicable, are now said to be communicable as properties to be "shared" and "given" by the Father to the Son and the Spirit. Furthermore, this appears to involve an act of divine will that by grace is additional to the Father's ontological sharing of the fullness of divine being with the Son and the Spirit as their "origin" and "cause." This additional functional or relational sharing of monarchical "authority and rule" is thus said to demonstrate the clear operation of a subordinationist dynamic in intra-Trinitarian relations, for the Father

6. Doyle, "Use and abuse," section on methodological errors 5. It may be noted that Giles's failure "*to take account*" of the meaning of the monarchy of the Father to mean "authority and rule" has become Giles's alleged positive "*denial*" of this.

"gives" what the Son and the Spirit must in logical terms hitherto lack. This they "receive," although allegedly without compromising or diminishing the quality of the equally shared divine nature, dignity, and status of their essential being. Unfortunately, all this is somewhat confusing and calls for some careful scrutiny.

~

In Doyle's review of chapter 7 of *Reflections in Glass* this same element of subordination is said to be logically implicit in the fact that the Father "delegates" something of this "authority and rule" to the Son and the Spirit. Doyle's thinking here seems to be that when powers are "delegated" it is logically implied that the one who delegates is superior to those to whom those powers are delegated (the Son and the Spirit). Likewise the one to whom power is delegated may *ipso facto* be said to be the subordinate of the one *from whom* it is delegated. Clearly, for Doyle the monarchy of the Father is not just to be understood in ontological terms as an equal sharing of divine being that ensures the essential divinity of the Son and Spirit with the Father; it is also said to involve an additional relational sharing of functions that indicates that the Son and the Spirit, although ontologically said to be fully equal in divinity with the Father, must necessarily *relate* to the Father as his willing subordinates. Once again properties that are initially said to be identifiably unique to the Father suddenly become properties that the Father by an act of will "shares with" or "delegates to" the Son and the Spirit. Incommunicable properties that are said rightly to belong essentially to the identity of the Father as properties appropriate to his monarchy suddenly become communicable properties.

In this way, Doyle insists that the meaning content of the idea of the "monarchy" of the Father goes beyond an ontological sharing of deity with the Son and the Spirit as their "origin" and "cause." Rather the divine nature that the Son and Spirit receive in terms of their very being is said to remain unsullied and undiminished, even though in need of an alleged additional relational sharing of functions by delegation, which is said logically to imply the subordination of the Son and the Spirit to the Father. This is what establishes the subordinationist differential in the interrelational dynamic found among the Trinitarian identities. Hence, we are all urged to accept the Father's relational superiority to the Son and the Spirit, and their resulting subordination to him as their divine monarch.

At this point in his argument, in order to sustain this extended functional meaning of the concept of the Father's "monarchy" so as to distinguish it from the characteristically Cappadocian notion of monarchy expressed in terms of "origin" and "cause" upon which Giles is said to have mistakenly relied, Doyle somewhat surprisingly turns to the heavyweight champion of Trinitarian theological orthodoxy—Athanasius of Alexandria.[7]

It has to be conceded that antecedents of the position popularized by the Cappadocians in the second half of the fourth century may already be found already in the writings of Athanasius, particularly in his discussions of the *arche* or eternal beginning of the Son, which he insisted was logically inseparable from the eternality of the Father. Athanasius's insistence on the eternality of the Son was designed to counter the noxiously compromising Arian teaching that the Son, as the incarnate "Word through whom all things were made," was *created* by the Father in an apparently second beginning by an act of the Father's will. Athanasius insists that for the Father to be Father eternally, he must have an eternally begotten Son, and *vice versa*; for the Son to be the only begotten Son eternally, he must have an eternal Father. This Athanasian emphasis on the eternal beginning of the Son is, however, effectively sidestepped by Doyle. Rather he shifts the focus from the monarchy of the Father as the eternal "origin" and "cause" of the eternally begotten Son (and of the procession of the Spirit) to his own preferred additional or "extended meaning" of the notion of the Father's monarchy by, once again, insisting that, over and above the concept of the Father as "origin" and "cause," the Father's monarchy may also be used to denote the "authority and rule" that is additionally "given" or "delegated" by the Father and "received" by the Son and the Spirit.

However, while the Father's monarchy understood in terms of his role as "origin" and "cause" of the Son and the Spirit is implicit in biblical references to the Father's "begetting" of the Son, and the Son's being "begotten" of the Father, and also to the Spirit's "proceeding" from the Father, this additional meaning of the concept of the Father's monarchy is not illustrated from Scripture but by directing attention to Athanasius's defense of monotheism in the treatise entitled *Against the Heathen*. In particular Doyle cites chapters 39–40 and 6–8 of this treatise, which Athanasius wrote quite early in his career. It may even be dated either

7. Born c. 296–298/died May 2, 373.

before or only very shortly after the Council of Nicaea, probably no later than 326/28.

Doyle's appeal to Athanasius to justify the giving of an "extended meaning" to the interpretation of the Father's monarchy is surprising for a number of reasons. First, Athanasius wrote a full generation *before* the Cappadocians sat down to do their work in the middle of the fourth century. Curiously, this means that Doyle finds his "extended meaning" of the concept of the "monarchy" of the Father in the *earlier* thought of Athanasius, in a treatise that is to be historically dated even before the flourishing of the Cappadocian interest in promoting this notion to signal the logical and ontological priority of the Father as the eternal "origin" and "cause" of the Son and the Spirit.

While Athanasius's treatise *Against the Heathen* is to be dated either before or, at the latest, very shortly after the Council of Nicaea in 325, the more characteristically Cappadocian ontological understanding of the monarchy of the Father as "origin" and "cause" comfortably belongs to the years leading up to the Council of Constantinople in 381. By this time, the theological focus had moved from the divine status of the Son to the deity of the Spirit, and to the role of the Father in the essential or immanent Trinity, as the "origin" and "cause" of them both—precisely to explain how both Son and Spirit share their divine being with the Father from all eternity. This was in the interests of asserting that all three Trinitarian identities possessed a commonly shared divine nature, status, and dignity. The divine nature, status, and dignity of the Son and the Spirit are to be understood as fully the equal of the Father's own divine nature, status, and dignity. Doyle's use of the earlier treatise of Athanasius to bring an "extended meaning" to the idea of the monarchy of the Father over and above the characteristically Cappadocia focus on "origin" and "cause" therefore seems a little awkward.

It would perhaps be more felicitous to say that the Cappadocians received notions of the Father's "authority and rule" as an implicit ingredient that fed into their own conceptual understanding of the Father's monarchy, rather than as an "extended meaning" that is to be added to their characteristic use of the term in the sense of "origin" and "cause." As we shall see, however, this would not be congenial to Doyle's argument, for it complicates his purpose insofar as he is intent upon *adding* an extended meaning to Giles's references to the monarchy of the Father so as to justify functional subordinationism *as an addition* to the divine being of the Son and the Spirit of which the Father is, as the Cappadocians would have us believe, the "origin" and "cause."

In any event, if this historical sequence of adding to the received Cappadocian meaning of the "monarchy of the Father" by reference to the earlier work of Athanasius sounds a little odd, any sense of awkwardness in drawing upon Athanasius is multiplied when it is observed that in *Against the Heathen* Athanasius does not actually use the term "monarchy" at all. Doyle is, of course, obliged to admit this, even though he turns to Athanasius to find an alleged "extended meaning" to the Cappadocian understanding of the Father's monarchy. He concedes that Athanasius does not use the term "monarchy" in this treatise, though he contends that it does appear elsewhere in Athanasius's writings, when he occasionally, and apparently approvingly, quotes it as a term used by others.[8]

Even so, although it does not rank a mention in *Against the Heathen*, this does not deter Doyle from appealing to this treatise in defining the term "monarchy" explicitly to mean, not just "origin" and "cause" but also, more functionally, and certainly additionally, the sharing of divine "authority and rule"!

He believes Athanasius can be called upon in this way because, in *Against the Heathen*, even while he does not refer explicitly to the notion of the Father's monarchy, he does discuss the importance of the ordering rule of One God in the course of defending monotheism as against polytheism. Athanasius's chief point in *Against the Heathen* is that belief in the unitary rule and power of one sovereign deity commends itself as a much more convincing explanation of the order of the natural world than belief in polytheism. He pertinently asks: If there were many gods how could the apparent order of the natural world be explained? Indeed if there were many gods there would be chaos. Athanasius concludes, therefore, that from the order of things in the created world it is "possible to perceive their Ruler, Arranger, and King."[9] Thus, even though Athanasius does not resort to the use of the term "monarchy" in this treatise, he does talk of the ordering rule of One God in the world.

Somewhat surprisingly, however, we are told by Doyle that the *arche* or ordering rule of God in relation to the created world means that for Athanasius the emphasis is on the creative rule of the Godhead as

8. Doyle cites its use by Athanasius in quoting Bishop Dionysius of Rome, *Defence of the Nicene Council*, 26; and his general approval of Dionysius in *On the Opinion of Dionysius*.

9. Athanasius, *Against the Heathen*, 8.

a whole. The divine ruling, arranging, and ordering includes the ordering intelligence of the Word of God in achieving its natural regularities, for it is the Word "through whom all things were made." Perhaps Doyle would agree with T. F. Torrance when, in discussing this aspect of the thought of Athanasius, he speaks in terms of a kind of horizontal sharing of the monarchy of the one God amongst all three Trinitarian identities: "The *monarche* for Athanasius is identical with the Trinity."[10] Likewise, Doyle makes essentially the same point, while in addition insisting that the participation of the Son and the Spirit in this divine "authority and rule" is explained by the fact that the Father "shares" or "delegates" the authority and rule that essentially belongs to his monarchy with the other two Trinitarian identities.

Now, Athanasius's view of the Father's rule in relation to creation appears to have been picked up by the Cappadocian fathers,[11] even though the focus of their own theological concern was less on the ordering rule of God the Holy Trinity in creation, and much more characteristically on the monarchy, specifically of the Father, in the internal life of the immanent Trinity, and hence, specifically on ontological relations between the Father and the other two Trinitarian identities as their eternal "origin" and "cause." Even so, and somewhat astonishingly, the earlier Athanasian emphasis is enough to allow Doyle to argue for his preferred "extended meaning" for the term "monarchy" *whenever* it is used by the early Fathers. "Monarchy," he says, "is a compound word comprised of the Greek words monos ('alone' or 'unique' or 'sole'), and arche ('origin' or 'rule', or both)." Doyle goes on: "[In] the writings of the fathers, including Athanasius, when the monarchy of God the Father is talked about, discussion about his unique rule is not far away."[12] This is said to be so of the early Fathers, "including Athanasius," even though the word "monarchy" is not actually used by Athanasius in *Against the Heathen*.

In other words, what Athanasius says in this treatise about the ordering rule of One God as against the potential chaos that would result from polytheism, is sufficient reason for Doyle to insist upon an "extended

10. Torrance, *Christian Doctrine of God*, 183.

11. For example, see Gregory of Nazianzus, *Orations* 3:2.

12. Doyle, "Use and abuse," section on Athanasius, 2. This very same sentence is important enough for Doyle to repeat it verbatim in his review of *Reflections in Glass* chapter 7: "In the writings of the fathers, including Athanasius, when the monarchy of God the Father is talked about, discussions about his unique rule or authority are not far away."

meaning" of the "monarchy" *explicitly of the Father*, including when it is used (as by Giles) in the manner more characteristic of the Cappadocians in discussions of the immanent Trinity. Indeed, the fact that Athanasius was addressing an entirely different set of issues in rebuttal of polytheism some fifty years prior to the Cappadocians does not deter Doyle from insisting that wherever reference is made to *the monarchy of the Father* in the writings of the early fathers, Athanasius's concept of "rule and authority" is "not far away."

It is important to note, however, that even if the Cappadocians were certainly aware of the earlier thinking of Athanasius, and even if notions of "authority and rule" were not far from their minds, in their own thinking the appeal to the Father's monarchy is for the ontological purpose of securing the equal divinity of Father, Son, and Spirit. The equality of their divine being, status, and dignity, that results from the begetting of the Son *by* the Father, and the procession of the Spirit *from* the Father, entails that the Father is to be identified as the "origin" and "cause" of the resulting undivided divine life. This understanding of the monarchy of the Father secures the integrity of the full divinity of all three Trinitarian identities. Nevertheless, Doyle's contention is that Giles is mistaken in confining his understanding of the Father's monarchy only to the characteristically Cappadocian notion of the Father as "origin" and "cause"; it must also include "authority and rule." Moreover, it is the transmission of the "authority and rule" from the Father, apparently as an act of will and grace, that Doyle contends grounds the superiority of the Father and leads to the logically consequent belief in the subordination of the Son and the Spirit to the Father. This is exactly the opposite to the point that the Cappadocians were concerned to teach and uphold.

⌒

Now it is important to note that when Doyle contends that the monarchy of the Father is expressed when the Father allegedly "gives" or "delegates" his "rule and authority" to the Son, this is not just a delegation of sovereign authority to the historical and raised Jesus Christ in the economy of salvation. Doyle quite explicitly says that the discussions of Athanasius in *Against the Heathen* about the ordering rule of one God as against belief in many gods of polytheism may also be said to apply to the internal relations of the immanent Trinity. His justification for this is that in that treatise Athanasius speaks of the importance of the unity of the Father *and his Word* in achieving the outcome of an ordered universe, and this is sufficient to allow Doyle to declare, "These are discussions about relations in the *immanent* as well as the economic Trinity." Apart from this, Doyle offers no specific justifying reasons in support of this assertion that the delegation of "authority and rule" is not just to the historical Jesus, but an eternal delegation within the internal relations of the immanent Trinity. Rather, what Athanasius has to say about the authority and rule of One God in the world over against polytheism, is sufficient to allow Doyle to insist that a similar "rule and authority" also applies when the word "monarchy" is used of *a kind of sharing or delegation of power by the Father*, even in the context of the discussion of the eternal relations of the immanent Trinity as well.

⤳

There can be little doubt that the basic strategy of Doyle's argument is to disengage the idea of the monarchy of the Father from its characteristic Cappadocian meaning as "origin" and "cause" to which Kevin Giles is said to be mistakenly wedded. This is achieved by appealing instead to this additional meaning of "authority and rule" so as then to allow talk of an alleged functional, or relational, delegation of power from the Father to the Son and the Spirit, apparently as an act of the Father's will by the free exercise of grace. This additional delegation of functional powers of "authority and rule" as an expression of the Father's monarchy, which is over and above the transmission of divine being and nature by the Father as the "origin" and "cause" of the deity of the other two Trinitarian identities, is then said to warrant belief in an alleged perfectly legitimate functional subordinationism within intra-Trinitarian relations.

It is important, however, to be aware that a subtle shift in Doyle's argument has necessarily been made in order to get to this point. He starts with his preferred focus on the *meaning* of the Father's monarchy as "authority and rule," which is said to provide what we may understand to be an additional *connotative content* to the concept. This is designed to correct Giles's (narrowly Cappadocian) focus *only* on the term's meaning as "origin" and "cause." Indeed, Giles is said actually to deny this additional meaning. But then this additionally preferred *meaning* imperceptibly morphs into a set of propositions about an alleged *actual* eternal "delegation" of "authority and rule" that is said to be a functional part of the relational life of the immanent Trinity *over and above* the communication of essential divine being and nature of which the Father is "origin" and "cause." Apart from *connoting (or meaning)* something in addition to "origin" and "cause," it appears unwittingly now to be asserting that the activation of some additional capacity involving the exercise of the Father's will is being *denoted* by the Father's monarchy understood as "authority and rule." In other words, it is being said that something is additionally delegated *in actuality* by virtue of the Father's monarchy. This is in addition to the transmission of divine being of which the Father is "origin" and "cause." Unfortunately, Doyle seems to have tricked himself into thinking that an additional notional *meaning* said to be connoted by the Father's monarchy (that was said either to be passed over or denied by Giles) somehow maps on to or *denotes* an actual endowment by the Father of the property of "authority and rule" to the Son and Spirit. This is an endowment that is additional to the fundamental eternal sharing of divine being and nature that is ontologically essential to the Trinitarian nature of God. In this way, Doyle conjures up the delegation of functions of "authority and rule" in the immanent life of the Trinity. These must necessarily be understood to be additional to, or over and above, the logically prior sharing of divine being resulting from the exercise of the Father's role as "origin" and "cause." This additional act of the Father's divine will seems logically to have occurred as something additional to the sharing of his (full?) divinity as the (eternal?) "origin" and "cause" of the Son and the Spirit, as though it were a point in a subsequent sequence of relational or functional transactions.

The result is a kind of bifurcation of the Father's monarchy whereby one outcome (the ontological communication of essential divine being and nature with the Son and Spirit) is apparently achieved by the Father's acting in his role as the eternal "origin" and "cause" of the other two Trinitarian identities, and then another outcome (a delegation of powers of "authority and rule" as an additional act of the Father's will) is achieved through an explicit act of grace by the Father through his functional relating or dealing with the Son and the Spirit. As we shall see, Doyle believes that one clear outcome of this additionally delegated power of "authority and rule" that is apparently *not* communicated by the exercise of the Father's monarchy as "origin" and "cause" is the "kingship" of the Son. Doyle insists that without this additional delegation of "authority and rule" we must either "establish an alternative basis for the Son's cosmic kingship, or surrender the Son's kingship."[13]

13. See his Review of "*Reflections in Glass*, Chapter 7."

Doyle is clearly of the view that without the allegedly additional delegation of "authority and rule" it could not be claimed that the Son is a divine king. This sounds suspiciously as though this alleged additional delegation of "authority and rule" makes up for something (kingly power and authority) that is lacking in the being of the Son (and the Spirit) as a consequence of the Son's begetting by the Father (or the Spirit's proceeding from the Father) as their eternal "origin" and "cause." We shall return to this point in what follows.

⮌

It is first important to note that, because this alleged actual additional delegation of "authority and rule" is said to be true of the intrapersonal life of the immanent Trinity, it must be thought to point to a standing subordination of the Son to the Father that may be understood to be eternal and thus timeless. The Son's subordination to the Father apparently cannot therefore really be thought to be *temporally* subsequent to the ontological sharing of divine being with the other two Trinitarian identities by the Father as their "origin" and "cause," even though Doyle's language seems to suggest that this delegation by the will and grace of the Father *is* a point in a functional or relational sequence. But, even if it is not *temporally* subsequent to the Father's sharing of his divine being with the Son and Spirit as their "origin" and "cause," it is nevertheless *logically* secondary to, and independent of, the Father's sharing of the essential divine being and nature with the other two Trinitarian identities. In this case the Father's sharing of the essential divine being and nature with the Son and the Spirit may be said to be *logically* prior (if not temporally prior) to his delegating of "authority and rule" to the Son and the Spirit. This means it is to be *thought of* as something "additionally delegated" or as something over and above the sharing in the one undivided "unity of being" of the three divine persons that is said to be attributed to the monarchy of the Father as the "origin and cause" of the deity of the Son and Spirit.

In other words, even if these functional properties of "authority and rule" were to be understood to be delegated eternally, and not *temporally* subsequent to the begetting of the Son by the Father as "origin" and "cause," they must be, as something additionally "delegated", at least *logically* independent of, and additional to, the exercise of the originating and causal role of the Father. The suggestion is that these functional powers may be *thought of* independently and additionally to the sharing "of one being" equally and without diminishment amongst all three Trinitarian identities through their being "of the same substance." If biblical language is to be preferred, this delegation of properties of "authority and rule" must be thought to denote something that is not temporally but logically independent of and additional to, the eternal *begetting* of the Son *by* the Father and the eternal *procession* of the Spirit *from* the Father. Furthermore, whereas the exercise of the Father's monarchy as "origin" and "cause" of the Son and the Spirit is a matter of the divine ontology, the alleged additional delegation of "authority and rule" is explicitly said to be a matter of will. Doyle unequivocally declares this: "the Father shares his monarchy willingly and the Son and the Spirit respond to it willingly."[14]

The difficulty of trying to sustain belief in the monarchy of the Father when it is explicitly understood to signal the delegation of "authority and rule" by the Father to the Son and Spirit, as something additional to and conceptually distinct from the logically prior sharing of divine being and nature as their "origin" and "cause" and therefore their being "of the same substance" (the *homoousion*), may be discerned in what Doyle has to say about its importance for Christian claims relating to the "kingship" of the Son. In his reviews both of Giles's *The Trinity and Subordinationism* and of my *Reflections in Glass*, chapter 7, Doyle relies upon the notion of the Father's functional or relational "delegation" of "authority and rule" over and above the ontological receiving from the Father as "origin and cause" of their divine being and nature, and their sharing of the same substance together as a consequence of this. This is in order to support belief in the Son's kingship. For that kingship is explicitly said to stem from the Father's explicit additional delegation of "authority and rule."

As if to clinch his argument that this "delegation" necessarily implies the relational or functional subordination of the Son to the Father, Doyle therefore demands an answer to a question: "Does the Father have the right to delegate authority to the Son (which because of delegation implies filial subordination)?"[15] In his review of *Reflections in Glass* chapter 7, the very same question is put: "*Does the Father have the right*

---

14. Doyle, Review of "*Reflections in Glass*, Chapter 7."
15. Doyle, "Use and abuse," section on methodological errors, 5.

*to delegate authority to the Son (which because of delegation implies filial subordination in the relations)?"*[16]

Doyle insists, furthermore, that denial of functional subordination amounts a denial of Christ's kingship! In relation to the alleged right of the Father to delegate his "authority and rule," Doyle says: "Since Carnley's treatment denies that right, then there are only two possible choices: either he must establish an alternative basis for the Son's cosmic kingship, or surrender the Son's kingship." *Touché!* It is clear that Doyle believes that claiming the kingship of the Son is only valid if God the Father delegates something of his "rule and authority" to him; the kingship of the Son depends upon this. This additional delegation of "authority and rule" apparently makes up something that is lacking in the Son's divine nature, in order that he may legitimately be addressed as "king." The property of kingship in other words is not a communicable property that is equally shared by all three Trinitarian identities as a consequence of the *homoousion*. In other words, it is not a communicable property shared by the Father as the "origin" and "cause" of the being and nature of the Son (and the Spirit). It depends upon a logically subsequent determination of the Father by the explicit exercise of his will intentionally to "share" or "delegate" something of his own "authority and rule" to the Son (and the Spirit). As such it is an act of grace on the part of the Father. Furthermore, he says: "If the Father does not have this right, then how is it possible to address Jesus as Lord?"

Unfortunately, Doyle fails to understand that the exercise of the monarchy of the Father, as "origin" and "cause" of the Son and the Spirit, means that they implicitly already share fully and equally in his Deity. This necessarily includes the faculties and the powers of "authority and rule" that are essential to the kingship appropriate to Deity. In orthodox Trinitarian description, this "authority and rule" of divine kingship is a nonnegotiable element of the divine nature, status, and dignity that the Father is said equally to share with the other two divine persons from all eternity. This is a consequence of his timeless communication of divine being and nature to them precisely as their "origin" and "cause." It is not something that is delegated at an additional point in a temporal sequence of the kind that would allow us to say that before that point the Son was lacking the properties necessary for him to be called "Lord" and "King" and that after that point this deficit was dramatically rectified.

16. Doyle, Review of *"Reflections in Glass*, Chapter 7," section on Athanasius, iii.

This means that we do not have to search for an "alternative basis for the Son's cosmic kingship" other than that which is appropriate to the "authority and rule" of the equally shared divine being and nature that is understood to have been fully received by the Son and the Spirit from the Father from all eternity. Given the equal sharing in the full deity of the Son and the Spirit with the Father as their "origin" and "cause" this is something already and implicitly possessed by them.

Clearly then, there is no need for an additional further endowment of "authority and rule" by the intentional exercise of the Father's will in order to compensate for some kind of deficit, and no basis for arguing on the basis of all this that the Son and the Spirit, as those to whom something additional is delegated, are rightly judged to be subordinate to the Father.

The point is, therefore, that there is no need either to "abandon belief in the kingship" of the Son, or to search elsewhere for "an alternative basis for the Son's cosmic kingship." Neither is it, by the same token, appropriate to invent an alleged additional "delegation" by the Father of "authority and rule" over and above the ontological communication of the fullness of deity as a consequence of the exercise of the monarchy of the Father as "origin" and "cause" of the divine being and nature of the Son and the Spirit from all eternity. This is particularly so if the "delegation" of an additional "authority and rule" is of a kind that would suggest the subordination of the one to whom this is allegedly delegated by the one who delegates, so as to subvert the unity of the equal sharing of full divinity by all three Trinitarian identities (the *homoousion*).

This is exactly why the Cappadocians relied upon the idea of the monarchy of the Father so as to secure and defend the equal divinity of all three Trinitarian identities. It is a very pertinent question whether the Cappadocians could have imagined an "extended *meaning*" of the concept of the monarchy of the Father so as to denote something called the property of "authority and rule" that could have been *added* to the (full) divinity that they believed was already equally shared amongst the Son and the Spirit and the Father as the "origin" and "cause" of the other two *hypostatic* identities.

↢

Somehow, it does not seem even to occur to Doyle that notions of the Father's monarchy, *including* an understanding of its meaning in terms of the exercise of sovereign faculties and powers connoted by the phrase "authority and rule," may already be *implicit* in the more characteristically Cappadocian insistence on the monarchy of the Father in the exercise of his ontological role as "origin" and "cause" of the other two hypostatic identities, and their consequent *full* sharing together of the same substance in one unity of being (the *homoousion*).

This is particularly the case if notions of sovereign "authority and rule" were inherited by the Cappadocians from Athanasius, even if originally this was in relation to achieving the harmony and order of creation by a single Creator. Admittedly, even though the Cappadocian focus moved to the role specifically of the Father as the ontological "origin" and "cause" of the deity of the other two Trinitarian identities, it is hard to exclude notions of "authority and rule" from an understanding of the faculties and powers of the essential divine being and nature that the Father was understood to share equally and without diminishment with the Son and the Spirit. If a specific meaning content of "authority and rule" is always "not far away" from the notion of divine monarchy in the usage of the early fathers, as Doyle himself says, it may in fact be even less far away than even Doyle himself imagines, for, indeed, it may always be implicitly and essentially present as a necessary and not just a contingent element of what was understood to be divine. For what is meant by the divinity of Father, Son, and Spirit, if it does not include the equally shared and infinite sovereign power of "authority and rule"?

In fact, when the post-Nicene fathers spoke of what was common to all three *hypostases* or persons, they famously spoke both of the *homoousion*, and of its nature (*physis*). Thus, the natural faculties and powers of the divine nature attaching to or inhering in the divine *hypostases* were original to them, not contingent possibilities that they might "grow into" or receive as an additional gift or delegation from the Father. Cyril of Alexandria famously said, for example, that the willing of the Father was "concurrent" with the divine *ousia*.[17] The properties, or sovereign faculties and powers, of the divine nature did not float free in search of a qualitatively neutral substance that was shared equally by the three hypostases or persons, in the manner of a homeless person in search of a place in which to lodge. The faculties and powers of the nature of divinity inhere equally in the shared *ousia* of all three Trinitarian identities from all eternity. We may thus say they are *inherent* properties being commonly

---

17. Cyril of Alexandria, *De Trinitate*, 2 (PG 75, 780b).

shared by Father, Son, and Spirit from all eternity. The Cappadocians could therefore use the terms "substance" and "nature" interchangeably.

This applies to all communicable moral or behavioral properties that are equally shared by all three Trinitarian identities, by contrast with the incommunicable properties that give each of the three *hypostases* a unique identity—that is to say, *begetting* with respect to the Father, being eternally *begotten* with respect to the Son, and ineffably *proceeding* with respect to the Spirit.

If the Cappadocians inherited notions of the divine sovereign powers of authority and rule of the One God already from Athanasius and appropriated them as integral elements of their own thinking specifically about the Father's monarchy, then they are also unlikely to have thought of a sharing of the *essential* deity of Father, Son, and Spirit that, in respect of the Son and the Spirit, was somehow lacking in sovereign "authority and rule." Indeed, in order that it might be imagined to be in need of being "added to" through an act of additional delegation by the Father's willing of functions expressive of divine "authority and rule," this would require some kind of logically prior understanding of the Godhead in which what was communicated to the Son and Spirit by the Father, as the "origin" and "cause" of their divine being, involved the sharing of a divine substance that in terms of its properties was *without* the sovereign faculties and powers of "authority and rule" so far as the Son and Spirit were concerned. This means, if Doyle is anxious to insist upon drawing a dichotomy between what is essential in the sharing of *divine being* by the Father with the other two Trinitarian identities as their "origin" and "cause" and divine properties or *functions* that allegedly operate within the interpersonal relations of the Father and the Son (and the Spirit), it would unfortunately be necessary to hold that sovereign faculties and powers of "authority and rule" are not an essential ingredient in our understanding of the being and nature of divinity.

As Gregory of Palamas said, however, the powers and faculties of God's "absolute and eternally pre-existing nature" inhere eternally in the divine essence, and must be eternally possessed by God, otherwise "the essence of God is not God."[18] This means that our understanding of what is shared amongst the Father, the Son, and the Spirit, as a consequence of the Father being the "origin" and "cause" of the other two hypostatic identities, must include *all* the communicable faculties and powers of

18. Gregory Palamas, *Triads*, III.ii.5.

divinity. These properties are eternally shared equally and without diminishment by the Father with the Son and the Spirit.

It follows that, when the Cappadocians insisted that the Father conferred *full and undiminished deity* on the other two Trinitarian identities as their "origin" and "cause," then in this case, no *additional* "delegation" of sovereign powers of "authority and rule" appears to be necessary. There can be nothing additional to or "over and above" the sharing of the defining faculties and powers of the divine nature "simultaneously" or better "timelessly" as an essential element of the eternal sharing of the divine being and nature in the undivided life of Father, Son, and Holy Spirit.[19]

An additional *meaning* of "authority and rule" might be said to be added to notions of "origin" and "cause" if the intention is to draw attention to specific aspects of the Father's monarchy that are implicit in the equally shared deity of Father, Son, and Spirit, but that might otherwise be overlooked or underemphasized. But even in this case the Father's equal sharing of "full deity" with the other two Trinitarian identities must nevertheless encompass all the communicable faculties and powers of divinity, including notions of "authority and rule" as elements of the essential nature of deity. This phrase cannot somehow here be used to denote *an added faculty or power and capacity* to what is already understood to have been communicated and fully shared without diminishment amongst Father, Son, and Holy Spirit, through the Father acting in his capacity as "origin" and "cause."

⤶

We have to conclude that the possession of "authority and rule" is not a contingent but a necessary ingredient in the exercise of the Father's monarchy; it is something essential to it. It is not an "add-on" to the nature of divine being and nature that can somehow be conceived without it. If the Father is the "origin" and "cause" of the full and equal divinity of the other two hypostatic identities, then references to "authority and rule" may in this case simply signal identifiable properties of the deity *equally shared* amongst all three persons of the immanent Trinity.

19. As Gregory Palamas pointed out in his famous Triad III.ii.5: God in his essence is all-powerful. If the essential being of God "possessed these faculties from eternity, it follows that not only is the divine essence unoriginated, but each of its powers are also."

It appears, then, that Kevin Giles was not remiss in not attending to "authority and rule" as an add-on to notions of the Father's monarchy as "origin" and "cause" precisely because he had "no need of this hypothesis."[20] Nor is it appropriate to accuse Giles of *denying* the additional meaning of "authority and rule"[21] in his focus on the Father as "origin" and "cause." This is because of the obvious reason that the undivided divine being and nature equally shared by Father, Son, and Spirit (the *homoousion*) already includes the shared capacity to exercise all sovereign divine faculties and powers, including the sovereign power of "authority and rule."

If God the Father's sovereign "authority and rule" is already an implicit defining quality of the divine being which the Father may be understood fully to share, equally and without diminishment, with the Son and the Spirit, then Doyle's talk of the "delegation" of an *additional* "authority and rule" is artificially manufactured and entirely unnecessary—except, of course, for the very dubious purpose of employing the Father's alleged "powers of delegation" in seeking to justify the entirely innovative and problematic notion of the functional or relational subordination of the Son and the Spirit to the Father as those to whom he delegates "authority and rule"!

⸺

Before proceeding to draw out further logical implications of Robert Doyle's basic argument, it may be useful to seek to understand how it was so apparently easy for him to start with an assertion about an alleged additional *meaning* of the Father's monarchy as "authority and rule," over and above his role as "origin" and "cause" of the other two Trinitarian identities, so as then to arrive at a set of assertions of a subordinationist kind about the actual internal relations of the immanent Trinity.

Apart from the mistaken assumption that an uncontested set of biblical texts may be summoned to the support of such a belief, the answer to this question appears to rest upon the assumption that this conclusion follows deductively from the contention that there are behaviors that may be said to be normative of fathers and sons generally, and further, that these stereotypical human functions or behaviors may simply be

20. Pierre-Simon Laplace to Napoleon.

21. As Doyle does when he says: "the denial that authority and rule is included in the monarchy of the Father, and not just origin, has very serious implications for Giles's doctrine of God." "Use and abuse," section on methodological errors, 5.

imported into an understanding of the relation of the divine Father and his equally divine Son. Somewhat surprisingly, the commanding function of the Father and the dutifully submissive function of his subordinate Son that are said to be appropriately stereotypical of fathers and sons generally, are then also specifically said by Doyle to arise from the very being of God the Father and God the Son respectively. Furthermore, the conclusion that the Son is eternally subordinate to the Father is then promoted in the belief that this is justified without compromising the unity of being which the divine persons are said unequivocally to share from all eternity. Doyle argues all this on the basis of the belief that the divine Father is a "real" father and the divine Son a "real" son.[22]

There is a concerning element of anthropomorphism in much of Doyle's language when he expresses his understanding of these relations amongst the Trinitarian identities. The specific understanding of the monarchy of the Father in exercising his "authority and rule," and also the specifically dutiful and obedient response of the Son as his subordinate, are said by Doyle to be "thoroughly appropriate" to fathers and sons generally. Furthermore, the divine Father's "providing/providence/rule" is said to be "what fathers do."[23]

The fact, then, that "authority and rule" is said to be "delegated" by the Father and "received" by the other Trinitarian identities, not just in the economy of salvation, but immanently in the inner life of the Godhead, is said by Doyle to be acceptable not because this is grounded in Scripture, but because it is "*proper* for the divine Father to 'give' and the divine Son to respond to that."[24] Doyle then says that this act of divine "giving" or "delegation" of authority and rule that is said to be perfectly "proper" to the Father/Son relationship, actually expresses "filial subordination" in the Son's relation to the Father. This, Doyle says, is "*because*" delegation "implies filial subordination in the relations."

This appears to mean that specific functions are not simply contingent or incidental or "accidental" functions that might or might not be assigned to the Father and the Son respectively. Rather, "the having of unique authority and the giving of it by the Father, and the wielding of it by the Son" is said to be "thoroughly appropriate to their divine, eternal

22. Doyle, Review of "*Reflections in Glass*, Chapter 7," section on Athanasius, iii.

23. Doyle, Review of "*Reflections in Glass*, Chapter 7," section on Athanasius, iii.

24. Doyle, "Use and abuse," section on Athanasius, 4. The Spirit is, of course, not to be excluded from this subordinationist dynamic, but it is easier to follow the drift of Doyle's argument by maintaining a focus on the relation of Father and Son.

Persons." Given that "a father cannot be a true father eternally unless he has a son eternally,"[25] Doyle, then expands upon this reference to "a true father": "the Father is really Father *in himself*" (i.e., ontologically).[26] Moreover, Doyle declares that the title "Father" as applied to God is not a merely figurative expression but "names who he actually *is* eternally."[27] He goes on: "The triune Father is a real father and the triune Son is a real son. Neither names are metaphorical."[28]

The very same thing had been said earlier in Doyle's review of Giles's *The Trinity and Subordinationism:* "It is proper for the divine Father to 'give' and the divine Son to respond to that. The triune Father is a real father and the triune Son is a real son. Neither names are metaphorical."[29] The repetition of this point makes it clear enough that Doyle is anxious to ground the functioning and relating of the Father and the Son in the actual hypostatic *being* of the Father *as* Father, and in the actual hypostatic *being* of the Son *as* Son.

⌐⟋

When he insists that the titles "Father" and "Son" are not being used metaphorically, it seems to be suggested that these titles are actually being used literally. However, if the titles "Father" and "Son" are not being used metaphorically, we must be aware that just as surely they cannot be being used literally, or univocally, as of the human fathers and sons of this world. Clearly, when these titles are taken from the arena of this finite world in which they may be used literally, and applied to the Infinite God, this must be in a way that respects the divine transcendence of a God who is "other" than all finite things.

It therefore seems obvious that, if these titles cannot be interpreted literally, and if we concede that in Doyle's terms they are strictly speaking not merely metaphorical figures of speech either, they must at least be acknowledged to be analogical. If they signal *some* similarities with the natural fathers and sons of this world by doing what fathers and sons stereotypically do, we have to be very careful also to acknowledge other

25. Doyle, Review of *"Reflections in Glass,* Chapter 7," section on Athanasius, i.

26. My italics.

27. Doyle, Review of *"Reflections in Glass,* Chapter 7." Once again, my italics.

28. Doyle, Review of *"Reflections in Glass,* Chapter 7," section on Athanasius, iii.

29. Doyle, "Use and abuse," section on Athanasius, 4.

important dissimilarities so as to avoid the charge of fashioning God in a purely human image. These will be dissimilarities appropriate to the ultimate transcendent mystery and unknowability of God and so these will be expressed in negative statements.[30]

It is acknowledged that, even if the terms "Father" and "Son" are not to be understood literally, nor as merely figurative or metaphorical images, but are in some way analogical, this is intended to signal something about the actual eternal being of the divine Father and Son respectively that is thought to be essential to their respective identities *as* Father and *as* Son.

In this way, Doyle argues that in functional and relational terms the Father relates to the Son episodically in a way that expresses the essential dispositional and ontological filial identity of the Son *as* Son and of the Father *as* Father. A move has clearly been made from a purely functional or relational submissiveness to an ontological state of affairs in which the Son *is* the subordinate of the Father. This means, however, that, for all his concern to try to avoid ontological language, especially about the essential being of the Father and Son so as to avoid the charge of Arianism by focussing only on the *functioning* of the Son as *relationally* subordinate to the Father, Doyle in this way slips easily by way of a kind of logical glissando into ontological language.

This is surprising, for it appears to be an admission that functions actually arise from, and may be sheeted back to, essences; i.e., to what is essential to their respective *hypostatic* beings and identities. In other words, despite Doyle's initial insistence that the subordination of the Son to the Father is *only* functional or relational but *not* essential or ontological, Doyle himself quietly slips from functional into ontological language.[31] This alerts us to the methodological difficulty of trying to work with some kind of bifurcation between (a) essential being and what is necessary to

---

30. If it is asserted that God is Father in the sense that he "begets" the Son, it must therefore immediately be said "*but not* in the sense that human fathers literally 'beget sons and daughters.'"

31. Doyle, Review of "*Reflections in Glass*, Chapter 7," section on Athanasius, i: "[T]he Father is really Father in himself. . . . 'Father' as applied to God is not a merely figurative expression but names who he actually is eternally."

the shared divine nature, and (b) functions and relational behaviors that are also said to be essential to the respective hypostatic identities.

In a sense a logical slide from functions to the standing essences that those functions exemplify is probably inevitable, for there is a necessary logical link between these two modes of discourse. It has already been noted that it is difficult not to say that a person who gardens regularly *is* actually a gardener, or to deny that a person who habitually murders people *is* not a serial murderer, and that it is difficult to say that the Son *functions* or *regularly behaves* as a subordinate but *is not* really a subordinate.[32] It may now be observed that this is because dispositional statements, such as the statements that a specific person is a gardener, or a murderer, or a subordinate, signal not that the person is at this instant so acting, but that the person in question is known for a proneness to act in such a way from time to time. A dispositional statement entails that there will be instances when he or she will be found to be gardening, or when he or she murdered people and may do so again, or when he or she is submissively obedient to the commands of another; dispositional statements entail a proneness to *function* or *relate* in a specific way. A person who is described as a gardener will be prone to be found gardening from time to time. Likewise, a person will naturally be described as a serial murderer if there have been episodes in which people have been murdered by him or her, with a likelihood of this happening again. Similarly, given episodes in which a person responds in dutiful submission to the commands of another, he or she is naturally and rightly described *as being* the subordinate of the other. Alternatively, when one says that a person is regularly and characteristically observed in situations in which he or she obeys a superior, it is impossible to deny that he or she may therefore rightly be said *to be* the subordinate of the one who is his or her superior. This means that to describe the Son as actually being the subordinate of the Father signals a disposition or proneness of a kind that entails that there will be instances in which he will be found to *function* as the subordinate of the Father, or to function in dutiful obedience to the Father. Conversely, to say that the Son's characteristic role as Son is to function and to relate to the Father in dutiful obedience signals that the Son is appropriately described as the submissively obedient subordinate of the Father. Clearly, the logical connection between dispositional statements and episodic

32. On page 28 above.

statements accounts for the inevitable tendency to drift from functional language into ontological language.

Doyle appears to find it impossible to maintain a clear distinction between the essential being of Father and Son, and those functional or relational properties that are said to belong to them as episodic instances of their *being* respectively Father and Son. This echoes the very same drift from functional to ontological language in the 1999 Sydney Doctrine Commission Report itself: "The Son's obedience to the Father arises from the very nature of his being as Son. . . . He is incapable of doing other than his Father's will."[33]

This means that we are no longer speaking of a purely functional or relational subordination of the Son to the Father while seeking to maintain adherence to belief in the essential equality of their divine being and nature in accordance with the *homoousion*, for the alleged functional or relational subordination of the Son to the Father is openly said to arise from his very being as Son. It is an ontological matter relating to the essence of the Son's hypostatic identity, just as properties of the shared divine nature are ontological matters essential to the very being of the Trinitarian identities.

In all this, the language has moved from functions and relations to the being and eternal identity that is *essential* to the Father *as* Father and to the Son *as* Son. The meaning that Doyle intends us to acquire from all this can only be that the divine Father and Son relate in a certain way *because* they are conditioned to do so by their *essential being and identity* as Father and Son respectively, for his argument is that they relate and function together in a complementary way *because of who they are.*

$$\backsim$$

Apart from the anthropomorphism of fashioning the divine in a human image, what then do these fundamental methodological commitments exactly entail that is theologically problematic? First, it is clear enough that Doyle believes that the ontological equality of the divine persons that is secured by the Father, exercising his monarchy as "origin" and "cause," may be affirmed simultaneously with the subordination of the Son to the Father. There is, indeed, a sense in which Doyle suggests that the equality of the divine persons and the subordination of the Son to the Father both

33. Report of the Sydney Doctrine Commission 1999, sec 4.2/para.18.

flow from the monarchy of the Father: in the first instance as the result of the exercise of the Father's monarchy as "origin" and "cause" and in the second instance as the result of the Father's monarchical power of delegation of "authority and rule."

Doyle draws upon the role of the Father as "origin" and "cause" to underline the point that the Son therefore fully shares the same divine nature as the Father but, insofar as the Father by an act of will allegedly delegates additional powers of "authority and rule," he also exercises his monarchy. If the Cappadocians drew upon the notion of the monarchy of the Father as "origin" and "cause" to establish their belief in the "unity of being" and the full and equal sharing of the same divine nature by all three Trinitarian identities, then the "additional meaning" that Doyle finds in the concept of monarchy is used to try to justify talk of the functional superiority of the Father. For his monarchy, understood as the exercise of sovereign "authority and rule" in the world, is also said to justify the view that the Father delegates "authority and rule" to the Son in the immanent life of the Trinity. It is important to underline that this is not just in his incarnate life in the world, but in the immanent Trinity.[34] This means that the Son is not just temporally, in the economy of salvation, but *eternally,* the subordinate of the Father. In other words, the Son is permanently and timelessly subordinate to the Father, and the specific instance of the "giving" or "delegating" of "authority and rule" to the Son is an episodic instance that demonstrates this eternal state of affairs.

In Doyle's understanding of these things, the end result is that the Father and Son relate as persons of *equal* status and dignity as a result of the exercise of the Father's monarchy when it is understood as "origin" and "cause," for they are "of the same substance" or "one in being" (in accordance with the *homoousion*). The very same Father and Son, however, relate as superior to subordinate of *unequal* status and dignity (even if in a complementary way), as a result of the exercise of the Father's monarchy when it is understood in this "additional sense" as "authority and rule." In arguing this proposal, Doyle therefore suggests that, *as divine persons* who share the same divine nature these Trinitarian identities relate together as equals, but *as Father and Son* these same persons relate together as superior to inferior. The same may be said, of course, of the Father and the Spirit. As persons, the Father and the Spirit are said to be equal in divinity, sharing the same essential nature, status, and dignity;

34. Doyle, "Use and abuse," section on Athanasius, 4: "the giving of authority to the Son by his Father belongs to the immanent Trinity, and not the economic alone."

but yet the person of the Spirit is said to be functionally inferior to the person of the Father.

It is important to note at this point that, in place of the more characteristically Cappadocian use of the notion of the Father's monarchy as the "origin" and "cause" of the Son and the Spirit that secures the principle of the *ontological equality* of the being, nature, status, and dignity of all three divine persons in the immanent Trinity, the notion of the Father's "monarchy" exercised *as an act of will* is actually used by Doyle to reach the opposite result: the Father's monarchy is used to secure belief in the Son's eternal subordination to the Father.

This outcome, in other words, is not just "additional to" but actually the opposite of the Cappadocian insistence that the Father's begetting of the Son, and the procession of the Spirit from the Father, as the "origin" and "cause" of their divine being, which results in their sharing equally in a common divine nature. Indeed, it is an outcome that is in logical tension with the belief that the Son and Spirit thus share a divine status and dignity that is unequivocally equal to the Father's own divine status and dignity—the belief that is secured by the definition of the *homoousion*.

The alternative would be to argue that Father and Son relate and function together in a complementary way insofar as in terms of their hypostatic identity they are Father and Son, but as divine persons sharing the same divine nature, they do not actually relate together at all. Rather, they simply share the same divine nature in much the same way as three human individuals share the same human nature by virtue of being members of the same species without necessarily relating together as persons. It is as though we are to conceive of three divine individuals with their unifying divine nature being understood as though they belong to a unique kind of species labelled "divine" as distinct from a "species of the animal kingdom," or as distinct from the specific animal species called "human beings." Alternatively, it is as though we are dealing with three individual instantiations of the same species, each being a different instantiation of the divine. The Father, Son, and Spirit are, however, quite definitely not three individual instantiations or members of the same species. That would clearly be a form of tritheism: the belief in three gods, all of whom may be said to be equally divine.

⌐

The next difficulty that automatically ensues from this leads to the same conclusion. It has to do with the implication that we must think in terms of multiple divine wills. It has already been noted that any complementarian talk of the subordination of the Son to the Father amongst Carillon Avenue theologians appears necessarily to presuppose two distinctly different wills—the commanding will of the Father and the obediently submissive will of the Son.[35] It is important to note that Doyle's concrete illustrations of the exercise of the alleged "extended meaning" of the Father's uniquely identifying monarchical role in the form of the Father's "giving" and "delegating" and the Son's being the recipient of this delegated "authority and rule," and also his "commanding" and the subordinate Son's obedience in "responding," leads to the unavoidable logical implication that two distinct wills must be presupposed. We are not, however, just hostage to the drawing of logical implications here; Doyle himself confirms that our presuppositions are in fact correct when he roundly declares that "the Father shares his monarchy *willingly* and the Son and the Spirit respond to it *willingly*."[36]

Once again, because a commanding will is said to be stereotypically appropriate to a father, and the obediently submissive will is said to be stereotypically appropriate to a son, this is a matter with ontological implications. It cannot be thought to be just a contingent matter of relations of an occasional or entirely incidental kind relating to the history of the humanly incarnate Jesus. As also in the original 1999 Sydney Doctrine Committee Report, this is not a passing or occasional episode but something permanent and ontological. Thus, the report asserts, "According to Scripture, the submission of Christ does not express a temporary and arbitrary arrangement, but the very nature of God in himself."[37]

As has already been noted in chapter 3, in orthodox Trinitarian description there is a clear determination to speak, not of two divine wills, and certainly not three, but of one divine will that is equally shared by all three persons of the Trinity. As Glenn Butner has alerted us, willing

35. The point made very forcefully by Glenn Butner specifically in relation to the proponents of "eternal functional submission" in the American electronic debates of 2016, that was noted in chapter 3 above.

36. Doyle, Review of "*Reflections in Glass*, Chapter 7," section on Athanasius, iii.

37. Report of the Doctrine Commission of the Diocese of Sydney 1999, sec 4.5/ para. 21.

is a unitary property of the shared divine nature. There is no "complementarity" of distinctly different wills exercised by individual *hypostatic*
identities in the immanent divine life but, as Basil of Caesarea said, a
"coincidence" of willing in the life of the Trinity.[38] In coming to this view
Basil was standing on the shoulders of Athanasius. As we have already
noted, in maintaining the unity of God and the indivisible nature of
the divine operations in the world, Athanasius, in the treatise *Against
the Heathen,* signaled the importance of the belief of monotheism in a
single divine will in order to explain the order of the universe. He was
convinced that multiple divine wills would result in disordered an-archy.

Likewise, Augustine was also adamant in insisting on the importance of a single divine will. There are not two distinct but complementary wills, for this would entail a division of divine operations in the world.
Rather, there is but one undivided divine will: "the will of the Father and
the Son is one, . . . their working (is) indivisible."[39] By way of citing the
biblical grounds for this, Augustine noted, for example, that though St.
Paul can say that the Father "spared not his own Son but delivered Him
up for us all" (Rom 8:32), he also says that the Savior himself "loved me
and delivered Himself for me" (Gal 2:20). In the Trinity there are not
individually different though complementary wills, but one divine will,
single and undivided.

It is because of the orthodox Trinitarian belief that there is but one
divine will that some serious questioning has therefore had to be raised
in relation to the subordinationist proposals of Carillon Avenue theology
generally relating to the complementarity of divine willing, the commanding will of the Father, and the obediently submissive will of the Son.
The same goes for the explicit proposals of Robert Doyle in relation to
the Father's delegation of "authority and rule" to the Son, and the Son's
willing obedience. Indeed, we may well say with Gregory of Nazianzus
that the Son "neither obeys nor disobeys."[40] Rather his and the Father's
will is single and undivided: if the Father wills the redemption of humanity, so the Son wills the redemption of humanity, and the Spirit wills
the redemption of humanity; all three act together for the redemption of

38. As Basil observed, "the Father finds his own will reflected back to himself by
the Son, like an image in a mirror." *On the Holy Spirit,* 8.20.

39. Augustine of Hippo, *On the Trinity,* II.5.9.

40. Gregory of Nazianzus, *Orations* 4.vi: "For in His character of the Word He was
neither obedient nor disobedient."

humanity. Christian monotheism demands the undivided unity of God in this respect and of the indivisibility of the divine operations in the world.

From the monotheistic perspective of the need to maintain adherence to the unity of God, we may even say that there is a sense in which, over and above the inappropriateness of speaking of the operation of different wills, the commanding will of the Father and the obediently submissive will of the Son, it is not even entirely appropriate to say that the Father willingly communicated properties of his divine nature to the other two as their "origin" and "cause." Rather, when the Son is said to have been "begotten" by the Father, and the Spirit is said to "proceeded" from the Father, this is a matter of ontology rather than an instance of the exercise of the Father's will. By contrast with the ontology of the Godhead, the divine will is exercised in relation to the creation of the world. Rather than say that the Father communicated the properties of the divine nature to the other two Trinitarian identities, it is therefore more appropriate to say that all three persons together simultaneously (though better, timelessly) share the one divine nature together from all eternity. This is what makes it inappropriate to speak, as Doyle does, of the "delegation" of the divine property of "authority and rule" (or any other communicable property for that matter) from the Father to the Son as though this were a point in a sequence. Sharing in the same substance entails a common ontological sharing of the same divine nature and thus a common and equal sharing in all the communicable properties of the divine nature. Otherwise this would already have dangerously subordinationist implications with vicious implications for the affirmation of the *homoousion*.

As a consequence, orthodox Trinitarian description avoids speaking of the three divine identities as individuals, each with an individual (even if complementary) will, for the really troubling implication of talk of differentiated wills amongst the Trinitarian identities necessarily understood as individuals, is that this must, once again, lead to a kind of tritheism. Indeed, even the concept of "complementarity" itself implies a necessary differentiation, and thus some kind of separation of individual wills.

⤶

All these difficulties rise because of Doyle's methodological commitment of beginning with the essential *differences* between natural fathers and sons that are said to apply, possibly literally, but if not literally, then analogically, to God the Father and God the Son. It is the essential *difference* of properties that are said to be respectively appropriate to each that allows Doyle to contend that God the Father "does what fathers do" and the Son responds in a way "appropriate to sons"; thus, the Father commands and the Son obediently responds. Likewise the Father, allegedly possessing functional properties of "authority and rule" not originally possessed by the Son (and the Spirit), is said to have delegated these monarchical properties to the Son, who could not be addressed as "Lord" or called "King" without them.

In all this Doyle works with the essential *difference* between properties that are appropriate respectively to the person of the Father and to the person of the Son. It is this difference that in turn allows him to defend the relational subordination of the Son to the Father, even if it is said to be exercised in a harmonious and complementary way. Although Doyle imagines that he is able to remain true to the definition of Nicaea by saying this subordination is purely "functional" or "relational" and not essential, it is (as we have seen) subverted by Doyle's own contention that the monarchy of the Father is essential to the identity of the Father as Father, just as submissiveness is said to be essential to the identity of the Son. It is thus a function that is implicitly admitted to be ontologically grounded. It is difficult, if not impossible to work with properties that are said to be *different* between the Father and the Son, and maintain an adherence at the same time to the Nicene belief that they share the very same divine substance and the very same fully and equally shared divine nature. Indeed, in this concentration of attention on the *essential difference* between the Father and the Son, it is hard not to hear a troublesome echo of the noxiously subversive undermining of the Son's equal divine status with the Father, which at Nicaea led to the definition of the *homoousion*.

⤶

Finally, we are now able to appreciate that something even more serious is at stake. If the "additional meaning" of the monarchy of the Father is said by Doyle to be expressed in the "delegation" of powers or capacities of "authority and rule," then it is logically implied that these powers and capacities were *not* innately or essentially possessed[41] by the Son and the Spirit as an element of the essential divine being and nature, which is eternally shared by them with the Father as a consequence of the fact that the Father is their "origin" and "cause." Obviously, as we have seen, if these divine powers and capacities of "authority and rule" had been implicitly and essentially possessed by the Son and Spirit as a consequence of the Father's being their "origin" and "cause," then there would be no need of any additional "delegation" from the Father as an additional act of grace and will. In other words, an act of grace and favor on the part of the Father, whom Doyle insists "has a right to delegate" what he wills, would be entirely unnecessary.

If the *homoousion* ensures that the very same faculties and powers are understood already to be possessed by the Son and Spirit as constituent elements of the *essential* divine being and nature is understood to have been originally shared by all three Trinitarian identities from all eternity, however, this means that all, and not just a portion of what is essential to their divine being and nature is shared by the Son and of the Spirit with the Father, as a consequence of the eternal exercise of his role as their "origin" and "cause." No additional logically subsequent endowment is necessary.

Gregory of Nazianzus put this point with commendable clarity when he argued that if a faculty or property is said to be received by the Son, whether it be "life, judgment, inheritance of the Gentiles, or power over all flesh, or glory, or disciples, or whatever else," then this is usually ascribed to the incarnate Jesus—i.e., "it belongs to the Manhood." Even so, says Gregory, "if you were to ascribe it to the Godhead, it would be no absurdity. For you would not so ascribe it as if it were newly acquired, but as belonging to Him from the beginning by reason of nature, and not as an act of favour."[42]

In other words, in the orthodox theology of the Trinity "authority and rule" is a communicable property of the shared divine nature. Furthermore, being subject to the requirement of the *homoousion*, all properties of the divine nature must be understood to be *fully and equally* shared by all three Trinitarian identities. If, as Doyle appears to contend,

---

41. In others words, they were not "ontologically" possessed.

42. Gregory of Nazianzus, *Orations* 4.ix.

however, "authority and rule" are not essential to the divine being and identity received from the Father as the "origin" and "cause" of the Son and Spirit, but something additionally "given" or "delegated" as an act of favor on the part of the Father (apparently at some point in a logical sequence), then these additional powers must be, at least in logical terms, independent of the divine nature. That is to say, independent of the divine nature originally shared with the Son and Spirit as a consequence of the exercise of the Father's monarchical role as their "origin" and "cause." But this would seem to mean that the divine being of the Son and the Spirit, of which the Father is "origin" and "cause'" must in logical terms *necessarily suffer from some kind of original deficit*. No doubt, Doyle would argue, this deficit is exactly what is made good by the additional "delegation" of "authority and rule"! But this simply concedes the point that, logically speaking, in Doyle's understanding of things there *is* an original deficit that needs to be made good. Unfortunately, in this case, the divine being of the Son and the Spirit of which the Father is "origin" and "cause" must be thought of as being in a significant respect essentially *less* than the divine being of the Father, for this original and eternal being is *without* (at least some of) the divine faculties and powers of "authority and rule."

Perhaps it might be said that the Father's "authority and rule" is simply more ample than the "authority and rule" originally, and from all eternity, shared with the Son and the Spirit, until by an act of will and grace the Father chooses to share his "surplus" of "authority and rule" with them, thus illustrating his superiority and their inferiority, but hopefully without implicitly suggesting that the divine being and nature eternally shared with them as their "origin" and "cause" is somehow lacking in these faculties and properties. In this case, however, the Son (and the Spirit) would nevertheless originally and ontologically inevitably still be *in some degree* "less" than the Father. The obverse would also hold: the Father could be said to be "greater" than the Son, not just in the sense that the Father is greater than the incarnate Jesus Christ of human history, but from all eternity. Gregory of Nazianzus would have something to say about this![43]

43. Gregory of Nazianzus, *Orations* 4.vii: "For that the same thing should be at once greater than and equal to the same thing is an impossibility; and the evident solution is that the Greater refers to origination, while the Equal belongs to the Nature; and this we acknowledge with much good will."

⤜⟋

In the 1999 Report of the Sydney Doctrine Commission it was argued (in sec. 4.7/para. 23) that the Cappadocian focus on the monarchy of the Father as the "origin" and "cause" of the Son and the Spirit ensured the "unity of being" of all three divine persons, and furthermore, that "if the Father is the source of the deity enjoyed by Son and Spirit" then "The danger of heresy is met by the insistence that the Son and Spirit are of one being with the Father." If, however, we were to accept the subsequent contention of Robert Doyle that it was necessary for the Father to delegate an additional power of "authority and rule" by the exercise of his monarchy (understood in a way additional to the exercise of his monarchy as "origin" and "cause"), and if this inevitably entails that something was ontologically lacking in the original exercise of the Father's monarchy as "origin" and "cause," then in this case, we may well ask what has happened to the Doctrine Commission's assurance that the monarchy of the Father as "origin" and "cause" of the Son and the Spirit ensures that the Trinitarian identities are "one in being" and that this meets "the danger of heresy"? If something is ontologically lacking in what is shared with the Father as a consequence of the exercise of his role as "origin" and "cause" of the Son and the Spirit, then what we were assured would meet the charge of heresy has become incapable of doing so, for the full and equal sharing of the same divine nature is no longer secured. Instead, the divine nature of the Son and the Spirit suffers from an ontological deficit that the Father is then said to remedy by an additional delegation of "authority and rule." If this ontological deficit is said to ground belief in the "eternal functional subordination" of the Son to the Father, we have to ask if this outcome of the defective exercise of the Father's monarchy as "origin" and "cause" is not the exemplification of the heresy it was supposed to meet.

⤜⟋

If, as Doyle contends, the Son could not be addressed as "Lord" nor referred to as "King" unless the Father were to delegate the faculty of "authority and rule" as something additional to the divine being and nature shared with both the Son and the Spirit as their "origin" and "cause," then something is indeed very seriously originally lacking in their shared divine being. An ontological deficit is said to be compensated for by the exercise of the Father's will in an act of grace and favor, but, if the Son and the Spirit are in ontological terms, and not just in occasional functional or relational terms, less than the Father because of their need from all eternity to receive an additional capacity to exercise "authority and rule," then as Doyle himself has assured us the resulting subordination of the Son and the Spirit to the Father would actually be heretical: "There is no Essential subordination. To assert that would be Arianism and contrary to the teaching of Holy Scripture."[44] But Doyle himself assures us that there is an essential subordination after all, given that the Father is said to share his divinity from all eternity with the Son and the Spirit *with a deficit* that has to be made up by the delegation of the additional grace and favor of "authority and rule." This power of delegation is exactly what is said by Doyle to demonstrate his monarchy and, at the same time, the alleged eternal subordination of the Son and the Spirit to him. Alas, talk of the divine being and nature of the Son and the Spirit that admits that it is somehow ontologically "less" than that of the Father, and in need of the delegation of additional powers to make up some kind of deficit, is used by Doyle to warrant the contention that the Son and Spirit are subordinate to the Father, but all this sounds suspiciously like an unwitting but alarmingly uncomfortable articulation of a contemporary form of the heresy of Arianism.

44. Doyle, Review of "*Reflections in Glass*, Chapter 7."

# Chapter 6

# Sidestepping the *Homoousion?*

KEVIN GILES, IN SUCCESSIVE publications, has not been coy in charging the authors of the 1999 Report of the Sydney Doctrine Commission on "The Doctrine of the Trinity and its bearing on the relationship of men and women" with the promotion of a kind of Arianism. In his first foray into this controversial arena, he roundly declared, "The idea that the Father commands and the Son obeys is an Arian error."[1] Ever since, he has consistently pointed out that the advocates of the "eternal relational subordination" of the Son to the Father are therefore guilty of a serious departure from the norms of orthodox Trinitarianism.

Giles's sustained argument has been that the subordination of the Son to the Father inevitably leads to a contemporary form of Arianism because it undermines the Nicene definition of the *homoousion*. By and large this argument has been pursued on historical grounds. He has maintained that subordinationism, whether ontological or relational or purely functional, is entirely out of kilter with the orthodox Trinitarian thinking of Athanasius, the Cappadocian fathers, Augustine, Aquinas, and Calvin. Drawing on this historical tradition, Giles has vigorously argued that the distinction between ontological and relational subordination is highly problematic. He notes, for example, that Athanasius, in his letters to Bishop Serapion, outlines "a doctrine that would become one of the basic planks of the pro-Nicene theology." He explains that "Athanasius speaks for the first time of the inseparable operations of all three divine persons" by saying that "The Father does all things through the Word in the Holy Spirit. Thus the unity of the Holy Triad is preserved."[2] In this way Athana-

---

1. Giles, *Trinity and Subordinationism*, 122.
2. Giles, *Jesus and the Father*, 143; see Athanasius, *Letters*, 1.28, 135.

sius first speaks of the "works" of the Father, Son, and Spirit, and then he says, "But if there is such co-ordination and unity within the holy Triad, who can separate either the Son from the Father, or the Spirit from the Son or from the Father himself?"[3] An undivided functional operation points to the ontological unity of being of the Trinity.[4]

Giles points out that the interrelated divine unity of *being and action* between the Father, Son, and Spirit, first spelled out by Athanasius,

> is a constant theme from this point on in the orthodox doctrine of the Trinity. On this basis it is held that to *eternally* subordinate the Son or the Spirit in work/operation/function by necessity implies their ontological subordination. If the Son (and the Spirit) on the basis of his personal identity alone must *always* take the subordinate role and always be obedient to the Father, then he must be a subordinated person, less than his superior in some way.[5]

It is clear that Giles believes that the charge of Arianism attaches to any doctrine that overtly insists upon the subordination of the Son to the Father in such a way as to fracture the unity of the Godhead. It is this outcome that Giles regards as the defining token of Arianism.

⤶

Giles is not alone in making this kind of accusation in relation to subordinationist views of the Trinity. In an initial article on "eternal functional submissiveness" that was published just prior to the electronic debates of 2016, D. Glenn Butner Jr. noted that the charge of Arianism has regularly been leveled against it. Even though Butner confessed that he was himself

3. Giles, *Jesus and the Father*, 142, 171. See *Letters of Saint Athanasius Concerning the Holy Spirit*, 1.20, 113 and "Discourses," *NPNF*, 3:3.4, 395. See also, "Discourses," *NPNF*, 4:3.9, 398–99, where Athanasius says, "For as the Father is first, so also is he [the Son] as the image of the first."

4. See Athanasius, "Discourses," *NPNF* 4:4.1 (433). "For the Word, being Son of the One God, is referred to Him of whom also He is; so that Father and Son are two, yet the Monad of the Godhead is indivisible and inseparable. And thus too we preserve One Beginning of Godhead and not two Beginnings, whence there is strictly a Monarchy. And of this very Beginning the Word is by nature Son, not as if another beginning, subsisting by Himself, nor having come into being externally to that Beginning, lest from that diversity a Dyarchy and Polyarchy should ensue; but of the one Beginning He is own Son, own Wisdom, own Word, existing from It." See further Giles, *Jesus and the Father*, 136; also, Ayres, *Nicaea and its Legacy*, 212–14.

5. Giles, *Jesus and the Father*, 142.

not actually impressed by the usual arguments of those who contend that this form of subordinationism amounts to a kind of Arianism (and we shall examine the arguments below), he acknowledged that the most prevalent philosophical and theological argument against it "charges the doctrine with undermining the fact that the Father is homoousios with the Son, and therefore claims that the advocates of EFS are Arians."[6]

The charge of the Arian character of contemporary Trinitarian subordinationism was raised in North America as early as 1997 by Gilbert Bilezikian, in "Hermeneutical Bungee-Jumping: Subordination in the Godhead."[7] Keith Yandell,[8] Millard Erickson,[9] and Thomas H. McCall[10] were among some of the most notable scholars who pursued the issue with an appropriate level of seriousness in publications through 2009 and 2010, and over this entire time the same charge has been heroically pursued with terrier-like tenacity from an Australian perspective by Kevin Giles.[11]

On the other side of the debate, the proponents of "eternal functional subordination" have been equally insistent that their views are perfectly in keeping with traditional formulations of Trinitarian belief, and not least with the definition of the *homoousion* of Nicaea. They therefore claim vehemently that they are thoroughly orthodox. Understandably, the charge of Arianism is thought by them to be misguided and entirely unjustified. It has consequently triggered a sustained and often hostile response. Indeed, it has even been said that Giles himself is the one who should be charged with heresy, and even with legal action![12]

6. Butner, "Eternal Functional Subordination," 131.

7. Bilezikian, "Hermeneutical Bungee-Jumping," 64. At the time of writing *Jesus as the Father* in 2006 Giles said that this was the only evangelical critique of eternal functional subordination known to him.

8. Yandell, "How Many Times Does Three Go Into One?," 160.

9. Erickson, *Who's Tampering with the Trinity?*

10. McCall, *Which Trinity? Whose Monotheism?* Butner also notes my own earlier passing reference in *Reflections in Glass*. See Butner, "Eternal Functional Subordination," 132n6.

11. See Giles's argument in *Jesus and the Father* and "Trinity without Tiers," 267, as well as *Rise and Fall*.

12. Giles, *Jesus and the Father*, 26: "The archbishop of Sydney, Peter Jensen, who had been on the doctrine commission, denounced my work as a 'hostile reading' of the report, I had numerous accusatory emails, there were letters to church papers claiming that I was the heretic, and I was even threatened with legal action—on what basis I cannot imagine." It may have been that the proponents of eternal functional subordination believed that Giles's charges were defamatory.

Robert Doyle, as one of the original authors of the Sydney Report, in his extended review of *The Trinity and Subordinationism*, spoke in a tone of incredulity when he asked: "Have we become heretics?"[13] This is actually a fair question.

It is certainly a question that must obviously be addressed, even though it has to be conceded that it may not be amenable to the production of an easy or straightforward answer. This is because of a deficit insofar as a precise and detailed account of Arius's actual views has to be pieced together with a degree of constructive ingenuity from fragments that come to us via the responses of his enemies. The mismatch between what Arianism originally involved and what it was perceived to have involved is made more complicated by the fact that speculative attempts to account for Arius's views in relation the influence of the theological and philosophical forces that he inherited from the contemporary culture have in the past tended to rely more on a degree of guesswork than on concrete evidence. As we shall see in the next chapter, even scholars of the caliber of Newman and Harnack have fallen victim to the complexity of the intellectual influences of the fourth century.

‿

In the absence of a clear presentation of Arius's actual teaching, and in the face of the variety of views that have been labeled and condemned as Arianism over the course of Christian history, it is understandable that in contemporary debates the terms "Arian" and "Arianism" have not necessarily been used to apply to theological positions of the modern world that are simply assumed to repeat what appears to have actually been articulated by Arius in the fourth century, let alone to retrace the precise logical route taken by Arius to get to them. Rather, these terms have tended to be used in relation to positions that are perceived to be in logical competition with the benchmark of the *homoousion,* which in the wake of Nicaea came to be regarded as the corrective to the views of Arius.

It is also a mistake to assume that this Nicene achievement was an overnight success. Different interpretations of exactly what the term *homoousios* actually entailed jostled for a hearing for some decades. It was only gradually that the forceful arguments of Athanasius came to

13. Doyle, "Use and abuse," Intro.

prevail and this probably did not occur until some twenty-five years after Nicaea.[14] Thus, though we today speak of the "Nicene definition of the *homoousion*," this is more a convenience of contemporary systematic theology than an accurate indicator of something that actually transpired instantaneously at Nicaea. At best Nicaea initiated a train of events that led to what R. P. C. Hanson has referred to it as an "apotropaic formula for resisting Arianism"[15] and hence to what we speak of today as "the Nicene definition."[16]

In any event, my point is that "Arianism" tends today to be defined in terms of its corrective—the Nicene definition of the *homoousion*—and what can be gleaned from the debates of the ecclesial crisis that eventually produced this definition. This implicit appeal to the benchmark of the *homoousion* is already apparent in the above quotations from Kevin Giles and Glenn Butner in their different assessments of whether "eternal functional subordination" is rightly categorized as a form of Arianism. However, if in present common usage "Arianism" tends to be understood in terms of what came to evolve in the wake of Nicaea as its corrective, this means that the term "Arianism" itself becomes capable of application to a variety of subordinationist and complementarian positions. What is categorized as "Arian" or an example of "Arianism" signals something much broader than a strict compliance with the detail of Arius's own fourth-century proposals—even if these could be articulated with confidence.

↬

The Nicene expression of the *homoousion* has thus come to be used as a code word for signaling the essential unity of being and consequently the qualitative sameness of divine nature that is fully and equally shared by the Father and the Son (and the Spirit), which Arius's teaching (as best we can discern it) was certainly perceived to challenge and even to deny.

14. See Ayres, *Nicaea and Its Legacy*, 144.

15. Hanson, *Search for the Christian Doctrine of God*, 172.

16. Thomas Torrance legitimately employs the *homoousion* as the organizing principle of his systematic theology in *Trinitarian Faith*, but unfortunately tends to use the term to "over organize" his historical accounts of the theological controversy out of which it eventually emerged. See Ludlow, *Gregory of Nyssa*, 37: "A debate about modern systematic theology is going on in the pages of what many have come to regard as textbook accounts of the development of early Christian doctrine."

In this way it has come to assume a normative place as the benchmark of orthodoxy over against a welter of views that are perceived to be broadly analogous with those first articulated by Arius. The promotion of belief in differences and inequalities in the divine life, that logically separate the essential being and nature of the Father from the essential being and nature of the Son after the apparent manner of Arius himself, so as to end by rendering the Son subordinate to the Father in a relationship of domination and submission, may obviously be judged to be logically vicious with respect to the requirements of the *homoousion*.

The understanding of "Arianism" in terms of a set of general characteristics based upon an assessment of the final outcome of Arius's thinking as its was perceived in the fourth century and which led to the corrective determination following the Council of Nicaea in 325 has thus assumed an important role in providing the normative benchmark of the tradition of Christian orthodoxy ever since.

Given that the terms "Arian" and "Arianism" tend today to be defined on all sides of the contemporary theological debate in terms of their Nicene corrective, so as to apply to a variety of nuanced beliefs that all challenge or deny the requirements of the *homoousion,* the current point of contention has come to focus on the question of whether "functional" or "relational" subordination leads to a set of logical entailments that fall under the same condemnation as Arius's own idiosyncratic teaching concerning the subordination of the Son to the Father .

⤸

It is important to acknowledge that the need for conformity to the standard requirements of the *homoousion* is vigorously affirmed, even by the contemporary proponents of Trinitarian subordinationism. David F. Wright helpfully noted, for example, that the confession of the co-equal divinity is affirmed "on all sides of the present debate."[17] The current issue is therefore about whether the "functional" or "relational" subordination of the Son to the Father can be held together with the Nicene definition of the full and equal sharing of the same divine being and nature by both Father and Son (and the Spirit) and is therefore not in breach of the standard requirements of the *homoousion*.

The first question to be asked is whether these beliefs are in logical competition. Does the affirmation of belief in the eternal subordination

17. Wright, "Dr. Carnley on T. C. Hammond and Arianism," 47.

of the Son to the Father lead to a set of logical entailments that in some way constitutes a challenge to, or implicit denial of, the *homoousion*? If it were to be demonstrated that the subordination of the Son to the Father may not necessarily be in competition with the requirements of the *homoousion*, and that therefore both beliefs may be held and affirmed simultaneously, then "eternal functional subordination" might not be said to fall under the same condemnation as Arius's idiosyncratic teaching.

Certainly, the proponents of the alleged "eternal functional subordination" of the Son to the Father are quite convinced that it is possible, not only to affirm this belief and simultaneously to uphold the requirements of the *homoousion,* but furthermore, that in doing so they stand in the historical tradition of Christian orthodoxy. Bruce Ware, for example, in responding from America to Kevin Giles's criticism of the Sydney Doctrine Commission Report, argued that an alleged "lethal failure" of Kevin Giles's first book, *The Trinity and Subordinationism*, was due to a "misreading" of the Bible and the theological tradition.[18] In reply to Giles, he said: "The church fathers, both west and east" taught "the primacy of the Father in the immanent Trinity," and that the Son "stood in a subordinate position to the Father while sharing in the one divine essence."[19] Unfortunately, as we have already seen, the primacy of the Father as the *origin* of the Son and Holy Spirit, which was energetically upheld by the early Cappadocian fathers, appears to have nothing explicitly to do with supposed relations of domination and submission involving the commanding will of the Father and the obediently submissive will of the Son, within the immanent life of the Trinity. We have to question, therefore, whether Ware's contention is in fact historically accurate, and whether these propositions relating to the Son's alleged relational subordination to the Father, and the equality of being, and hence the equal sharing of the properties of the same divine nature required by Nicaea, may justifiably be said to be simultaneously true.

⌒

While many, like the Australian Carillon Avenue theologians, and Ware and many others beside him in the United States, all tend to assume that belief in the Son's subordination to the Father, while at the same time being equal to the Father in terms of his essential divine being and

18. Ware, "Trinity and Subordinationism," 355.
19. This is noted by Giles in *Jesus and the Father*, 11.

nature, is nothing but traditional Christian orthodoxy, an actual closely argued theological defense of this proposition is actually quite difficult to come by. Likewise, the quest to find a credible systematic examination of whether the contention that both the relational subordination of the Son to the Father, and an adherence to the requirement of the Nicene definition of the *homoousion* may be held together as simultaneous truths, is somewhat elusive. The majority of defenses of subordinationism in response to those who have raised the charge of Arianism tend to fall back on to assumptions and assertions without really pursuing a cogent argument.

Two notable exceptions have been provided by Paul C. Maxwell and Glenn Butner, both of whom produce sophisticated arguments with a claim to be taken with the utmost seriousness.

In both cases, the basic strategy of argument is effectively to detach the property of the Son's subordination from his divine nature (where it would be in logical competition with the requirements of the *homoousion* and thus open to the charge of being Arian) and to associate it instead with the hypostatic identity that is unique to the Son in relation to the Father. This strategy of argument is congenial to the proposals of the proponents of the "eternal functional subordination of the Son," including Australian Carillon Avenue theologians, insofar as they contend that the Son's subordination is purely functional or relational and associated with the hypostatic identity of the Son with respect to the Father, but not ontological in the sense that it would impact negatively on the shared divine being and nature. Whether the arguments of Maxwell and Butner can be sustained so as to constitute a positive help to the proponents of Carillon Avenue theology and others, particularly in the United States, who defend belief in the "eternal functional subordination" of the Son to the Father, remains to be seen.

∽

In a very speculative and high-flying piece of Trinitarian theology,[20] Maxwell sets up a dogmatic schema or "taxonomy" in which he classifies the properties of the Son into four different categories. The graphic presentation of Maxwell's taxonomy is reproduced below.

20. Maxwell, "Is There an Authority Analogy?"

FIGURE 1

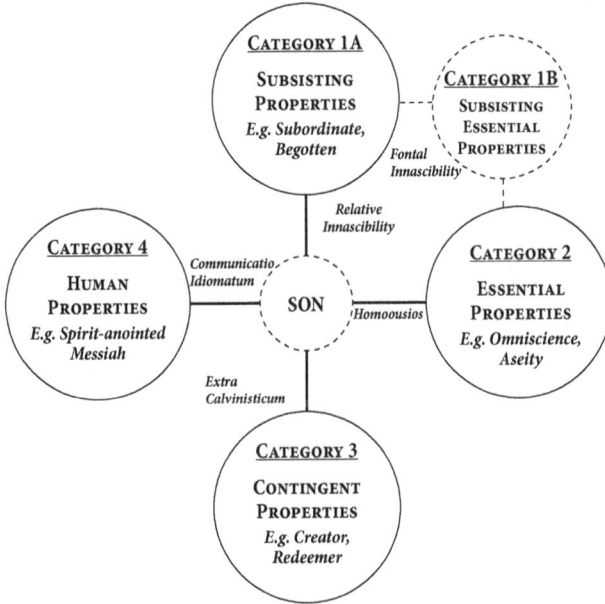

Maxwell begins as a matter of course by assuming the validity of the subordinationist contention that the property of submissiveness may legitimately be classified as a property pertaining to the unique identity of the person of the Son in relation to the Father, rather than as a shared property of his divine nature (that would fall under the provisions of the *homoousion*). Being "Subordinate" is simply listed as an incommunicable property that is said to be unique to the identity of the *hypostasis* of the eternal Son. He therefore categorizes it along with the traditional incommunicable property of the Son's having been "begotten" as one of the "Subsisting Properties" relating to the personal and individual identity of the Son.

These properties of the *hypostatic* identity that are said to be unique to the Son are placed under a label of Maxell's devising, which he designates Category 1A. His Category 1A properties are explicitly described as "that unique class of properties which ontologically differentiate the Son from the Father, and the Son from the Spirit."[21] It is in this sense that they are, as a matter of theological custom, usually spoken of as "incommunicable" as distinct from the "shared" or "communicable" properties

---

21. Maxwell, "Is There an Authority Analogy?," 544.

of the essential divine nature that are subject to the requirements of the *homoousion*.

The *hypostatic* or personal property of the Son's "subordination" to the Father, along with his "having been begotten" by the Father, is understood by Maxwell to contrast with the Father's corresponding incommunicable property of "innascibility"—meaning his being "without source" or ontologically "unborn."[22] In other words, the unique, incommunicable, and defining characteristic of the Father's identity is said to be his being "unsourced" or "unbegotten" by contrast with the Son's "being begotten." Because there is a sense in which the Father is answerable to no one, he cannot therefore be said to be subordinate, or submissively obedient, because there is no one to whom to be subordinate, or to claim his obedient submissiveness. The Father's innascibility and his closely associated "power of command" (possibly in the first instance exercised in begetting the Son?) thus "go together." In relation to this, the Son is both begotten by the Father and is said necessarily to be subordinate to the Father.

Maxwell then highlights two different approaches to the Father's "innascibility": a purely negative or "Relative Innascibility" is said to be characteristic of Aquinas; this is classified under Category 1A as a "subsisting property" of the *hypostasis* of the Father. Maxwell terms a variation on this, which is no less associated with the *hypostasis* of the Father, the "fontal innascibility" of God. This is said to be peculiar to Bonaventure, and is characterized by a focus on the positive role of the Father who, though himself "unsourced," is the origin or "font" of the Son (and the Spirit). In order to distinguish it from Category 1A "subsisting properties" attributed to Aquinas, this is placed under Category 1B to denote "subsisting essential properties."[23] At this stage, this distinction between Aquinas and Bonaventura, and Maxwell's nuanced classification of Category 1A and 1B properties, need not claim too much of our time

---

22. In the fourth-century debates of Greek-speaking Christianity the equivalent term is "unoriginated" (ἀγέννητος). On the other hand, the negative concept of being "unsourced" or "unoriginated" implies the more positive concept that God has his being "from himself," possessing absolute ontological independence. This is usually referred to in classical theism as God's aseity, from *a se esse*, "being from oneself."

23. Given that "begottenness" is the property that distinguishes the Son from the Father, inversely, the property which distinguishes the Father from the Son is called "innascibility," meaning "without source." By "fontal innascibility" Maxwell means to refer to the eternal originative role of the Father, as the "font" or source of the divinity of the Son and the Spirit of Bonaventure, whereas the "relative innascibility" attributed to Aquinas is said to be the purely negative concept of being "unsourced."

or mental energy. As we shall see, it is the use to which Maxwell puts the concept of innascibility as such, rather than these medieval permutations on the exposition of it, that are of immediate concern to us.

Meanwhile, in addition to Maxwell's Category 1 (A and B) classification of incommunicable "subsisting properties" that have to do with the uniquely innascible identity of the Father, and the matching properties that are unique to the Son (the Son's subordination and being begotten), are what he refers to as the "essential properties" of the divine nature, such as omniscience and aseity, that are equally shared with the Father by both the Son and the Holy Spirit. These are said by Maxwell to belong to a second category, which Maxwell terms Category 2. The Son's Category 2 properties are "truths necessarily predicated about the Son because he is God. In other words, they are properties of the divine nature, and are predicated of the Son by virtue of his being *homoousios*—of the 'same substance' or 'shared essence'—with the Father."[24] The same may be said of the Holy Spirit. As properties that are understood to be equally shared by all three Trinitarian identities, these are the properties that are usually spoken of as "communicable."

Somewhat curiously, however, Maxwell says, "Properties in this category include communicable and incommunicable attributes such as omnipotence, omniscience, aseity, and all other divine attributes common among the divine persons because of their shared essence." Unfortunately, he does not clearly identify any examples of the incommunicable properties that he places in this category. However, perhaps this is simply a mistake, as all equally shared properties are, as a matter of theological custom, usually understood simply as "communicable" (i.e., being equally shared).

To these Maxwell then adds "contingent properties" as Category 3 Properties. These are also shared by the Father with the Son and the Holy Spirit. They include properties relating to the exercise of the divine creative and redemptive will, and so are contingent rather than necessary either to the identities of the Trinitarian persons of Father, Son, and Spirit (Category 1 properties) or necessary to the shared divine nature or the shared essence (Category 2 properties). Instead, they simply have to do with creation of the universe and salvation history, rather than being

---

24. Maxwell, "Is There an Authority Analogy?," 545.

essential to the divine nature. In the Reformed tradition these are apparently known as properties of "the Extra Calvinisticum."[25]

Then finally, there are the properties that belong to the incarnate Christ's human nature, which Maxwell labels as "Category 4" properties. Human properties such as being Spirit-anointed, and being the Messiah, as well as being hungry and thirsty, or exercising a human willing obedience in response to the Father, etc., may unequivocally be placed in this category.

It is not necessary at this stage to pursue the detail of Maxwell's taxonomical schema of the classification of properties; and we may certainly be spared from having to spend time analyzing the distinction he draws between the Category 1A and 1B variations of the Father's innascibility, which he finds in Aquinas and Bonaventura respectively. Also, a discussion of the contingent properties of the Son and the Father relating to creation and redemption of Category 3 will not immediately concern us. It will be sufficient for our present purpose to focus on his placing of "subordination" in Category 1 as an incommunicable property of the *hypostatic* identity that is said to be unique to the Son, and that he argues helps to justify the distinction between the persons of the Son and the Father. This maneuver is crucial to his argument, for by placing it in his Category 1 he hopes to keep it well clear of Category 2, where it would potentially come into conflict with the *homoousion*. To be frank, this appears to be a strategy of argument that is designed to sidestep the requirements of equality and sameness of nature of the *homoousion*.

At the outset there is a fundamental problem: Although Maxwell classifies "subordination" as a Category 1 property right at the very outset in constructing his taxonomical schema, he offers no satisfactory explanation for doing so. Rather, the validity of his placing "subordination" in Category 1 of this classification of Trinitarian properties appears to be somewhat arbitrarily assumed. No biblical warrant is cited for doing this, for example, though perhaps this is not a surprise, because, as we noted in chapter 3, Glenn Butner has demonstrated there *are* no uncontested biblical references to the alleged eternal subordination of the Son to the Father. The biblical tradition of the Son's submissiveness has to do with his incarnate life as the Second Adam, who as one who is *homoousios* with humanity in the economy of salvation exercises a human will in obedience to the God whom he naturally addresses as "Father." In this

25. The apparent derivation of this categorization from Calvin need not concern us.

case, "subordination" or "submissiveness" should properly speaking fall
with the "human properties" of Maxwell's Category 4. By simply assuming that the "submissiveness" of the Son relates, not to his incarnate human nature, but to his unique personal identity as the eternal Son, and
so placing it in his Category 1 as a property of the eternally subsisting
*hypostasis* of the Son, Maxwell assumes exactly what needs to be proved.

↬

When we look carefully for the reasoning for mounting this innovative
proposal it is significant that Maxwell appears openly to admit the deficit
of a biblical warrant: "Whether or not subordination is a true and biblical
predication of the Son is another question entirely" but "on a charitable
read . . . The very term 'subordination' . . . may simply be a semantic
specification of the term 'Son.'"[26] Maxwell's "charitable read" here apparently invites us to assume that the concept of subordination is a kind
of definitional or analytic truth that is implicit in the very concept of
"sonship." Just as all bachelors are by definition unmarried, so it seems
to be assumed that, at least ideally, all sons are subordinate and obediently submissive to their fathers. In this way, a "charitable read" allows
submissiveness to be understood as something that tends to come with
the semantic baggage as part of the meaning communicated by the concept of a "son." We should note in passing that, as it happens, this is also
the position of Robert Doyle insofar as he argues that the Son is a "real"
son and the Father is a "real" father. Likewise, the 1999 Sydney Doctrine
Commission Report had argued that the idea of the subordination of the
Son arises out of the "very being" of the Son.

Further to this, Maxwell then suggests that the subordination that
he regards as a unique property of the Son answers to the innascibility
that is correspondingly said to be unique to the identity of the Father.
Thus, he says: "The point that has been clarified by a taxonomical nuanc-
ing of the doctrine of innascibility is this: the subordination of the Son
is a theologically non-heretical Category 1A predicate. In other words,
it does not so far appear to entail the denial of *homoousios*."[27] Put differently, the pairing of the Son's subordination, especially with Aquinas's
account of the Father's innascibility, is important to Maxwell because

---

26. Maxwell, "Is There an Authority Analogy?," 554.
27. Maxwell, "Is There an Authority Analogy?," 554.

it allows him to assume that the Son's subordination may be spoken of as a unique incommunicable property of the person of the Son, just as innascibility is spoken of as a unique incommunicable property of the hypostatic identity of the Father. For just as the Father is innascible or unbegotten or ungenerate, so the Son is begotten or generated by the Father. He is therefore said to be subordinate and submissive to the Father.

By associating subordination with the Son's hypostatic identity in this way, Maxwell endeavors to isolate it from the communicable (or equally shared) properties of the *homoousion* that he places in his Category 2. By this strategy of argument the Son's alleged eternal subordination to the Father is affirmed as an essential identifying personal or *hypostatic* property that is unique to the Son's identity, just as innascibility is said to be the corresponding unique identifying personal property of the Father. As a consequence, it is imagined that the charge of heresy is therefore avoided "by sidestepping" (to use Maxwell's own phrase) the *homoousion*.[28]

᠃

The problem with this deceptively neat attempt to classify the subordination of the Son in relation to the Father's innascibility is that Maxwell appears to have tricked himself into assuming that the relation of the Son to the Father is to be understood as the relation of one who is begotten (the Son) with one who is unbegotten or unsourced (the Father—for this is the essence of the Father's innascibility). The relation is thus defined in terms of semantic opposites—the Son's being begotten, dependent, and subordinate, and the Father's being unbegotten, unsourced, and ontologically independent.

However, if we were to be persuaded to use Maxwells taxonomy of properties in this way it would be a mistake. It is in fact not the innascibility or unbegottenness that defines the unique identity of the Father *in relation* to his only begotten Son. Rather, the property that is unique to the Father's identity *in relation* to the Son is that of being the begetter of the Son; conversely in the relation of the Father as the begetter of the Son,

---

28. Maxwell, "Is There an Authority Analogy?," 554. This "specification of the term 'Son' . . . evades the heresy of subordinationism." It is pertinent to note that Maxwell himself acknowledges that Ware's strategy of associating the subordination of the Son with his *hypostatic* or personal identity in order to avoid compromising the *homoousion* amounts to "sidestepping." "Is There an Authority Analogy?," 562.

the Son himself is "the only begotten of the Father." In the relation of the Son as the "only begotten" of the Father, the Father is not himself necessarily unbegotten (or innascible) but necessarily the begetter of the Son.

In other words, in the Father-Son relation the key defining concepts are the Father's "eternal begetting" and the Son's "being eternally begotten," not the Father's "being *un*begotten" (or innascible) and the Son's "being begotten." This means that the Father's role of "eternal begetting" and the Father's being by definition "unbegotten," "unsourced," or "innascible" are to be distinguished as two different properties.[29] The relation between the Father and the Son, which grounds the conviction that the Father is the origin of the Son (and the Spirit), is between the Father's "eternally begetting" and the Son's "eternally being begotten," or, in the case of the Spirit, the Father's "spiration" and the Spirit's "proceeding" from the Father. It is not between "being *un*begotten" and "being begotten" and "proceeding."

It is of some interest that the contrast between the unbegotten being of the Father and the begotten being of the Son was exactly the basis of the alleged difference between them that was exploited by Eunomius in the development of an extreme form of Arianism that, contrary to the Nicene *homoousion*, insisted that the Father and Son were unlike.[30] It is significant that Athanasius particularly disliked the Arian designation of God as "the Unoriginate" (ἀγένητος), though the title was regularly equated with "the Unbegotten" (ἀγέννητος). He could accept that compared with his works in creation God may be called "the Unoriginate," but not in relation to the Son. Athanasius appears to have been wary of the use of term "unoriginate" in speaking of the Father in relation to the Son on scriptural grounds. For this reason alone he preferred to speak of the Son as "begotten of the Father" and hence of the Father as the

29. Confusion here probably lies at the heart of the difference of opinion between Aquinas and Bonaventure at this point.

30. Eunomius, in the course of articulating what is often spoken of as an extreme form of Arianism, based his views on the radical *difference* that he alleged between the Father and the Son. As it happens Eunomius held that this difference was constituted by the fact that while the Son was "begotten" the Father was "unoriginated" or "unbegotten" (effectively innascible). This alleged relational difference based upon the contrast between the "unoriginated" Father and the "begotten Son" was effectively rejected at Nicaea in favor of the affirmation of the sameness of divine nature equally and fully shared by Father and Son, by virtue of the fact that the relation between them is established by the Father's "begetting" of the Son as his "only begotten." See Ayres, *Nicaea and Its Legacy*, 144–49, especially 146.

"begetter" of the Son. But apart from the scriptural warrant for using the terms "begetter/begotten" rather than "unbegotton/begotten," there are logical grounds for not introducing the term "unoriginate" or "unbegotten" in the discussion of the relation of the Father to the Son.

Perhaps at this point we can unpack this insight of Athanasius by exploring the logic of relations. Aquinas would have said that the relation of the Father to the Son is a real and not just a nominal relation. In the philosophical terminology of more recent times this distinction is perhaps more likely to be made by speaking of internal relations and external relations. In a nutshell, real or internal relations are relations in which the terms are affected or changed by virtue of the relation, whereas nominal or external relations are relations in which the terms are not similarly affected. For example, in the relation of a knower to an object known, the knower may be said to be a really or internally related term, because the knower is affected by virtue of knowing the object known (in the sense of being internally changed by virtue of the specific content of the knowing experience). But the object known, let us say a rock, is in no way affected by virtue of the fact that it is known by the (internally related) knower. It is therefore said to be only a nominally or externally related term.

Now, in applying these logical distinctions to the relation of the Father and the Son, both terms may be said to be really or internally related terms. When the Father is said to be the begetter of the Son, he is a really or internally related insofar as his identity is affected by virtue of his role in relation to the begotten Son, and he would not be the Father or begetter of the Son if he were not so related to the begotten Son. And likewise the only begotten Son would not be the only begotten Son were it not for the real relation to the Father as his begetter. In the case of really related and not just a nominally related terms, there is thus a real interdependence, for one necessarily implies the other. Moreover, the fact that the Father *eternally* begets the Son means that the Son is *eternally* begotten.

However, as "unoriginated," the Father is not really or internally related to the Son as the "only begotten." Indeed, in logical terms, as "unoriginated" the Father does not have to be related to anything. Certainly, the Father could be defined as "unoriginated" without the Son even existing. The Father's identity as unoriginated does not necessarily imply that there is a begotten Son. To speak of the Son as "only begotten" may certainly imply the begetter, who is also for this very reason in this real or internal relation and called "the Father." On the other hand, to speak of the Father as "unoriginated" and the Son as "begotten," or even "origi-nated," is to speak of polar opposites, and one term does not necessarily imply the other.

⤸

It is true that the Father may rightly be said to be "*un*begotten" or "un-originated." However, this is not so much an incommunicable property that is unique to the Father's identity, but a property of the divine nature. God *as such* is by definition unoriginated or innascible; for God is not dependent upon any being for God's divine life other than Godself. In this way, God by definition is absolutely ontologically independent, hav-ing the divine "being from Godself." This is the divine *aseity*. As it hap-pens Maxwell correctly places in Category 2 as an essential property, an equally and fully shared property of the divine nature that is subject to the *homoousion*!

Although dictionaries often assume that innascibility and aseity are simply synonymous, aseity as such is the more positive alternative ex-pression, whereas innascibility carries the essentially negative meaning of unsourced. God's having his being from Godself (or aseity) is in effect the other side of the penny of God's innascibility, for as unsourced the ulti-mate divine reality is one whose being necessarily derives "from himself." Both innascibility (being unsourced) and aseity (having one's being from oneself) are therefore interrelated properties of the divine nature that are shared by all three *hypostases*. In other words, these associated properties refer to the absolute ontological independence, not just of the Father but of God the Holy Trinity.[31]

This means that while it is acceptable that the Father's begetting of the Son might be categorized according to Maxwell's schema as an incom-municable Category 1 property associated with the unique identity of the *hypostasis* of the Father, the innascibility of the Father is not likewise an incommunicable property that is unique to the Father's personal identity. On the contrary, while the real relation of the begetter to the one begotten signals differences of *hypostatic* identity, the relation of innascibility or

---

31. At the Council of Florence (1438–45) it was agreed that "all that the Father is, and all that he has, he does not derive from another, but from himself, he is the principle that has no principle." The Son's aseity is in turn received from the Father as a shared divine property as a consequence of the eternal begetting of the Son *by the Father*.

being divinely "unoriginated" or unsourced signals a communicable or shared property of the divine nature.[32] Now, this means that innascibility as a communicable property that is essential to the divine nature is a property that (in accordance with the *homoousion*) is shared fully and equally by the Father with the Son and the Spirit. It is a property unique to the identity of God the Holy Trinity, rather than a property that is exclusive to the identity of the Father alone by contrast with the other two Trinitarian identities.[33]

In the debates of the fourth century it was held by Arius and his supporters that God (the Father) alone is ἀγέννητος (unoriginated or unsourced) whereas all else, including the Word incarnate, was created out of nothing by the exercise of God's free will. In endeavoring to defend this, the Arian bishop Eusebius of Nicomedia, in his Letter to Paulinus,[34] equated "to beget" with "to create" but acknowledged that if the Son were not created out of nothing but begotten out of the substance of the Father the property of ἀγέννητος would automatically be shared with him. Inevitably, he would possess the ταυτότης τῆς θύσεως with the Father. Precisely!

In other words, the ultimate property of absolute ontological independence signaled by the divine innascibility/aseity is a property of the divine; it is what defines God as God. It does not define the Father over against the Son. Furthermore, as a communicable property of the divine nature that is subject to the requirement of the *homoousion*, even though it is a property that has its origin with the monarchy of the Father (as "origin" and "cause" of the Son and the Spirit), it is a property of divinity

32. As we have already noted, Maxwell (correctly) attributes aseity along with omniscience as a Category 2 property of the Son. These are both shared properties of the divine nature as such. However, while Maxwell categorizes aseity as a property of the Son which, as a consequence of the *homoousion,* is shared with the Father, innascibility is by contrast said to be an incommunicable property of the Father alone. We would do well to avoid being drawn into this confusion.

33. John Zizioulas has argued that this sharing is the consequence of the monarchy of the Father and of the ontologically free exercise of the will of the Father. See his "Father as Cause." But this raises the problematic suggestion that the Son and the Spirit have individual wills, whereas orthodox theology insists upon a single indivisibly shared divine will.

34. Paulinus (died in 358) was bishop of Trier and a supporter of Athanasius in the conflict with Arianism.

that is equally shared, not a property that is reserved uniquely and exclusively to the identity of the Father in a relation of opposition *over against* the Son (and the Spirit). That would surely be Arianism pure and simple.

Maxwell tacitly recognizes this by correctly categorizing the property of aseity as a Category 2 Property of the Son that is shared with the other two Trinitarian identities, while incorrectly (and somewhat confusedly) categorizing innascibility as an incommunicable property of the Father alone. Whether we speak of innascibility or aseity, as a property of the divine nature of the ultimate reality of God as the absolutely independent and unconditioned all-conditioning conditioner of all, this refers to what makes God ontologically and uniquely God. It follows that, by a paradox, the only begotten Son who has his origin from the Father who eternally begets him, by this very fact thus equally shares the divine properties of innascibility and aseity that are as a consequence common to Father, Son, and Spirit.

Given all these logical issues, it is entirely inappropriate to take the concept of the innascibility of the Father (alone) as the basis for arguing for a fundamental *difference* between Father and Son in the way Maxwell has done. Furthermore, it is therefore entirely inappropriate to ground talk of an alleged dependence of the Son on the Father on the basis of the Father's innascibility and to press it into service as a warrant to justify belief in the eternal subordination of the Son to the Father. This can only be achieved by resorting to the theological fiat of associating the property of innascibility with the unique identity of the Father and "subordination" with the unique *hypostatic* identity of the Son, thus separating the Son's alleged subordination from the communicable properties of the divine nature that all three Trinitarian identities equally share, and by this strategy, sidestepping the requirements of the *homoousion* in the hope of avoiding the charge of Arianism.[35]

Though he does not directly refer to Maxwell's taxonomy, Glenn Butner adopts a similar strategy of argument when he self-identifies as one who

---

35. Though Maxwell acknowledges that Bruce Ware's strategy of associating the subordination of the Son with his *hypostatic* or personal identity in order to avoid compromising the *homoousion* amounts to "sidestepping," this charge also applies to the strategies of argument of Maxwell himself. See Maxwell, "Is There an Authority Analogy?," 562.

is somewhat reluctant to categorize those who defend "eternal functional submissiveness" specifically as "Arian."[36] This is despite the fact that Butner has himself convincingly demonstrated that the proponents of "eternal functional submissiveness" have to face an apparently insuperable set of other theological difficulties.[37] Indeed, Butner is to be credited with highlighting an interrelated set of subordinationist errors, even though the charge of falling into the heresy of Arianism is not one of them.

The first problem for the proponents of the Son's subordination to the Father to which Butner draws attention arises from the Third Council of Constantinople's definition of Christ's willing in terms of two wills, a human and a divine will belonging respectively to his human and divine nature. The tendency of the proponents of the Son's eternal subordination to fail to take account of this, and their novel identification of the Son's willing obedience as a unitary property of the *eternal* pre-incarnate Word as well as a property of the human nature of the incarnate Christ tends to lead to a misreading of the biblical evidence. Butner has convincingly demonstrated that there are no uncontested scriptural texts that refer to the *eternal* subordination of the Son to the Father in the immanent life of the Trinity. Rather, the overwhelming weight of the uncontested evidence favors an understanding of the incarnate Son's *human* willing obedience in the economy of salvation.[38]

The second problem that Butner highlights then logically follows: the same subordinationist tendency to concentrate on the "eternal functional submissiveness" of the Second Person in the immanent life of the Trinity, necessarily implies the operation of *two divine wills* instead of one. Insofar as the eternal Son's *willing obedience* is said to be responsive to the specific divine commands of the Father, the will of the Son is obviously distinct from, and set in logical opposition to, the commanding will of the Father. Butner sees this problem clearly. In the course of arguing

36. Maxwell published his article "Is there an Authority Analogy?" in 2016. Butner's *Son Who Learned Obedience* followed in 2017. However, given the lag between writing and publishing, Butner may not have had access to Maxwell's article at the time of writing his own book. Even so, there had been some collaborative exchange between them. Maxwell, who had been a PhD student in 2016, actually thanks Butner for his encouragement and advice. Certainly, Butner and Maxwell are of a common mind in relation to the categorizing of subordination as a personal or *hypostatic* property of the Son, rather than as a shared property of the divine nature.

37. As has been acknowledged with appreciation in chapter 3 of this book.

38. Whether this may legitimately be said to reveal something about the eternal willing obedience of the Son to the Father will be addressed below.

what is in fact the major thesis of *The Son Who Learned Obedience*,[39] he recruits the support of Kyle Claunch: "In order for the Son to submit *willingly* to the *will* of the Father, the two must possess distinct wills."[40] Butner points out that, given that Christian orthodoxy affirms belief in a single undivided divine will, equally shared and exercised indivisibly together by all three Trinitarian identities as an essential requirement of the divine unity, this differentiation of willing within the Trinity immediately signals a disastrous tritheism. Perhaps Butner thinks that this is a heresy enough!

Certainly, though he is prepared to argue vigorously that the allocation of separate wills to the *hypostatic* identities of the Trinity amounts to a form of tritheism, Butner is equally convinced that this is not correctly categorized as a form of Arianism. This is precisely because of his conviction that by treating the property of the Son's subordination as an incommunicable property that is unique to his hypostatic or personal identity (thus tacitly agreeing with the Maxwell's categorization of it as a property belonging in Category 1 of his taxonomy) and not as a property of the Son's divine nature, it is automatically quarantined from the requirements of the *homoousion*. In this way the property of submissiveness is kept well away from the shared properties that are said to be essential to the divine nature (which Maxwell places in his Category 2). What to Butner's mind delivers the proponents of the submissiveness of the Son from falling into the heresy of Arianism is therefore that eternal submission is not a property of the divine essence but an incommunicable property of the person of the Son that plays a part in defining his intra-Trinitarian relationships. Thus, he declares: "it is simply not true that claiming the Son eternally submits to the Father entails a denial of the *homoousios*, provided that whatever is said of the Son submitting is said of the *person* of the Son through relational predication and not the shared divine nature or essence through substantial predication."[41] Indeed Butner cites a list of like-minded colleagues who promote a similar theological commitment.[42] This allows him to argue with confidence that, even though

39. Butner, *Son Who Learned Obedience*, 26.

40. Claunch, "God is the Head of Christ," 88.

41. Butner, *Son Who Learned Obedience*, 23.

42. This is regularly insisted upon by the supporters of eternal functional subordination. There are multiple examples of scholars who categorize eternal submission as "a property exclusively of the Son," "strictly and only a personal property," and a "property of his personhood in relation (and only in relation) to the Father." Ware,

222 ARIUS ON CARILLON AVENUE

he has convincingly demonstrated that the eternal subordination of the Son to the Father is not supported by any uncontested biblical tradition, it cannot properly be described as "Arian" or correctly categorized a form of "Arianism."

⤸

That said, Butner has not been entirely consistent in relation to this crucial point. With regard to the question of whether subordinationists are guilty of undermining adherence to the requirements of the *homoousion*, he is in fact on occasion somewhat equivocal. He initially admitted, for example, that "the conclusion that EFS entails a rejection of homoousian-ism ultimately holds true" even though he nevertheless went on to say, "I do not find the standard argument against EFS compelling."[43] In other words, it is the *argument* leading to the charge of "Arianism" that is found wanting, rather than the charge itself.

It is clear that what provides Butner with his basic reasoning for entertaining reservations about *the standard argument* of those who charge "eternal functional submission" with Arianism depends on the strategy of classifying "eternal functional submissiveness" as a defining *hypostatic* property of the *person* of Son in relation with the Father. Thus, in the face of the charge that a kind of neo-Arian assault has been made on the *homoousion*, Butner acknowledges that the advocates of eternal functional submissiveness in fact generally seek to abide by the obligation to affirm the *homoousion* in the interests of claiming to conform to the requirements of Christian orthodoxy. This is certainly true of Australian Carillon Avenue theologians who follow the lead of T. C. Hammond at this point.[44] As we have already noted, this is exemplified in the Sydney Doctrine Commission's 1999 Report insofar as it seems to have imagined that

"Denial of *Homoousios*?," 244. See also Gons and Naselli, "Examination of Three Recent Philosophical Arguments," 204–5; Smail, *Like Father, Like Son*, 169: "the eternal subordination of the Son is a 'willing responsiveness' of eternal submission and 'the defining hypostatic characteristic' of the Son"; Horrell, "Complementarian Trinitarianism," 352: subordination is the Son's "distinguishing personal characteristic"; and Frame, *Systematic Theology*, 501: "There is no subordination within the divine nature . . . there is subordination of role among the persons, which constitutes part of the distinctiveness of each."

43. Butner, "Eternal Functional Subordination," 132.

44. As Hammond summarizes the basics of Trinitarian faith in *In Understanding Be Men*, 56.

its orthodoxy could be secured simply by declaring its belief in the equal status and authority of the Trinitarian identities, even while promoting subordinationist and complementarian doctrines at the same time.

In a similar way, in a sympathetic presentation of the subordinationist contentions of Bruce Ware, Glenn Butner concludes that "Ware is not saying anything at all about the divine nature or essence, so he cannot possibly be jeopardizing the *homoousion*."[45] Though Butner originally acknowledged that the rejection of the *homoousion* might be something that "ultimately holds true" in the thinking of subordinationists, his argument therefore is that, to be fair, it has to be acknowledged that articulations of eternal functional subordination do not have to do with the *homoousion* and the shared divine nature of the Trinitarian persons, so much as with the actual definition of their hypostatic identities as such.

In this way Butner seems to accept the subordinationists' view that they at least *intend* to uphold the integrity of the *homoousion* by associating the willing obedience of the Son with his unique *hypostatic* identity while detaching it from his fundamental divine nature. Clearly, the proponents of eternal functional submissiveness are well aware of the danger of associating this with the essential properties of the shared divine nature, for this would bring them into conflict with the acknowledged requirement of equality and sameness that is secured by the definition of the *homoousion*.

Glenn Butner has already made it more than clear that the often confidently expressed assumption that there is actually a biblical tradition that grounds belief in eternal functional subordination is entirely misplaced. As was already noted in chapter 3 of this book, Butner has convincingly demonstrated that there are no uncontested biblical texts that support the notion of the eternal functional subordination of the Son to the Father in the immanent life of the Trinity. Rather, the overwhelming weight of the biblical tradition has to do with the submissiveness of the historical Jesus in his incarnate human life, by contrast with "eternal submissiveness" as an interpersonal dynamic of the internal life of the immanent Trinity.

As a consequence, while Butner is to be credited with making a very significant contribution to this debate by convincingly demonstrating (a) that there is no uncontested biblical text that warrants belief in the eternal functional subordination of the Son to the Father, and (b) that belief

45. Butner, *Son Who Learned Obedience*, 24.

in eternal functional subordination inevitably leads to the error of tritheism, he is nevertheless prepared to acquiesce in the contention of the proponents of eternal functional subordination that they are not guilty of the charge of Arianism, because they quite explicitly associate the eternal submissiveness of the Son with his personal or *hypostatic* identity rather than with the essential divine nature that he shares with the Father and the Spirit.

&#8765;

Generally speaking, Butner appears to be disinclined to be accusatory in relation to his fellow evangelical Christians. For example, he is reluctant even to speak of "a complementarian Trinity" as against an "egalitarian Trinity"; instead, he appears to want to discourage evangelicals from thinking of themselves in adversarial terms whether as "complementarians" or "egalitarians." He therefore insists that there is no such thing as the "complementarian Trinity" or the "egalitarian Trinity." This begs a question as to whether the terms "complementarian" or "egalitarian" ever lend themselves to any meaningful use either in the context of Trinitarian theology, or by implication perhaps also even in relation to the alleged biblical understanding of the interpersonal gender dynamics and the need for wives to be submissive to their husbands. In any event, though Butner does not necessarily object to the contemporary use of the terms "Arian" or "Arianism," he resists any temptation to speak of eternal functional submissiveness as an Arian heresy, and further declares that it does not amount to a form of "Arianism" because, "in all fairness," it has to be acknowledged that when subordinationists argue in favor of the view that the Son is eternally submissive to the Father, they do so while at the same time earnestly expressing the belief that this does not entail any adverse implications so far as the *homoousion* is concerned.

Instead, the focus of the alleged submissiveness of the Son to the Father is on the *hypostatic* relation of the *persons* of the Son and the Father: the submissiveness of the Son to the Father and the power of command of the Father in relation to the Son, is a way of establishing (or bolstering?) the respective unique identities of the Father and the Son. But this is said to allow for the continuing affirmation of the *homoousion,* for all other behavioral properties of the Father and Son are said to be equally possessed as shared elements of the same divine nature. This is what allows him to conclude that the "problem with EFS is not Arianism, but the fact that it entails tritheism."[46]

⌒

This is in fact the standard position of many, if not the majority, of proponents of eternal functional subordination. Though few are prepared to argue the theological case in the way Maxwell and Butner have done, it is clear that most subordinationists are entirely convinced that "subordination," as an incommunicable property, is not just accidental but necessary or essential to the unique identity of the Son. Furthermore, as both essential and unique to the eternal Son's personal identity, it is regularly held that this may be believed simultaneously with their continuing allegiance to the requirements of the *homoousion*.

It is also clear that in promoting this belief they are quite convinced that they stand squarely in the tradition of the Bible and historical Christian orthodoxy. The Carillon Avenue authors of the Sydney Doctrine Commission Report of 1999, for example, are immovably firm in their convictions—not only in their belief in the relational subordination of the Son to the Father, but in their conviction that this in no way conflicts with the shared equality of essential divinity required by the *homoousion* and that both propositions are scriptural. They thus conclude "that the concept of 'functional subordination,' of equality of essence with order in relation, represents the long-held teaching of the church, and that it is securely based on the revelation of the Scriptures."[47] This is understandable in view of the overwhelming influence that T. C. Hammond has had on Australian Carillon Avenue theology through the teaching instrument of his book *In Understanding Be Men*, with its much-quoted belief which clearly and quite unequivocally insists that the doctrine of the Trinity requires *both* the affirmation of the subordination of the Son to the Father and the "full deity" of all three Trinitarian identities (in accordance with the *homoousion*). These are to be held together.[48]

Likewise, without relying on any direct dependence on Maxwell's taxonomy of the categorization of the divine Trinitarian properties,

46. Butner, "Eternal Functional Subordination," 132.

47. Sydney Doctrine Commission Report 1999, sec. 6.4/para. 45. Also see the endorsement of this by Jensen, *Sydney Anglicanism*, 132.

48. Hammond, *In Understanding Be Men*, 56, quoted in the 1999 Sydney Doctrine Commission Report 1999, sec. 3.2/para. 15.

Butner somewhat surprisingly also assumes that the property of subordination may rightly be associated with the person of the Son, thereby tacitly agreeing with Maxwell's placement of the Son's subordination as a Category 1 property. Like Maxwell, Butner believes that eternal submissiveness, being allegedly a *hypostatic* property that is unique to the person of the Son,[49] is to be treated as something quite separate from the shared properties of his essential divine nature, which Maxwell places in his Category 2. In this way it is allegedly quarantined from other properties that the Son possesses by virtue of his sharing in the divine nature,[50] and so is kept well clear of the requirements of the *homoousion*.

It also has to be said, however, that the classification of subordination as an eternal incommunicable property of the Son is a novel innovation that is incongruent with respect to the traditional understanding of the theology of the Holy Trinity, as Kevin Giles's sustained historically based critique over the last two decades has surely demonstrated. The challenge is to try to untangle the theological argument that has led to this all too apparent disjunction of the conflict of ideas.

The crucial issue is whether the "standard argument" for classifying "eternal functional subordination" as a form of Arianism is as faulty as Butner imagines it to be, and, furthermore, whether there is in fact any theologically convincing justification for categorizing the Son's alleged eternal subordination to the Father as an incommunicable property that is unique to his hypostatic identity as the Son. The question is: can all this be theologically justified?

⤳

The first thing to note is that, while Maxwell simply assumed at the outset of his argument that subordination may be categorized as a Category 1 property that is unique to the personal identity of the Son, on the slender basis of a belief that it is implicit in the idea of "sonship" generally conceived, Butner goes a step further. In the course of signaling his disenchantment with the arguments of those who categorize eternal functional submissiveness as a form of Arianism, he actually seeks quite positively to defend this proposition. The reason given for his allocation of the specific incommunicable identifying property of submissiveness to the

49. In Maxwell's taxonomy, a Category 1 property.
50. The shared divine properties of Maxwell's Category 2.

unique hypostatic identity or person of the Son (effectively in Maxwell's Category 1) is said to be because "if one cannot apply a unique word to each hypostasis—at the very least the terms 'Father,' 'Son,' and 'Spirit'—then there is no way to distinguish the persons."[51] In other words, it is implied that the Son's submissiveness to the Father *is positively needed* to establish the unique identity of the Son as distinct from the Father. This means, however, that Butner defends the allocation of the specific identifying property of submissiveness to the *hypostasis* or person of the Son, over and above the usual appeal to his "being begotten" for this explicit identifying purpose. In the case of the Spirit, it is being "brought forth" or "proceeding" from the Father that fulfills this purpose. In both cases these identifying characteristics respectively of the Son and the Spirit are grounded in the biblical textual tradition.

We therefore have to ask whether there is either need or justification for assigning any *additional identifying criteria* either to establish or to bolster the *hypostatic* identities of the Trinitarian persons over and above the biblically sanctioned qualities of "begetting, being begotten, and proceeding." After all, it was to this biblically based formula that the early fathers regularly appealed in order to secure the unique identifying property of the Father as the "origin" and "cause" of the other two Trinitarian identities. Likewise, the fact that the Son is "eternally begotten" of the Father and the Spirit "proceeds" from the Father *are* the biblically sanctioned incommunicable properties that establish the unique identities of the Son and the Spirit in relation to the Father. And given that Butner has himself impressively demonstrated that there is no clearly uncontested biblical warrant in favor of belief in eternal functional submissiveness in the immanent life of the Trinity, we are obliged to ask the very pertinent question as to whether there is any textual warrant for applying *additional behavioral properties* that might distinguish the identity of the Father from the Son and the Spirit over and above this traditional biblically sanctioned appeal to the Father's "begetting," the Son's "being begotten," and the Spirit's "proceeding"?

While each of the three Trinitarian persons is uniquely identified and described by appeal respectively to the properties of "begetting, being begotten," or "proceeding," it is quite another thing to import alleged additional behavioral properties relating to "permanent roles, functions,

---

51. Butner, "Eternal Functional Subordination," 132.

command structures, and obedience between the Father and the Son"[52] that are also said to be essential to the definition of their unique identities. To contend that the eternal Father necessarily commands and the eternal Son always willingly obeys, in a way that introduces a relationship of domination and submission into the triune life even in the absence of uncontested biblical reasons for doing so, and to insist nevertheless that this is somehow essential to secure the unique identities respectively of Father and Son (and Spirit) is exactly what is at issue.

Curiously, once again exhibiting a strange tendency to equivocate, at one point Butner at least initially acknowledged this: "Advocates of EFS," he says, "are correctly using classical trinitarian metaphysics but incorrectly replacing terms like 'unbegotten' and 'begotten' with the ideas 'authority' and 'submission.'"[53] Indeed Butner has himself demonstrated that this would introduce the quite disastrous outcome of a multiplicity of willing, and so fracture the unity of the divine life. This surely suggests that whether this can be theologically justified is highly questionable. Moreover, whether this can be done without compromising the definition of the *homoousion* may be more problematic than Butner imagines. After all, the definition of the *homoousion* acts as a discouragement from doing exactly this kind of thing on the dogmatic grounds that this would introduce inequalities and divisions into the divine life. The indications are that such inequalities and divisions would in the end therefore lead logically to a form of subordinationism of the kind that historically has attracted the epithet "Arian." In a way, that would render the assurances of the proponents that they uphold the *homoousion* somewhat empty.

⤚

While there is a tendency amongst proponents of Trinitarian subordinationism simply to assume that they stand in the historical tradition of Christian orthodoxy, without engaging in theological argument to demonstrate this, many of them have necessarily been pressed to respond on dogmatic grounds to those who have charged them with the heresy of Arianism. Among the most notable critics of belief in the Son's eternal submissiveness that have called forth a response are Thomas McCall and Millard Erickson, both of whom contend that the chief problem with

52. Robert Doyle's formula relating to what is involved. See his Introduction to "Use and abuse."

53. Butner, "Eternal Functional Subordination," 132.

belief in "eternal functional submissiveness" (and the same applies to "eternal relational subordination") is that *it does lead* logically to a form of Arianism precisely because it is ultimately inimical to the Nicene definition of the *homoousion*. Millard Erickson's statement of the standard argument against "eternal functional submissiveness" is put in a usefully succinct form:

> The problem is this: If authority over the Son is an essential, not an accidental, attribute of the Father, and subordination to the Father is an essential, not an accidental, attribute of the Son, then something significant follows. Authority is part of the Father's essence, and subordination is part of the Son's essence, and each attribute is not part of the essence of the other person. That means that the essence of the Son is different from the essence of the Father. . . . That is equivalent to saying that they are not homoousios with one another.[54]

This is explicitly the kind of argument that Glenn Butner has found wanting and that grounds his conviction that while "eternal functional subordinationism" leads to a form of tritheism, insofar as it necessarily involves belief in multiple divine wills, it does not constitute an assault on the *homoousion* and therefore does not qualify to be categorized as an example of Arianism.

In any event, Thomas McCall sets out essentially the same argument as Erickson in the form of a series of logical steps:

(1) If Hard EFS is true, then the Son has the property of being functionally subordinate in all time segments of all possible worlds.

(2) If the Son has this property in every possible world, then the Son has this property necessarily. Furthermore, the Son has this property with *de re* rather than *de dicto* necessity.

(3) If the Son has the property necessarily (*de re*), then the Son has it essentially.

(4) If Hard EFS is true, then the Son has this property essentially while the Father does not.

(5) If the Son has this property essentially and the Father does not, then the Son is of a different essence than the Father. Thus the Son is *heteroousios* rather than *homoousios*.[55]

54. Butner, "Eternal Functional Subordination," 131, citing Erickson, *Who's Tampering with the Trinity?*, 172.

55. McCall, *Which Trinity? Whose Monotheism?*, 179–80. "Hard EFS" is McCall's way of referring to the Son as being eternally functionally subordinate to the Father in the internal life of Trinity. See also Ware, "Does Affirming an Eternal

Paul Maxwell responded explicitly to this argument in the course of his taxonomical classification of properties within the immanent life of the Trinity by charging McCall with the fundamental mistake of not distinguishing different categories of divine properties, notably the properties that he himself identifies as Category 1A and 1B (the subsisting properties essential to the identities of the Father and the Son) as distinct from Category 2 properties (the essential properties of the Son equally shared with the Father and Holy Spirit by virtue of the definition of the *homoousion*). By failing to observe what to Maxwell's mind is this important distinction, McCall was said to be guilty of sliding promiscuously from his own Proposition 4 to his Proposition 5 in the argument set out above, i.e., from a focus on the property of submissiveness/subordination as an incommunicable Category 1A or 1B property attaching to the *hypostasis* of the Son by moving to the *homoousion* (which properly applies *only* to the communicable or shared properties governed by the requirement of sameness and equality appertaining to the divine nature but not with the incommunicable properties relating to the Son's unique identity).

As we have already seen, however, Maxwell's delineation of submissiveness as an incommunicable property attaching to the *hypostasis* of the Son (in his Category 1) assumes what has to be proved. Submissiveness as an eternal personal property that is unique to the Son as Son is, as Butner has shown, exactly what cannot be demonstrated from Scripture in any unequivocally clear or uncontested way. Apart from the Son's "being eternally begotten" of the Father there is no warrant for allocating additional identifying properties to him or to any of the Trinitarian identities. Rather, all the essential properties of the divine nature of the Son are equally shared by the Father, Son, and Holy Spirit and are therefore communicable. They thus properly fall not in Maxwell's Category 1 (as incommunicable hypostatic properties) but in his Category 2 (as equally shared properties of the divine nature).

Maxwell's allocation of "submissiveness" from the outset as a Category 1 property attaching to the hypostatic identity of the Son that is thereby said to be independent of the *homoousion* is at best the result of what he speaks of as a "charitable reading" of texts relating to the Son and at worse the result of an entirely arbitrary allocation of "innascibility" to the Father not just as the polar opposite of the Son's being begotten,

---

Authority-Submission Relationship in the Trinity Entail a Denial of Homoousios?"

but (mistakenly) as logically implying the Son's being begotten, which he accepts as the basis of a fundamental difference between the Father and the Son and hence of belief in the Son's subordination to the Father. He assumes what needs to be proved. Then, having constructed the high-flying apparatus of this trapeze theology, Maxwell requires McCall to ascend to the same high platform, off which he is then nudged—at the same time being urged to grab the swinging bar of "eternal submissiveness" as an arbitrarily fabricated Category 1A incommunicable property allegedly attached to the *hypostasis* of the Son. McCall should rightly be encouraged not to swing with this problematic apparatus, and to hold his ground.

On the other hand, Glenn Butner entertains some additional serious reservations explicitly in relation to the stated positions of Erickson and McCall. His particular complaint focuses upon their use of the terms "essentially" and "essence." McCall's argument, for example, is that, if the Son has the property of eternal submissiveness not accidentally but eternally and "essentially" and the Father does not, then the Son is of a different essence, and that this amounts to an attack on the *homoousion*. In response to this, Butner points out that this use of the word "essential" (for which McCall recruits the support of Alvin Plantinga[56]) and then the use of the cognate term "essence" is at variance with the way the early Fathers used the term "essence." His complaint is not so much with the definitional meaning given to the term by Plantinga and McCall as with the use of the term "essence" specifically in relation to the person of the Son, for, he says, in the usage of the Fathers this term relates explicitly *not* to the person of the Son but to the equally shared divine nature. In other words, "essence" has to do with what is necessary or "essential" *to the nature of divinity,* but not with the *hypostasic identity* of the Son. It follows that the property of submission, if it "does *not* apply to the divine essence, but only to the person of the Son,"[57] is not one of the "essential" properties

56. Plantinga argued that a property is held essentially "if and only if [a thing] has [that property] and could not possibly have lacked it." See McCall, *Which Trinity? Whose Monotheism?*, 179n15.

57. Butner, *Son Who Learned Obedience*, 23. He cites multiple examples of scholars who categorize eternal submission as "a property exclusively of the Son," "strictly and only a personal property," and "a property of his personhood in relation (and only in

of the divine nature governed by the *homoousion* and therefore cannot be held to be in conflict with its requirements of sameness and equality. It therefore follows that, if it does not conflict with the requirements of the *homoousion*, the charge of Arianism is inappropriate.

All this, however, is something of a quibble. Even if Butner is right in his contention that the Fathers used the term "essence" of the divine nature but not in relation to the *hypostatic* identity of the Son, he knows perfectly well that if asked, they would certainly have said that "being begotten" *is* of the essence of the person of the Son, and quite necessary to his identity as Son. But perhaps they did not apply the words "essence" or "essential" to other *hypostatic* properties of the Son, such as his alleged subordination in relation to the Father, precisely because they did not so much as speak of "additional properties" as being necessary to secure the unique identity of the Son over and above the fact of his having been begotten by the Father! They did not apply the word "essential" to additional incommunicable properties because they were not in the business of talking about additional properties! Butner's point is empty.

᠆ꝗ

In the course of signaling that he does not find the arguments of either McCall or Erickson compelling, Butner willingly accepts that the proponents of "eternal functional submissiveness" affirm their belief in the essential properties of the divine nature that are shared by all three of the Trinitarian identities in accordance with the *homoousion*. Furthermore, he apparently accepts the contention that these can be kept logically independent of the affirmation also of the "eternal submissiveness" of the Son as an additional defining property of his unique hypostatic or personal identity.

It can readily be acknowledged that, by this strategy of thought, the "eternal submissiveness" that is said to be expressive of the Son's subordination to the Father is *conceived and spoken of* in a way that is imagined to quarantine it from having any negative impact on the standard

---

relation) to the Father" (Ware, "Does Affirming an Eternal Authority Submission?," 244); "the defining hypostatic characteristic of the Son" (Smail, *Like Father, Like Son*, 169); the Son's "distinguishing personal characteristic" (Horrell, "Complementarian Trinitarianism," 352). See also: "There is no subordination within the divine nature . . . there is subordination of role among the persons, which constitutes part of the distinctiveness of each." Frame, *Systematic Theology*, 501.

requirements of the *homoousion*. However, *to think or speak* of something in a specific way does not make it so. It is one thing *to say* that the property of "submitting to the Father" is a personal incommunicable property of the Son in relation to the Father while the Father lacks this property, and in addition *to say* that this is affirmed in such a way that the *homoousion* is not brought into play so that it is not in any way affected. Nevertheless, regardless of what the proponents of "eternal functional submission" may *think and say*, it is, even so, not necessarily the case that the definition of the *homoousion* in fact remains unsullied.

While Butner is content to accept the validity of the assumption that "claims made about the divine *hypostases*" are "not claims about the essence,"[58] the crucial question is whether these specific claims made about the *hypostasis* of the Son, which are said to apply explicitly only to his personal identity, may actually be made without generating logical implications that have a noxious impact on the definition of the *homoousion*. In other words, we are obliged to ask if it is really possible that what is said to be the Son's defining behavioral property of willing obedience in response to the Father's defining property of commanding, can actually be understood to be entirely separate from, or other than, the essential properties of the divine nature that were defined at Nicaea by the *homoousion* as being equally shared and the same.[59]

↜

Clearly, a great deal depends upon the attempt of the proponents of eternal functional submissiveness to tie the property of the Son's subordination to his *hypostatic* identity (with which Butner is content to acquiesce) in a way that "sidesteps" and so quarantines it from the requirements of the definition of the *homoousion*. This demands some very careful scrutiny.

---

58. Butner, *Son Who Learned Obedience*, 22.

59. Another example of the assumption that it is possible to affirm the eternal functional or relational subordination of the Son to the Father and at the same time to confess belief that all three persons of the Trinity share one and the same divine nature as required by the *homoousion*, was provided by David F. Wright, who insisted that, though some affirm the "eternal function or relational subordination" of the Son to the Father, "on all sides in the present debate" the three persons of the Trinity are "confessed to be co-equally divine." Wright, "Dr. Carnley on T. C. Hammond and Arianism," 47.

At the outset it has to be noted that, in order to avoid the charge of the heresy of Arianism, the proponents of "eternal functional submissiveness" are obliged to distinguish the sonship of the Son from his divinity by saying that the Son *as Son* is obediently submissive, but the Son *as divine* is not eternally submissive, because he is by virtue of his divine nature "of the same substance" as the Father (the *homoousion*). In other words, when the "submissive obedience" of the Son is classified independently of the equally shared properties essential to the divine nature that are subject to the *homoousion*, and instead classified as a unique property of his *hypostasis*, it is understood as a property that has to do with the identity of the Son *as Son* rather than with the identity of the Son as divine.[60] This point is clearly made by Philip Gons and Andrew Naseli, who argue that eternal submission "inheres in what it means for the Son to be Son, not in what it means for the Son to be God."[61] It is in this way that it is hoped that both the obedient submissiveness of the Son and the authoritative power of command of Father may be classified as unique incommunicable properties respectively of the persons so as to (help) define their intra-Trinitarian relationship, and may therefore be kept well clear of any reference to the *homoousion*.[62]

It is significant that this proposition is of a piece with Maxwell's allocation of submissiveness in addition to the fundamental defining property of "being eternally begotten" also as a Category 1 property to the hypostatic identity of the Son. Unfortunately, it is no less arbitrary and lacking biblical warrant than we have already noted in relation to Maxwell's proposals. But let us follow the logical route to the outcomes to which it leads.

The proposal at issue is designed to exempt the respective behavioral properties of the Father's commanding and the Son's submissive obedience from the requirements of the Nicene definition of the *homoousion*, by insisting that these properties are *separate* from the shared properties of the divine nature that are subject to the Nicene definition. In this way, as Butner says, "provided that whatever is said of the Son submitting is said of the *person* of the Son through relational predication and not the shared divine nature or essence through substantial predication," no challenge is posed to the Council of Nicaea's definition of the

---

60. See the exposition of this in Butner, *Son Who Learned Obedience*, 22–25.

61. Gons and Naselli, "Three Recent Philosophical Arguments," 204–5.

62. Gons and Naselli, "Three Recent Philosophical Arguments," 204–5.

*homoousion*. The hope is that this allows both propositions to be entertained at the same time without logical competition, and that belief in the "eternal functional subordination" of the Son to the Father is therefore impervious to the charge of Arianism. Once again, the end result of this strategy of argument is effectively to sidestep the *homoousion*.

⌐⌐

Perhaps an analogy may help to unpack the conceptual knot that this actually involves, not to mention the logical and theological pitfall it harbors. It might be said, for example, that a sock *as a sock* is *essentially* foot-shaped, especially when a foot is in it, and that this is what gives it its identity as a sock, but a sock *as made of wool* might be said to be warm—in the sense of possessing the property of being capable of generating warmth. In this way, different predicates are applied according to whether the sock is being referred to and *identified* as an item of apparel, or whether it is being spoken of by reference to the *substance* of which it is made, along with the warming properties associated with that substance. Both propositions may be affirmed simultaneously without logical competition; no self-contradiction is involved. In a sense, the shape *defines* the sock; that it is made of wool distinguishes the substance of which it is made from other alternatives (cotton or some kind of synthetic).

Similarly, on analogy with the sock, in the case of the identity of the divine Son, one property (submissiveness/subordination) is said to be unique to his hypostatic identity which, along with his "being eternally begotten," assists in defining the Son over against the Father. But the nature of the essential substance of the Son and Father is said to be a separate and altogether different matter. As with the properties of the sock, both the Nicene insistence on the sameness and equality of the communicable properties of the divine nature that are of the essence of the substance of divinity, and the incommunicable properties involved in the relational subordination of the Son to the Father and his identity as Son, may therefore be held together. As the authors of the Sydney Doctrine Commission Report of 1999 put it, it is possible for "eternal relational subordination" to be promoted because "equality of essence with order in relation" may be entertained as simultaneous truths. Undoubtedly, the authors of the report hoped that "eternal functional subordination" would therefore pose no challenge to the Nicene affirmation of the essential equality and sameness of the shared divine substance and its nature.

The analogy of the woolen sock, however, harbors a set of logical difficulties. Insofar as it can be said that a sock may be *identified* as a sock because it is foot-shaped, and at the same time that as made of the substance of wool it is warm, without generating any logical competition, it has to be remembered that as foot shaped it takes on that identifying shape that identifies it as a sock, particularly in a three-dimensional sense, when a foot is in it. To speak of it as being made of wool and therefore as warm may be to speak of properties that are separate from its shape, but unfortunately in *saying* that they are separate in this way, this does not mean that *as made of wool* the substance of which it is made is somehow *actually separate* either from the sock or separate from the foot that wears the sock. Likewise, it cannot be said that the property of obedient submissiveness is associated with the *hypostasis* of the Son, but that other behavioral properties (those that are equally shared with the Father and the Spirit as properties of the divine nature and therefore subject to the *homoousion*) are somehow *not* actually associated with the *hypostasis* of the Son (or the *hypostases* of the Father and the Spirit for that matter). They may be *thought of* as being separate from the incommunicable properties that are thought to be associated with the identity of the *hypostasis* of the Son, and so as being different enough *to be spoken of* separately, but that does not mean that they have some kind of actual existence that is independent of the *hypostasis* of the Son. Indeed, the Fathers would have said that there can be no divine substance (*ousia*) without a *hypostasis*. The divine substance and its nature that is subject to the requirements of the *homoousion* do not float free, as it were, in independence of the divine *hypostases,* while the specific property of submissiveness or subordination *is* associated with the *hypostasis* of the Son, just as the power of command *is* associated with the *hypostasis* of the Father.[63]

In other words, in responding to the insistence of proponents of eternal subordination that the alleged incommunicable property of submissiveness is associated with the *hypostasis* of the Son rather than being a property of the shared divine nature, we should not be beguiled into thinking that the shared properties of the same divine nature that are secured by the *homoousion* somehow float free as though entirely detached from the *hypostasis* of Son (or of the Father, and the Holy Spirit). As even Arius well knew, there can be no divine nature without a *hypostasis*.

63. See the classic statement of Letter 38.2 (whether attributed to Basil or Gregory of Nazianzus) that the substance never exists in a "naked" state, without a *hypostasis*. *Patrologia Graeca* 32, 325, and following pages.

This means that, while submissiveness is said by the proponents of "eternal functional subordination" to be associated with the person of the Son and also that this is important to his *hypostatic* identity, but is not to be spoken of in association with the behavioral properties of the Son that he shares with the Father and the Spirit as properties of his essential divine nature, this does not mean that these properties have some kind of existence in independence of the *hypostasis* of the Son. In both cases, these respective properties—one the incommunicable behavioral property of submissiveness allegedly associated with the *hypostasis* of the Son and with the Son's filial identity in relation to the Father, and the other, the behavioral properties of the equally shared divine nature—are all associated with the *hypostasis* of the Son. Divine nature and *hypostasis* belong together as much as the property of eternal functional submissiveness and the *hypostasis* of the Son are said allegedly to belong together.

⮑

Now, if it is said that the Son's unique identity precisely as Son (rather than as divine) is to be "obediently submissive" and furthermore that it is not accidental but an eternal identifying *hypostatic* property of the Son, then it seems to follow that we are able to say that "obedient submissiveness" to the Father comes by nature or naturally to the Son. Indeed it is necessary to the Son's identity as Son. However, this is in effect to furnish the *hypostasis* of the Son with a nature that is separate from or in addition to the divine nature that is shared with the Father (and that is subject to the requirements of the *homoousion*). We might well speak of it as his "filial nature" as distinct from his "divine nature." Likewise, if the power of command, as a kind of commanding authority, is said to be an incommunicable defining property of the *hypostatic* identity of the Father in relation to the Son, so that "commanding" is not just accidental, but something that comes by nature or naturally to the Father, then it logically follows that "commanding" is a property of the Father's paternal nature. This means that the Father is also furnished with a nature that is uniquely specific to his identity in addition to the divine nature constituted by the communicable properties that he shares equally with the Son and the Holy Spirit. The net result of furnishing the *hypostases* of the Father and Son with these specific properties is that both Father and Son must be said to possess natures in which the power of command and obedient submissiveness respectively are incommunicable. These properties therefore that are natural to them, or that come by nature to them, may be said to endow their respective *hypostases* with their essential and defining relational identities.

But if it is said that the Son is, by virtue of his nature as Son, and as a matter of his personal or *hypostatic* identity, naturally and necessarily and not just accidentally eternally submissive to the Father (even in terms of function or relationality), so that submissiveness comes by nature to the Son, or is natural to the Son and his personal identity, just as the power of command comes by nature or is natural to the Father's personal identity, then this means that both Father and Son possess natures that are definitive of their specific identities in addition to and in some way separate from the set of communicable properties of the divine nature that they both share (and that are subject to the requirements of the *homoousion*).

Specifically in the case of the Son, this means that the allocation of an incommunicable property (submissiveness) to the *hypostasis* of the Son *as Son*, and separate or contrasting communicable properties to the *hypostasis* of the Son *as divine*, would mean that the *hypostasis* of the Son possesses two separate sets of properties that come by nature to him or that are natural to him—with some properties falling under the provisions of the *homoousion* while another (allegedly being submissively obedient) does not.

Butner may well be right in saying that the early church fathers did not use the term "essence" (or "essential" for that matter) in the sense in which Erickson and McCall use it, but only in relation to the equally shared divine nature. Indeed any inclination that the Fathers may have entertained to speak of "submissiveness" as an incommunicable property relating to the identity of the Son was logically suppressed (and perhaps quite intentionally avoided) by their concentration on the biblically based appeal exclusively to the properties of "begetting, being begotten, and proceeding" for this purpose. But the important point here is that this is a logical not a historical matter. The point is not that the early Fathers did not use the language of Erickson and McCall; Erickson and McCall may well assent to that. The point is that Erickson and McCall make the point that the proponents of eternal functional submission, by claiming that submissiveness is a defining property that is necessary to the identity of the Son, cannot avoid the *logical* implication that it is essential or "of the essence" of the Son's identity precisely as Son. Even if the early church fathers did not use the term in this way, the proponents of "eternal functional submissiveness" *do* speak of the property of submissiveness as "*essential*" or "of the essence" of the identity of the Son as Son. Furthermore they do speak of the power of command, not as something that is accidental to the identity of the Father, but as something that is *essential* to the identity of the Father. It is said to be a property that defines the Father's identity and is unique to him. In other words, we may say that it is essential to his paternal nature in the sense that "commanding" comes by nature or naturally to him. Likewise obedient submissiveness is said to be essential to the Son in relation to the Father as a property of his nature as Son, in the sense that "being obedient" comes necessarily and by nature or naturally to him. Moreover, this is the *divine* Son whose *hypostasis* is also furnished with a nature that is one and the same as that of the Father. This means that to furnish the Son with the property of "eternal functional submissiveness" is to furnish him with a property that logically implies a nature *in addition to* the divine nature of shared properties that are subject to the requirements of the *homoousion*.

It follows that if two distinguishable eternal natures are associated with the *hypostasis* of the Son, one his divine nature and the other what I have termed his filial nature, so that what comes naturally or by nature to him as divine is one thing and what comes naturally or by nature to him as Son is quite another, then we may be a little less confident about the belief that "eternal functional subordination" can somehow actually be held apart from the properties of the divine nature that are subject to the definition of the *homoousion*, even if it is *said* that they are. To say that submissiveness is associated with the *hypostasis* of the Son and not his divine nature does not make a good deal of sense if the properties of the divine nature are also associated with his *hypostasis*. Furthermore, simply *speaking* of the eternal Son's filial nature as somehow different from his eternal divine nature, does not necessarily entail that the Son actually *has* two different eternal natures (one filial and one divine).

Moreover, we may find that talk of the Son's eternal filial nature and his eternal divine nature may be entirely unjustified on scriptural grounds, and that, rather, they are one and the same (unsurprisingly in accordance with the requirements of the *homoousion*!). We may also find that, by virtue of his filial identity, being eternally begotten of the Father, the Son is not the subordinate of the Father, but the Father's equal, simply sharing one and the same divine nature.

⌐

But let us not get ahead of ourselves, for there is yet another troubling implication of the attempt to associate the property of submissiveness with the *hypostasis* of the Son so as to sidestep the *homoousion*. An additional logically related issue arises in relation to the use of the terms "functional" and "relational" when it is said that the incommunicable properties of the power of command and obedient submissiveness are to be associated with the *hypostases* respectively of the Father and the Son (in distinction from the properties that are said to be essential to the divine nature that is equally shared by all three *hypostatic* identities of the Trinity). For the suggestion is that these latter properties that are subject to the provisions of sameness and equality required by the *homoousion* are somehow *not* relational or functional in the way that the alleged incommunicable properties of command and obedience are said to be relational. Bruce Ware explicitly says, for example, that these properties are distinguished by virtue of the fact that subordination "is a property of the person of the Son, and it is a property that could exist only in relation to another person."[64] The suggestion is that the properties of the divine nature that are subject to the requirements of the *homoousion* are somehow *not* similarly relational.

However, the requirement of sameness and of the equal sharing of properties of the definition of the *homoousion* are a signal of the fundamental relationality of the *hypostases*. When one thing is said to be the *same* as another, the two terms are necessarily conceived in a relationship of comparison if not of identity. Clearly, when the communicable properties that are subject to the requirements of the *homoousion* are said to be "essential" to the shared divinity of all three of the Trinitarian identities, this does not signal a want of relationship. For example, the love of the Father, which is one and the same as the love of the Son, and shared equally by both of them, signals the relational unity of their interpersonal communion precisely as *hypostatic* identities.

This should alert us to the fact that while the proponents of eternal functional subordination appear to believe that they are making a valid distinction between "equality of essence with order in relation"[65] this formula actually masks an illusion. After all, "relationality" is of the *essence* of divinity. If God is understood as three persons and one interpersonal

64. Ware, "Does Affirming an Eternal Authority Submission?," 244.

65. The formula of the authors of the Sydney Doctrine Commission Report 1999.

communion of love, then this relationality is of the essence of divinity. The relationality of mutual self-gift in the life of the Trinity is not something somehow belonging to the *hypostases* of the Trinitarian identities in some way that is distinct or separate from their shared divine nature. Rather, relationality is fundamental to the understanding of the unity and Trinitarian character of the divine nature. Moreover, the same will would be exercised by the Son in being obediently submissive in relation to the Father, as is exercised when the Son willingly loves the Father. After all, some sons do love their fathers as well as obey them. How is it that being submissively obedient is said to be an act of will associated with the *hypostasis* of the Son in relation to the Father, while by an act of will the Son's loving of the Father is said to be not a relational or functional hypostatic property of the Son but an essential ontological and equally shared property of the divine nature?

Furthermore, according to Butner's own argument the divine property of willing should be placed under the umbrella of the *homoousion*, along with all other communicable properties of the divine nature, and not taken from under this umbrella and located separately in some kind of isolated association with the *hypostasis* of the Son as an incommunicable property unique to him in distinction from the willing of the Father and the Holy Spirit. Otherwise, as Butner rightly points out, talk of different individualized willing amongst the Trinitarian identities leads to a tri-willing tritheism. Divine willing is a property of the divine nature that is equally shared by all three *hypostases*; because the Trinity does not involve three wills, but one and the same will, the three Trinitarian identities act together and in unison. This is essential to the unity of the One God. But being eternally submissive is a matter of willing. If, as Butner says, willing is a property of the divine nature (and not an incommunicable property relating to the hypostatic identities of the Trinitarian persons) then in this case it must be subject to the provisions of the *homoousion*. It is therefore puzzling that Butner expresses sympathy for the proponents of eternal functional submissiveness in their determination to keep well clear of the requirements of the *homoousion* by classifying the Son's alleged submissiveness as an incommunicable property that is said to be necessary for establishing the unique *hypostatic* identity of the Son, and by associating this specific property with his *hypostasis*, rendering it no longer a property of the divine nature that he shares with the Father. At the same time, however, Butner insists that willing cannot be an incommunicable *hypostatic* property but must be a communicable property of the shared divine nature. There is obviously some confusion here. How can both these propositions be true when eternal functional submissiveness is an eternal *willingness* of the Son to be obediently submissive to the Father?

⤺

We are now in a position to ask a very important question: Why is it important to resist the innovative pressure of Maxwell, Butner, Grudem, and Ware, and many others including Australian Carillon Avenue theologians, to classify the property of submissiveness as a *hypostatic* property that is unique to the identity (and will?) of the Son? For the answer to this question we must first return to Scripture.

When we turn to the scriptural evidence relating to the theme of submissive obedience what we find in the Gospels is the account of the *human* willing obedience of the Son. This is the willing obedience that Butner himself has so convincingly brought to our attention as exactly what the overwhelming weight of the scriptural tradition invites us to contemplate regarding the submissiveness of the Son in relation to the Father. Insofar as he is submissively obedient to his God-given vocation, even unto death on the cross, the Son is the paradigm of self-giving than which there is none greater.[66] This is the "ultimate sacrifice." As Butner has successfully demonstrated, this is to be understood in terms of the exercise of the human will of the historical Jesus.

In addition to this, the Christian conviction is that this human Jesus is by virtue of the incarnation the revelation of God. Given the doctrine of the *communicatio idiomatum*,[67] key aspects of the unique character of the human Jesus are understood to reveal important aspects of the nature of the divine. This is why Athanasius insisted that the Son must be of the very same substance as the Father. He must be *homoousios* with the Father, for only so can he truly reveal God. Though Chalcedon declared

---

66. John 15:13: "There is no greater love than this: that a person would lay down his life for the sake of his friends."

67. The idea is first found in Ignatius of Antioch (c. 100) and developed by Tertullian (c. 155–220). See Kelly, *Early Christian Doctrines*, 151–2, quoting Tertullian as one of the first theologians to tackle the question of the relationship between Christ's two natures (*Adversus Praxean*, 27). This was endorsed at the Council of Ephesus in 431 and the Council of Chalcedon twenty years later with the articulation of the doctrine of the hypostatic union of the two distinct natures of Christ, one *homoousios* with the Father, and the other *homoousios* with humanity.

that he is also *homoousios* with humanity, it is as *homoousios* with God the Father that the truly human Jesus can truly reveal the nature of divinity.[68]

One of the favorite texts of Athanasius in his engagement with Arius was therefore found in the tradition of Jesus' engagement with Philip in John 14:8–10. In response to Philip's request to "show us the Father," Jesus replied: "the one who has seen me has seen the Father" (John 14:9). Insofar as the "submissive obedience" of the human Jesus "shows us the Father" we are obliged to reflect on the possibility that his "submissive obedience" of his human willing has an eternal dimension, not in the sense that it shows us the "eternal functional submissiveness'" of the Son alone but rather something that is shared with the Father—thus it does not just show us the eternal Son or Word; it "shows us the Father." In other words, the suggestion of Athanasian Trinitarianism is that the submissiveness that was known in the human Jesus revealed a property of the divine nature that is shared by all three of the Trinitarian identities.

Furthermore, because it is equally shared and the same, this means that it must be a kind of interpersonal "mutual submissiveness"—the selfless, other-regarding willingness to be of service to others, that is fully and equally shared by all three Trinitarian identities. The three are indivisibly one by being other-regarding and submissive to the other in an interpersonal communion of love and mutual concern. This means that Jesus as "the man for others" shows us something of a God who is the "God for others." He is one who came amongst us as "the one who serves" and so reveals a God not as a kind of self-concerned absolute potentate of coercive commanding power, but a God whose essential nature is equally and truly the same across all three Trinitarian identities—a God who is disposed graciously to serve the well-being of those who put their trust in him. In this case, "submissiveness" or "self-effacing subservience" is thus central to the revelation of *the divine nature* in and through the humanity of the incarnate Word.

Now, this means that there are good scriptural grounds for arguing that if the property of "submissiveness" is to be submitted to the kind of taxonomical classification of the kind pursued by Paul Maxwell, it is not arbitrarily to be placed in his Category 1, as an incommunicable property associated exclusively with the *hypostatic* identity of the Son in relation to the Father's *hypostatic* identity understood as a power of command, but in the first instance in Maxwell's Category 4 as a natural property of the

---

68. In accordance with the formula of the two natures defined at Chalcedon.

human Jesus, and then in his Category 2 as the revelation of a fundamentally key communicable or equally shared property of the divine nature. As such it conforms to the requirements of the *homoousion*. In other words, the self-effacing, other-regarding property of humble submissiveness as that was definitively known in the life and death of the human Jesus is to be taken seriously as the express image of the invisible God.

~

The appropriateness of this classificatory outcome is further enhanced by the fact that it is often said, even by proponents of "eternal functional subordination," that the Father shares his power and authority with the Son and the Spirit. In this case power and authority, including specifically the power of command, must be understood also as a communicable property. Robert Doyle, for example, points out that "the Father is the Ruler over all things" and "the Father's authority/rule" is a property "which he gives to the Son as the eternal Son."[69] In this case the power of command of the Father should not be classified using Maxwell's categories as a Category 1 incommunicable property that is essential to the Father's identity as Father and therefore unique to the Father, but as a Category 2 communicable property of the equally shared divine nature. It too is subject to the requirements of the *homoousion*.

This means that on both sides of the equation, the specific property of obedience that is said by the proponents of the "eternal functional subordination" to be a unique property of the Son in response to the power of command, which in turn is to be understood as being unique to the Father, that are classified as incommunicable properties associated with their respective *hypostases*, so as to be somehow independent of the *homoousion*, are in fact entirely misclassified.

On the contrary, they are both communicable properties of the divine nature that are equally shared by all three Trinitarian identities. In this case, if the other-regarding interpersonal "submissiveness" of the communion of persons of the Trinity in love is regarded, not as an incommunicable property that is unique to the identity of the Son (which Maxwell classifies in his Category 1), but as an equally shared divine property of "mutual submissiveness," a kind of self-effacing willingness to be of

69. Doyle, "Use and abuse," section on Athanasius, 2 (Doyle's italics). As we have seen, unfortunately in Doyle's understanding of things this is not ontological, however, but by an act of will a matter of the Father's grace and favor.

service to the other in love, it should be classified in Maxwell's Category 2. This means that, whereas the property of submissiveness/subordination, when it is thought of as a unique personal incommunicable property of the Son in relation to the power of command of the Father (so as to fall within Maxwell's Category 1) is said not to conflict with the *homoousion*, if it is understood as an equally shared property of "mutual submissiveness" we touch the very opposite truth. As a communicable property of the divine nature "mutual submissiveness" is thoroughly in accord with the requirements of the *homoousion*. "Submissiveness," as a consequence, is transformed from being unique to the Son and essentially different from its polar opposite, the power of command of the Father, into a kind of mutually other-regarding love and respect, an equally shared interpersonal deference to the "other" as a key property of the divine nature.

‌⤳

Moreover, though Glenn Butner has very persuasively shown us that there are no undisputed biblical texts that teach the "eternal functional subordination" of the Son to the Father of the kind that would warrant thinking of their relationship in terms of the power of command and obedient subordination as polar opposites in a relationship of domination and submission, there *is* undisputed biblical warrant for the belief that the obediently submissive human Jesus does indeed "show us the Father" as having the essentially same divine character. Indeed, the Jesus who said "the one who sees me has seen the Father" may be understood in faith to show us the Father in a definitive sense. He quite positively does not point us to his own alleged eternally submissive self from which we may infer the nature of the Father as his polar opposite, in the way the existence of a commanding master might to be inferred from the life of a servant. Instead, the incarnate life of the historical Jesus, through the mystery of his passion and death, reveals the nature of divinity in the form, not of the coercive power of this world, but in the form of the humbly submissive, suffering servant. In other words, the submissively obedient servant reveals God's own divine character as the essentially noncoercive but persuasive power of self-effacing love. As Barth perceptibly declared, the high and holy God who inhabits eternity is known in the humility and obedience of the cross of Jesus Christ: "It is in the light of the fact of his humiliation . . . that all the predicates of his Godhead, which is the true Godhead, must be filled out and interpreted."[70]

Wolfhart Pannenberg has correctly pointed out:

> The biblical witness tells us about the personal relationship between Father, Son and Holy Spirit, that constitutes the different persons of the Trinity. It tells us about the mutuality of their personal relations, and if mutuality is indispensable to all personal communion, the trinitarian communion of Father, Son and Holy Spirit must be understood to be the eternal source and model of mutuality in all personal communion.[71]

In these words Pannenberg is at pains to make the point that the interpersonal mutuality of sharing equally and fully in the same divine nature actually assists in securing the personal identities of all three Trinitarian persons as against all forms of modalism, given that it is a mutuality of distinct persons: "The mutuality of personal relations, then, secures the personal distinctions as well as the communion between the persons." In their personal distinctions as Father, Son, and Spirit, the begetter, the only begotten of the Father, and the one proceeding from the Father, they enjoy a set of relations that "are not reversible" but this constitutes their personal distinctiveness as well as their communion with one another as persons. Thus, the self-distinction of Father, Son, and Spirit that is known in the economy of salvation is matched by the revelation of the mutuality of their interpersonal relations of love that constitutes their "*perichoretic communion.*"[72] What is revealed of the divine in the economy of salvation is not only something about the unique personal identities of Father, Son, and Spirit, but something about their mutually shared divine nature.

St. Paul effectively makes this point in Philippians 2, in which "the mind that was in Christ Jesus" (v. 5) is characterized in terms of "self-emptying" (v. 7). In much traditional exegesis of this kenotic passage it is as though this self-employing involved a setting aside of divine power and authority in the interests of becoming human; the divine nature was in a sense withdrawn and not brought into play during the course of Jesus' incarnate life, in much the same way as the undercarriage of an aircraft is withdrawn during the course of a flight. This self-limiting condescension has been regarded as what was involved in the divine becoming man.

70. Barth, *Church Dogmatics*, IV/I, 130.

71. Pannenberg, "Divine Economy and Eternal Trinity," 84.

72. Pannenberg, "Divine Economy and Eternal Trinity," 85.

However, in contemporary exegesis[73] this kenotic passage is understood not in terms of the divine condescension of "becoming man" so much as in the first instance the human condescension involved in Jesus' life of becoming *a particular kind of man*. It is precisely a particular kind of humanity that is revelatory of the divine. The condescension of the "mind that was in Christ Jesus" was exhibited by the historical Jesus in choosing to pursue a specific form of humanity—the humble life of an other-regarding and always dutiful servant—which in turn is said by Paul to reveal "the form of God" (v. 6).[74] It is not that something is hidden or withdrawn from view, but the very opposite. The form of Jesus' servant humanity, even unto death on the cross, reveals something of the true nature of God.

In a similar way, in the second half of his Gospel, St. Mark makes it clear that Jesus is quite positively not a messiah of coercive power, even though this may have been the messianic hope of his day, but the humbly submissive one who is even prepared to be mistreated at the hands of others,[75] and who calls his true disciples to take up their cross and follow in the same way (Mark 8:31–34; 9:31–35; 10:32–45).[76] Despite the blindness of the scribes and Pharisees, his very own family, and even the inner circle of his first disciples (Mark 3:6; 6:1–5a; 8:14–21), which Mark sets out in the first half of the Gospel, by the miracle of sight, Bartimaeus becomes the paradigm of the true disciple who "sees clearly" and follows Jesus "in the way" (Mark 10:46–52). The passion narrative then follows. Mark's message about the true nature of Jesus' messiahship, and the

73. See for example, Moule, "Further Reflections on Philippians 2.5–11"; Schoonenberg, "'He Emptied Himself,'" and "Kenosis or Self-Emptying of Christ."

74. For a more detailed discussion of Philippians 2:.5–11, see Carnley, *Reconstruction of Resurrection Belief*, 291–98.

75. The essential passivity of having to "allow" or "permit" things to happen to oneself being the essence of suffering (as in Jesus' words "Suffer the little children to come to me"). This sense of the meaning of the Greek word *pascho* informs our understanding of Jesus "passion," which begins when he falls into the hands of others and thus becomes "patient of suffering." Physical pain may be part of suffering, but suffering is a much more inclusive category, signaling a passive "being done to" rather than being in command and acting coercively. The mystery of the cross of Christ in this way speaks of the nature of God.

76. The fact that this teaching is presented by Mark as Jesus' "plain" teaching (Mark 8:32) by contrast with the more enigmatic parables of the first half of the Gospel, and that it is repeated three times, with illustrations of the misunderstandings of the nature of messiahship on the part of the disciples who mistakenly think in terms of coercive power, is of course of the utmost revelatory significance.

nature of Christian discipleship, speaks unmistakably of the lowly and submissive humanity that is revelatory of the nature of God.

∽

If this scriptural tradition of the Christian good news is about the definitive nature of the messiahship of the human Jesus as truly revelatory of the divine nature of God and the values of his kingly reign, then in our systematic theological understanding submissiveness should rightly be placed, not in Paul Maxwell's taxonomical Category 1, as an eternal incommunicable property that is unique to the person of the Son, but in his Categories 4 and 2—first as a property of Christ's human nature (Category 4) that is then revelatory of the equally shared divine nature (Category 2) of the Triune God. Sadly, the proponents of eternal functional subordination, by arbitrarily associating it not with the divine nature of God, but instead uniquely with the *hypostasis* of the Son in relation with God the Father's power of command, effectively join Maxwell himself in removing it from Maxwell's Category 2 and placing it in his Category 1. This effectively (and disastrously) means that the property of "eternal submissiveness" is taken from under the umbrella of the divine nature where it is subject to the requirements of the *homoousion* as a property that is shared by all three of the Trinitarian identities, and associated instead uniquely (and mistakenly) with the *hypostasis* of the Son.

Maxwell candidly acknowledges that this strategy of argument amounts to an attempt to "sidestep" the Nicene definition of the *homoousion* so as to avoid compromising it. He notes that Ware's defense in response to McCall's critique holds that if "subordination is a Category 1 predicate—then he sidesteps the compromise of *homoousios*."[77] In pursuing an essentially similar strategy of argument, the 1999 Sydney Doctrine Commission Report expresses the hope that by separating belief in the eternal functional or relational subordination of the Son from the ontological divine substance and its nature, thus removing it from the requirements of the *homoousion*, it avoids falling to the charge of the heresy, while allowing for a hierarchical conception of God.[78]

---

77. Maxwell, "Is There an Authority Analogy?," 562.

78. Sydney Doctrine Commission Report 1999, sec. 4.7/para. 23: "The danger of heresy is met by the insistence that the Son and Spirit are of one being with the Father, but the position of the Father ensures a hierarchical mode of conceiving God."

≤⌐

However, the removal of the property of "mutual submissiveness" from the company of other properties of the divine nature that are subject to the requirement of sameness under the umbrella of the *homoousion* (from Maxwell's Category 2) and replacing it with the submissiveness of the Son to the Father that is unique to the *hypostasis* of the Son (in Maxwell's Category 1) obviously seriously compromises the integrity of the *homoousion*. Even worse, if submissiveness is subtracted from the set of shared properties governed by the *homoousion* and separately associated with the *hypostasis* of the Son alone, with the Father then being identified by the complementary property of the power of command, then we have on our hands relational properties of domination and submission that, far from being the same, are in fact polar opposites. Even if they are regarded as binary and complementary rather than equal and the same, as polar opposites they are properties that are not only different but are radically unalike.

It seems clear that these attempts to "sidestep" the provisions of the *homoousion* in the interests of promoting "Trinitarian complementarianism" mean that "eternal functional submissiveness" has a seriously negative impact on the requirements of sameness of substantial divine being and nature that are shared by all three *hypostases* of the Trinity. This means that the attempted removal of the property of mutual submissiveness from under the umbrella of the *homoousion* leads to a serious diminishment, not only of the *homoousion* itself, but of a fundamental understanding of the Christian revelation of the nature of God. This is living very dangerously from the point of view of Christian orthodoxy. For, if the Son is not *homoousios* with the Father in this specific respect, so that Father and Son (and Spirit) are no longer "mutually submissive" and "other-regarding," but on the contrary, so that an eternal obedient submissiveness that is said to be unique to the Son is rendered essentially different from, even though complementary to, the Father's commanding authority, then the result is theologically disastrous. For in this case there is a sense in which the Son is not only different from the Father, but *less than* the Father, just as a servant is necessarily less than his master. How is this not a form of Arianism?

# Chapter 7

# Is This Arianism?

If the terms "Arian" and "Arianism" are to be used to classify contemporary theological proposals as being in some way analogous to the views of Arius and his friends in the fourth century, we are naturally obliged to say a little more about the precise nature of their original views so as to be able to understand why it was that emerging Nicene orthodoxy found them offensive. Only so will we be in a position to say in more positive terms whether the drawing of a contemporary analogy may be justified.

Given that the *homoousion* has come to be accepted on both sides of the current debate as the benchmark of Christian orthodoxy, the precise nature of the heresy it was intended to correct remains somewhat unclear. It is one thing to define what may be described as "Arian" or classified as "a form of Arianism" by starting with what was intended to be its corrective. This means that what it originally *was* that might be described as "Arian" or classified as "a form of Arianism" tends to be "defined" negatively, and indeed, by a paradox, *in*definitely—as "whatever it was" that led the 318 assembled bishops at Nicaea between May and August in 325 to initiate the process that eventually led to the definition of the *homoousion*. To insist that all three persons of the Trinity fully and equally share the same divine nature is one thing; but to define what exactly it was that was perceived to pose such a threat to this standard of belief is a task that is not amenable to a simple or straightforward answer.

It is indisputable that the much-maligned Arius gave his name to what has come to be identified as arguably the most grave of Christian heresies. The bishops who assembled at Nicaea in 325 went back to their homes believing that they had dealt with Arius reasonably satisfactorily by deciding upon a standard of christological belief that eventually came to be accepted and thence known as the *homoousion*. But what exactly was "Arianism"? The fact that this question is so often asked signals that the quest for a clear answer faces something of a challenge.

⌇

In the first instance we have to contend with some historical problems associated with defining Arius's own original theological proposals with settled accuracy. The fragmentary nature of his surviving writings, and the fact that the picture we have of him and his views is filtered to us through the perceptions of his enemies, means that we are obliged to proceed with some caution. The received outline of the teaching with which others found fault comes to us *via* Alexander, his bishop, and others in Alexandria in the years that led up to Athanasius's championing of the rebuttal of Arius that triumphed all but unanimously at Nicaea in 325. Unfortunately, even if unwittingly, his critics tended to massage their presentations of Arius's alleged errors into sympathetic congruence with their own arguments. In the heat of argument some distortion appears to have become inevitable.

Apart from the fragmentary and sometimes problematic nature of the evidence at the point of origin of the controversy, over the centuries there has also been considerable disparity across successive historical versions of what has been condemned as "Arianism," even to the point of giving rise to speculation as to whether Arius was actually himself really an Arian.[1]

In the years immediately following Nicaea there was no organized movement of card-carrying "followers of Arius" who may be said to have promoted a specific agenda that can be accepted today as the definitive form of "Arianism." On the contrary, by default any anti-Nicene view tended to attract condemnation as a form of "Arianism" even in the apparent absence of detailed similarities with the views of Arius himself. This was the case, for example, in relation to Eunomius, bishop of Cyzicus, whose views appear to have been a good deal more extreme than those of his mentor.[2]

1. Rebecca Lyman notes that "'Arians' therefore inhabited different theological and rhetorical spaces . . . in the shifting imperial orthodoxy of the fourth century." "Topography of Heresy," 62.

2. See Ayres, *Nicaea and Its Legacy*, 106–7. By contrast Basil of Ancyra tended to be less extreme and so is often classified as a "semi-Arian."

Eunomius openly and insistently subordinated the Son to the Father on the basis of what he judged to be an essential difference between Father and the Son. In this case, the different identifying properties that are understood to be essential respectively to the Father and the Son are obviously understood to be incommunicable—the *unbegottenness* of the Father and the *begottenness* of the Son, which he said define the Father as Father and the Son as Son. These properties were acknowledged to be essential to the identity respectively of the Father and the Son, and on the basis of this difference Eunomius argued, contrary to Nicaea, that these two Trinitarian identities were of unlike substance. Similarly, the Anomoean decree of the Synod of Antioch in 362 explicitly set forth the doctrine that, because of the essential difference between the unbegotten Father and the begotten Son "the Son is in all things unlike (*kata panta anomoios*) the Father, as well in will as in substance." This emphasis on difference went well beyond the original proposals of Arius himself insofar as he seems to have treated the Logos, if not ontologically the same as the Father, having been created by the Father for the work of the creation of the material universe, as at least quasi-divine.

↜⟩

These problems have been compounded by the fact that there has been considerable speculation, particularly through the last two centuries, as to the precise nature of the formative intellectual forces that are alleged to have led Arius to the views that undeniably disturbed the lives of those who heard him. It is not easy to get a grip on the exact flow of his argument in view of the complexity of intellectual life in that era, both theological and philosophical, to which he might well be imagined to have been exposed.

It is understandable that what have been thought in the past to be the formative influences that explain Arius's views have therefore tended to be unhelpfully speculative. For example, John Henry Newman was convinced that Arius had received his ideas from an Antiochene source, and pointed in particular to Paul of Samosata as the author of a Christology with a Nestorian coloring. This led Newman to conclude that a Christology that effectively stressed the humanity of Jesus at the expense of the revealed mystery of his divinity was what lay at the heart of Arius's heretical views. This in turn allowed him to pillory Arius mercilessly as the author of the prototype of a kind of theological liberalism with which

Newman did battle in his own day. Newman was suspicious of the emerging biblical criticism in Germany, which he tended to identify as a liberalizing concentration on an all-too-human rationalistic temper of mind that minimized the importance of revelation. All this he believed could be traced back to a paradigm said to have been articulated first by Arius.

In the past many commentators have also pointed to the Neoplatonism of Plotinus, who in the century before Arius had taken Plato's doctrine of the ideal forms that were thought to be changeless, eternal, and transcendent, and prized them entirely apart from their material exemplifications in the shadowy, finite world of change and passing time. Plotinus then characteristically inserted a ladder of steps in between the resulting antithesis to produce a polarized worldview characterized by gradations of being between the ideal world of matterless form and the chaos of formless matter. Adolf von Harnack, as one notable heir to this tradition, believed that Arius was therefore led into a basic mistake through the influence of Greek philosophy. Even if it were tempered by the constant use of Holy Scripture, Greek philosophy was the real culprit.

In particular, Harnack concluded that Arius was "dominated by the thought of the antithesis of the one inexpressible God, a God remote from the world, and the creature" that called for gradations in the created order and intermediaries between God and creation.[3] Harnack almost certainly underestimated the importance for Arius of some key biblical texts, but Arius certainly shared a Plotinian insistence on removing God far from the world. In the light of this schema the incarnate Word "through whom all things were made" was said to have become necessary as a kind of intermediary to bridge the gap between God and the material order. Hence, at the beginning of Creation the Son was said to have been begotten or created to carry through the work of creation. By being "begotten timelessly"[4] at a particular point in a sequence prior to the material creation, the Word is accordingly conceived to be necessarily "less" than the Father, at best a quasi-divine subordinate of the ineffably remote and transcendent God.

However, despite the fact that Arius lived in close temporal proximity to Plotinus, the evidence, such as it is, imposes constraints on the

3. Harnack, *History of Dogma* IV, 39.

4. As Arius himself appears to have argued. Hanson quotes Arius as saying: "the Son begotten by the Father and created and established (Proverbs 8:22) before the ages did not exist before he was begotten, but being begotten timelessly, before everything . . ." Hanson, "Who Taught *ex ouk onton*?," 80.

degree of Arius's openness to influence from the inheritance of Neoplatonism. It can now be appreciated that, though Arius shared Plotinus's view of a God remote from the world, the Neoplatonic philosophical and spiritual quest to shake free of the downward pull of the constraints of this world to move by stages towards the ideal vision of the One, which was so important to Plotinus himself, does not seem to have been a feature of Arius's religion. Indeed, for him, even the begotten Word was cognitively removed from an intimate knowledge of the creative source of his own being. This obviously made it difficult for humans to get to him!

On the other hand, Harnack believed that we cannot understand Arianism "unless we consider that it consists of two entirely disparate parts."[5] One is the metaphysic that has its basis in cosmology. This Harnack puts down to Hellenism and specifically to the God/world antithesis of Neoplatonism, but this, he believed, has no necessary connection with soteriology. Independently of this metaphysic, Harnack perceived that "Arianism" has first of all "a Christ who gradually becomes God, who therefore develops more and more in moral unity of feeling with God, and progressively attains his perfection by divine grace." Harnack noted that such a Christ who acquires properties in this way is being understood essentially in terms of a kind of adoptionism.[6]

Harnack noted that the orthodox Nicene view was, by contrast, that the Son was not made, still less created by an act of divine will and grace, but was "*eternally* begotten." This eternal begetting is itself a quite necessary element in the divine nature of God, for it brings with it the equal sharing of divine being and an unqualified sharing of the essential properties of the divine nature *from all eternity*.[7] In Harnack's estimate, Arius's problem was to think of the Son as "created by an act of divine will and grace," probably at a particular point in a sequence, rather than being "*eternally* begotten." In this way, he thus tended to understand the final outcomes that were formally corrected by the Nicene definition of the *homoousion* as orthodox Christianity's response to a kind of adoptionism.[8]

---

5. Harnack, *History of Dogma* IV, 39.

6. Harnack, *History of Dogma* IV, 39.

7. There was apparently a period when the citizens of Alexandria could hear the Arian chant on their streets: "There was a time when he was not."

8. Since the work of H. M. Gwatkin (*Studies in Arianism*, 1882) it is no longer possible simply to cast Arius as a player in the articulation of a form of adoptionism. See Williams, *Arius*, 11.

The somewhat speculative work of Newman and Harnack are only two representative samples, even though they undoubtedly bulk large as probably the most noteworthy, among many such attempts to come to terms with the precise teaching of Arius by appeal to what was alleged to be its intellectual and cultural inheritance. All this has naturally clouded the perception of how it was that Arius reached the conclusions that Nicaea deemed to be erroneous, and this has even further complicated the task of saying exactly what those conclusions were.

⌐

Given this inherited lack of precision about the exact nature of what is to be described as "Arian" or categorized as an example of "Arianism," it is understandable that some have expressed misgivings about the appropriateness of using these terms in contemporary debate at all. The late David F. Wright, who was clearly uncomfortably defensive about the suggestion that T. C. Hammond's theology might be so classified (and perhaps sensing some awkward vulnerability in relation to Hammond's work) proposed that the term "Arianism" should only be used in relation to the "historical particularity" of ideas that were actually promoted by Arius himself in the first half of the fourth century (whatever they might have been). In other words, the use of this term should be reserved to the particular discussion of the historical views of Arius, but not used at all with reference to theological positions that might be espoused in the modern world. "As a church historian," Wright said,

> I am sometimes tempted to protest against the violation of the integrity of this or that ancient heresy. They have a right to be treated in their own specific identity and not abused in the interests of belabouring one's theological opponent. Pelagianism suffers the most frequent abuse, but Arianism too deserves to be left alone in its own historical particularity. Sound contemporary theology is not best served by unhistorically fixing the labels of past heresies on those we disagree with in the present.[9]

Thus, Wright urged that the term "Arianism" should not be brought to the identification of inadequacies in, and condemnation of, what some judge to be similarly deviant theological views in the contemporary world. Instead, the use of the descriptive term "Arian" and the noun

9. Wright, "Dr. Carnley on T. C. Hammond and Arianism," 47.

"Arianism" must be circumscribed for use exclusively with regard to a phenomenon of ancient time.

⟿

It is, however, very problematic whether it is possible to confine the use of these terms strictly with respect to what might be termed their classical and original use in relation to Arius's own views, even if these could be clearly and definitively identified. This is not how language works. After all, even when the historical reference is in the past, the language is in use by historians who are living in the present; historians who write about the past from the perspective of the present are communicating today with others with the intention that the meaning of the terms they use will be understood. Furthermore, there is no such thing as a private language. No individual is privileged to decide that a word is to be used in only one way approved by him or herself. The meanings of words are conventionally agreed upon by linguistic communities, and the hard fact is that the terms "Arian" and "Arianism" have been used by many and various linguistic communities over time, and are still in contemporary use with, at least in broad terms, a conventionally agreed-upon set of meanings. Only so do those who use them mean something by what they say and discern a meaning in what they hear.

Were it not for some basic understanding of the general outline of what was condemned following Nicaea by the eventual definition of the *homoousion*, and what is meant when the terms "Arian" and "Arianism" are used today, the prospects of understanding the thought processes, communications, and theological debates of the past from the perspective of today would obviously be fairly dismal. Some conventionally agreed-upon meaning must necessarily be assumed in order to permit the continued use of these terms. Indeed those who use them today appear to find them not only helpful, but in fact necessary, both in communication and theological argument. They are shorthand terms for the identification of theological views that may need to be considered inadequate or misleading, and for indicating the general nature of the reasons why this is considered to be so. And this is not to mention their usefulness in identifying views that are judged to be so dangerously erroneous as therefore to be carefully avoided for falling well beyond the boundaries of a tolerable diversity of Christian doctrine.

෨

It is pertinent to note that even those who promote the notion of the eternal functional subordination of the Son to the Father, while insisting at the same time that they are quite definitely *not* Arian, must also have a basic notion of what being "Arian" means as it is conventionally used today. It is therefore perfectly understandable that when David Wright himself insists that T. C. Hammond was *not* Arian because Hammond affirmed the essential equality of the Father and the Son (even while at the same time promoting the relational subordination of the Son to the Father), this twentieth-century use of the term "Arian" (and by implication "Arianism") is apparently as meaningful as its use by the critics of T. C. Hammond in charging that he *was* essentially Arian.[10] Unfortunately, Wright seeks to have his cake and eat it insofar as he urges that the term "Arianism" cannot be used outside the fourth century to condemn a specific contemporary theological view as "heretical" but that it may legitimately be used outside the fourth century (i.e., by Wright himself in 2005) to insist that a specific theological point of view is definitely *not* heretical because *it is not Arian.*

If these terms are in contemporary use on both sides of the current debate, they must necessarily have acquired a conventionally agreed-upon set of meanings, at least of a general kind. Nevertheless, we can take the point that the checkered and fluid history relating to views that have been labeled as "Arian" or categorized as "a form of Arianism" should act as a cautionary warning. We should accept David Wright's advice—not necessarily to abandon the use of these terms—but at least not to bandy them about lightly. Equally, it is not possible for us to make a judgment as to whether theological speculation in our own day is to be fairly and correctly described as "Arian" or categorized as "a form of Arianism" until we at least attempt to clarify what it is that we are talking about.

෨

It is obviously not appropriate, or even possible, for anybody to charge contemporary theological thinkers simply with producing a verbal replica

---

10. Wright says: "It is nothing short of outrageous to accuse T. C. Hammond of Arianism or Arianising tendencies." "Dr. Carnley on T. C. Hammond and Arianism," 47. We understand Wright to mean something by what he says when he uses the terms "Arianism" and "Arianising."

of Arius's thinking as though such a thing might be transported through the centuries and deposited in a twenty-first century context by a kind of direct transference. Whatever the formative influences on Arius actually were, we can be sure that they differed radically from the way they might be heard in the intellectual environment in which we live and work today. We inevitably think differently. However, that does not prevent us from drawing an analogy. Given that the terms "Arian" and "Arianism" are in contemporary use, and are in fact regularly employed on both sides of the current debate, they obviously signify something of importance that might not be communicated otherwise. If we mean something by what we say, this seems to suggest, at the very least, that, if pressed, it should be possible to give some account of the intended meaning of what is said, and of what it is that invites the drawing of an analogy with the fourth-century proposals of Arius and those who sympathized with him.

The pressing question is therefore whether a sufficiently clear picture of the key characteristics of the teaching that was condemned following Nicaea by the eventual acceptance of the definition of the *homoousion* will permit the drawing of an analogy upon which a categorization of a contemporary set of beliefs might justifiably be described as "Arian" or at least "neo-Arian" or as "a *form* of Arianism."

⸏

Fortunately, despite the historical variety in the use of the terms, in recent years a good deal of very impressive scholarly work has been done, both in relation to Arius's own views and the inherited intellectual forces that produced them, as well as work in relation to the shortcomings of historical accounts of what has been condemned, often along with the unfair vilification of Arius, as the "heresy of Arianism." Since the Ninth International Conference on Patristic Studies at Oxford in September 1983, old assumed certainties have given way to new lines of enquiry, with the result that a fresh picture of the controversy that was triggered by the teaching of Arius has emerged.

It was already apparent in the consciousness of the scholars who met at Oxford in 1983 that there was a need to make "distinctions between types of Arians and phases of Arianism" and to pursue a scholarly reassessment of the nature of the original controversy that would be "adequate to the complexity of Arianism (or the several forms and expressions of

Arianism) and the complexity of the era in which it emerged."[11] Over the last forty years that promise has been amply fulfilled, largely through the work of British scholars such as Maurice Wiles, Rowan Williams, and Lewis Ayres.[12]

A much clearer perception of mistaken assessments of the past in relation to the fourth-century controversy has now emerged, including considerable agreement about what in the past has been attributed to Arius unfairly and mistakenly, along with a degree of consensus in relation to the general outline of the key teachings of Arius himself. This consensus has provided a new standard upon which some critical judgments may be made.

For example, though the Sydney Doctrine Commission ventured to identify Arius's fault in terms of an "overemphasis" on subordination, apparently in the forlorn hope that an "underemphasis" might be trouble free, the more scholarly recent work on Arius has shown that this is not only incorrect but unhelpfully simplistic. Arius was certainly responsible for articulating a form of subordinationism with its own distinctive coloring given the philosophical presuppositions with which he seems to have worked, and his own reading of some key biblical texts that he regarded as being of particular importance. But it has become clear that the issue was not one of *degrees* of subordination. If Arius overemphasized anything, the current consensus is that it was the sublime ineffability of God and the transcendent remoteness of God from the created order, which Harnack seems to have got more or less right, even if his characterization of Arius's adoptionist Christology may have been speculatively wayward. Thus, when Arius read of the role of the Word of God in the work of creation in the prologue of St. John's Gospel, this necessarily mundane involvement in the world of material things entailed for him that the Word could not be exactly of the same dignity and authority (or of the same substance) as that of the ineffable God. As the product of the creative will of God at the time of the creation of the material universe the Divine Word could only subsist (even if timelessly) at some stage removed from God. Understandably some of Arius's later followers came to conclude that it was therefore only possible to speak at best of a "like substance" to God, but this obviously necessarily implied a status and authority less than and subordinate to the ineffable God. Certainly, we can be confident

11. Gregg, Foreword to *Arianism*, iii.

12. Wiles, "In Defence of Arius" and *Archetypal Heresy*; Williams, *Arius*; Ayres, *Nicaea and Its Legacy*.

that the fourth-century controversy triggered by the views of Arius did not just focus on an alleged overemphasis in relation to the Son's subordination to the Father, which implies that some kind of "lite" emphasis on subordination may be thought to be perfectly acceptable. After all, any degree of subordination to the Father would call in question the full divinity, and the equal status and authority, of the Son.

⤚

The emerging general consensus about the need for a revised assessment of Arius and the nature of Arianism suggests that while the historical traditions relating to Arius and Arianism have been complex, diverse, and often confused, it has at least become possible to sort matters of historical speculation from matters that appear to be somewhat more secure. In particular, while the current wave of historical scholarship on Arius and Arianism remains very sensitive to "types of Arians and phases of Arianism," this has at the same time made it possible to discern some of the more characteristic commonalities that have been shared across time and in different cultural circumstances. Robert Gregg, while underscoring the need to attend to distinctions between "types of Arians and phases of Arianism," acknowledges, for example, that this quest goes on "even while continuities are sought."[13] In other words, the admitted fact of the historical variety in perceptions of what have been thought to constitute examples of "Arianism" through time, even though with contextually conditioned nuances, also raises the possibility that a persisting shared meaning of a general or stereotypical kind has made it possible nevertheless to continue to use the terms "Arian" and "Arianism" and to mean something by them. Indeed, even to speak of "types of Arians" and "phases of Arianism" implies that these terms are meaningfully used in relation to a commonality that is perceived despite the heightened awareness of historically and culturally conditioned nuances that can be detected through the complex history of church doctrine since the original controversies of the fourth century.

Likewise, when the terms "Arian" or "Arianism" are used today in relation to what has been judged to be a specific kind of deviation from the historical tradition of Christian orthodoxy, some such shared stereotypical meaning is presupposed. This has made it possible to give some

13. Gregg, Foreword to *Arianism*, iii.

justifying account of the meaning that is assigned to these terms as they are currently used in the modern world. Hence there has been a growing consensus about what may justifiably be described as "Arian" or categorized as "a form of Arianism."

⤻

Rowan Williams, for example, after a very careful reconstruction and analysis of Arius's writing and thinking, insofar as these can be pinned down, was prepared to express his basic conclusions in terms of three syllogisms. His considered judgment is that Arius appears to have held that:

1. The Logos of God is the ground and condition, the rational or intelligible structure of the world. But that structure has no ex istence independent of the world which it structures; therefore the Logos does not exist prior to the divine decision to make the world . . .
2. God the Father is absolute unity . . . but absolute unity cannot be conceptualized by any knowing subject without being distorted into multiplicity (as something existing over against a subject). Therefore the Son can have no concept of the Father's existence . . .
3. The Logos truly exists as a subject distinct from the Father. But the defining qualities, the essential life of one subject cannot as such be shared with another.

It follows that for Arius the Logos was not eternal. Having been created immediately prior to the creation of the world, the attributes scripturally applied to the Son as the incarnate Word must be true of him in a sense quite different from that in which they are true of the Father.[14]

Williams's findings have been largely responsible for structuring the general outline of a current consensus, at least in relation to the key aspects of the thought of Arius. In his spirited defense of the alleged orthodoxy of T. C. Hammond, for example, David F. Wright actually reflects this consensus when he says that "Arius's teaching can be summarised as a monotheism of the Father alone, since for him the divine being was by definition incommunicable. Hence from the beginning the Son and the Spirit were outside the being of God."[15] On the other side of the Atlantic, Glenn Butner expresses a similar grasp of what appears to be this

14. See Williams, *Arius*, 231–32.
15. Wright, "Dr. Carnley on T. C. Hammond and Arianism," 47.

emerging general consensus regarding the key beliefs of Arius: "Arius sought to make Christ the preeminent creature of the Father by affirming what might be called monotheistic homoiousianism, a stance insisting that only the *ousia* of the Father was divine, and that the Son was created with a different, non-divine *ousia* at some point in time."[16]

Despite the long history of confusion over the exact nature of the actual beliefs and the logical detail of the arguments of Arius himself, if we are prepared to work with some broad brushstrokes, it is clear that Arius necessarily subordinated the Son to the Father, hence denying him the enjoyment of any kind of equal status and authority. To speak of the Father and the Son in terms of a single "unity of being," fully sharing the qualities of the very same nature, was anathema to him. We may then say that this outcome was achieved not only by denying the eternality of the Son, but by denying the very possibility of his intimate knowing of the Father. In this way it has therefore become possible to distill some basic characteristics from Williams's summary of Arius's idiosyncratic beliefs with some confidence.

$$\backsim$$

If "meaning is use," as Wittgenstein has taught us, then we may discern something of the meanings that by convention have come to be assigned to the terms "Arian" and "Arianism," both historically and currently, by observing their actual use in the context of specific linguistic communities. Perhaps one of the most obvious examples of an implicit appeal to a set of general characteristics for identifying what might justifiably be described as "Arian" or classified as "a form of Arianism" may be discerned in what is in fact a celebrated discussion of John Milton's alleged espousal of an apparently analogous form of heresy in the context of the seventeenth century.

A. D. Nuttall has observed that it once used to be said that though Milton's *De Doctrina Christiana*, which was not published in his lifetime,[17] might exhibit "a generally Arian Christ" who is "God's great Vice Regent" though not fully and unequivocally divine, this is not the case in *Paradise Lost*.[18] Already it is clear that a "generally Arian" Christ is understood by

16. Butner, "Eternal Functional Subordination," 132. (*Homoiousios*=like substance, rather than of the very *same* substance—*homoousios*.)

17. It was not found until 1823 and was published in 1825.

18. Which was first published in 1667.

Nuttall, for whatever specific reason, to be "not fully or unequivocally divine." However, in the course of what has been a very lively and classical debate about Milton's alleged "Arianism," Nuttall unpacked this contention in further detail. He first pointed out[19] that in fact there was a chorus of voices complaining of heresy long before *De Doctrina Christiana*.[20] He further notes that even in *Paradise Lost* Milton's orthodoxy was already somewhat problematic. On one hand Milton describes the Son as

> throned in highest bliss
> equal to God, and equally enjoying
> Godlike fruition . . .[21]

Yet, says Nuttall, Milton "does not fully affirm the *homoousion*." Rather, Milton suggests that the Son's enjoyment and bliss *will be equal*, not that the Son's essence is *timelessly* equal to that of the Father. Two lines later we find the words: "by merit more than birthright Son of God."[22] This prompts Nuttall pertinently to declare that "these words are, precisely, Arian."[23]

Quite apart from any attempt to go into the specifics of Arius's own reasoning, or to account for Arius's idiosyncratic views by appeal to formative influences of a philosophical or theological kind to which he could well have been exposed, Nuttall simply appealed to the benchmark of the *homoousion* in judging whether Milton's portrayal of the Son presents him as "timelessly equal" to the Father or essentially unequal and thus "not fully and unequivocally divine." Nuttall's discussion of Milton's views at once illustrates what he understood in general terms to be the key characteristics of the Arian heresy as distinct from an explicit appeal to the precise teachings of Arius himself, and at the same time his grasp of the basic reasons that triggered the determination of the orthodox bishops at Nicaea to correct them by what has come to be regarded as the definition of the *homoousion*: the problem is that the Son is not timelessly equal to the Father, but is elevated to "Godlike fruition" as something earned by merit rather than enjoyed by birthright.

In all this, what is described in broad terms as "Arian" or as a "form of Arianism" is defined by reference to the general subordinationist

---

19. Following Bauman, *Milton's Arianism*, 279.
20. Late in the seventeenth century.
21. Milton, *Paradise Lost*, iii, 305–7.
22. Milton, *Paradise Lost*, iii, 309.
23. Nuttall, *Alternative Trinity*, 138.

conclusions to which Arius seems to have come, rather than to the specifics of the logical route he took to get to them. Clearly, the detailed specifics of the logical route taken by Arius to reach this more general outcome is one thing, the outcome itself is another. And while there may be much historical debate about the specifics of the arguments of Arius on the way to the final more general outcome, it is the final subordinationist outcome itself that is of more concern to contemporary systematic theology. Indeed, even in the years immediately following Nicaea those who applied the benchmark of the *homoousion* as a formula for resisting Arianism actually employed it to cover a variety of different manifestations of a general problem that was believed to have originally been derived from Arius. Certainly, the definition of the *homoousion* may well be as useful today, as it was then, in identifying and countering views that in general terms are understood to be analogous to those attributed to Arius in the fourth century, and therefore to be theologically suspect.

꜀

Curiously, those who have come to the view that the proponents of the eternal functional subordination of the Son to the Father are "flirting with a kind of Arianism"[24] have sometimes tended to take the opposite course of seeking to match up the perceived problems of present-day theology, not with the general subordinationist nature of an Arian outcome, but with one or other of the historical nuances on the Arian theme of the ancient past.

Michael Bird,[25] for example, who originally took issue with Kevin Giles, has more recently come to the conviction that what the chief American proponents of the eternal functional subordination of the Son to the Father have proposed resembles "a species of semi-Arianism."[26] He had earlier precipitated a controversy by the publication of "One God in Three Persons" on a blog, which raised the ire of Southern Baptist Church theologians in America. Bird wrote, "Given the centrality of this school of thought around Wayne Grudem and Bruce Ware, I propose—for discussion–whether it is apt to start referring to "Southern

24. Bird, "Theologians of a Lesser Son" (Preface to Bird and Harrower, *Trinity without Hierarchy*), 9.

25. An Anglican priest/theologian of Ridley College, Melbourne.

26. See Grudem, *Systematic Theology,* esp. 250–51; Ware, *Father, Son, and Holy Spirit;* and Ware and Starke, eds., *One God in Three Persons.*

Baptist Homoianism."[27] Since then a major discussion has ensued, notably between Bruce Ware, Malcolm Yarnell, Matthew Emerson, and Luke Stamps, precisely in relation to whether an alleged "homoianism" has in fact become domiciled in the Southern Baptist Church in the United States.[28]

Whereas Glenn Butner called Arius's concluding position "homoiousianism," Bird confidently calls what he detects as its modern-day equivalent "homoianism"[29] or sometimes even "quasi-homoianism."[30] Bird had initially been reluctant to join Giles in categorizing contemporary subordinationists simply as "Arian" because, as far as he could tell, they "were clearly not Arians; they did not deny the eternality of the Son, they affirmed that the Son was of the same substance as the Father, and they believed in their own minds that they were orthodox Trinitarians."[31] His more recent view, however, is that he is "now convinced that Grudem, Ware, and others were arguing for something analogical to a semi-Arian subordinationism." He notes, "The Trinitarian relations being advocated by such scholars are not identical to Arius, since proponents identify the Son as coeternal with the Father and sharing the same substance as the Father." However, he goes on to say that he thinks "it is fair to say neither are Eternal Functional Subordination (EFS) advocates pure semi-Arians, because they do not think Jesus is merely like the Father nor do they consider the Son to be the Father's creature."[32]

Putting these caveats aside, Bird then concludes that they *resemble* a species of semi-Arianism, that he calls "homoianism."[33] He then justifies this by identifying three basic things in the writing of subordinationist theologians such as Wayne Grudem, Bruce Ware, and others. These are: (1) an overreliance on the economic Trinity in Scripture for formulating immanent Trinitarian relationships, (2) leading to a robust subordinationism characterized by a hierarchy within the Godhead, (3)

27. For the history of this episode see Whitfield, ed., *Trinitarian Theology*, 8.

28. See the series of exchanges in Whitfield, ed., *Trinitarian Theology*.

29. For an introduction to what he means by *homoianism*, he refers to Hanson, *Search for the Christian Doctrine of God*, 348–86. The *homoians* taught that the Son was like the Father, but not equal to the Father in divine essence.

30. Bird, "Theologians of a Lesser Son," 11.

31. Bird, "Theologians of a Lesser Son," 9.

32. Bird, "Theologians of a Lesser Son," 10.

33. Bird, "Theologians of a Lesser Son," 10.

consequently identifying the Son as possessing a lesser glory and majesty than the Father.[34]

While Bird speaks of these characteristics more specifically as tokens of what he calls "homoianism," these three characteristics might well be said to be the general characteristics that are fundamental to all specific instances of Arianism! This alerts us to the fact that what might obviously be of historical interest might not justify the attempt to match forms of quasi-Arian belief with modern-day equivalents.

Specific nuances ultimately arising from a particular historical argument, or the precise logical route taken to get to a generally Arian outcome, might obviously be of historical interest. The language of "degrees of Arianism" or of "semi-Arian" or "quasi-Arian belief," or whether an essential problem is best spoken of as "homoiousianism," or "homoianism," or "quasi-homoianism," as distinct from the post-Nicene preference for the "*homoousion*," is clearly of importance to the historical quest to identify differences within the variety of ancient Arian belief. However, for the purpose of our present concern with contemporary systematic theology, all this might best be submitted to the simplification of Occam's razor. After all, what is ultimately of concern to us today is not so much the historically and culturally conditioned nuances and permutations on the theme of Arianism, as much as what is common to all of them. It is the more general characteristics that are shared across the historical spectrum of various "kinds of Arianism" that are more likely to be of use in assessing whether or not a phenomenon of current experience and controversy fits the same general label. In other words, it is the commonly shared nature of the more general Arian error, rather than the historically and culturally expressed nuances on the Arian theme, that impacts negatively on orthodox Trinitarian belief.

On the other hand, it has to be conceded that, from the point of view of *historical theology* the application of the terms "Arian" and "Arianism" are sometimes thought to be so general as to be of no positive use. Derrick Peterson has recently drawn attention explicitly to the fact that the use of the concept of "Arianism" as a proper designation for anti-Nicene views is thoroughly suspect, at least for directing *historical* enquiry. Peterson

34. Bird notes that a similar observation is made by McCall, *Which Trinity? Whose Monotheism?*, 186.

corrals the use of "Arianism" along with such other fashionable scholarly tropes as "Hellenization" or "Eastern versus Western Trinitarianism." The use of such highly generalized concepts, he says, has recently been exposed as vacuous, for overgeneralized concepts "are often less than useless."[35] Similarly, Morwenna Ludlow has expressed some impatience specifically with regard to Thomas Torrance's use of the *homoousion* as an organizing principle for interpreting the history of patristic doctrinal development, particularly in relation to the thought of Gregory of Nyssa.[36] In a similar vein, Lewis Ayres also self-consciously pursued his own discipline of historical theology, while registering suspicion of systematic theology, in his monumental *Nicaea and Its Legacy*.[37] All this appears to involve some suspicion of systematic theology on the part of historians of Christian doctrine, not unlike that which has already been noted in the case of David F. Wright's expressed impatience with the practice of "unhistorically fixing the labels of past heresies on those we disagree with in the present." Indeed, Wright is explicitly condemning of "the Torrances." He avers that "they have not been known for their prowess as historians. In particular, the account of patristic theology they have generally given has tended to be viewed by patristic scholars as informed as much or more by dogmatic interests as by secure historical interpretation."[38] It seems fairly clear that here is a divergence of opinion between historians of doctrine and systematic theologians.

↫

This apparent difference of linguistic approach that is found between historians of doctrine on one hand and systematic theologians on the other, has been noted by Paul Maxwell. In a useful footnote comment he has helpfully drawn attention to the fact that historians of doctrine and systematic theologians often diverge over this very point.[39] Understandably, historical theology, seeks to examine the course taken by religious thinkers of the past by taking an interest in the inevitable coloring of contemporary influences on their thought and the specific perspectives

35. Peterson, "Loud Absence."
36. See Ludlow, *Gregory of Nyssa, Ancient and (Post)modern,* 15–36.
37. Something that Sarah Coakley has questioned in "Introduction."
38. Wright, "Dr. Carnley on T. C. Hammond and Arianism," 47.
39. Maxwell, "Is There an Authority Analogy?," 550n26.

and prejudices of their time, in what David F. Wright rightly calls their "historical particularity." The identification of any idiosyncratic nuances that appear to have been peculiar both to individuals of past time and to the context within which they lived and worked, is par for the course for the historian of Christian doctrine. Historical theology thus examines the *specific* form in which a concept is embodied in the context of a particular historical period.

Likewise, in the case of biblical theology, the quest is to understand and expound the meaning of a text in the context of its original use as best we can, so as to seek to understand the meanings of words as the authors intended them to be heard, difficult though this might sometimes be. It is well recognized that we always bring with us some coloring from the perspective in which we ourselves stand as readers; what is heard or understood to have been communicated may not conform exactly to "authorial intent." Even so, the biblical quest is to understand the utterances and thoughts of those who have lived in past times with as much objectivity as possible. This means attending to the specifics of historically and culturally determined linguistic differences.

Systematic theology, by contrast with both biblical and historical theology, views the same things from a different and much more generic perspective. While historians naturally take an interest in identifying nuances and distinctions of the kind that are produced in different cultural circumstances or at the hands of a specific historical personages, it is important to remember that the less descriptive and more constructive discipline of systematic theology necessarily aims at pursing an argument and clarifying conceptual outcomes in search of theological truth in the context of today. Inevitably, while noting deviations of linguistic and conceptual detail wherever they appear to have been of importance in relation to previous historical contexts, in this contemporary work, systematic theology may be more content to work with acknowledged stereotypical definitions with a more general or generic meaning.

This certainly appears to be the case in relation to contemporary attempts to justify the categorization of a theological position as "Arian" or to classify it as a form of "Arianism." In seeking to unpack a concerning tendency towards a kind of Trinitarian subordinationism, it is helpful to draw similarities with the problems posed by subordinationism in the past without it being necessary to distinguish precise forms of subordinationism or the specific arguments pursued in the past in reaching them. Thus, it may be sufficient to draw attention to a "form of Arianism" without the need to distinguish the many different stripes of Arianism that may historically be identified in the messiness of the post-Nicene world.[40]

This means that the enterprise of systematic theology is to be distinguished from historical theology, given that systematicians forsake a necessary historical concentration on detailed nuances that any particular theological theme may have taken in the historical context of a quite specific time and place. By contrast with scientific historiography, systematic theology may be obliged to deal with a more general or stereotypical understanding of things in the pursuit of clarity of expression and the articulation of truth in the formulation of doctrine for today. From a purely historical point of view this may have the appearance of a kind of oversimplification that obscures rather than reveals the desired truth; but this is par for the course.

~

In his footnote, Paul Maxwell makes this point specifically in relation to the characterization of the respective theological positions of Bonaventure and Scotus as authors of distinctive types of theology.[41] In relation to the contrasting "general" or characteristic theological approaches respectively of Bonaventura and Scotus, specifically in relation to the Trinity, he says:

> We should . . . recognize that "Bonaventure" and "Scotus" are typologies—names, by which we call certain general concepts—and constructive theology is dependent on these sorts of historically reductionistic typologies for the sake of synthesizing concepts, otherwise the entire dialogue about the metaphysics of the Trinity is hindered to the degree that the full historically accurate picture of "Bonaventure" and "Scotus" require constant readjustment. While good systematic theology will be in conversation with the history of Christian theology, systematic theology should not be at the direct mercy of the discipline

40. It is curious that despite his plea in favor of "historical particularity" David F. Wright himself somewhat inconsistently concedes that he does not want to "rule out appropriate analogies in theology." "Dr. Carnley on T. C. Hammond and Arianism," 48.

41. As it happens in relation to nuances of language having to do with the distinctive quiddities of the persons of the Trinity, and whether these are to be identified by appeal to "relation" or "origin."

of historical theology. For that purpose, we, by academic
convention, must endorse and assume a degree of historical
reductionism.[42]

Clearly, there must be a set of core criteria connoting the generic
meaning of a term, or the distinctive characteristics of a theological position, in order to establish a conventionally agreed-upon stereotype. Let
us, for the sake of this discussion, say that there might be seven different
elements pertaining to the identification of a particular theological position, and that it might be that three or four of these are regarded as basic
characteristics, while others might not feature in some specific historical
manifestation along with the four points that are regarded as fundamentally important to the same position. In other words, while some fundamental characteristic modes of thought might be shared, and noted
as being analogous to the manifestation of essentially the same general
position in other times and places, historically specific differences nevertheless have to be noted. Historical theology has a duty to identify these
differences in the interests of accuracy in the work of explicating what
was once the case at a specific time. The theological systematician, on the
other hand, may focus simply on the four basic or shared characteristics,
as the more general or stereotypical meaning commonly held across the
historical spectrum. These, indeed, may be viewed as the "defining" or
"generally shared commonality" amongst what is in fact a range of slightly differing uses of the same term. When asked, it should be possible to
unpack these fundamental or characteristic elements of the shared meaning content of a term that has been used with nuances over time, and to
cite them as justifying reasons for continuing to use it. Hence, we speak
of "Calvinism" and clearly communicate something of importance by it,
even while distinguishing the specific kind of Calvinism originally taught
by Calvin himself from subsequent historically conditioned variants of
his basic or characteristic ideas, such as, for example, those taught by Ursinus in the specific historical phase that is often identified as "scholastic
Calvinism." Despite the identifiable difference between classical Calvinism and scholastic Calvinism, a general similarity or analogy between the
two allows for an easy contrast to be drawn with, let us say, "Thomism"
or "Arminianism."

Likewise, in identifying a particular deviant theology as a form of
"Arianism" we are associating it, by virtue of some of its fundamental

42. Maxwell, "Is There an Authority Analogy?," 550n26.

characteristics that are discerned to be analogous to a general understanding of the ancient heresy originally articulated by Arius. In this
understanding of things the Son is understood to be subordinate to the
Father in a way that is inimical to the affirmation of the full and equal
divinity of the Son, and which therefore challenges the Nicene insistence
on the unity of the divine being and nature that is identically the same,
and equally possessed by Father and Son (and Spirit)—the *homoousion*.

⸺

This tendency of systematic theology to work with stereotypes seems
reasonable enough. While the understanding of what may be described
as "Arian" or a form of "Arianism" may have incorporated historically
conditioned variations and nuances of meaning through time, in the actual use of these terms from age to age and from linguistic community to
linguistic community there must inevitably be what Wittgenstein called
a "family likeness" of a general or stereotypical kind that runs through
all of them. Indeed, it is in the light of the continuity of the generally
or conventionally agreed upon meanings of the terms "Arian" and "Arianism" that specific instances of their use today may be deemed to be
either grammatically meaningful and acceptably useful, or else entirely
mistaken and unhelpfully misleading.

While there is no one dictionary definition of the meaning of a word
to which it must always and in all respects strictly conform and against
which its use in all other situations, perhaps with nuances of meaning,
may simply be judged to be illegitimate, at least a general "family likeness" may be discerned against which its specific use at any one time may
be judged to be appropriate or otherwise. Just as the descriptive use of the
word "red" is employed in ostensive definition despite the many, many
variations of the color "red" that present themselves to human experience, so there is necessarily no single definition of "redness" that limits
its use to only one instantiation on the spectrum of "reds." The word "red"
as it is used in the linguistic communities of English-speaking people,
obviously works with reasonably broad conventionally agreed-upon
boundaries that either allow or prohibit its meaningful use in a variety of
specific sets of circumstances.

In the natural world there is clearly a very wide range of differences
of the color "green" that present themselves to human experience from
age to age—from a yellowy lettuce green, to a deep "British racing car"

green, but all of them despite sometimes obvious, but at other times very subtle differences, nevertheless fall under the generic description of "green." Problems of communication only arise should somebody choose to identify something that is conventionally called "red" by calling it, for some entirely idiosyncratic and inexplicable reason, "green"—with obvious potentially disastrous consequences at traffic lights. Hence, the practical importance for life today of Wittgenstein's appeal to the linguistic concept of "family likenesses."

In a similar way, the concepts of systematic theology are expressed in words within boundaries set by their conventional use, but we must expect them to apply across a range of specific and slightly different instantiations of what may be at issue. It may be in some circumstances that a theological term may be used in a way that is in some respects different from the use of the same term in another historical context while nevertheless carrying a valid freight of shared meaning.

For all practical purposes, the more general meaning of a word to indicate a "family likeness" among various possible actual differences will usually suffice to serve the purposes of communication. After all, we are not normally plunged into confusion at traffic lights while we sort through a color chart of different shades of red, from vermillion, to crimson, to cherry red, in search of the specific one that means we must apply the brakes. It is sufficient to respond to what in more general terms we simply identify as "red." Likewise, the flashing red light of heresy serves the practical purpose of warning us to "stop" and "not go there"—on the grounds that the church has been somewhere similar in the past and found it wanting. It would be wise not to repeat it. The exercise of the more specific interests of a historiographical mentality is of course a perfectly legitimate and useful enterprise. But for systematic theology in the service of the church today, the more general meaning of terms such as "Arian" and "Arianism" is certainly not "worse than useless" but in terms of definition and fundamental boundary setting, eminently helpful.

⸎

We are now in a position to turn to the contemporary use of the terms "Arian" and "Arianism" in the context of this current debate about the validity or otherwise of a subordinationist and complementarian approach to the understanding of intra-Trinitarian relations in the promotion of belief in the eternal functional subordination of the Son to the Father. If the meaning of a term is established by its use, it is pertinent to notice, for example, that Kevin Giles, in signaling that my own categorization in 2004 of the undisputed subordinationism of the Sydney Doctrine Commission Report as apparently a kind of "Arianism," also drew attention to some justifying reasons that were cited at the time for making this judgment. In *Jesus and the Father*, he noted that I had "accused the Sydney evangelical theologians of falling into 'the ancient heresy of Arianism' by selectively quoting from the Bible, setting the will of the Son of God in opposition to that of the Father, and calling into question the Son's equal status with the Father."[43] I am not entirely convinced that I was actually quite as systematically precise as this; however, I am gratified that Giles himself was apparently willing to identify these three basic characteristics as an indication of what was thought to be basically wrong with the position taken by the Sydney Doctrine Commission, and which at the same time constituted a reasonably acceptable "working definition" of "Arianism."

It has to be said that, while it is true that the proponents of the eternal functional subordination of the Son to the Father, no less than Arius himself, have relied upon a selection of key biblical texts to try to justify their position, "textual selectivity" is hardly a problem that can be said to be exclusive to, or uniquely characteristic of, Arius or Arianism. And though Glenn Butner has convincingly demonstrated that there is no undisputed textual tradition that can justify the contemporary "eternal subordinationist" reading of them, which certainly raises some very serious questioning of the Sydney Report's argument, this does not warrant the identification of it as definitely "Arian."

Likewise, the "setting of the will of the Son of God in opposition to that of the Father" mentioned by Giles may, as Butner has argued, at least in the first instance be said to be a token of tritheism rather than of Arianism. Tritheism is obviously problematic enough to the ears of Christian monotheists, but as Butner rightly says, it is not really a characteristic of Arianism. Arius certainly did not believe in three *divine* wills, signaling three equally divine gods.

On the other hand, if a difference in willing is asserted in such a way as to set the Father's power of command in a binary relation to the Son's willing obedience, so as to make the Son subordinate to the Father in a relationship of authoritative domination and compliant submission,

---

43. Giles, *Jesus and the Father*, 26.

then something more than the bare numerical diversity of wills of trithe-ism is at stake. Something even more serious than tritheism seems to be involved, given that what is being described is not just a numerical distinction but a qualitative difference. In the case of the subordination of the Son to the Father, when the commanding will of the Father is lined up against the obediently submissive will of the Son, in a binary relation of domination and submission such as is known between a master and his servant, the Nicene claim to the Son's equal status and authority with the Father immediately becomes problematic. It is not just that the numerical distinction of willing leads to the tritheism to which Butner has alerted us. The sharing of the very same essential nature is inevitably called in question by the assertion of a qualitative imbalance between different wills. This is not to mention the fact that the simplicity of the divine unity of willing and acting is also challenged if not seriously compromised, as is the revelatory capacity of the Son to "show us the Father." In general terms this disastrous outcome does appear to be reminiscent of what it was about the proposals of Arius himself that raised the alarm and con-cern of those who were moved to oppose him, and that were deemed to necessitate the definition of the *homoousion*.

It is therefore the third of these three defining qualities of Arianism cited by Giles—that relating to "the calling into question the Son's equal status with the Father"—that is of most significance in the quest to define the meaning of the terms "Arian" and "Arianism." This third justifying reason is what more clearly invites the initial drawing of the analogy with the controversy triggered by the views promoted by Arius. Once again, even if the detailed reasoning leading to the articulation of this working definition of "Arianism" may differ from the specifics of the philosophi-cal route taken in the idiosyncratic reasoning of Arius himself, it is the similarity of this final outcome that, in more general terms, is sufficient to trigger seriously troubling concerns, and to raise the possible analogy with Arianism.

∽

In the chapter of *Reflections in Glass* to which Giles referred I could well have added specifically that the Doctrine Commission's failure to uphold and defend this fundamental identifying characteristic of this working definition of "Arianism" amounts to a tacit, if unwitting, assault on the Nicene definition of the *homoousion*. As has already been noted on a number of occasions, the *homoousion* is regularly used as a code word to signal the essential ontological sameness that secures the single divine nature that is shared fully and equally by the Father and the Son (and the Spirit) in one unity of being. The seriousness of dissent from this is openly acknowledged, even by the proponents of Carillon Avenue theology. It would be an instance of "Arianism."[44]

However, insofar as their argument is that the postulation of alleged purely *relational* or *functional* inequalities that are said to be essential, are associated not with the equally shared divine nature, but only to the personal or *hypostatic* identities of the Father and the Son, the forlorn hope is that the charge of Arianism may be avoided. Apart from the fact that this attempt to sidestep the requirements of the *homoousion* fails to convince for all the reasons that were cited in the previous chapter, when the eternal functional subordination of the Son in relation to the Father is said to arise from *"the very being of the Son,"*[45] thus suggesting an ontological subordination of the Son to the Father, any reliance on an alleged *purely* functional or relational subordination evaporates, and the Son's equal sharing of essentially the same nature as the Father continues to be called into question.

This remains problematic because even the functional or relational subordination of the Son to the Father, based upon the fundamental difference between their respective paternal and filial natures, also obviously compromises the Son's status and authority in relation to the Father.

This means that, even if the Carillon Avenue argument seeks to speak only of a functional or relational subordination, the ensuing personal or *hypostatic* difference of status and authority between the Father and the Son appears unavoidably to entail an unwelcome outcome. For a Son who is said to be, by virtue of his filial nature, compliantly obedient to the authoritative command that is in turn said to be unique to the Father's paternal nature, is clearly subordinate to the Father in authority, and hence in status and dignity. In this respect the outcome is obviously analogous to that perceived to have been championed by Arius himself that eventually led to the corrective definition of the *homoousion*.

44. As acknowledged by Doyle in his Review of *"Reflections in Glass,* Chapter 7."
45. As it certainly is in the 1999 Report of the Sydney Doctrine Commission.

෨

In any event, as it happened I did not mention the *homoousion* in *Reflections in Glass* because my basic concerns were driven by a slightly different issue. It was not just the apparent diminishment in the *hypostatic* status and dignity of the Son as such, even based upon an alleged subordination of a purely functional or relational kind, that struck me as being troublesome as a contemporary deviation from the requirements of the formal definition of the *homoousion*. Apart from the report's apparent failure to sufficiently secure the equal status and dignity of the Trinitarian identities, I was in fact concerned to point to some of the extended practical implications of these Carillon Avenue proposals.

Although contemporary scholarship has been concerned to explore the historical details of what went on *behind* the formal definition of the *homoousion,* with the aim of achieving a more accurate historical understanding of the views of Arius and what led to them, the exploration of what *currently goes on,* as it were, *in front of the homoousion* and the historical controversy that led to it, in terms of its continuing practical implications for faith and worship, also invites the drawing of the analogy with the controversy of the fourth century. At the same time this throws further light on the meaning of the term "Arianism" and the seriousness of it for today.

In *Reflections in Glass* I was particularly concerned to note the implications of an extended set of issues that appear to be analogous to issues and concerns thrown up by the fourth-century views of Arius, that further justify the drawing of the analogy with them. I noted, for example, that among those who were disturbed by the views of Arius, the perceived diminishment in status and dignity of the eternal Son immediately appeared to entail the outcome that the Son was not available as an object of worship along with the Father. The very same issue is entailed even by contemporary talk of a *relational* or *functional* differential between the Father and the Son. Insofar as Carillon Avenue theology goes on to argue that this functional or relational difference flows from *the very being* of the Father as Father and the Son as Son, this problem is of course even further compounded.

It is of some significance that the implications of introducing belief in the eternal subordination of the Son to the Father for the practicalities of faith and worship have from the beginning been an important consideration in the identification and rejection of Arianism. As John Henry

Newman pointed out in relation to fourth-century Arianism, the views of Arius did not just become the subject of the definitive judgment of the 318 Nicene bishops alone, or just precipitate the formal conciliar definition of the *homoousion* and the anathematization of his views as heretical. On the contrary, while the bishops voted at Nicaea in condemnation of the views of Arius, over time the laity also played an important role in the exercise of ecclesial authority by "voting with their feet," as it were. In other words, the laity exercised their vote by refusing to attend the worship of Arianizing bishops. Indeed Newman was convinced that, for all the importance of the definitive judgment of an ecumenical council of bishops, the church's judgment on the novel proposals of Arius was much more broadly based. This was sufficiently important to be construed by Newman as a matter of ecclesial principle: "technicality and formalism are . . . inevitable results of public confessions of faith."[46] Hence, Newman's insistence on the importance of "consulting the faithful in matters of doctrine."[47]

Faithful resistance to the innovative views stemming from Arius surfaced precisely for the reason that it was publicly perceived that a Christ who was somehow subordinate to the Father, and therefore of unequal status and dignity, did not measure up to the practical requirements of the standing practice of the worship of Christ as God. From the outset of the controversy about what came to be referred to as "Arianism," what provided the laity with good reasons for accepting, upholding, and defending the corrective of the *homoousion* was their perception of the impact that the lack of a full and equal sharing of the essential divine nature, status, and authority, had for the religious availability of the Son as an object of faith and worship. Such an understanding meant that the Son was effectively less than fully divine. Thus, in celebrating the "Christian heroism of the laity," Newman observed, perhaps with a touch of hyperbole, that in the aftermath of Nicaea when some bishops failed to sustain the determinations of the council, "The Catholic people, in the length and breadth of Christendom, were the obstinate champions of Catholic truth and the bishops were not."[48]

46. Newman, *Arians of the Fourth Century*, 36–37.

47. The title of his 1859 contribution, even as a Roman Catholic, to the then current public debate about the possible inclusion of laypeople in synods and councils of the Church—something that his former colleague E. B. Pusey opposed.

48. Newman, *Arians of the Fourth Century*, 445.

Fortunately, there were significant episcopal exceptions, and eventually the arguments of Athanasius prevailed, but Newman's point is that we should not underestimate the role of the faithful laity and their insight that the diminishment of the Son in status and authority would also entail that it would no longer be appropriate to address the Son as "Lord" along with the Father in the context of prayer and worship.[49]

On the basis of what has become known as the theological principle of *lex orandi, lex credendi*[50] the laity instinctively refused to attend worship led by Arianizing bishops because they were quick to perceive that subordinationist views seriously compromised the appropriateness of addressing Christ along with the Father as their worshipful "Lord." They did not have to get their heads around the high-flown philosophical concepts of the debate of Athanasius with Arius, not least the subtleties of the notion of the *ousia* and its divine nature that the Nicean bishops insisted was fully and equally shared by all three Trinitarian identities. Nor was it necessary to understand the details of the theological reasoning that led Arius to his conclusions. Rather, it was the final subordinationist outcome and the perceived implications of it for the practicalities of religious observance that held authoritative sway.[51]

⤺

In addition to this problem of diminishing the Son's religious availability as an object of worship, Athanasius would also want us to raise a concern about how it could be possible for the Son to "show us the Father." If the eternal Son were to be understood to be somehow less than the Father and not precisely equal to the Father as fully the same by virtue of the sharing of the very same nature, then his capacity to be the supreme revelation of divinity is very seriously compromised. This remains so whether this

49. See the references to this in Carnley, *Reflections in Glass*, 234, 241.

50. *Lex orandi, lex credendi*—the rule of prayer is the rule of faith. See the catalogue of ups and downs in the fortunes of the *homoousion* in the decades following Nicaea provided by Newman in "Orthodoxy of the Body of the Faithful During the Supremacy of Arianism," first published in *The Rambler*, July 1859; republished as Note V in the third edition of *Arians of the Fourth Century*.

51. There are many instances of refusal to attend worship led by Arianizing bishops. Even as late as 360, when the father of Gregory Nazianzus became persuaded of the Arian confession on the basis of its apparent scriptural credentials, he found himself suddenly deserted by a large portion of his flock. Newman, *Arians of the Fourth Century*, 357.

perceived inequality is because of an apparent diminishment of his divine nature (contrary to the *homoousion*) or a diminishment of his personal status and authority based upon functional and relational considerations. Either way, the revelatory capacity of the incarnate Son to reveal the divine nature that is shared with the Father is seriously impacted. Indeed, if the humanly willing subordination of the Son in the economy of salvation is said to reveal the "eternal functional subordination of the Son to the Father" in the immanent life of the Trinity, then it is not the Father who is revealed, but precisely something of *the eternal filial nature of the Son himself.* By sidestepping the *homoousion* and associating the property of subordination uniquely with the person of the Son, the Son does not "show us the Father"; at best he is said to show us himself as "eternally functionally subordinate." This means the commanding authority that is said to be unique to the Father's paternal nature and identity has to be indirectly inferred from this. Alas, by contrast, in the thinking of orthodox Christianity, as the agent of the revelation of God, Jesus "shows us the Father" in the sense of his unsurpassed communication of the divine nature that the Father fully and equally shares with the him and the Spirit.

Clearly, both the religious availability of the Son as an object of worship equal to the Father, and the revelatory capacity of the Son to show us the divine nature that he equally and fully shares with the Father become matters of concern when the Son is judged to be subordinate to, and thus less than, the Father. Whether this subordination is expressed in ontological terms relating to his essential divine nature, or alleged functional and relational terms essential to his hypostatic identity, is immaterial. Either way, the Son's subordination cannot be affirmed without affecting his status and dignity in relation to the Father. This deficit is what grounds the drawing of an analogy with the perceived subordinationist outcome of the views of Arius.

⮑

The significance of this is that the description of a set of theological proposals as "Arian" or its categorization as an instance of "Arianism" is not in this case based on meeting the requirement of strict conformity to the exact *details* of Arius's own fourth-century theological and philosophical views. Nor is this judgment determined in the light of some kind of comparison with the formative influences of an essentially historical account of the complex of intellectual forces that might explain how it was that

Arius reached his conclusions, even if we could be sure of them. Nor is the justification of the charge of "Arianism" simply a matter of demonstrating the shortfall of uncontested scriptural texts that might be deemed to teach the "eternal subordination of the Son to the Father." A shortfall in terms of the biblical warrant certainly raises questions as to the wisdom of entertaining the possibility of assent to a theological proposition, but it does not itself necessarily demonstrate the appropriateness of categorizing the outcome as "Arian." In identifying a contemporary set of proposals as "Arian" or as an instance of a kind of "Arianism," an assessment has to be made of the general nature of the proposals themselves, their chief characteristics, and whether these in logical terms in fact fracture the substantial unity of being of the Trinity in a way analogous to the perceived outcome of the fourth-century proposals of Arius.

On the other hand, when the terms "Arian" or "Arianism" are currently used in the debates of today they are not just bandied about, or used emptily or unthinkingly. Rather, reasons are regularly given to justify the appropriateness of their use. The use of the term "Arianism" is rarely just an apotropaic signal of the bald assertion that the definition of the *homoousion* has been challenged or compromised. Instead, reasons are assembled for the purpose of providing a considered and rational justification for making this judgment. By unpacking the specific offending characteristics of subordinationist and complementarian proposals and their negative implications for the orthodox theology of the Trinity, an analogy may be drawn with the controversy triggered by the idiosyncratic proposals of Arius. Alarm bells ring when we hear a contemporary echo of the fourth-century concern about the shortfall from the requirements of faith and worship that went hand in hand with the dogmatic corrective of the Nicene definition itself.

↜

Finally, this does not mean that there are not factors within the contemporary debate about the impact of eternal functional subordination on the integrity of the doctrine of the Trinity that are peculiar to our time. While it is possible to discern analogies with the fourth-century controversy triggered by Arius, there are also issues that are unique to this contemporary phenomenon. When the historians of the future write their accounts of this theological saga they will undoubtedly tell the story of an almost one-hundred-year development in Australian ecclesial history that I have called Carillon Avenue theology. As noted earlier, this was first imported into Australian Anglicanism from Ireland in the decade prior to the Second World War. Its parallel in the United States is found notably amongst Presbyterians of the Westminster tradition and Baptists, for whom the seminal influence of the federal theology of Charles and his son A. A. Hodge at Princeton seems *prima facie* to be of particular significance. These factors that are unique to this contemporary phenomenon will include such items as the attempt to sidestep the *homoousion* by distinguishing eternal functional subordination of the Son from an ontological subordination associated with the divine nature, and talk of a complementarian as against an egalitarian set of interpersonal relationships within the Trinity, and of the significance of this for gender relations of husbands and wives and so on. All this is obviously historically unique to the present age.

Meanwhile, the chief problems raised by the novel proposals of complementarian subordinationism that invite their classification as a kind of Arianism, may be set out in four points:

First, unfortunately, the forging of an essential difference between the personal nature essential to the Father, and the personal nature essential to the Son, such as is entailed by talking in the manner of the proponents of Carillon Avenue theology of the commanding will of the Father and the eternally submissive will of the Son, immediately raises a number of problems. Even though the commanding will of the Father and the obediently complaint will of the Son may in a sense be said to be binary and harmoniously complementary, the very notion of complementarity itself necessarily entails that they are nevertheless not the same but different. Furthermore, this does not just lead into tritheism, as Glenn Butner has rightly argued, for this difference is not just numerical: the differential between the commanding will of the Father and the obediently submissive will of the Son introduces a qualitative difference. An eternal inequality is entailed in terms of status and dignity, and hence in terms of authority. This inevitably in turn entails that the Son must be judged to be in some sense less than, or inferior to, the Father in terms of his divine authority, status, and dignity. This is a theological disaster precisely of the kind that, in the fourth century, the definition of the *homoousion* was intended to remedy in relation to the novel proposals of Arius.

Second, the attempted removal of the property of the Son's subordination from under the umbrella of the *homoousion* by the proponents of his eternal functional subordination to the Father, in the interests of associating it instead with the *hypostasis* of the Son in a way that is in-dependent of the full complement of properties belonging to the equally shared divine nature, is also a serious mistake. For, while the full and equal sharing of the properties of the divine nature that is required by the *homoousion* is imagined to secure the essential hypostatic equality of the Trinitarian identities in terms of their divine status and dignity, so as to avoid the charge of heresy, unfortunately this is self-defeating. For a start, and unavoidably, the very status and dignity of their *hypostases* or *persons* is negatively impacted by this strategy of argument. Although the requirements of the *homoousion* are relied upon precisely as a corrective buffer against the charge of heresy, the attempt to remove the property of submissiveness from under the requirements of the *homoousion*, thus separating it from this corrective buffer, ironically triggers an additional set of problems. Even if the property of the subordination of the Son is said to be dissociated from his divine nature in a way that is intended to deflect it from impacting negatively on the definition of the *homoou-sion*, by its more immediate association with the Son's filial identity it not only therefore immediately impacts negatively on the Son's *hypostatic* authority, status, and dignity, but diminishes the *homoousion* itself. This is because the removal of the property of "submissiveness" from under its requirement of "equality and sameness" means that the other-regarding property of "mutual submissiveness" is lost from the divine nature.

Third, when it is said that an ontological defect of the exercise of the Father's monarchy as the "origin" and "cause" of the Son and the Spirit has to be compensated for by his delegation of an additional "authority and rule" through a determination of the Father's will, and as an act of grace and favor of the Father, the outcome is even more disastrous. This is because this is said allegedly to demonstrate the Son's subordination in relation to the exercise of the monarchy of the Father. Arius's error was to deny that the Logos was eternally begotten and *ontologically related* to the being of the Father, but instead created as an act of will of the Father at the time of creation. Robert Doyle's suggestion with regard to the delegation of "authority and rule" by an act of will of the Father to the Son is parallel to this. His contention is that an ontological deficit has to be compensated for by an act of will of the Father who delegates "authority and rule" to the Son and so ensures that he has a status as Lord and King. Whether this is to be understood temporally or timelessly, it implicitly denies an original ontological status of the Son equal to that of the Father. Adolf Harnack might well have drawn our attention to a kind of adoptionism in this additional delegation of "authority and rule" to make good this ontological deficit.

Fourth, the undeniable diminishment of the status and dignity of the *hypostasis* or person of the Son with respect to the Father has disastrous consequences with respect to the Son's availability as an object of faith and worship. It is the *hypostasis*, the person, of the Father, and the *hypostasis*, the person, of the Son (and the Spirit), who are together called "Lord" in the context of the address of prayer and worship. It is not the shared divine nature that is secured by the *homoousion* (however important this may be) that is worshipped; rather, it is the Divine Persons who are the object of worship. Thus, and very importantly, in the identification of "eternal functional subordination" as an "Arian" notion, or an instance of a form of "Arianism," consideration must be given to the apparently unavoidable logical implications of the alleged possession of different and *unequal hypostatic* properties by the Father and the Son (and the Spirit) in relation to the practicalities of faith and worship.[52]

In drawing upon the significance of all this in giving an account of what is at stake when we describe "eternal functional subordination" as "Arian" or categorize it as "a form of Arianism," a direct analogy is being drawn between these novel contemporary subordinationist and complementarian proposals and their practical implications for faith and worship with those of the fourth-century phenomenon triggered by the theological proposals of Arius.

⌣

In Arius's day there does not seem to have been anything like an organized troupe of supporters with an agenda of belief sufficiently systematized and coherent to be labeled as "Arian" and as an example of "Arianism." But it can nevertheless be accepted that these terms came to be borrowed for use as labels in relation to the identification of a deviation from the norms of Christian orthodoxy for which in the post-Nicene world the *homoousion* became the accepted corrective. This has meant that the terms "Arian" and "Arianism" have come to be used with the conventionally

---

52. It is significant that the 1999 Sydney Doctrine Commission Report acknowledges this requirement: "The Church doctrine states that the Father and the Son and the Spirit are of the same substance, or essence, equal in power, dignity, worship and praise." (sec 2.4/para. 8). It nevertheless imagines that the "eternal functional subordination" of the Son to the Father does not affect this.

agreed meaning that signals the problematic nature of any belief package, whether systematized and institutionalized or not, and arrived at by whatever intellectual route, that is perceived to introduce a fracture into the unified life of the One God by subordinating the Son to the Father. In other words, the suggestion that the eternal Son is somehow subordinate to the Father, and therefore less than the Father in terms of authority, status, and dignity, in such a way as to appear to compromise his full divinity, may fairly be identified as "Arian" or as an example of "a kind of Arianism." In general terms this basic issue is what was perceived in the fourth century to be dangerously inadequate, both amongst the bishops who assembled at Nicaea in 325 and those across Christendom who continued to worship Christ as fully and equally divine with the Father.

By contrast with the situation of Arius's time, we clearly have on our hands today a very well defined and well organized "movement" of overt, committed proponents of the novel teaching of the "eternal functional subordination" of the Son to the Father within the immanent life of the Trinity. There is no suggestion that this is not a very sincerely held conviction particularly amongst Australian Carillon Avenue theologians and very large numbers of their like-minded evangelical counterparts across North America. Similarly, there is no suggestion that the authors of the 1999 Sydney Doctrine Commission Report doubted that the concept of "functional subordination" of "equality of essence with order in relation" is anything but the long-held teaching of the church, and that it is securely based in the revelation of the Scriptures.

Kevin Giles reports an extended correspondence with Robert Forsyth, one of the authors of the report, in the course of which Forsyth said that what he wanted to make emphatically clear is that none of the members of the 1999 commission "consciously intended" to embrace key elements of Arianism, or to deny what the creeds teach, or directly contradict the basic theological principle enshrined in the Nicene and Athanasian Creeds. "In particular" Giles reports that "they did not 'consciously' intend to deny that the three divine persons are 'one in being' (homoousios) by speaking of 'differences of being.'" When Giles asked Forsyth if he would "now like to reword anything in the Report," or admit that some comments were, to say the very least, unhelpful, he declined. Instead, Forsyth said that "properly understood" the report teaches "what 'we' believe."[53] It appears that the theological substance of the report was reaffirmed.

53. Giles, *Jesus and the Father*, 26–27.

Michael Jensen, who apparently himself agrees with the commission's teaching,[54] reports that the succeeding Sydney Doctrine Commission reviewed the 1999 Report and also reaffirmed its conclusions. According to Jensen:

> In 2004–2005, the Sydney Doctrine Commission indeed met to reconsider their report in the light of correspondence from Giles and Carnley but determined that there was no need to change the view of the 1999 report. The chairman of the Commission, John Woodhouse, wrote to the archbishop that "the Commission is of the opinion that no substantial case has been made that the 1999 Report on the Doctrine of the Trinity is in serious error . . . The Doctrine Commission therefore supports the teaching of the 1999 Report although in the light of subsequent debate it would elaborate some points more fully today and possibly express some matters in clearer language."[55]

Given that this report was formally received by the Synod of the Diocese of Sydney in 1999 without a motion of dissent, Giles justifiably understands it as having ecclesial authority as a "synod-endorsed statement of faith."

Almost certainly, Robert Doyle did not anticipate an answer in the affirmative when, on behalf of his Carillon Avenue colleagues, and specifically in response to Kevin Giles's charge of the report's apparent Arianism, he posed the poignant question: "Have we become heretics?"[56] Unfortunately, an affirmative answer seems unavoidable.

54. Jensen, *Sydney Anglicanism*, 132.

55. Jensen, *Sydney Anglicanism*, 143. On this point Jensen cites Frame and Treloar, *Agendas for Australian Anglicanism*, 156.

56. See Robert Doyle's review of Kevin Giles's *Trinity and Subordinationism*, "Use and abuse," Intro.

# Bibliography

Abelard, Peter. *Exposition of the Epistle to the Romans* (An Excerpt from the Second Book). In *A Scholastic Miscellany: Anselm to Ockham*, edited and translated by Eugene R. Fairweather, 276–87. The Library of Christian Classics X. London: SCM, 1956.

Adam, Peter. "Honouring Jesus Christ." *St Mark's Review* 1/198 (2005) 11–17.

Agourides, Savas. "Can the persons of the Trinity form the basis for personalistic understandings of the human being?" *Synaxis* 33 (1990) 67–78.

Aristotle. *Metaphysics*. Translated with notes by Christopher Kirwan. Oxford: Oxford University Press, 1971.

———. *Politics*. Translated by Ernest Barker and R. F. Stalley. Oxford: Oxford University Press, 1995.

Armitage, Chris. "The Memorialists." *The Anglican Historical Society, Diocese of Sydney, Journal*, 55/2 (2010) 18–25.

Athanasius. *Against the Heathen*. Kindle ed. N.p.: Fig Classics, 2013.

———. *Defence of the Nicene Council*. In *The Nicene and Post Nicene Fathers of the Christian Church (NPNF)*. Edited by Philip Schaff and Henry Wace. Grand Rapids: Eerdmans, 1971.

———. "Discourses Against the Arians." In *The Nicene and Post Nicene Fathers of the Christian Church (NPNF)*. Edited by Philip Schaff and Henry Wace. Grand Rapids: Eerdmans, 1971.

———. *Letters of Saint Athanasius Concerning the Holy Spirit*. Translated by C. R. B. Shapland. London: Epworth, 1951.

———. *On the Opinion of Dionysius*. In *The Nicene and Post-Nicene Fathers*, second series, IV. N.p.: Fig Classics, 2013.

Augustine of Hippo. *On the Trinity*. In *A Select Library of the Nicene and Post-Nicene Fathers of the Christian Church*, vol. 3, edited by Philip Schaff, translated by the Rev. Arthur West Haddan, with an introduction by William G. T. Shedd, and edited by Paul A Böer Sr. Buffalo: Christian Literature, 1886.

Awad, Najeeb G. "Between Subordination and Koinonia: Toward a New Reading of the Cappadocian Theology." *Modern Theology* 23/2 (April 2007) 181–204.

———. "Personhood as Particularity: John Zizioulas, Colin Gunton, and the Trinitarian Theology of Personhood." *Journal of Reformed Theology* 4 (2010) 1–22.

Ayres, Lewis. *Nicaea and Its Legacy: An Approach to Fourth Century Trinitarian Theology*. Oxford: Oxford University Press, 2004.

Barnes, Michel René. "Augustine in Contemporary Trinitarian Theology." *Theological Studies* 56/2 (1995) 237–50.

————. "De Régnon Reconsidered." *Augustinian Studies* 26/2 (1995) 51–79.

Barnes, Michel René. and Daniel H. Williams, *Arianism After Arius: Essays on the Development of the Fourth Century Trinitarian Conflicts*. Edinburgh: T. & T. Clark, 1993.

Barth, Karl. *Church Dogmatics* IV, *The Doctrine of Reconciliation*. Translated by G. W. Bromiley, edited by G. W. Bromiley and T. F. Torrance. London: T. & T. Clark, 1956.

Basil of Caesarea. *On the Holy Spirit*. Introduction by David Anderson. Crestwood, NY: St. Vladimir's Seminary Press, 1980.

Bauman, Michael. *Milton's Arianism*. Frankfurt: Peter Lang, 1987.

Bilezikian, Gilbert. "Hermeneutical Bungee-Jumping: Subordination in the Godhead." *Journal of the Evangelical Theological Society* 40/1 (1997) 57–68.

Billings, Todd. *Calvin, Participation and Gift: The Activity of Believers in Union with Christ*. Oxford: Oxford University Press, 2007.

Bird, Michael F. *Evangelical Theology: A Biblical and Systematic Introduction*. Grand Rapids: Zondervan, 2013.

————. "Theologians of a Lesser Son." Preface to *Trinity without Hierarchy* by Michael F. Bird and Scott Harrower, 9–11. Grand Rapids: Kregel Academic, 2019.

Bird, Michael F., and Scott Harrower. *Trinity without Hierarchy: Reclaiming Nicene Orthodoxy in Evangelical Theology*. Grand Rapids: Kregel Academic, 2019.

Bird, Michael F., and Robert Shillaker. "The Son Really, Really Is the Son: A Response to Kevin Giles." *Trinity Journal* 30 (2009) 257–68.

————. "Subordination in the Trinity and Gender Roles: A Response to Recent Discussion." *Trinity Journal* 29/2 (2008) 267–83. Also in *The New Evangelical Subordinationism: Perspectives on the Equality of God the Father and God the Son*, edited by Dennis W. Jowers and W. Wayne House, 288–310. Eugene, OR: Pickwick, 2012.

Blocher, H. *Original Sin*. Nottingham: Apollos, 1997.

Boersma, Hans. *Heavenly Participation: The Weaving of a Sacramental Tapestry*. Grand Rapids: Eerdmans, 2011.

Boethius. *Against Eutyches and Nestorius*. Translated by W. V. Cooper. London: J. M. Dent, 1902.

Boff, Leonardo. *Trinity and Society*. Maryknoll, NY: Orbis, 1988.

Brent, Alan. *Hippolytus and the Roman Church in the Third Century: Communities in Tension before the Emergence of a Monarch-bishop*. Supplements to Vigiliae Christianae. Leiden: Brill, 1995.

Bromiley, G. W. "Eternal Generation." In *Evangelical Dictionary of Theology*, edited by Walter A. Elwell. Grand Rapids: Baker, 1984.

Bugár, István M. "The making of personhood: crossroads around 400 AD." *Interdisciplinary Research in Humanities,* edited by Gergely Angyalosi et al. Constantine the Philosopher University. https://www.academia.edu/3816223/The_making_of_personhood_crossroads_around_400_AD?auto=download&email_work_card=download-pap.

Bull, George. *Defensio Fidei Nicaenae,* I and II. University Press, 1685. Oxford: J. H. Parker, 1851–1852.

Burkert, Walter. *Homo Necans: The Anthropology of Ancient Greek Sacrificial Ritual and Myth*. Berkeley: University of California Press, 1983.

Butner, D. Glenn, Jr. "Eternal Functional Subordination and the Problem of the Divine Will." *Journal of the Evangelical Theological Society* 58/1 (March 2015) 131–49.

———. *The Son Who Learned Obedience: A Theological Case Against the Eternal Submissiveness of the Son.* Eugene, OR: Pickwick, 2018.

Cable, K. J. "Hammond, Thomas Chatterton (1877–1961)." *Australian Dictionary of Biography* 14 (1966) 376–68. https://adb.anu.edu.au/biography/hammond-thomas-chatterton-10406.

———. "The Memorialists." *Anglican Historical Society, Diocese of Sydney, Journal* 58/2 (2013) 10–24.

Carnley, Peter. "Godfellows." *The Bulletin*, May 22, 2001, 38–40.

———. "In the Beginning." *The Bulletin*, September 3, 2002, 34–35.

———. "In Praise of Hierarchy—A Response to Jürgen Moltmann." *Common Theology*, edited by Maggie Hellas, I/1 (July 2002) 9–15. Also available at commontheology.com, archive of vols 1–3.

———. "Introduction to the Colloquium." *St Mark's Review* 1/198 (2005) 3–4.

———. "King on a Cross." *The Bulletin*, April 17, 2001, 33–35.

———. *The Reconstruction of Resurrection Belief.* Eugene, OR: Cascade, 2019.

———. *Reflections in Glass.* Sydney: HarperCollins, 2004.

———. *The Subordinate Substitute: Another Wrong Turn on Carillon Avenue.* Eugene, OR: Cascade, forthcoming.

———. "Such is Life." *The Bulletin*, April 16, 2002, 36–38.

———. "T. C. Hammond and the Theological Roots of Sydney Arianism." *St Mark's Review* 1/198 (2005) 5–10.

———. "Theory of the Atonement Makes God Look Cruel." *Anglican Messenger*, Perth (March 1991) 12.

———. "The rising of the Son." *The Bulletin*, April 25, 2000, 40–43.

———. "The Ultimate Sacrifice." *The Bulletin*, April 2, 2002, 26–29.

Carson, D. A. "Review of *Evil and the Justice of God*, by N. T. Wright." *Review of Biblical Literature*, April 2007. http://www.bookreviews.org/pdf/5581_5877.pdf.

Cave, William. *Ecclesiastici: or, The History of the Lives, Acts, Death and Writings of the Most Eminent Fathers of the Church.* London: Printed by R. J. for Richard Chiswel, 1683.

Chalke, Steve. "Cross Purposes." *Christianity* (September 2004) 44–48.

Chalke, Steve, and Alan Mann. *The Lost Message of Jesus.* Grand Rapids: Zondervan, 2003.

Claunch, Kyle. "God is the Head of Christ: 1 Corinthians 11.3." In *One God and Three Persons: Unity of Essence, Distinction of Persons, Implications for Life*, edited by Bruce A. Ware and John Starke, 65–93. Wheaton, IL: Crossway, 2015.

———. "What God Hath Done Together: Defending the Historic Doctrine of the Inseparable Operations of the Trinity." *Journal of the Evangelical Theological Society* 56/4 (2013) 781–800.

Coakley, Sarah. "Afterword: 'Relational Ontology', Trinity and Science." In *The Trinity and an Entangled World*, edited by John Polkinghorne. Grand Rapids: Eerdmans, 2010.

———. "Introduction: Disputed Questions in Patristic Trinitariaism." *Harvard Theological Review* 100/2 (2007) 125–38.

———. "'Persons' in the Social Doctrine of the Trinity: Current Analytical Discussion and 'Cappadocian Theology.'" In *The Trinity—An Interdisciplinary Symposium*, edited by Stephen Davis, Daniel Kendall, and Gerald O'Collins, 123–44. Oxford: Oxford University Press, 1999.

Cocceius, John. *Summa doctrinae de foedere et testamento Dei* (1648).Lugduno-Batava: Ex Officinâ Elseviriorum, 1654.

Cranfield, Charles E. B. *A Critical and Exegetical Commentary on the Epistle to the Romans.* 2 vols. Edinburgh: T. & T. Clark, 1975.

Cross, F. L., and E. A. Livingstone, eds. *Oxford Dictionary of the Christian Church.* 3rd ed. Oxford: Oxford University Press, 1974.

Cvetkovic, Vladimir. "The Oneness of God as Unity of Persons in the Thought of St. Maximus the Confessor." In *Maximus the Confessor as a European Philosopher*, edited by Sotiris Mitralexis, Georgios Steiris, Marcin Podbielski, and Sebastian Lalla, 304–15. Eugene, OR: Cascade, 2017.

Cyprian of Carthage. *On the Unity of the Church.* In *The Complete Works of Saint Cyprian*, edited by Phillip Campbell. https://patristics.info/cyprian-on-the-unity-of-the-church.html.

Del Colle, Ralph. "'Persons' and 'Being' in John Zizioulas' Theology: Conversation with Thomas Torrance and Thomas Aquinas." *Scottish Journal of Theology* 54/1 (2001) 70–86.

Denaux, Adelbert. *Looking Towards A Church Fully Reconciled.* Edited by Nicholas Sagovsky and Charles Sherlock. Mahwah, NJ: Paulist, 2016.

Devlin, Patrick. *The Enforcement of Morals.* Oxford: Oxford University Press, 1968.

*Doctrine in the Church of England.* London: SPCK, 1938.

Dorner, I. A. *A History of the Development of the Doctrine of the Person of Christ* 3. Translated by D. W. Simon. Edinburgh: T. & T. Clark, 1889.

Doyle, Robert. "God in Feminist Critique." *Reformed Theological Review* 52/1 (1993) 12–22.

———. Review of "*Reflections in Glass*, Chapter 7: Women in the Episcopate." *sydneyanglicans.net*, September 3, 2004.

———. "Sexuality, Personhood, and the Image of God." In *Personhood, Sexuality, and Christian Ministry, Explorations: Moore Papers No. 1*, edited by B. Webb, 43–46. Sydney: Lancer, 1987.

———. "Use and abuse of the fathers and the Bible in trinitarian theology." Review of Kevin Giles, *The Trinity and Subordinationism. The Briefing*, April 1, 2004, 11–19. http://thebriefing.com.au/2004/04/use-and-abuse-of-the-fathers-and-the-bible-in-trinitarian-theology/.

Dunn, James D. G. *The Theology of the Apostle Paul.* London: T. & T. Clark, 2003.

Eberhart, Christian. "Sacrifice? Holy Smokes! Reflections on Cult Terminology for Understanding Sacrifice in the Hebrew Bible." In *Ritual and Metaphor: Sacrifice in the Bible*, edited by Christian Eberhart, 17–32. Atlanta: Society of Biblical Literature, 2011.

Emerson, Matthew Y. "Response to Bruce A. Ware and Malcolm B. Yarnell III." In *Trinitarian Theology*, edited by Keith S. Whitfield, 157–73. Nashville: B & H, 2019.

Emerson, Matthew Y., and Luke Stamps. "On Trinitarian Theological Method." In *Trinitarian Theology*, edited by Keith S. Whitfield, 95–128. Nashville: B & H, 2019.

Erickson, Millard. *Who's Tampering with the Trinity? An Assessment of the Subordination Debate.* Grand Rapids: Kregel, 2009.

Faith and Order Advisory Group of the Church of England (FOAG). *"Church as Communion*: Briefing for General Synod." 2008, GS Misc 1713. www. churchofengland.org/media/1236810/gs1713.pdf.

Farrow, D. "Person and Nature: The Necessity–Freedom Dialectic." In *The Theology of John Zizioulas: Personhood and the Church*, edited by D. H. Knight, 109–24. Aldershot: Ashgate, 2007.

Fee, Gordon D. *The First Epistle to the Corinthians*. Grand Rapids: Eerdmans: 1987.

Fenner, Dudley. *Sacra theologia, sive veritas quae est secundum pietatem*. Geneva: Eustache Vignon, 1585.

Fiddes, Paul. *Past Event and Present Salvation: The Christian Idea of Atonement*. London: Darton, Longman and Todd, 1989.

Field, Richard. *Of the Church: Five Bookes*. London: Imprinted by Humfrey Lownes for Simon Waterson, 1606. https://www.google.com/books/edition/Of_the_Church_Five_bookes_An_appendix_co/e-NhAAAAcAAJ?hl=en&gbpv=0.

Filonenko, Alexander. "The Theology of Communion and Eucharistic Anthropology." In *Philosophical Theology and the Christian Tradition: Russian and Western Perspectives*, edited by David Bradshaw, 177–85. Washington, DC: Council for Research in Values and Philosophy, 2012.

Fokin, Alexey. "Models of the Trinity in Patristic Theology." In *Philosophical Theology and the Christian Tradition: Russian and Western Perspectives*, edited by David Bradshaw, 31–52. Washington, DC: Council for Research in Values and Philosophy, 2012.

Forsyth, Robert. "It's Negative Theology." *Market-Place*, April 8, 2004, 6–12.

Frame, John. *Systematic Theology: An Introduction to Christian Belief*. Phillipsburg, NJ: P & R, 2013.

Frame, Tom. *Anglicans in Australia*. Sydney: University of New South Wales Press, 2007.

———. "The Dynamics and Difficulties of Debate in Australian Anglicanism." In *Agendas for Australian Anglicans: Essays in Honour of Bruce Kaye*, edited by Tom Frame and Geoffrey Treloar, 139–70. Adelaide: ATF, 2006.

Gilders, William K. "Jewish Sacrifice: Its Nature and Function (According to Philo)." In *Ancient Mediterranean Sacrifice*, edited by Jennifer Wright Knust and Zsuzsanna Varhelyi, 94–105. New York: Oxford University Press, 2011.

Giles, Kevin. *The Eternal Generation of the Son: Maintaining Orthodoxy in Trinitarian Theology*. Grand Rapids: Zondervan, 2012.

———. "In Praise of Egalitarianism." *Common Theology* 1/2 (Advent 2002) 13–15.

———. *Jesus and the Father: Modern Evangelicals Reinvent the Trinity*. Grand Rapids: Zondervan, 2006.

———. "Response to Michael Bird and Robert Shillaker: The Son is not Eternally Subordinated in Authority to the Father." *Trinity Journal* 30/2 (2009) 237–56.

———. "Review of *The Holy Trinity in Scripture, History, Theology and Worship*, by Robert Letham." *Evangelical Quarterly* 78/1 (2006) 85–94.

———. *The Rise and Fall of the Complementarian Doctrine of the Trinity*. Eugene, OR: Cascade, 2017.

———. "The Trinity and Subordinationism." *St Mark's Review* 1/198 (2005) 19–24.

———. *The Trinity and Subordinationism: The Doctrine of God and the Contemporary Gender Debate*. Downers Grove, IL: InterVarsity, 2002.

———. "The Trinity without Tiers." In *The New Evangelical Subordinationism? Perspectives on the Equality of God the Father and God the Son,* edited by Dennis W. Jowers and H. Wayne House, 262–87. Eugene, OR: Pickwick, 2012.

Giles, Kevin, and Robert Letham. "Is the Son Eternally Submissive to the Father?" *Christian Research Journal* 31/1 (2008) 10–21.

Global Anglican Futures Conference (GAFCON). Jerusalem Declaration, June 2008. https://www.gafcon.org/about/jerusalem-declaration.

Goligher, Liam. "Is It Okay to Teach Complementarianism Based on Eternal Subordination?" *Mortification of Spin,* June 3, 2016. http://www.alliancenet.org/mos/housewife-theologian/is-it-okay-to-teach-a complementarianism-based-on-eternal subordination#.WGGyLfB96Ul.

Gons, Philip, and Andrew Naselli. "An Examination of Three Recent Philosophical Arguments Against Hierarchy in the Immanent Trinity." In *One God in Three Persons: Unity of Essence, Distinction of Persons, Implications for Life,* edited by Bruce Ware and John Starke, 195–213. Wheaton, IL: Crossway, 2015.

Grabowski, John. "Person: Substance and Relation." *Communio* 22 (Spring 1995) 139–63.

Green, Joel B. "Must We Imagine the Atonement in Penal Substitutionary Terms? Question, Caveats and a Plea." In *The Atonement Debate: Papers from The London Symposium on the Theology of Atonement.* edited by Derek Tidball, David Hilborn. and Justin Thacker, 153–71. Grand Rapids: Zondervan, 2008.

Green, Joel B. and Mark D. Baker, *Recovering the Scandal of the Cross,* 2nd ed. Downers Grove, IL: IVP Academic, 2011.

Gregg, Robert C., ed. *Arianism: Historical and Theological Reassessments, Papers from The Ninth International Conference on Patristic Studies,* Oxford, September 5–10, 1983. Philadelphia: Philadelphia Patristic Foundation, 1985.

Gregory of Nazianzus. *On God and Christ: The Five Theological Orations and Two Letters to Cledonius.* Crestwood, NY: St. Vladimir's Seminary Press, 2002.

Gregory Palamas. *The Triads.* Classics of Western Spirituality. Translated by Nicholas Gendle with an introduction by John Meyendorff. London: SPCK, 1983.

Grudem, Wayne. "Biblical Evidence for the Eternal Submission of the Son to the Father." In *The New Evangelical Subordinationism? Perspectives on the Equality of God the Father and God the Son,* edited by Dennis W. Jowers and H. Wayne House, 223–61. Eugene, OR: Pickwick, 2012.

———. *Evangelical Feminism and Biblical Truth: An Analysis of More Than 100 Disputed Questions.* Wheaton, IL: Crossway, 2004.

———. *Systematic Theology: An Introduction to Biblical Doctrine.* 2nd ed. Leicester, England: Inter-Varsity, 2020.

Grudem, Wayne, and J. Piper, eds. *Recovering Biblical Manhood and Womanhood: A Response to Evangelical Feminism.* Wheaton, IL: Crossway, 1991.

Gunton, Colin. *The Actuality of Atonement: A Study of Metaphor, Rationality, and the Christian Tradition.* London: T. & T. Clark, 1998.

———. "Eastern and Western Trinities: Being and Person." In *Father, Son, and Holy Spirit: Toward a Fully Trinitarian Theology,* 32–57. Edinburgh: T. & T. Clark, 2003.

———. "Persons and Particularity." In *The Theology of John Zizioulas: Personhood and the Church,* edited by D. H. Knight, 97–108. Aldershot: Ashgate, 2007.

Gwatkin, H. M. *Studies in Arianism Chiefly Referring to the Character and Chronology of the Reaction which followed the Council of Nicaea.* Cambridge: Deighton Bell, 1882, 1900.

Halcrow, Jeremy. "Passionate response to atonement attacks." *sydneyanglicans*.net, September 25, 2007, http://your.sydneyanglicans.net/sydneystories/cross_concern_debated/.

Hammond, T. C. *Authority in Religion. Irish Church Quarterly* 9/36 (1916) 287–99.

———. *In Understanding Be Men* (1936). Edited and revised by David F. Wright. London: Inter-Varsity, 1976.

———. *The New Creation.* London: Marshall, Morgan & Scott, 1953.

———. *One Hundred Texts of the Society for Irish Church Missions.* 3rd ed. Society for Irish Church Missions. London: Marshall, Morgan & Scott, 1950.

———. *Perfect Freedom: An Introduction to Christian Ethics.* London: InterVarsity Fellowship of Evangelical Unions, 1938.

———. "Post-Reformation Theology in the Church of Ireland." In *The Church of Ireland AD 432–1932: Report of the Church of Ireland Conference Held in Dublin, 11th–14th October, 1932, (with an account of the Commemoration by the Church of Ireland of the 1500th Anniversary of the Landing of St Patrick in Ireland)*, edited by W. Bell and N. C. Emerson, 97–105. Dublin: Church of Ireland, 1933.

———. "The Significance of the Death of Christ." In *From the Manger to the Throne: Outstanding Events in the Life of Our Lord*, edited F. Donald Coggan, 39–49. London: Inter-Varsity, 1936.

Hanson, R. P. C. "The Arian Doctrine of the Incarnation." In *Arianism: Historical and Theological Reassessments, Papers from The Ninth International Conference on Patristic Studies*, Oxford, September 5–10, 1983, edited by Robert C. Gregg, 181–211. Philadelphia: Philadelphia Patristic Foundation, 1985.

———. *The Search for the Christian Doctrine of God: The Arian Controversy 318–381.* Edinburgh: T. & T. Clark, 1988.

———. "Who Taught *ex ouk onton*?" In *Arianism: Historical and Theological Reassessments, Papers from The Ninth International Conference on Patristic Studies*, edited by Robert C. Gregg, 79–83. Philadelphia: Philadelphia Patristic Foundation, 1985.

Harnack, C. G. Adolf. *History of Dogma.* 7 vols. Translated by Neil Buchanan, E. B. Speirs, J. Millar, and W. MacGilchrist. London: Williams & Norgate, 1894–99.

Hennessy, Kristin. "An Answer to De Régnon's 'Accusers': Why We Should Not Speak of 'His' Paradigm." *Harvard Theological Review* 100/2 (2007) 179–97.

Hick, John. *Evil and the God of Love.* Cambridge: Cambridge University Press, 1967.

Hilary of Poitiers. *On the Trinity.* Electronic ed. N.p.: Fig Classics, 2012.

Hilborn, David. "Atonement, Evangelism and the Evangelical Alliance: The Present Debate in Context." In *The Atonement Debate: Papers from The London Symposium on the Theology of Atonement*, edited by Derek Tidball, David Hilborn, and Justin Thacker, 15–33. Grand Rapids: Zondervan, 2008.

Hippolytus of Rome. *Contra Noetum.* Edited by R. Butterworth. London: Heythrop College, 1977. N.p.: Fig Classics, 2012.

Hodge, A. A. *Outlines of Theology.* New York: Robert Carter and Brothers, 1866.

Holmes, Stephen R. *The Quest for the Trinity: The Doctrine of God in Scripture, History, and Modernity.* Downers Grove, IL: IVP Academic, 2012.

Horrell, J. Scott. "Complementarian Trinitarianism: Divine Revelation is Finally True to the Eternal Personal Relations." In *The New Evangelical Subordinationism? Perspectives on the Equality of God the Father and God the Son*, edited by Dennis W. Jowers and H. Wayne House, 339–74. Eugene, OR: Pickwick, 2012.

House, H. Wayne. "The Eternal Relational Subordination of the Father to the Son in Patristic Thought." In *The New Evangelical Subordinationism? Perspectives on the Equality of God the Father and God the Son*, edited by Dennis W. Jowers and H. Wayne House, 133–82. Eugene, OR: Pickwick, 2012.

Huttinga, Wolter. *Participation and Communicability: Herman Bavinck and John Milbank on the Relation of God and the World*. Academisch Proefschrift, Theologische Universiteit van de Gereformeerde Kerken in Nederland te Kampen, 2014.

Ignatius of Antioch. *The Epistles of St. Ignatius of Antioch*. Edited by J. H. Srawley. London: SPCK, 1910.

Ivánka, E. von. *Plato Christianus: Übernahme und Umgestaltung des Platonismus durch die Väter*. Einsiedeln: Johannes Verlag, 1964.

Jeffery, Steve, Michael Ovey, and Andrew Sach. *Pierced for Our Transgressions: Rediscovering the Glory of Penal Substitution*. Nottingham: Inter-Varsity, 2007.

Jensen, Michael P. *Sydney Anglicanism: An Apology*. Eugene, OR: Wipf & Stock, 2012.

Jensen, Peter. "The Good News of God's Wrath." *Christianity Today*, March 1, 2004. http://www.christianitytoday.com/ct/2004/march/5.45.html.

———. "T. C. Hammond No Arian: A Response to Peter Carnley." *St Mark's Review* 2/199 (2005) 44–46.

Jensen, Phillip. "Defining the Evangelical." August 12, 2008. *sydneyanglicans.net*, http://www.sydneyanglicans.net/archive/indepth/defining_the_evangelical/.

Jewett, P. K. *Man as Male and Female*. Grand Rapids: Eerdmans, 1975.

John, Jeffrey. *Lent Talks: Jeffrey John*. BBC Radio 4 Lent Talks, April 4, 2007, https://web.archive.org/web/20070607085657.

John of Damascus. *Exposition of the Orthodox Faith*, translated by S. D. F. Salmond. Oxford: J. Parker, 1899.

Judd, Stephen, and Kenneth Cable. *Sydney Anglicans*. Sydney: Anglican Information Office, 1987.

Kariatlis, Philip. "The Exercise of Primacy in the Church: An Orthodox Theological Perspective." *Phronema* 26/1 (2011) 27–47.

———. "St Basil's Trinitarian Doctrine: A Harmonious Synthesis of Greek *Paideia* and the Scriptural Worldview." In *Cappadocian Legacy: A Critical Appraisal*, edited by Doru Costache and Philip Kariatlis, 131–54. Sydney: St Andrew's Orthodox, 2013.

Kasper, Walter. *Theology and Church*. Translated by Margaret Kohl. New York: Crossroad, 1989.

Kelly, J. N. D. *Early Christian Doctrines*. Rev. ed. San Francisco: HarperCollins, 1978.

King, William. *De Origine Mali*, 1702, translated into English with extensive notes by Edmund Law as *An Essay on the Origin of Evil*. London: Printed by F. Stephens for W. Thurlbourn, 1739.

Kirk, Kenneth. *Commentary of the Epistle to the Romans*. Oxford: Clarendon, 1937.

Klawans, Jonathan. *Purity, Sacrifice, and the Temple: Symbolism and Supersessionism in the Study of Ancient Judaism*. New York: Oxford University Press, 2006.

Knight, Douglas H., ed. *The Theology of John Zizioulas: Personhood and the Church*. Aldershot: Ashgate, 2007.

Knight, George W., III. *The New Testament Teaching on the Role Relationship of Men and Women*. Grand Rapids: Baker, 1977.

Knox, D. Broughton. *Selected Works 1, The Doctrine of God*. Edited by Tony Payne. Kingsford: Matthias Media, 2000.

———. *Selected Works 2, Church and Ministry*. Edited by Kirsten Birkett. Kingsford: Matthias Media, 2003.

Koutloumousianos, Chrysostom. *The One and the Three: Nature, Person and Triadic Monarchy in the Greek and Irish Patristic Tradition*. Cambridge: James Clarke, 2015.

Lattier, Daniel J. "John Henry Newman and Georges Florovsky: An Orthodox-Catholic Dialogue on the Development of Doctrine." PhD diss., Duquesne University, 2012.

Leibniz, Gottfried Wilhelm. *Théodicée*. Chicago: Open Court, 1985.

Leslie, Charles. *History of Sin and Heresy* (1698). In *Milton: The Critical Heritage*, vol. 1, edited by John T. Shawcross. London: Routledge, 1970.

Letham, Robert. "The *Foedus Operum*: Some Factors Accounting for Its Development." *The Sixteenth Century Journal* 14/ 4 (Winter 1983) 457–67.

———. *The Holy Trinity, in Scripture, History, Theology and Worship*. Phillipsburg, NJ: P & R, 2004.

———. "The Man-Woman Debate: Theological Comment." *The Westminster Theological Journal* 52/1 (2009) 65–78.

———. "Reply to Kevin Giles." *Evangelical Quarterly* 80/4 (2008) 339–45.

———. *The Westminster Assembly: Reading Its Theology in Historical Context*. Westminster Assembly and the Reformed Faith. Phillipsburg, NJ: P & R, 2009.

Letham, Robert, and Kevin Giles. "Is the Son Eternally Submissive to the Father?" *Christian Research Journal* 31/1 (2008) 10–21.

Libolt, Clayton. "Synod Affirms Penal Substitutionary Atonement, Does Not Call Denial Heresy." *The Banner*, September 11, 2022, www.thebanner.org/news/2022/06/synod-affirms-penal-substitutionary=atonement.

Lieb, Michael. "Milton and 'Arianism.'" *Religion & Literature* 32/2 (2000) 197–220.

Loke, Andrew T. "Review of *The Reconstruction of Resurrection Belief*." *Journal of Theological Studies* 72/2 (2022) 1055–57.

Lossky, Vladimir. *The Mystical Theology of the Eastern Church*. Crestwood, NY: St Vladimir's Seminary Press, 1976.

———. *Orthodox Theology: An Introduction*. Translated by Ian and Ihita Kesarcodi-Watson. Crestwood, NY: St Vladimir's Seminary Press, 1989.

———. "Redemption and Deification." In *In the Image and Likeness of God*, edited by John H. Erickson and Thomas E. Bird, 97–110. Crestwood, NY: St. Vladimir's Seminary Press, 1974.

———. "The Theological Notion of the Human Person." In *In the Image and Likeness of God*, edited by John H. Erickson and Thomas E. Bird, 111–23. Crestwood, NY: St. Vladimir's Seminary Press, 1974.

———. "The Theology of the Image." In *In the Image and Likeness of God*, edited by John H. Erickson and Thomas E. Bird, 125–39. Crestwood, NY: St. Vladimir's Seminary Press, 1974.

———. *The Vision of God*. London: Faith, 1964.

Louth, Andrew. "Recent Research on St Maximus the Confessor: a Survey." *SV Theological Quarterly* 42 (1998) 67–84.

Lubardic, Bogdan. "Orthodox Theology of Personhood: A Critical Overview, Part I." *The Expository Times* 122/11 (2011) 521–30.

———. "Orthodox Theology of Personhood: A Critical Overview, Part II." *The Expository Times* 122/12 (2011) 573–81.

Ludlow, Morwenna. *Gregory of Nyssa, Ancient and (Post)modern.* Oxford: Oxford University Press, 2007.

Lyman, Rebecca. "A Topography of Heresy: Mapping the Rhetorical Creation of Arianism." In *Arianism After Arius: Essays on the Development of the Fourth Century Trinitarian Conflicts,* edited by Michel R. Barnes and Daniel H. Williams, 45–62. Edinburgh: T. & T. Clark, 1993.

Marshall, I. Howard. *Aspects of the Atonement: Cross and Resurrection in the Reconciling of God and Humanity.* Colorado Springs: Paternoster, 2007.

Matelescu, Sebastian. "Counting Natures and Hypostases: St Maximus the Confessor on the Role of Number in Christology." In *Studia Patristica* lxxxix: Papers presented at the Seventeenth International Conference on Patristic Studies held in Oxford 2015, 15: The Fountain and the Flood: Maximus the Confessor and Philosophical Enquiry, edited by M. Vinzent & S. Mitralexis, 63–78. 2017.

Maxwell, Paul C. "Is There an Authority Analogy between the Trinity and Marriage? Untangling Arguments of Subordination and Ontology in Egalitarian-Complementarian Discourse." *Journal of The Evangelical Theological Society* 59/3 (2016) 541–70.

McCall, Thomas. *Which Trinity? Whose Monotheism? Philosophical and Systematic Theologians on the Metaphysics of Trinitarian Theology.* Grand Rapids: Eerdmans, 2010.

McClymond, Kathryn. *Beyond Sacred Violence: A Comparative Study of Sacrifice.* Baltimore: Johns Hopkins University Press, 2008.

McGowan, Andrew. "Philo and the Materialization of Sacrifice." *Studia Philonica Annual,* 183–204. Atlanta: SBL, 2020.

———. "The Shadow of Arius: Subordinationism Then and Now." *St Mark's Review* 1/198 (2005) 25–28.

McGowan, Andrew T. B. *The Federal Theology of Thomas Boston.* Dissertation thesis, University of Aberdeen, 1990, Rutherford Studies in Historical Theology. Edinburgh: Paternoster, 1997.

McIntosh, John A. *Anglican Evangelicalism in Sydney, 1897 to 1953: Nathaniel Jones, D. J. Davies, and T. C. Hammond.* Australian College of Theology Monograph. Eugene, OR: Wipf & Stock, 2018.

McIntyre, John. *The Shape of Soteriology: Studies in the Doctrine of the Death of Christ.* Edinburgh: T. & T. Clark, 1992.

McWilliam, Joanne. "Augustine at Ephesus?" In *One Lord, One Faith, One Baptism: Studies in Christian Ecclesiality and Ecumenism in Honor of J. Robert Wright,* edited by Marsha L. Dutton and Patrick Terrell Gray, 56–67. Grand Rapids: Eerdmans, 2006.

Mercer, Calvin. "*Apostelein* and *Pempein* in John." *New Testament Studies* 36/4 (1990) 619–24.

Mesyats, Svetlana. "Does the First have a hypostasis? Some remarks to the History of the term hypostasis in Platonic and Christian Tradition of the 4th–5th cent. AD." *Studia Patristica* LXII, Papers presented at the Sixteenth International Conference on Patristic Studies held in Oxford, 2011, edited by Marcus Vinzent, 10 (2013) 41–56.

Millare, Roland. "Towards a Common Communion: The Relational Anthropologies of John Zizioulas and Karol Wojtyla." *New Blackfriars* 98/1077 (August 2016) 599–614. https://doi.org/10.1111/nbfr.12056.

Milton, John. *De Doctrina Christiana*. In *The Complete Works of John Milton*, Vol. VIII, edited by John K. Hale and J. Donald Cullington, Oxford: Oxford University Press, 2012.

———. *Paradise Lost*. In *The Complete Prose Works of John Milton*, 8 vols., edited by William Alfred et al. New Haven: Yale University Press, 1953–1982.

———. *A Treatise on Christian Doctrine*. Translated by Charles R. Sumner. Cambridge: Cambridge University Press for Charles Knight, 1825.

Moltmann, Jürgen. "Political Theology." *Theology Today* 28 (1971) 6–23.

———. *The Trinity and the Kingdom*. Translated by Margaret Kohl. London: SCM, 1981.

Morris, Leon. *The Apostolic Preaching of the Cross*. Grand Rapids: Eerdmans, 1965.

———. "Atonement." In *New Dictionary of Theology*, edited by Sinclair B. Ferguson and David F. Wright, 54–57. Leicester: Inter-Varsity, 1988.

———. "Atonement." In *Evangelical Dictionary of Theology*, edited by Walter A. Elwell, 113–14. Grand Rapids: Baker Academic, 2001.

———. *The Atonement: Its Meaning and Significance*. Leicester: Inter-Varsity, 1983.

———. *The Cross in the New Testament*. Exeter: Paternoster, 1976.

———. *The Epistle to the Romans*. Grand Rapids: Eerdmans, 1988.

———. *New Testament Theology*. Grand Rapids: Zondervan, 1990.

Moule, C. F. D. "Further Reflections on Philippians 2.5–11." In *History and the Gospel*, edited by W. Ward Gasque and Ralph R. Martin, 264–76. Exeter, UK: Paternoster, 1970.

Mounier, Emmanuel. *The Personalist Manifesto*. London: Longmans, Green, 1952.

Müller, D. "Apostle." In *New International Dictionary of New Testament Theology* 1, edited by Colin Brown, 126–35. Grand Rapids: Zondervan, 1971.

Nelson, Warren. *T. C. Hammond: Irish Christian—His Life & Legacy in Ireland and Australia*. Edinburgh: The Banner of Truth Trust, 1994.

Newman, John Henry. *The Arians of the Fourth Century*. London: Basil Montagu Pickering, 1876.

———. *An Essay on the Development of Christian Doctrine*. https://www.newmanreader. org/works/development/index.html.

*On Consulting the Faithful in Matters of Doctrine*. 1859. Edited by John Coulson. London: Collins, 1986.

Nicole, Roger. "Postscript on Penal Substitution." In *The Glory of the Atonement: Biblical, Theological and Practical Perspectives: Essays in Honor of Roger Nicole*, edited by C. E. Hill and F. A. James III, 445–52. Downers Grove, IL: InterVarsity, 2004.

Normann, F. *Teilhabe-ein Schlüsselwort der Vätertheologie*. Münster: Aschendorff, 1978.

Novatian. *On the Trinity*. Translated by Robert Ernest Wallis, from *Ante-Nicene Fathers* 5, edited by Alexander Roberts, James Donaldson, and A. Cleveland Coxe. Buffalo, NY: Christian Literature Publishing Co., 1886.

Nüssel, Friederike. "Die Sühneverstellung in der Hassischen Dogmatikund ihre neuzeitliche Problemutisierung." In *Deutengen des Todes Jesu in Neuen Testament*, edited by Jörg Frey and Jens Schriter, 73–94. WUNT 181. Tübingen: Mohr Siebeck, 2005.

Nuttall, A. D. *The Alternative Trinity: Gnostic Heresy in Marlowe, Milton and Blake*. Oxford: Clarendon, 1998.

Olivetti, Marco M., ed. "Biblioteca dell' 'Archivio di Filosofia.'" *Intersubjectivité et théologie philosophique*. Milano, 2001.

Otto, Randall. "Moltmann and the Anti-Monotheist Movement." *International Journal of Systematic Theology* 3/3 (2001) 293–308.

Ovey, Michael, Steve Jeffery, and Andrew Sach. *Pierced for Our Transgressions: Rediscovering the Glory of Penal Substitution*. Nottingham: Inter-Varsity, 2007.

———. *Your Will Be Done: Exploring Eternal Subordination, Divine Monarchy and Divine Humility*. London: Latimer Trust, 2016.

Owen, John. "The Death of Death in the Death of Christ." In *The Works of John Owen*, vol. 10 of 24, edited by William H. Goold, 140. Edinburgh: The Banner of Truth Trust, 1967.

———. "Federal Transactions between the Father and the Son." In *The Works of John Owen*, vol. 19 of 24, edited by William H. Goold, 77–97. Edinburgh: T. & T. Clark, 1862.

Packer, J. I. "Anger." In *New Dictionary of Biblical Theology*, edited by T. Desmond Alexander and Brian S. Rosner, 381–83. Downers Grove, IL: InterVarsity, 2000.

———. "The Atonement in the Life of the Christian." In *The Glory of the Atonement: Biblical, Theological and Practical Perspectives: Essays in Honor of Roger Nicole*, edited by C. E. Hill and F. A. James III, 409–25. Downers Grove, IL: InterVarsity, 2004.

———. "What Did the Cross Achieve? The Logic of Penal Substitution." In *The J. I. Packer Collection*, edited by Alister McGrath, 109–11. Downers Grove, IL: InterVarsity, 1999.

Panagopoulos, John. "Ontology or Theology of Person." *Synaxis* 13–14 (1985) 35–47, 63–79.

Pannenberg, Wolhart. "Divine Economy and Eternal Trinity." In *The Theology of John Zizioulas*, edited by Douglas H. Knight, 79–86. Aldershot: Ashcroft, 2007.

Papanikolaou, Aristotle. *Being with God: Trinity, Apophaticism, and Divine-Human Communion*. Notre Dame: University of Notre Dame Press, 2006.

———. "From Sophia to Personhood: The Development of 20th Century Orthodox Trinitarian Theology." *Phronema* 33/2 (2018) 1–20. www.https://fordham.academia.edu/AristotlePapanikolaou.

———. "Is John Zizioulas an Existentialist in Disguise? Response to Lucian Turcescu." *Modern Theology* 20/4 (October 2004) 601–7.

———. "Personhood and its exponents in twentieth-century Orthodox theology." In *The Cambridge Companion to Orthodox Christian Theology*, edited by M. B. Cunningham and E. Theokritoff, 232–45. Cambridge: Cambridge University Press, 2008.

*Patralogia Graeca*. Edited by J. P. Migne. Paris: Imprimerie Catholique, 1857–1866.

Perkins, Harrison. *Catholicity and the Covenant of Works: James Ussher and the Reformed Tradition*. Oxford: Oxford University Press, 2020.

Perkins, William. *The Works of Mr William Perkins*, edited by Randall J. Pederson and Ryan M. Hurd. Grand Rapids: Reformation Heritage, 2017.

Peterson, Derrick. "A Loud Absence: T. F. Torrance in Light of Recent Patristic Scholarship." *Participatio: The Journal of the T. F. Torrance Fellowship* 11 (2023) forthcoming.

Peterson, Erik. *Der Monotheismus als politisches Problem: Ein Beitrag zur Geschichte der politischen Theologie im Imperium Romanum.* Leipzig: Jakob Hegner, 1935.

Portaru, Marius. "Gradual Participation According to St Maximus the Confessor." *Studia Patristrica* lxviii, Papers presented to the Sixteenth International Conference on Patristic Studies, Oxford, 2011, edited by Markus Vinzent, 281–93. Leuven: Walpole, 2013.

Porter, Lawrence B. "On Keeping 'Persons' in the Trinity: A Linguistic Approach to Trinitarian Thought." *Theological Studies* 41/3 (1980) 530–49.

Rahner, Karl. *The Trinity.* Translated by Joseph Donceel. Tonbridge Wells: Burns & Oates, 1970.

Reid, Duncan. "The Trinity and Subordinationism: The Doctrine of God and the Contemporary Gender Debate." In *The Australian Theological Book Review OnLine,* August 2003. www.atbr.openbook.com.au.

Rengstorf, K. H. *"apostello (pempo)."* In *Theological Dictionary of the New Testament* 1, translated by Geoffrey W. Bromiley and edited by Gerhard Kittel, 398–406. Grand Rapids: Eerdmans, 1964.

Richardson, Alan, ed. *A Dictionary of Christian Theology.* London: SCM, 1969.

Rimmer, Chad. *Poetic Participation: Re-narrating a Lutheran concept of faith and works by comparing the writings of John Milbank and Tuomo Mannermaa.* MTh diss., University of Edinburgh, 2010.

Rollock, Robert. *Tractatus de vocatione efficaci.* Edinburgh: Waldegrave, 1597. English translation, *Select Works of Robert Rollock,* 2 vols., translated and edited by William Gunn. Edinburgh: The Wodrow Society, 1849.

Rosenthal, James M., and Nicola Currie, eds. *The Virginia Report.* In *Being Anglican in the Third Millennium: The Official Report of the 10th Meeting of the Anglican Consultative Council,* 211–81. Harrisburg: Morehouse, 1997.

Rumrich, John P. *Milton Unbound: Controversy and Reinterpretation.* Cambridge: Cambridge University Press, 1996.

Sanders, Fred. "A Plain Account of Trinity and Gender." June 17, 2016. http://scriptoriumdaily.com/a-plain-account-of-trinity-and-gender/.

———. *The Image of the Immanent Trinity: Rahner's Rule and the Theological Interpretation of Scripture.* New York: Peter Lang, 2004.

Schoonenberg, Piet. "'He Emptied Himself': Philippians 2:7." *Concillium* 1/1 (1965) 47–66.

———. "The Kenosis or Self-Emptying of Christ." *Concillium* 1/2 (1966) 27–36.

Schreiner, Thomas R. "Head Coverings, Prophecies and the Trinity: 1 Corinthians 11.2–16." In *Recovering Biblical Manhood and Womanhood: A Response to Evangelical Feminism,* edited by John Piper and Wayne Grudem, 124–39. Wheaton, IL: Crossway, 2006.

———. "Penal Substitution View." In *The Nature of the Atonement: Four Views,* edited by James Beilby and Paul R. Eddy, 67–98. Downers Grove, IL: InterVarsity, 2006.

Schreiner, Thomas R. and Andreas J. Koestenberger, eds. *Women in the Church: An Interpretation and Application of 1 Timothy 2:9–15.* 3rd ed. Wheaton, IL: Crossway, 2016.

Shiner, Rory. *One Forever: The Transforming Power of Being In Christ*. Sydney: Matthias Media, 2015.

Shiner, Rory, and Peter Orr. *The World Next Door, A Short Guide to the Christian Faith*. Sydney: Matthias Media, 2021.

Sinnema, Don. "The Heidelberg Catechism at the Synod of Dort (1618–19)." https://www.canadianreformedseminary.ca/img/site/Conference/Sinnema%20Heidelberg%20Cat%20at%20Dort.pdf.

Skliris, Dionysios. "Synodical Ontology: Maximus the Confessor's proposition for Ontology, within History and in the Eschaton." In *Christian and Islamic Philosophies of Time*, edited by Sotiris Mitralexis and Marcin Podbielski, 85–117. Wilmington, DE: Vernon, 2018.

Smail, Tom. *Like Father, Like Son: The Trinity Imagined in Our Humanity*. Grand Rapids: Eerdmans, 2005.

Stamps, Luke. "The New Evangelical Subordinationism? Perspectives on the Equality of God the Father and God the Son." *Journal of the Evangelical Theological Society* 59/4 (2016) 874–81.

Steenson, J. N. "Basil of Ancyra on the Meaning of Homoousios." In *Arianism: Historical and Theological Reassessments, Papers from The Ninth International Conference on Patristic Studies*, Oxford, September 5–10, 1983, edited by Robert C. Gregg, 267–79. Philadelphia: Philadelphia Patristic Foundation, 1985.

Stott, John. *The Cross of Christ*. Downers Grove, IL: InterVarsity, 1986.

———. "The Patriarch (Abraham)." A Sermon from Genesis 12:1–9, preached on April 6, 1986. London: Langham Place Media, 1986.

Sullivan, F. A. "Comment on *Church as Communion*." Pontifical Council for Promoting Christian Unity, *Information Service* 77 (1991–1992) 97–102.

Swinburne, Richard. "Christ's Atoning Sacrifice." In *Philosophical Theology and the Christian Tradition: Russian and Western Perspectives*, edited by David Bradshaw, 21–29. Russian Philosophical Studies, V, Christian Philosophical Studies, III, Series IVA, Eastern and Central Europe, Volume 44, Series VIII, Christian Philosophical Studies, Vol. 3, general editor George F. McLean. Washington, DC: The Council for Research in Values and Philosophy, 2012.

Sydney Doctrine Commission. "The Doctrine of the Trinity and its bearing on the relationship of men and women." Reports to Synod, document 18, 1999. https://www.sds.asn.au/reports-received-synod-1999.

———. "Penal substitutionary atonement." Report to Synod, Referral 36/07, 2010. https://www.sds.asn.au/sites/default/files/PenalSubstitutionaryAtonement.DocCommission.%2836.07%29%20%282010%29.pdf?doc_id=NDE1NTA=.

Sykes, S. W. "Outline of a Theology of Sacrifice." In *Sacrifice and Redemption: Durham Essays in Theology*, edited by S. W. Sykes, 282–98. Cambridge: Cambridge University Press, 1991.

Synod of Dort. *The Canons of Dort*. Electronic ed. Pensacola, FL: Chapel Library, available at www.chapellibrary.org.

Tidball, Derek, David Hilborn, and Justin Thacker, eds. *The Atonement Debate: Papers from The London Symposium on the Theology of Atonement*. Grand Rapids: Zondervan, 2008.

Tilling, Chris. *Beyond Old and New Perspectives on Paul: Reflections on the Work of Douglas Campbell*. Cambridge: James Clarke, 2014.

Tinkham, Matthew L., Jr. "Neo-Subordinationism: The Alien Argumentation in the Gender Debate." *Andrews University Seminary Studies* 55/2 (2017) 237–90.

Tollefsen, Torstein Theodore. *The Christocentric Cosmology of St Maximus the Confessor.* Oxford: Oxford University Press, 2008.

———. "Did St Maximus the Confessor have a Concept of Participation?" *Studia Patristica* 37 (2001) 618–25.

Torrance, Alan J. *Persons in Communion: Trinitarian Description and Human Participation.* Edinburgh: T. & T. Clark, 1996.

———. "The Trinity." In *The Cambridge Companion to Karl Barth,* edited by John Webster, 72–91. Cambridge: Cambridge University Press, 2000.

Torrance, James B. "Covenant or Contract? A Study in the Theological Background of Worship in Seventeenth-Century Scotland." *Scottish Journal of Theology* 23 (1970) 51–76.

Torrance, Thomas F. *The Christian Doctrine of God: One Being Three Persons.* Edinburgh: T. & T. Clark, 1996.

———. *The Trinitarian Faith.* Edinburgh: T. & T. Clark, 1988.

Treloar, Geoffrey R. "T. C. Hammond the Controversialist." *Anglican Historical Society, Diocese of Sydney, Journal* 51 (2006) 20–35.

Turcescu, Lucian. "'Person' versus 'Individual', and Other Modern Misreadings of Gregory of Nyssa." *Modern Theology* 18/4 (October 2002) 97–109.

Ullucci, Daniel C. *The Christian Rejection of Animal Sacrifice.* New York: Oxford University Press, 2012.

Ussher, James. *Answer to a Jesuit: With Other Tracts on Popery.* Cambridge: Pitt, 1835, reproduced by BiblioLife.

———. "Eighteen Sermons Preached at Oxford." In *The Whole Works of the Most Rev. James Ussher, XIII.* Electronic ed. Miami: HardPress, 2017.

———. *The Whole Works of The Most Rev. James Ussher, D.D. with a life of the author and an account of his writings by Charles Richard Elrington.* Dublin: Hodges and Smith, 1847–1864.

Van Asslet, W. J. *The Federal Theology of Johannes Cocceius (1603–1669).* Translated by Raymond A. Blacketer. Studies in the History of Christian Thought 100. Leiden: Brill, 2001.

Van Dixhoorn, Chad B., ed. *Minutes and Papers of the Westminster Assembly, 1643–53.* Oxford: Oxford University Press, 2012.

Wainwright, Geoffrey. *Doxology: The Praise of God in Worship, Doctrine and Life.* London: Epworth, 1980.

Ware, Bruce A. "Does Affirming an Eternal Authority-Submission Relationship in the Trinity Entail a Denial of *Homoousios?*" In *One God in Three Persons: Unity of Essence, Distinction of Persons, Implications for Life,* edited by Bruce A. Ware and John Starke, 237–48. Wheaton, IL: Crossway, 2015.

———. "Equal in Essence, Distinct Roles." In *The New Evangelical Subordinationism? Perspectives on the Equality of God the Father and God the Son,* edited by Dennis W. Jowers and H. Wayne House, 13–38. Eugene, OR: Pickwick, 2012.

———. *Father, Son, and Holy Spirit: Relationships, Roles, and Relevance.* Wheaton, IL: Crossway, 2005.

———. "The Trinity and Subordinationism: The Doctrine of God and the Contemporary Gender Debate by Kevin Giles." *Religious Studies Review* 4/29 (2003) 355.

Ware, Bruce A., and John Starke, eds. *One God in Three Persons: Unity of Essence, Distinctions of Persons, Implications for Life.* Wheaton, IL: Crossway, 2015.

Weir, David. *The Origins of the Federal Theology in 16th-Century Reformation Thought.* Oxford: Clarendon, 1990.

*Westminster Confession of Faith.* https://reformed.org/master/index.html?mainframe=/documents/wcf_with_proofs/contents.html.

Whitehead, A. N. *Process and Reality.* New York: Harper and Row, 1929.

Whitfield, Keith S., ed. *Trinitarian Theology.* Nashville: B & H, 2019.

Wiles, Maurice. *Archetypal Heresy: Arianism Through the Centuries.* Oxford: Oxford University Press, 1966.

———. "In Defence of Arius." *Journal of Theological Studies* XIII/10 (1962) 339–47.

Williams, Garry J. "Penal Substitution: A Response to Recent Criticisms." *Journal of the Evangelical Theological Society* 50/1 (March 2007) 71–86.

Williams, Rowan. *Arius: Heresy and Tradition.* Rev. ed. London: Darton, Longman and Todd, 1987.

Wood, Maxwell Thomas. "Penal substitution in the construction of British evangelical identity: controversies in the doctrine of the atonement in the mid-2000s." PhD diss., Durham University, 2011.

Wright, David F. "Dr. Carnley on T. C. Hammond and Arianism." *St Mark's Review* 1/199 (2005) 46–48.

Wright, N. T. "The Cross and the Caricatures: A Response to Robert Jenson, Jeffrey John, and a New Volume Entitled Pierced for Our Transgressions." Eastertide 2007, https://www.fulcrum-anglican.org.uk/articles/the-cross-and-the-caricatures/.

———. *Evil and the Justice of God.* London: SPCK, 2006.

———. *Jesus and the Victory of God.* London: SPCK, 1996.

———. "Redemption from the New Perspective? Towards a Multi-Layered Pauline Theology of the Cross." In *The Redemption,* edited by Stephen T. Davis, Daniel Kendall, and Gerald O'Collins, 69–100. Oxford: Oxford University Press, 2004.

———. *What Saint Paul Really Said: Was Paul of Tarsus the Real Founder of Christianity?* Oxford: Lion, 1997.

Yandell, Keith. "How Many Times Does Three Go Into One?" In *Philosophical and Theological Essays on the Trinity,* edited by Thomas McCall and Michael C. Rea, 151–68. Oxford: Oxford University Press, 2009.

Yang, Hongyi. *A Development Not a Departure: The Lacunae in the Debate of the Doctrine of the Trinity and Gender Roles.* Phillipsburg, NJ: P & R, 2018.

Yates, Roy. "Colossians 2.15: Christ Triumphant." *New Testament Studies* 37/4 (October 1991) 573–91. DOI: https://doi.org/10.1017/S0028688500021962.

Zachuber, Johannes. "Individuality and the Theological Debate about 'Hypostasis.'" In *Individuality in Late Antiquity,* edited by Alexis Torrance and Johannes Zachuber, 91–109. Burlington, VT: Ashgate, 2014.

Zizioulas, John D. *Being as Communion.* London: Darton, Longman and Todd, 1985.

———. "The Being of God and the Being of Anthropos." *Synaxis* 37 (1991) 11–35.

———. "The Father as Cause: Personhood Generating Otherness." In *Communion and Otherness,* edited by Paul McPartlan, 113–54. London: T. & T. Clark, 2006.

———. "Human Capacity and Human Incapacity." *Scottish Journal of Theology* 28 (1975) 401–8.

# Subject Index

Abelard, Peter, 287
Abraham, 300
  God's covenant with, 50–51, 72
  distinct from covenants with
    Adam, Noah, 69
  its unconditional nature 50, 72
  not "contractual", 69, 72
  *protevangelium*, 50
Adam,
  God's alleged contract with,
    43–52, 43n15, 52n29, 63–65,
    69–78, 69n100, 76
    (alleged conditional nature)
      45–51, 59–61, 60n62, 63,
      66, 69, 69n102
  as "federal head of the human
    race", 43n15, 48, 50, 60, 61,
    66, 70
  in understanding of Ussher,
    59–60, 60n62, 63–65
  in understanding of Hammond,
    60–74
    (as historical person) 69,
      69n100, 71n106/107/
      108/109/110/111
  in understanding of Michael
    Bird, 66n86
"Adamic Christology", 77, 91, 93–94
Agatho, Pope, 125–26
Alexandria, 171, 182, 182n17, 251,
  254n7
Anselm, 287
  atonement as essentially *human*
    offering, 119, 119n85
Anthropomorphism, 50

in the thought of Thomas
  Schreiner, 84–85, 94n27
in language of Doyle, 99, 186–
  88, 190
leading to tritheism, 192, 195
Antinomianism, 64–65
Antioch, Synod of (Anomoean), 252
ARCIC, Agreed Statement on Mary,
  xiii
Aristotle, 4n11, 99n22, 108n54, 287
Arius, xvii, xxii, xxiv–xxv, 4, 11, 13,
  218
  on the absolute sovereignty of
    one God, 149
  on the Word as (timeless)
    product of the will of God,
    157, 253n4, 254, 254n8
  his views according to Newman,
    252–53, 255
  his views according to Harnack,
    253–55, (as a form of
    adoptionism) 254
  his views according to Maurice
    Wiles, xxiv–xxv, xxivn18,
    259n12
  his views according to Rowan
    Williams, 108, 108n54, 259,
    259n12, 261–62, 261n14
  his views according to
    the Sydney Doctrine
    Commission, 83, 259
  his views according to Doyle,
    99–100 (on Athanasius's
    response)

# Author Index

Adam, Peter, xx, xxn10/11, xxi, xxv,
19–20, 20n30, 53, 144, 287
Agourides, Savas, 287
Armitage, Chris, 287
Awad, Najeeb G., 287
Ayres, Lewis, 202n4, 205n14,
215n30, 251n2, 259, 259n12,
267, 287

Baker, Mark D., 292
Barnes, Michel René, 288, 296
Barth, Karl, 41, 44, 44n18, 142,
245–46, 246n70, 288, 301
Bauman, Michael, xxiiin15, 263n19,
288
Beilby, James, 299
Bell, W., 293
Bilezikian, Gilbert, 203, 203n7, 288
Billings, Todd, 288
Bird, Michael F., 66n86, 264,
264n24, 265–66,
265n30/31/32/33, 266n34,
288, 291
Bird, Thomas E., 295
Blocher, H., 66n86, 288
Boersma, Hans, 288
Boff, Leonardo, 288
Brent, Alan, 288
Bromiley, G. W., 135, 288, 299
Bugár, István M., 288
Burkert, Walter, 288
Butner, D. Glenn, Jr., 1, 1n2, 33,
33n54, 109, 128, 220n36,
238, 242–45, 261–62,
262n16, 265, 289

critique of "eternal functional
submissiveness" (EFS), 85,
85n8, 193–94, 193n35
its tritheism, 33, 85, 85n8, 223–
25, 274, 281
its "missing Scriptural Case", 88–
98, 89n15, 91n21, 95n29/30,
102–3, 103n47, 111, 111n70,
208, 212–13, 227, 230, 242,
245, 273
on importance of Christ's two
wills (*dyothelitism*), 125,
125n96, 126–28 (engaging
with Grudem), 193–94,
193n35, 220–28, 228n53,
241
EFS not necessarily Arian, 33,
33n54, 202–3, 203n6/10,
205, 208, 219–29, 220n36,
221n39/41, 222n43, 223n45,
225n46, 227n51, 228n53,
229n54, 231–42, 231n57,
233n58, 234n60

Cable, Kenneth J., xviiin8, 289, 294
Carnley, Peter, 285, 289
life in Sydney, 38–40
as student of theology, 40–41
as Primate of Australia, ix, ixn1,
xi, xiv, 11–16, 145
on Arianism of Sydney Doctrine
Commission, 13, 13n23, 19,
30, 32.
on T. C. Hammond, 16–20,
53n30, 54n32, 55, 55n39,

www.ingramcontent.com/pod-product-compliance
Lightning Source LLC
Chambersburg PA
CBHW030921150426
42812CB00046B/444